PENGUIN BO(
SOVEREIGNS OF

Seema Alavi is a professor of history at Ashoka University, Sonipat, Haryana. She earned her PhD from Cambridge University, England, and has twice been a Fulbright Scholar and a Smuts Visiting Research Fellow at Cambridge. In 2010, she was at the Radcliffe Institute for Advanced Study at Harvard, USA, as the William Bentinck-Smith Fellow.

Alavi specializes in early modern and modern South Asia, with an interest in the transformation of the region's legacy from Indo-Persian to one heavily affected by British colonial rule. She has written books on the military, medical and religious histories of India. Her most recent book is the Albert Hourani Award (Honourable Mention) winner *Muslim Cosmopolitanism in the Age of Empire* from Harvard University Press, USA.

Celebrating 35 Years of
Penguin Random House India

SOVEREIGNS OF THE SEA

Omani Ambition in the Age of Empire

SEEMA ALAVI

PENGUIN BOOKS

An imprint of Penguin Random House

PENGUIN BOOKS

USA | Canada | UK | Ireland | Australia
New Zealand | India | South Africa | China | Singapore

Penguin Books is part of the Penguin Random House group of companies
whose addresses can be found at global.penguinrandomhouse.com

Published by Penguin Random House India Pvt. Ltd
4th Floor, Capital Tower 1, MG Road,
Gurugram 122 002, Haryana, India

First published in Allen Lane by Penguin Random House India 2023
This paperback edition published in Penguin Books by Penguin Random House India 2023

ISBN 9780143464280

Typeset in RequiemText by Manipal Technologies Limited, Manipal

www.penguin.co.in

Contents

Introduction

The Context

In 1866, Lewis Pelly, the British Resident in the Persian Gulf, commented on a murder most foul at the port city of Sohar, north of Muscat on the Al Batinah coast of Oman. He said, 'The horrors of Macbeth pale beside this tragedy of Sayyid Salim.'[1]

He was referring to the murder of Sayyid Thuwayni, the Sultan of Muscat and the son of the Omani patriarch Sultan Sayyid Sa'īd, who ruled from 1806 to 1856. Thuwayni was allegedly murdered by his son Salim. Soon after this macabre deed, Salim successfully installed himself as the Sultan of Muscat.[2]

Pelly alleged that Thuwayni was shot in the head with a double-barrelled pistol. A Wahhabi named Bashir assisted Salim in the job, and later both of them secretly buried him in the fort with the assistance of the Baluchi Governor and a man called Rajab, the Baluchi guard. It was officially declared that he died of fever. Salim then imprisoned Sayyid Turki, the Governor of Sohar and the elder brother of Thuwayni, and also his confidential servant, Marhom. And once the job was over he rode off to Muscat for his coronation.[3]

Pelly was disappointed that, despite his scathing opposition, the British recognized Salim as Thuwayni's successor. Fearing a period of instability, he warned the British Indian subjects and the Christians at Muscat to guard their specie and jewellery and embark on board their *buglas*, or boats. He also intervened to get Sayyid Turki released. Salim lasted as the Sultan only for a few years; his

Ibāḍī allies expelled him from Muscat and elected his relative Azzan bin Qais as Sultan.[4]

Thuwayni's mausoleum at the Sohar Fort is a stark reminder of this gruesome incident. And his son, Salim, pops up in the archival records shrouded in mystery and despised by later British officials. However, such stories of open rancour, competitiveness, fratricide, violence, murder, conspiracy and deceit, involving the Omani princes caught in succession battles, are rarely factored into the telling of the story of the world of the Indian Ocean.

Indeed, the narrative on the ocean's political culture is marked by the general invisibility of the Sultans. In conventional narratives, the Omani patriarch Sultan Sayyid Sa'īd is discussed mostly as a mere ally and friend of the British. His sons, who dominate the ocean in the latter half of the century, fare worse. Princes Hilal and Khalid are portrayed as failed heroes unworthy of discussion.[5] And the more successful ones such as Thuwayni, Turki, Majid and Barghash are dismissed for being competitive, creating familial discord or ending up as mere friends of the British wallowing in their consumerist material culture.[6] The missing Sultans in the historical narrative of the Western Indian Ocean appear to suggest that they were inept and consumed by in-house factionalism. They bound themselves in iniquitous treaties with the imperial powers and were witness to the eventual loss of the Sultanate to Western nation states.

I

The Missing Sultans in Indian Ocean Historiography

Historians have moved away from viewing the Western Indian Ocean as a geographically marked physical entity that remained dominated by Europeans through its long history. They see it more as a socially produced space very much in line with Ferdinand Braudel's historically constructed Mediterranean arena. This shift helped decentre the Eurocentrism that framed the Indian Ocean world. It restored the centrality of South Asia and the significance of Africa in its making.⁷ Michael Pearson, the renowned historian of the Indian Ocean, viewed the range of people located in the Indian Ocean rim as constituting the 'littoral society which was socially and economically distinct in its cultural diversity and its dependence on the ocean'. This characterization, when used as a unit of analysis, conceptualized the ocean as a seamless world crowded with a range of both European and non-European actors who shaped its political culture.⁸

The story of this socially and culturally heterogeneous ocean was enriched with Enseng Ho's inspiring insights, which focused on mobility and diasporas as a window into understanding its political culture. Ho's studies put the spotlight on the itinerant Asian contenders for the ocean's spoils who refused to be silenced by the capitalist surge of the nineteenth century: Arab and Indian merchants and Hadhramaut scholars and jurists, among others. Viewed from this perspective, the ocean emerged as a critical space for 'inter-Asian' connections that predate Empire and globalization, but which survived through the long nineteenth-century period of economic integration, lending resilience to the littoral society.⁹

Many younger scholars, inspired by Ho's influential scholarship, explored the history of the non-European protagonists who straddled the ocean in the early modern period, leaving their indelible imprint on the destination ports. Historians such as Sebastian Prange and Mahmood Kooria focused on the Arab Muslim merchants, who arrived in Malabar, heeled themselves in local society and transformed it by integrating the region to the Islamic tinged 'Monsoon Asia'.¹⁰ Mahmood Kooria elaborated on the dependence of the Hindu ruling dynasts in the Indian Ocean littoral on the itinerant communities of Arab Muslim littérateurs and merchants as they battled the foreigners, in particular the Portuguese.¹¹

The story of itinerant communities, mobility, obligation and connections was taken forward into the long nineteenth century in the works of Fahad Bishara. Bishara highlighted the important role of the non-European legal and financial networks that both powered the economic integration of the ocean and energized

the local polities. His influential research highlights the mobility
of Indian merchant communities, bankers and Arab jurists who
criss-crossed the ocean and encountered Western courts and
financial networks. Their networks successfully pushed the Omani
Sultans to the fringe, making them entirely dependent on the legal
expertise, capital and influence of this ethnically diverse diaspora.
This happened to such an extent that the Sultans, argues Bishara,
presided over an 'Empire of people, of texts, of deeds, of capital
and of power, if not of political authority'.[12] Indeed, in Bishara's
work, the diaspora powered the ocean while the political sovereigns
occupied its margin. Not surprisingly, the Arab Sultans remained
outside his story of the ocean. At best, they operated in the shadow
of the imperial political sovereigns who crowded the ocean.

Other legal historians did indicate the continued relevance of
the Arab political sovereigns in the Western Indian Ocean. They
highlighted the mobility of the Arab Sultans who embodied distinct
legal traditions that derived from multiple contexts that they accessed.
Indeed, their mobility and the reference points they touched reflect
the many non-European sovereignties and jurisdictions that operated
in the ocean.[13] Most recently, Nurfadzilah Yahaya's work points to
the sophisticated awareness in the Arab diaspora in Southeast Asia
of the existence of distinct European and Arab sovereignties and
legal jurisdictions—colonial and Islamic—that people tapped into in
self-interest.[14] However, with the notable exception of Iza Hussin,
whose work forefronts the political acumen of the Malay Sultan
of Johar as he moved around and entangled with imperial powers
to carve out his sovereignty, the critical role of the non-European
sovereigns in shaping the ocean's political culture remains absent in
the scholarship.[15]

This absence is particularly true of the littoral society's most
visible political actors—the maritime Arab kingdoms. They are
generally projected as the unsuspecting victims who got crushed
under aggressive imperial hegemony.[16] In British records, some of
them, such as the chiefs of Ra's al-Khaimah, Sharjah and Lingah,
are viewed as encouraging 'piracy' and mentoring the Wahhabis,
the dreaded Islamic reformists from northern Arabia.[17] Other

polities, such as Oman, are projected as pliable allies of the British in controlling maritime violence.[18] Very rarely are they studied in their own right. The overwhelming silence and the invisibility of the Arab polities and dynasts in the historiography reflects its unabashed Eurocentrism when it comes to dealing with structures of state power that shaped the ocean's political culture. Imperialism sans the Arab-Islamic tint becomes the received wisdom.

Thomas McDow's work began to change the trend by pointing out that the Arab Sultans were not entirely external or unaffected by mobility, debt and the social relationships of obligations in the ocean. Nor were they just pawns in the hands of Western powers that crowded the ocean. Rather, they had their own distinct imperial aspirations, which they materialized with their exceptional mobility across the treacherous waters. He highlights the mobility of the Omani Sultan Sayyid Sa'īd and views it as integral to the Sultan's Arab style of governance. The technicalities of his 'mobile governance' included his own physical mobility to perform a range of tasks: settle disputes, establish subsidies, dole out pensions, sign commercial treaties with foreigners and strike alliances with Western powers. Mobility became a 'temporizing strategy' that allowed both the Sultan and his people to 'buy time' when faced with ecological, financial and political challenges. His political sovereignty was constituted by his involvement in both the imperial and the Asian networks of power and finance that he accessed as he straddled Muscat and his new outpost of Zanzibar in East Africa.[19]

However, McDow's focus on Sayyid Sa'īd restricts the exploration of mobility to the Muscat–Zanzibar arc. According to him, the synergy that the Sultan injected in the Sultanate petered out after his death (1856), which was also followed by the high period of imperialism and capitalist integration. The Sultanate was weakened further by the British-engineered 1861 bifurcation of Oman into the two independent kingdoms of Muscat and Zanzibar. These developments are viewed as pushing the Sultans to political irrelevance in what is known as the period of counter-revolutionary imperialism.

The Omani Sultans in the Indian Ocean World

This book puts the spotlight on this late nineteenth-century moment of imperial hegemony through the micro-optic on the life of not just Sayyid Sa'īd but four of his sons, who were significant protagonists navigating the ocean in the high period of imperialism. Collectively, these careers cover the period of the counter-revolutionary imperialism and stretch into the period of the proliferating nation states that marked the end of the century.[20] They show how Omani Sultans engaged with the imperial world and simultaneously dug their heels in local society in the long nineteenth century, until Zanzibar and Oman became British protectorates in 1890 and 1891, respectively.

Those like Sayyid Thuwayni and Sayyid Majid, who held sway in the mid-nineteenth century, appear as counter-revolutionaries in their own right, negotiating the political and economic winds of change in their favour. Whereas others, like Sayyid Barghash and Sayyid Turki, who ruled in the period of the fast-proliferating nation states, refashioned the Sultanate as a 'modern monarchy'.[21] This was produced in conversation with imperial powers, with whom they deliberated over global agendas such as abolition and the political threat from the Wahhabis, depending on their location.

However, the new 'modern monarchies' put in place by Barghash and Turki were differently produced, even if they both remained entangled in imperial conversations and agendas. Barghash, based at the slave hub of Zanzibar, engaged with imperial conversations on slavery and travelled around the Western world articulating what the slave meant to his society. His mobility and sea-facing politics fashioned a Sultanate that had a specific Zanzibarian cultural core and a Western outlook. In contrast Turki, at Muscat, remained heeled in the bricolage of tribal alliances and cultivated his base in the Wahhabis who posed a threat to imperial powers. His Wahhabi social capital brought him in close conversation with Britain and involved him in imperial politics. The British exiled him to Bombay early in his career. This fired his political imaginary and made British Indian cities integral to his political geography. On becoming the

Sultan, he tapped into the politics of exile to deal with rival siblings. The manufacturing of the new style of monarchy by both Barghash and Turki was in sync with similar trends that were visible in the monarchies in Britain, Europe and parts of Asia.[22]

The Sultanic careers offer a rich micro-history of the ocean that textures our understanding of Asian imperialism as it evolved in interaction with and at pace with a world fast changing with economic integration, imperial clampdowns and the rise of the nation states in Europe. The analysis of these individual lives reveals that the 'age of revolution', characterized by the more familiar narrative of political and economic reforms in Europe, had a non-European angle as well. The highlighting of its Arab agents of change reveals its parallel life and a longer temporality in the ocean. It reveals that the Sultans were no unsuspecting victims when the waves of counter-revolutionary imperialism gained momentum in the late nineteenth century. Their careers draw attention to Arab/Asian imperialisms that flourished outside but in interaction with Western imperialisms.

Sayyid Sa'īd belonged to the Al Busaidi dynasty that ruled Oman since the late eighteenth century. The dynasty had illustrious non-European contemporaries: the Qajars in Iran (1797–1925), Muhammad Ali Pasha, the Ottoman rebel Governor and the ruler of Egypt, the Al Saud dynasty in Saudi Arabia, the Ottoman Sultans Abdal Aziz and Hamid and a string of Arab rulers on the Persian Gulf, including the most formidable one—Sagar of Ra's al-Khaimah. Each one of these powers had specific engagements with imperial powers that were contingent on their geopolitics. Nasir al-Din Shah of Iran (1848–96) had an indirect connect with Europeans via Iranian littérateurs, students and merchants travelling to Britain or to India and bringing back ideas of military reforms and printing technology. Muhammad Ali Pasha rebelled against his Ottoman masters after ousting Napoleon from Egypt and became the ruler of Egypt, charged with French ideas of military and administrative reforms. And the intermittent periods of Ottoman rule in the Hijaz gave the taste of the railways and steamship technologies to the Al Saud dynasts in Arabia.[23]

However, the Al Busaidis stood out in this non-Anglophone imperial circuit for their exceptional engagement with Western powers. They were not merely influenced by the technologies and consumer culture that streamed into their region; rather, they stood tall in the imperial assemblage as active participants in the discussions on slavery and the Wahhabis that obsessed the Western powers. Indeed, their spatial location at Muscat and Zanzibar—the hotspot of Wahhabi politics and the slave trade respectively—coloured their engagement with the imperial powers in a specific hue. The imperial powers gravitated to their doorstep hungry for slaves, and they emerged as the most sought-after Arab rulers that were needed to keep the wheels of both commerce and political stability going. The Al Busaidis made the most of the spatial advantage they enjoyed and cashed in on the temporal moment, when the anti-slave rhetoric of the British in particular made both local and British slavers and merchants swing towards them. These exceptional geopolitics made them exceptionally mobile as they travelled across the ocean to as far as Bombay, London, Paris, Cairo, Jerusalem and Damascus, sought after by Western powers to negotiate and ratify slave treaties and strategize on the Wahhabis in particular. They squeezed themselves into the imperial drawing board, making the most of the spotlight on them, and became globally visible. Unlike their Asian contemporaries, they emerged more as counter-revolutionaries firmly on board in imperial discussions on slavery and the Wahhabis, which they made locally legible.

Indeed, Sayyid Sa'īd confirmed his sovereignty by involving himself in imperial politics centred in particular on slaves and the Muslim reformists—the Wahhabis. His location at Muscat, which he projected as his principal political unit, and the constant mobility between this port city and the East African outpost of Zanzibar, framed his politics as he stepped into the imperially crowded world. After his death, his sons fought their succession battles on the Muscat–Zanzibar political canvas that he had charted. They aspired to be rulers of a united Oman using the expertise they had gained as Governors in his lifetime. The sheer economic wealth offered by the ocean, its geographic seamlessness and its social diversity of people, combined with the assets of the tribal interiors, offered them both challenges as well as huge opportunities. And the rapidly rising wealth of the Sultanate from the profits in particular of the slave trade, centred at Zanzibar, accommodated princely restiveness and enabled all contenders to carve out a space for themselves. Muscat and Zanzibar remained the territorially marked arenas for brothers Thuwayni and Turki and Majid and Barghash, respectively.

These two locales became critical in their struggle to survive in the high period of imperialism. It is from Muscat and Zanzibar that they tapped into the emotive issues of the earlier age and used them to insinuate themselves into imperial politics much more than the patriarch Sayyid Sa'īd. Indeed, like their father, they too continued to cash in on the Wahhabi reformist politics, focused on Muscat as the new political unit and competed for the profits of slave trade. But they travelled far more expansively, visited British and Ottoman imperial cities and engaged with the new ideas of urban planning, print technology, the sugar press, the telegraph and steamships. They used the imperial networks and moved around, borrowing from multiple contexts as they balanced their regional politics with imperial agendas.

The lives of these later Sultans show the playing out of the spirit of the 'age of revolution' in the long nineteenth century that made it possible for them to circumvent the surveillance of the counter-revolutionary Empire.[24] Their careers reveal that the Omani engagement with the imperial powers was temporally and spatially contingent. The book elaborates on these contingencies to show the limitations of concepts such as 'mobile governance' and 'buying time', coined specifically to understand the ocean's political culture in the reign of Sayyid Sa'īd. It draws attention to the relevance of factoring into the narrative of the ocean the string of temporalities and historical moments that shape its politics.

The micro-history of individual Omani Sultans offers us a non-Eurocentric view of the ocean's political culture in which the royal political aspirants appear as active agents very much in control of their destiny.[25] The analysis of these individual sons of the dead Sultan unravels the many different political aspirations and experiences that shaped the ocean's politics. Indeed, the varied responses of the aspiring Sultans impacted by the same event—the death of their father—but located in different geographical, social and political contexts offers a thick connectedness of things on scales both small and large.[26] The book brings this more textured optic of micro-history in conversation with the embracive and flexible frame of analysis of Indian Ocean studies to narrate the story of the ocean in more contingent ways.[27]

It alerts us to the utility of micro-history—with its emphasis on materiality, individual experience and the contingent nature of space and time—for writing the big, bold macro-history of the ocean.[28] The bringing together of the micro stories of the Al Busaidi Sultans to tell the big story of the ocean is revealing, as it makes them stand distinct from their Arab contemporaries in having lofty imperial aspirations that rubbed shoulders with those of Western powers. The ocean attracted them with its lucrative slave trade just as much as it lured the European powers to its shore for similar reasons. The Sultans made the most of this crowding of their shores. They shared the imperial dream with the European powers, successfully stepped into their boardroom, tapped into its multiple contexts and actively participated in global deliberations on the pressing issues of ocean politics. These micro-histories show the Sultans rubbing shoulders with the Western powers as they collectively shape the ocean's political culture. The detailing of their lives decentres the European- and American-driven nature of change in the age of capitalist expansion and imperial hegemony.

The stories of each of the protagonists in the book are distinct. And yet all the five Sultans discussed here share the genealogical reference point to the Al Busaidi dynasty. Their internal familial power struggle helped them articulate in clear terms what they stood for as Al Busaidi dynasts. And the royal household played a critical role in the launch of each of their political careers. Indeed, this private sphere remained a constant reminder of their familial roots and became their critical conduit to the more public political world. In their political moves, they blurred the private and the public spheres, and thus their lives offer a specifically non-European style of governance, with implications for Indian Ocean studies. They remained not merely recipients of abstract ideas and material goods from the Global North but active agents of change who engaged with their rapidly transforming world in exceptional ways. Their stories reveal the limitations of using Anglophone models of state building to capture non-European political experience. And their fascinating careers disrupt the binaries of the Global North, as the manufacturer of abstract theory and political ideas, and the South as the recipient and the site of experience.

The late nineteenth-century context of high imperialism and economic integration ensured that these successive Sultans moved far more than their father, who straddled Muscat and Zanzibar alone. Paradoxically, the politics of the imperial world both tightened its embrace on them and gave them easy access to imperial cities in British India, Persia, Britain and the Ottoman Empire. Their temporally contingent mobility made many of them visible in Bombay, Cairo, Jerusalem, Damascus, Mecca, Bandar Abbas, Paris, Marseilles and London, and for reasons not only guided by deportation or exile. Many of these visits were made to explore urban development, lobby against rival siblings, establish their foothold in the Persian Gulf to offset the British, tie up with Muslim reformists and very often for mere entertainment.[29] Indeed, their exceptional mobility established enduring connections across the Asian and African port towns in the Indian Ocean littoral. This had its own political and cultural implications for the Sultanate. The most important of these was the lateral flow of capital, knowledge of urban planning, architecture, navigation, shipbuilding technology, printing techniques and reformist ideas.[30]

And yet, as the career of Sayyid Turki shows, the mobility of the Sultans was not always voluntary. They were often forced into exile. Ironically, this coerced mobility under duress increased their exposure to the oceanic world and became a political asset. Turki, who preferred overland movements into the tribal interiors, was deported from Sohar to Muscat and then to faraway Bombay across the Indian Ocean. Unlike his brothers, he was never particularly interested in a berth in the imperially crowded world. But these

xviiiIntroduction

sojourns drew him into the imperial assemblage. They connected him to the imperial cities and politics from which he derived immense political capital for his bid to be Sultan.

The book draws on the concept of translation as a 'multidirectional and generative' knowledge production process that helped the Sultans consolidate their sovereignty. They derived freely from the multiple knowledge hubs and contexts that they accessed,[31] and appear as ingenious navigators who selectively picked up on the knowledge flows even as the imperial networks remained enabling conduits that brought these influences closer home. They 'forum shopped' and negotiated their way in the imperially crowded ocean, translating Western obsessions with technology, slavery and radical Islam, in particular, to their advantage.[32]

The exceptional mobility of the Sultans, both overseas and overland into the tribal interiors, made them engage with a range of contestants who flourished in the Indian Ocean littoral. They made spatially and temporally contingent alliances with both the Western imperial networks, tribal factions and the vast diaspora of merchants, bankers, sailors, jurists, littérateurs that spawned the ocean. The Omani royals appear as bricoleurs, whose alliances with the Arab, Swahili, Indian and European protagonists of different hues wove a fascinating bricolage of political and social relations that carpeted the ocean.[33] Like all bricoleurs, they too suffered from political precarity. But this precarity lent a tinge of adventure to their entrepreneurship, making it different and exceptional.

With all its limitations, the bricolage became the critical site from where they translated Western obsessions, such as slavery, radical Islam, the steamship, the mail service and the telegraph, making them locally accessible. They tempered the Western material and ideological influences that streamed into their world with the experiences they brought home from the Indian Ocean port towns they straddled: Bombay, Cairo, Damascus, Muscat and Zanzibar. This translation politics became the way of defining their political sovereignty in the age of Empire.

The Sultans brought together imperialism, slavery and reformist Islam in temporally and spatially contingent ways to carve out their political sovereignty. Mobility was indeed the engine that powered this sovereignty. It enabled princes to draw from a repertoire of referents in multiple contexts and establish their sovereign status locally even as they looked globally.[34] However, the mobility of both the Sultan and his sons was more than the deft diplomacy implicit in the idea of 'buying time'. It was also not always voluntary and also not only about crossing the ocean to sign treaties with Western powers. Rather, it included both land and sea sojourns, forced deportations, exiles, as also the use of their creative imaginary to satiate political aspirations, as some of them strove to squeeze themselves into the crowded imperial assemblage.

They made their entry into the imperial public sphere in different spatial and temporally contingent ways. Those in Zanzibar, such as Majid and Barghash, found themselves at the heart of the slave trade. They were more 'sea sovereigns' with the imperial interest in them, as they were perceived as the overseers of the slave trade. This made it relatively easy for them to connect with imperial powers and articulate what slavery meant to them. Others such as Thuwayni and Turki, based in Muscat, made their global presence felt via their dealings with the Muslim radical Wahhabis—the great Western obsession—and by using the outreach the imperial powers made to them in the laying of the telegraph line and the steamship-driven mail service that passed through their territory. Unlike their Zanzibar siblings, they moved more over land, as they consolidated their alliances with the tribes to meet the Wahhabi challenge in their territory. And yet, the directions of mobility notwithstanding, each one of them translated burning global issues and gave them local legibility.

The 'new' temporally and spatially contingent mobility, as reflected in the political aspirations of the Sultans, can be viewed as a form of 'careering'. Lester and Lambert introduced the concept of 'imperial careering' to describe British officers who moved across the Empire and used the experience they collected to further not just imperial interest but their own careers.[35]

However, careering had a life outside Anglophone imperialism as well. This is best exemplified in the careers of Ottoman

Governors, such as Muhammad Ali Pasha in the Middle East, who rebelled against his master to became the independent ruler of Egypt; or the Thais who, along with the French and British colonists in Thailand, made careers competing at mapping territory and legitimizing power using the European practice of cartography and cadastral surveys;[36] or the Japanese, who similarly produced their geo-body, which invoked both tradition and mimicked aspects of Western modernity in greater East Asia.[37] These instances reveal that the experience that was gained in being in contact with Western imperial political culture often empowered individuals to chart out independent careers, either as rebels as with Muhammad Ali Pasha, or as agents of home-grown imperial projects, as in the case of the Thai and Japanese cartographers.

Omani careering makes a useful imprint in this collection of cases outside Anglophone imperialism. However, it stands out in this constellation for evolving firmly heeled in imperial politics, entangled in its networks, and yet not replicating its political practice. The Sultans in the imperial assemblage appear distinct in their political practice. There is certainly little effort of constructing an imagined geo-body with a public sphere separated from 'private' issues such as religion, ethnicity, race as in the case of other Asian imperialisms. This was possible because of their unique geographical location that brought slave-hungry imperial powers to their doorstep and made them sought-after rulers integral to global strategies concerning the ocean. The Sultans engaged with the Western powers from a position of strength and forum shopped to cannibalize their array of material cultures at will. This level of engagement gave the Sultans huge opportunities to travel as they engaged in deliberations with Western powers. Their exceptional mobility as visitors, participants and interlocutors to discuss global issues energized their political sovereignty and made them visible as significant Arab imperialists in the assemblage of Western powers normally viewed as the white man's club that framed the ocean.

The Sultans' presence in the white man's club did not mean they turned away from engaging with the many sovereignties and jurisdictions they navigated in the tribal interiors. Indeed, imperial entanglements intensified their links with the tribal societies. Omani princes used their political and military experiences, gathered from their younger days as Governors, to negotiate both the religion-inflected tribal politics of the interior Omani towns as well as the imperial networks and intellectual hubs to carve out their political sovereignty. With the Western capitalist noose tightening around them, they moved more expansively than their father to balance their politics with that of the imperial powers. Some of them, such as Thuwayni and Turki, moved internally to consolidate their hold on tribal factions, and Majid and Barghash sailed the ocean to British and Ottoman cities.

As they moved, they borrowed from a range of referents in multiple contexts to consolidate their sovereign status. Some, such as Turki, ingeniously engaged in tribal politics and economy. Others, such as Majid and Barghash, purposefully translated Islam, slavery and imperialism, making them locally meaningful.[38] The Muslim reformist influences of the Arab Ottoman cities, which some of them visited, made them liberal interpreters of Ibāḍī Islam. They welcomed Muslims of other sects and aspired for unity in the face of the Western challenge. At the same time they defined slavery, slave trade and labour in local terms so as to justify their use as they competed with imperial powers to garner the profits of slavery. And they gave their own spin to global events that impinged on their world: the British arbitration in settling the subsidy between Muscat and Zanzibar; the abolition rhetoric and the 1873 slave treaty; the sinking of private European capital in agriculture to monopolize clove and date plantations; the laying of the telegraph line; the sinking of capital in the steamship companies and the establishment of the coal depots to service the steamship and the registration of British subjects residing in their territory.[39] All these issues offered them the perfect canvas to assert their sovereign status by both connecting to the world outside as well as garnering local support.

Indeed, they used many of these issues for instant global visibility in an imperially crowded world. Many such as Barghash, who lived in a period of burgeoning nation states, refurbished monarchy as a modern political form that projected him as the modern Sultan who was at once both a father figure to all his people, including slaves, and also someone very visible on international forums articulating forcefully his views on slavery and the Wahhabis. Barghash travelled all the way to London in connection with the slave treaty ratification and made himself visible on the global stage. He enjoyed the spotlight in London, accepting honours, sightseeing and attending state banquets. Back home, his vast exposure was most visible in his interest in the construction of royal yachts in Zanzibar, which were modelled on steamships produced in Portsmouth in Britain but tempered with his local taste. And the tapping into the expertise of William Mackinnon, the founder of the British India Steamship Navigation Company, for many of his road and transport projects needed to pull up Zanzibar to global urban standards. His sibling, Majid, responded to global pandemics, such as cholera, in ingenious ways, shifting their capital to the new town of Dar as Salaam on the mainland. This port town became the centre of slave and ivory collection, as the overland slave and ivory trade from the African interiors was rerouted to it avoiding Zanzibar, where British surveillance was intense.

As the Sultans moved around a world crowded by Western powers, they ingeniously tapped into its internal tensions and contestations. The Eurasian imperial assemblage that framed the Western Indian Ocean and that comprised Britain, Europe and Qajar Iran, offered them opportunities of forum shopping.[40] Their purposeful engagement with the imperial powers resulted in their success in carving out a sub-political culture within this assemblage. This was a space that reflected their political and commercial vision and became their lasting legacy when, in 1890, Zanzibar became a British protectorate and Oman followed suit in 1891.

This political space stretched like a seamless corridor linking the Omani towns of the tribal interior to the ports of Muscat and Sohar. It pushed in to the Persian Gulf and the east coast of Africa with Bandar Abbas, Zanzibar and Dar as Salaam as its important footholds. In the lifetime of their father, each of these princes had gained experience managing the affairs of these tribal towns and maritime ports as Governors. In the long nineteenth century, struggling to make their independent careers, they dug their heels into their respective niches and strove to consolidate their social base locally and globally push further their political ambit. As they moved in this corridor, they established temporally contingent relationships with each other and with the tribal and port societies. These flexible alliances lent porosity to the Omani political culture and made both sovereignty and jurisdictions open-ended and slippery.

In the late nineteenth century, the European effort to establish control over Muscat and Zanzibar further intensified.[41] In this period of increased global economic integration and imperial hegemony, the Omani Sultans tightened the link between the coast and the interior that their father had forged in order to meet military exigencies. They crafted a seamless space that contained within it a plurality of geographies and ethnic and linguistic communities that sprawled from the interior tribal society to their extended maritime frontier in the Persian Gulf. This corridor of support was not only for moments of political crisis. Rather, it was for all times and duly integrated into their politics with sustained interest and investments in its dates and indigo economy as well.[42]

II

The Protagonists: Sultan Sayyid Sa'īd in the Age of Revolution

Thomas McDow projects the Sultan as an astute diplomat, signing treaties and 'buying time' as he straddles between Muscat and his new maritime post of Zanzibar, balancing his rule with imperial politics. It is indeed noteworthy that Sayyid Sa'īd's 'mobile governance' was characterized by his techniques of alliance making, negotiation and deals with imperial powers, which played a key role in the constitution of his political sovereignty. However, the Sultan had a loftier political ambition that went beyond treaties and deals with the imperial powers. He was very much the Sultan who inaugurated new kinds of political practice in keeping with the spirit of the 'age

of revolution' in which he lived and to which he contributed in no
small measure.

In keeping with the tide of the 'revolutionary age', he made a
break from his family tradition and shifted his base of power from
the tribal interior to the port town of Muscat. He powered the 'age
of revolution' from the coast, pushing his maritime frontier to the
Persian Gulf and setting up his base on the island of Zanzibar to
maximize the profits of the slave trade. He recalibrated existing
traditions and religious beliefs to integrate the socially diverse
communities in his expanded territorial ambit. He blurred the private
and the public lines in his political practice and defined his legal
jurisdiction on the waters in specific ways; he successfully balanced
his politics with the loftier European agents of the revolution. He
tapped into imperial agendas, cashing in on the Western fears of the
Wahhabis, and exploiting the Anglo-French rivalries, over slaves in
particular, to his advantage. He clearly envisaged for himself a wider
role in the vast globalizing world system.

Indeed, he very much wanted to be visible on global platforms
and get into the European public gaze as an energetic ruler
who was at par with them. In 1837, he very proudly accepted
honorary membership of the Royal Asiatic Society in London.
This honour was bestowed on him among other things for, 'the
encouragement . . . to the arts and sciences among his people . . .
particularly to those of shipbuilding and navigation . . . and
of the friendly feelings he has on all occasions exhibited to all
subjects, Asiatic as well as European of the British Empire'.[43] This
accomplished his long-standing aspiration.

Sayyid Sa'īd perfected a distinctly non-European style of
functioning in which his household remained central to politics.
Its centrality made the Sultanate the exemplar of a distinctly
Islamic political practice that marked the royal family as the
'inner' sphere that constantly powered the 'outer' political realm of
action. He established matrimonial alliances keeping in mind his
political predicaments. His most favourite Persian Queen used her
Iranian contacts to handle the slave traffic from Persia in the age
of heightened anti-slave trade rhetoric. But most importantly, he

governed through his sons—the princes. They were integral to his sovereignty and shaped the frontiers of the Sultanate. He personally trained them in military and political matters. They were made in charge of military campaigns to expand his maritime frontiers in the Al Batinah coast as well as the Persian Gulf.

Sayyid Sa'īd's ties with the tribal interior remained intact even if the Sultanate became more sea facing. In the early nineteenth century, as the British influence in the Western Indian Ocean increased, both Muscat and Zanzibar felt the heat, as they were transit points for the lucrative trade in slaves and arms. This meant that Sayyid Sa'īd maintained a continued interest in the interior to garner military labour and forge alliances to meet the political challenge on the maritime coast.[44] He recruited military labour from the tribal interiors, Persia and the Swahili coast to both defend and expand the maritime frontier. He connected with tribal Baluchi chiefs for commanders. And indeed, he augmented it on occasions by the sepoys shipped from Bombay by the British.[45]

The Sultan's refreshingly new political practices were in sync with the spirit of reforms that marked the 'revolutionary age' in world history. His political sovereignty was powered by his imaginative and roving mind that was ever engaged in stitching together what are traditionally seen in the Western political practice as dichotomies: the private household and the public political space, the inward-looking tribal society and the more outward-leaning port cities, the local issues and the global concerns.

The Counter-Revolutionary Sultan: Sayyid Thuwayni at Muscat

Thuwayni, who ruled from 1856–66, represents a different temporal moment in the Indian Ocean world when the British influence was at its peak and the waves of counter-revolutionary imperialism were gaining traction. As the favourite son of the dead Sultan, heeled at Muscat, he aspired to step into his father's boots as the sovereign of a united Oman that included Zanzibar. His hopes were dashed with the British-sponsored division of the Sultanate into Muscat and Zanzibar in 1861. He lamented this unjust division—he claimed that it economically favoured Zanzibar, with the subsidy promised to him being irregular and erratic. He attributed the depleting economy of Muscat to the loss of the lucrative slave trade profits that flowed from the island in his father's time. He loathed his brother Majid at Zanzibar and regarded him as his political subordinate, even though the 1861 division had declared him the independent ruler of Zanzibar.

Thuwayni made the most of his political predicaments, balancing his rule with imperial agendas and circumventing the clouds of imperial clampdown on Oman. He maintained a foothold in the Persian port of Bandar Abbas, renewing the lease signed by his father. He also used his political capital for leverage with Western imperial powers. His rule was marked by the playing off of Asian imperialism as represented by Qajar Iran with the politics of the Western powers.

As compared to his father, Thuwayni leaned less on the household and on the practice of striking matrimonial alliances to fashion his politics. Instead, he relied more on the tribal interiors for political and economic sustenance. The substantive losses in the slave trade that followed his father's death made him turn inwards to the tribal areas for support. He continued to maintain a foothold in Bandar Abbas, but used it more to offset the increasing British influence in the Gulf. The tribal alliances powered his politics more than the cementing of matrimonial liaisons leading to the diversification of the household. He made strategic alliances with tribal factions and recruited military labour from their ranks with an eye to fulfil his expansionist political aspirations. With his tribal support base intact, he also invested in the dates and indigo economy in the interior.

However, it was the Wahhabis who offered him the perfect launching pad to step on to the global stage. His political sovereignty was carved by striking alliances with the tribes to dent the Wahhabi expansion into his territory.[46] The social capital he gained in the interior made him an attractive ally and negotiator for the British, who wished to check the Wahhabi menace too. He used this clout to squeeze into the imperial space and get global visibility. The Wahhabis became the conduit for his entry into the imperial circuits as he deliberated over them with the British officers. It also made him strike close relations with Lt Col Pelly, the British agent in the Persian Gulf. Such relationships knitted him closely into the imperial networks. With his political sovereignty grounded firmly in the military labour and economy of the tribal interior and his engagements with the imperial powers intact, he often put his political sovereignty on display. More than his siblings, he was the warrior prince, well known for his constant military campaigns and celebratory marches along the Al Batinah coastline and the Persian Gulf. These showcased his sovereign status and its deep rooting in the tribal interior.

Thuwayni put this political confidence to effective use in the British-led arbitration to resolve the subsidy dispute between him and his brother Majid. The arbitration was led by the British Consul at Zanzibar, Lt Col Rigby, who mediated between the brothers. He leaned on precedent, history and customary practice to divide political sovereignty between them. Such interventions manufactured the Omani tradition. Thuwayni not only participated in the process but also turned it to his advantage.

Indeed, arbitration became a welcome forum whose legalities Thuwayni used for careering.[47] Thus, he cashed in on the rejection of the practice of primogeniture and the emphasis on unigeniture that underlay the manufactured 'tradition'. He extended the logic of the open-ended succession that unigeniture guaranteed to assert his sovereign status over Zanzibar as well. He found arbitration particularly attractive as he 'forum shopped' in the imperial assemblage comprising the British, French, Germans and the Americans. He dragged in the imperial powers, exploiting in particular the Anglo-French rivalry, to complicate its legal wrangles to his best advantage. Navigating the tribal and the imperial webs became his characteristic feature in firming up his sovereign status. This marked his signature political practice to dent the waves of counter-imperialism that shrouded the ocean in the long nineteenth century.

Sayyid Majid at Zanzibar: Slave Trade, Cholera and the Bombay Inspiration

Thuwayni's rival brother, Sayyid Majid, remained no unsuspecting victim to his machinations. He was located at Zanzibar, the centre of imperial interest because of the profits of slave trade. This spatial context made his politics distinct from Thuwayni's. His career underlines the importance of factoring not just the temporal but also the spatial context in the narrative of the Indian Ocean.

Indeed, the sibling rivalry with Thuwayni became Majid's entry point into the web of relationships involving both imperial powers and the Indian, Arab and Swahili merchants, slavers and bankers who carpeted the ocean. He made the most of the historical conjunction at Zanzibar that brought imperial hegemony, the rivalries for slave profits and the cholera pandemic together. This rare moment launched Majid at the centre of imperial politics that was characterized by the jockeying for the profits of slavery as well as the efforts to combat the ravages of the cholera pandemic that struck the island with ferocity.

This instant visibility on the global scale made him strike friendships with British officers. His father and brothers had done this too. But he did so from a position of greater strength and bargaining power, fully aware that from the British Consul in Zanzibar, Lt Col Rigby, to the British agent in the Persian Gulf, Pelly, all needed him in their slave trade politics, as also in their cholera containment mission. He was fully aware that so many of these Western imperial careers rested on his manoeuvres. He cleverly cashed in on this moment and used this dependence to extend his political ambit to British India, which boosted his political sovereign status.

Majid's link with Bombay was unprecedented, as neither his father nor his brother Thuwayni had included the city in their political aspirations. He visited the city and carved his career on a more extended political canvas that included this British Indian port city. This lent him a much higher standing in the imperially crowded world than his father or brother Thuwayni. The extension of his Indian Ocean frontier to British India brought huge dividends. He used the friendships made during his Bombay stint, with officers such as Pelly, to explain to the European powers what slavery meant to him and his people. The local rendition of slavery not only made him justify it for his use but also made him an active participant in the ongoing discussions in imperial circles on what was a truly global issue. He justified the practice of slavery in local society and signed agreements with the British, making it legal within his territory. This projected him as the local guardian defending the legitimate rights of his people to deal with slaves. He even registered his subjects and documented them so that they could exclusively avail the hard-fought concessions he obtained for them from the British to carry on with the slave trade. In doing so, he underlined his sovereignty as he defined their legal status and his own jurisdiction.

Additionally, he used the ambiguities and the angularities of the abolition rhetoric to create a niche for himself in the imperially crowded oceanic world. He exposed the hypocrisy of the prohibition narrative that clamped down on the slave trade and yet turned a blind eye to the sinking of British private capital in the island's sugar and clove plantations, which were driven by slave labour.[48] He exploited the Anglo-French imperial rivalries over the profits of the slave trade and refused to let the Western powers monopolize the trade.

As cholera ravaged his island and the British launched their critique of his urban planning and highlighted the poor sanitation conditions, he looked for refuge in a new urban site—Dar as Salaam. This newly founded city of his dream was strikingly similar to Bombay. It epitomized the centrality of this British port city in his oceanic imaginary. It encapsulated beautifully his embracive political imaginary and the expansive Indian Ocean topography even as it exuded his standing as a sought-after tall leader in the imperial assemblage.

Barghash and the Making of the 'Modern National Monarchy'

Of all the Omani royals, it was Barghash (1871–89), Majid's younger brother, who was the most mobile in a world that was still very imperial. He built his sovereignty using a repertoire of referents from multiple contexts. The constant sibling rivalries for succession, the European politics for control of the Western Indian Ocean, and the discussions on the 1873 slave ban treaty ensured that he moved across Bombay, Muscat, Zanzibar, Cairo, Palestine, Jerusalem, Paris, Marseilles and London in many capacities: exile, negotiator, lobbyist, reformist and simple royal visitor.

In the course of these travels across the maritime cities of the Indian Ocean littoral, Barghash familiarized himself with the ideas of Islamic reformists advocating unity, imbibed notions of urban planning and picked up new technologies like that of print. He projected himself as a 'just' Sultan who derived his jurisprudence from an array of Islamic Ibāḍī legal texts that he got printed for larger circulation. His exposure to reformist hubs such as Cairo made him welcoming to Islamic scholars from the Hadhramaut as well. And his various stints in Bombay, in close association with British society, made him learn the art of diplomacy and negotiation. Indeed, these friendships led him to a visit to London escorted by the British Consul John Kirk to discuss the slave treaty of 1873. The visit was dotted with honours and state banquets, and it gave him instant visibility on a global stage. He was quick to use this stature once he was back in Zanzibar. He cashed in on global flashpoints—such as the hysteria over the slave trade abolition, the mail and telegraph service linking Zanzibar to Britain via Aden and the steamship fuelling depots and routes—for the realization of his own political aspirations. He also expanded his vision for commercial expansion, making the east coast of Africa the premier market for the Bombay export trade, particularly for an unbleached *merekani* lookalike cloth.

Barghash's ingenious fusion of Islam, slavery and imperial agendas enabled him to refurbish monarchy as a 'modern' political form that was produced by his entanglements with imperial powers. The production of such new forms of 'modern' monarchy that projected him as the 'symbol of nationhood' was a balancing act that ensured his status as the Sultan in an age of proliferating nation states.[49] His figuring of slavery as a familial system different from the Atlantic slavery and he as the father figure of his people, including the slaves, was one such gesture.[50]

The new 'modern national monarchy' was produced in particular through his participation in global conversations and experiments on slavery. He opposed the 1873 slave treaty that banned the export of slaves from the island and warned the British interlocutor, Bartle Frere, of an insurrection like the one that had 'happened to the Americans'. He not only showcased his awareness of global politics but reflected an even stronger connect with the local political economy and geography. He put forward a sophisticated argument based on the exceptional character of Zanzibar's political culture and economy to justify slave labour on the island even as he pledged his support for the ban on slave export.

This 'modern monarchy' lent the island a cosmopolitan modernity that was religiously inclined, imperially entangled and firmly grounded in slave labour. This cosmopolitan modernity was old in the sense that it had the embracive Islamic reformist culture and slavery at its core. But it was also 'new', as it experimented with ideas of urban planning and governance, used the print and engaged in the art of diplomacy and negotiation with Western powers. Barghash saw no contradiction between his modernizing agenda—characterized by Bombay-style buildings, railways, waterworks, powerhouses and the telegraph— and the promotion of Islamic reform and culture in sync with similar trends in the Ottoman cities that he visited.

Barghash projected himself not only as a 'just' Sultan rooted in the Ibāḍī religious and legal intellectual tradition but also as a 'modernizing' Sultan. He was exiled to Bombay very early in his career during the succession struggle with his rival brother, Sayyid Majid. It was here that he was exposed to British material and political culture. His architectural hallmark—the *Bayt al-'Ajā'ib* or the house of wonders—reflects British Indian influences, as do his infrastructure projects, such as electrification, roads, the telegraph and railway line. He brought to Zanzibar the printing press from Bombay and used it to disseminate his religious views across the island. He even used these material and ideational moorings to project himself as the 'symbol of nationhood'. In 1890, a year after his death, when Zanzibar became a British protectorate, his political and commercial legacy was tough to dismiss.

Sayyid Turki at Sohar: The Land-Oriented Sovereign

In 1871, Sayyid Turki, the fifth son of Sayyid Sa'īd, marched overland from Soor to Muscat to install himself as the Sultan. His terrestrial rather than sea gaze marked him out from his father and contemporaries, such as his brother Barghash. Turki's career offers insights into the political dividends reaped by a land-facing Sultan and the difference that his terrestrial spatiality makes to our understanding of the Indian Ocean political culture.

Turki's overland conquest of Muscat was made possible by the array of support bases he tapped into his march: the Banī Bū Hasan tribes helped him. The British did not obstruct him. He had support from Zanzibar, where both his brothers Majid and Barghash remained allies. And once settled as the Sultan of Muscat, he reached out via matrimonial ties to his brother Thuwayni's family as well.[51]

Not surprisingly, Turki's sovereignty was rooted in the tribal society, continued to derive from his extended household and interacted with imperial networks. He sustained this social base by his constant mobility across the tribal interiors. He struck alliances with its influential members, such as the Wahhabis. Unlike his brother Thuwayni, who forged anti-Wahhabi alliances, his careering remained dependent on these radical Islamic reformists of the north who held considerable clout. Simultaneously, he also dug his heels into the date- and indigo-driven agricultural economy of the tribal interior. Indeed, dates and the Wahhabis entangled him in imperial politics. He used the Wahhabis in particular as his social capital to leverage with imperial powers that dreaded their disruption to maritime commerce.

His political strides in the interior were determined by his deep local knowledge of the vagaries of weather and its impact on the date orchards and the markets. In 1878, he sailed northwards from Muscat in his yacht—the *Dar el-Salam*—to occupy the fortress town of Burka and consolidate his tribal foothold. He knew this was the perfect time to consolidate his hold, as heavy rains and flooding had destroyed the date crop in the whole of Oman. There was a lurking fear of famine as well. The tribes and the date plantation owners were facing hardships due to this unprecedented economic crisis. Similarly, other towns, such as Al Rustaq, were taken over by intercepting their date trade. Turki's meddling with the politics of the tribal interior produced a realm of contested sovereignty and flexible jurisdictions. Muslim reformists such as the Wahhabis from northern Arabia slipped into Oman using these porous crevices in his governance. Their influence on society was most evident in his reign.

However, the Wahhabi connection also made him the most influential of the Sultans. Both his brothers and the imperial powers despised him but could not do without him. The heeling in the tribal lands made him a sought-after figure in his sibling networks, who leaned on him for help. Indeed, he never lost track of his Al Busaidi moorings epitomized in the household. The strengthening of the household through carefully chosen sibling alliances, matrimonial alliances and gift exchanges remained central to his political moves even as he leveraged the imperial politics to his own diplomatic manoeuvring.

Turki's firm grounding in the tribal society made him enter the imperial world from a position of strength. This was increased by his influential position with the Wahhabis, who were viewed as the biggest political challenge. Turki also tapped into the rampant Persophobia in the imperial assemblage to become close with Qajar Iran. He entrenched himself in Muscat and built on the Omani footholds, such as Bandar Abbas, in the Persian Gulf. Like his brothers, he too mapped his politics on the wide imperial ambit that carpeted the region; and he also held British Indian cities integral to his political world. But unlike them, he was more oriented inwards—to the tribal interiors—from where he bargained with relatively greater strength with the imperial powers. His clout with the Wahhabis and other tribes in the interior sharpened his political sovereignty as he continued to engage with the imperial powers on the political challenges they posed. Turki's machinations revealed the continuing relevance of the inland terrestrial politics in shaping the political culture of the ocean.

III

Murders, Coups and Violence: Energizing the Omani Political Practice

The stories of rancour, conspiracy and deceit that marked Omani careering after the death of the patriarch Sayyid Sa'īd were dismissed as mere scandals and dropped from the pages of both Omani and Indian Ocean history. Thus, the murder of Sultan Thuwayni allegedly by his son, Prince Salim, and Salim's subsequent coronation as the Sultan, followed by his sudden expulsion from Muscat by Azzan bin Qais, rarely met with historical scrutiny.[52] At best, such episodes were considered aberrations from the relatively stable rule of Sayyid Sa'īd. However, when viewed from the temporally and spatially contingent nature of Omani careering, they reflect the exceptional political culture of the region, whose many contingencies and the intersections of the local and the imperial allowed political adventurism.

The Omani royals' political practice, which brought together religion, slavery, family, tribal and imperial politics, could always backfire on individual Sultans, as rivals could dip with equal gusto into its many strands to test their political fortunes. Such contestations only lent traction to the region's political culture. Royal coups and misdemeanours did not necessarily amount to political crisis and instability. Rather, they reflected the healthy functioning of the new style of political practice that the Sultans had perfected and that made them active agents of change even in the high period of imperialism.

As we saw, Thuwayni lost his life in one such political challenge to his rule. And his son Salim, who installed himself as the Sultan, did not last for too long as the ruler either. Again, in 1873, Turki experienced a similar political threat, from his brother Aziz, soon after his installation as Sultan. And at Zanzibar, Majid lived in continuous fear of political challenge from his brother Barghash. But these contestations for power lent traction to both the Omani and the Indian Ocean politics. They only energized the political culture as rival contestants wallowed in the Omani political practice that derived from multiple contexts, both local and imperial: the Arab tribes, the Wahhabis and slaves and the entanglements with imperial politics. Thus, for instance, Turki and the rival brother Aziz both fought with their respective tribal support base and both tapped into the imperial assemblage to the best of their abilities, with Aziz relying on the Banī Runeyah alongside the Bedouins and Turki on the Ghāfirīs.

The flexible and contingent nature of Omani careering also saw innumerable instances of sibling cooperation, especially when there was no apparent conflict of interest. This was most evident when Turki bonded with Barghash in Zanzibar, as he saw him as someone with no imperial ambition for Muscat. Indeed, the cordiality between them resulted in many gift exchanges that proved particularly useful for the cash-starved Turki. Despite his financial woes, Turki emerged as a much-feared and yet sought-after ally in the Western Indian Ocean because he successfully grounded himself at the intersection of the tribal, the imperial and the family networks and drew huge dividends.

Not surprisingly, individual setback and ousters never extinguished political aspirations or the appetite for power. The seamless waters of the Western Indian Ocean and the diverse range of people who crowded its space offered endless opportunities for a second chance. Indeed, the ocean nurtured Omani politics, as it became the perfect canvas for political dabbling by the Sultans. Thus, Thuwayni's son, Salim, continued to pose difficulties to Turki even after he was expelled from Muscat and replaced by Qais. Salim was a wanderer on the Omani littoral and had taken refuge in Bandar Abbas after being ousted from Muscat. In order to end his nuisance value, Turki was willing to grant him, his nephew, a monthly allowance of $300 on condition that he would reside in British territory and abstain from interfering in Muscat affairs. But Salim refused the offer. He not only claimed a larger allowance but also the unrestricted right to certain property in Muscat. Basically, like all his other relatives, he was not willing to quit careering as he dabbled in the politics of the imperial assemblage and moved along its intersections with the tribal and family networks.

Salim located himself in the ports of the Persian Gulf on the other side of Muscat—Gwadar, Jashk and Qishm—to keep watch on Muscat events. He hopped around the Persian and British port towns, straddling the imperial assemblage and never losing an opportunity to use its networks, just as all others of his family had done. He arrived in Bombay in 1873 and asked for British support, playing the victim: he said he had been ousted from Muscat by Qais in 1868. He was forced to flee Muscat with his mother, brother and sisters and remain in hiding in foreign lands, he claimed. Later, he sent his mother and sisters to Zanzibar in the hope that they would get aid there.

But Turki, who had created a comfortable niche for himself both in the imperial assemblage and the tribal networks of Al Batinah, elbowed him out. In 1875, the British government arrested Salim while he was making an attempt to revisit Oman with a band of armed followers on the mission to raise disturbance against Turki. Salim was captured and removed to Karachi and later to the fortress of Hyderabad in Sindh, where he was detained by a warrant issued under Regulation III of 1818. While at Hyderabad, Turki consented to allow Salim a monthly allowance of $100 for his maintenance. He also ordered that the prisoner was to be subjected to such a degree of restraint as would 'prevent his escaping or carrying on intrigues'.

I

Sayyid Saʻīd: The Arab Sultan in the Age of Revolution

The Context

In 1842, Sayyid Saʻīd (1791–1856), the Sultan of Oman and Zanzibar, checked with the British Consul at Muscat if it would be disrespectful to recycle to the Nizam of Hyderabad, in India, a carriage and harness that was gifted to him by Queen Victoria. He said he had not made any use of it, as there were no roads of any description in Zanzibar where he could use it. As a result, the carriage remained in its packing case. He once got it taken out to have a look at it and then got it repacked.

The carriage was a gift on the exchange of the Ratifications of the Convention of Commerce between him and Her Majesty. The Sultan was recycling it as his gift to the Nizam because of the 'extraordinary good treatment all Arabs met with' at Hyderabad. He said he was constantly hearing of the Nizam's kindness to all Arabs. Once he got the permission, he sent the carriage, along with other gifts, to the Nizam via Bombay. The Bombay government assisted in its onward journey to Hyderabad. The Sultan kept a constant link with Bombay as, among other things, this was a contact point for the purchase, repairs and management of his fleet of ships. Ali Muhammad, one of the Queen's Justices of Peace in the city, received the carriage and arranged for its transport to Hyderabad.[1]

The Queen's gift of a carriage to an island with poor roads revealed her ignorance of Zanzibar's urban infrastructure despite many treaties of cooperation she had signed with the Sultan. And the Sultan's request to forward the carriage as a personal gift to the Nizam of Hyderabad, in India, via his many contacts at Bombay, reflected his wide networks, political vision and the aspiration to engage with the wider politics of the Indian Ocean. The incident best exemplifies that there was more to the Sultan than met the eye beneath the diplomatic bonhomie and treaties of cooperation he signed with the British. He was most certainly lending the Asian slant to the 'age of revolution' as it played out in the Indian Ocean.

The Argument

Sayyid Saʻīd, who reigned from 1806 to 1856, can be situated in what is known in world history as the 'age of revolution'. This temporal categorization has been a valid tool of analysis to scrutinize European political and economic reforms in the period leading up to the late nineteenth-century waves of economic integration and globalization. What is less known is the role of the Arab and Asian rulers who dotted the Indian Ocean littoral and were equally effective agents of change. As a result, the analytical category becomes heavily Eurocentric, leading to the assumption that the Indian Ocean world became an unsuspecting victim to imperial hegemony in the decades that followed.

Sayyid Saʻīd's career corrects this imbalance. This critical period of world history—marked by a widening crisis in Eurasian land empires, the end of Persian dominance, the Ottoman crisis and the rise of Russophobia in the imperial circles—offered Sultans like him the perfect context to step in as critical agents of change in the region. His economic interaction with the winds of globalization and his political aspiration as he engaged in conversations with the imperial powers, on slaves and the Wahhabis in particular, reflects the complex play of the 'age of revolution' which had a distinct feel and a particularly long temporality on the ocean.

Sayyid Saʿīd, in keeping with the spirit of the 'revolutionary age', made a break from his family tradition of ruling from the interior tribal town of Al Rustaq. Instead, he made the port city of Muscat his seat of power. He recalibrated existing traditions and religious beliefs and set up his base on the island of Zanzibar to maximize the profits of maritime trade in slaves. He clearly envisaged a wider role for himself in the fast-globalizing world system. And yet, he powered the 'age of revolution' in distinctly non-Western ways. The household remained the powerhouse of his forays into imperial politics. He diversified it to include a Persian princess, whom he married to get a foothold into the Persian Gulf and offset the control of the slave trade, in particular, by Britain.

His mobility was restricted to his straddling between Muscat and Zanzibar. It is in this corner of the Western Indian Ocean that he carved his political sovereignty by successfully bringing together imperialism, the politics on slavery and reformist Islam to his self-interest. His ingeniousness lay in balancing his specific sociological understanding of these issues to imperial agendas and in the embedding of Western material culture to local society. Together, these gestures lent a distinct cosmopolitan modernity to his Sultanate and gave the 'age of revolution' its Asian slant.

I

The Al Busaidi Dynasty in Oman: Dates, Indigo and the Ibāḍī Faith

Sayyid Saʿīd was born in 1791 and belonged to the Al Busaidi dynasty of Oman. The dynasty had a distinguished history in the region. It began its innings in the region by combining temporal and spiritual powers. Ahmad bin Saʿīd Al Busaidi (1749–83), the founder of the dynasty, was the son of a coffee merchant from Sohar, a port town north of Muscat. Among other military feats, his successful ouster of the Persian warlord Nadir Shah from Sohar and the tribal

interiors clinched for him the leadership of the family. In 1741, with
the support of the Ghāfirī and the Hināwī tribes, he was elected the
first Al Busaidi Imam of the Ibāḍī faith. This marked the beginning
of the Omani political tradition that fused temporal and spiritual
power. This fusion lent it the name Imamate.

The Ibāḍī Imamate was based at the tribal town of Al Rustaq.
Ahmad ruled for thirty-four years and, although located in the
interior, his strength came from a range of economic activities,
both in the agricultural sphere and in maritime trade. He kept
his gaze on the two fronts and was sensitive to any reports of
high-handedness in the exercise of his temporal leadership. He
always attended to complaints of extortion against his son with
alacrity. This was apparent very early in his reign, in the lucrative
indigo production sector where the lure of profits often led to
improprieties. He disapproved of the innovations his son, Saʻīd,
made in setting up monopolies in the indigo production and
dyeing prevalent in the towns.

Ahmad had made Saʻīd the Wālī (Governor) of Nizwa. Saʻīd
began to set up his monopoly in the indigo dyeing industry in that
town. He erected a building and decreed all dyers to dye there,
forbidding them to dye elsewhere without his permission or without
paying him a certain tax. The people of the town complained to
their Shaykh Sayyid al-Sāʼighi. The Shaykh went to the marketplace
and ordered the monopolist to remove his set-up. Saʻīd complained
to his father, who was at Al Rustaq, naturally hiding from him the
fact that he had established a monopoly. The Imam said, 'I believe
you have introduced some illegal novelty at Nizwa and the people
there have contended with you about it.' He removed him as Wālī
of Nizwa. But later, the Imam marched against the tribals to Hujrah
al-Akr and destroyed their date plantations in retaliation to their
protest against his son Saʻīd bin Ahmad.[2]

In 1783, Saʻīd bin Ahmad succeeded his father as Imam. And
like his father, he remained the temporal head as well of the Omanis.
He remained focused on the dates and indigo economy of the tribal
towns of Al Rustaq and Nizwa. Free from the restraints of his father,
he initiated his pet economic reforms: taxes and monopolies on

indigo dyeing. This made him very unpopular. It offered the perfect opportunity to his son, Hamad, to galvanize support against his rule.

Hamad's revolt triggered the beginnings of the separation of temporal and spiritual power in the Sultanate. Eventually, Hamad set himself up at Muscat and let his father Saʿīd function as the Imam from Al Rustaq. Saʿīd continued as the Imam until his death in 1821, while Hamad and his successors battled it out for the control of Muscat. The tension triggered by his attempt to separate the spiritual and temporal seats of power continued to simmer.

Saʿīd bin Ahmad's Imamate was known for its rootedness in the tribal interiors where his officials and governors reigned supreme, garnering support for him. The tribes upheld the Ibāḍī faith. They remained premier recruits also for military labour. And the ancient towns of Al Rustaq and Nizwa remained the seat of the Imam's power. Significantly, Nizwa was not only the seat of the Ibāḍī Imamate but also an important indigo-producing town. Located about 175 km from Muscat, its bazaars traditionally had dyers, and the blue dye produced was used to colour the imported cotton from Bombay and America that flooded its markets.[3]

Indeed, the profits from the dates and indigo dyeing and manufacture oiled the Imamate's political economy. Along with the date plantations, indigo manufacture and dyeing constituted the key revenue-bearing activities that sustained the Imamate. The nearby town of Bat also had about 400 Beni Kalban tribals who cultivated indigo and were dyers. They made the dye in large earthen vats called *kabaia*.[4] Indeed, this part of the tribal interior was dotted with villages, such as Mohaira, involved in indigo cultivation and production.

A lot of indigo was cultivated in the district of Al-Dhahirah too. S.B. Miles, a British army officer who served as a diplomat in various Arabic-speaking countries like Oman and who travelled through the region, noted that he was surprised at 'the extent of ground under it [indigo]'[5]. The town of Dhank in Al-Dhahirah had small indigo-making and dyeing industries. People had their own indigo dye vats and dyed imported cotton cloth from America and Bombay along with local homespun stuff. Similarly, the town of Ibri was both a dye manufacturing centre as well as a dyeing hub.[6]

In 1792, Hamad was ousted by his uncle Sultan bin Ahmad Al Busaidi (1792–1804). When Ahmad died, Badr bin Saif became the Regent for a brief period, as the Sultan's sons, including our protagonist, Sayyid Sa'īd, were very young.

II

Sayyid Sa'īd Becomes the Sultan (1806)

A New Form of Political Practice: Muscat, the Sea-Facing Political Unit

In 1806, Sayyid Sa'īd became the Sultan, ending the two-year period of Regency of his uncle Badr bin Saif. It was widely alleged that his uncle was murdered to pave the way for his political takeover. However, in typical Omani fashion, stories of such misdemeanours posed no deterrent to his political stride. He was a very young Sultan known to be a 'good-looking young man of moderate stature and florid complexion'. His personal life exemplifies archipelagic thinking. He spoke Arabic, Persian and Hindustani and had many concubines from cultures ranging from Central Asia, Iran to Malabar in India and Turkey, Ethiopia, Nubia, the Swahili coast and the Black Sea. His few legal wives were of Arab and Persian origin.[7] Indeed, his private household space reflected the web of relations he crafted with the world outside via marriage and concubines: from India to Iran, the Swahili coast and Ethiopia to Assyria and Circassia.

Sayyid Sa'īd inherited the Al Busaidi political legacy that combined spiritual and temporal powers, albeit replete with internal turmoil. This was epitomized by the Imam—the temporal and religious head—who governed while located at the interior towns of Al Rustaq. Several attempts in the past to separate the fusion of these powers in one person had failed even if they left a lingering tension.

However, in sync with the revolutionary fervour of his age, Sa'īd broke his family tradition—he located his base at Muscat and projected himself as the temporal head of Oman. He allowed Sa'īd bin Ahmad to continue as the Imam until his death in 1821. And yet, the tribal interiors remained integral to his military and economy. He posted his oldest son Hilal as the Governor of Al Rustaq. The area offered not just agricultural revenue but also served as the nursery for military recruits. These were needed in times of crisis to defend the expanding maritime frontiers, which included the Persian Gulf ports of Bandar Abbas, Gwadar and Meena.

However, it was the turn to the sea that best characterized his reign. Sayyid Sa'īd was keener on building his maritime presence at a time when the European powers were hovering over the Gulf with an eye to control its slave traffic. Muscat and Zanzibar were particularly attractive to the Europeans, as they were major slave depots and transit points in the slave journey to Europe. The Sultan was not keen on giving them a free way. He focused on Muscat and Zanzibar as his maritime frontier, which was to be adequately strengthened. The emergence of Muscat as the principal political unit of governance heralded his new sea-facing political practice.

From the time he took charge in 1806, he launched himself as a 'merchant prince' and began building a maritime empire, often in a subtle conflict and outright competition with the British. He focused on the shipping industry in Muscat as the source of his revenue and power. He put together a fine naval fleet to sustain his dream maritime empire. He initiated a rigorous drive to develop Oman's maritime economy. He cultivated Muscat and the entire length of the Al Batinah coast, where this port city was located, so as to underline his global gaze.

The Muscat customs were farmed to an Indian Bania for $1,80,000 annually; he was paid annually $5000 as permission to export salt from the mines at Ormuz. He got the same amount from the ports on the Persian side of the Gulf– Bandar Abbas, Larek and Qishm. And the Baluchi chiefs of the Makran coast also sent him a small tribute.[8] Indeed, Jairam, the Indian Customs Master, invested heavily in the building of the Customs House at Muscat.[9]

Sa'īd presided over an economy marked by gift exchanges that spread out to the British and the European world and embraced Bombay and the Nizam of Hyderabad in India.[10] Horse chariots, ships, clocks and glassware were some of the important gift articles he received and recycled to his contacts. The example of this was the gift of the beautiful vessel *The Liverpool*, built in Bombay in 1826, to King William IV. The vessel was rechristened *The Imam* by the recipient in honour of its donor.[11] In 1842, when the pressure on him to ban the slave trade was mounting, he sent a representative to London with gifts for Queen Victoria. These included two pearl necklaces, two emeralds, an ornament made like a crown, ten cashmere shawls and four horses. He bargained with her, asking for Bahrain in exchange for the abolition of slavery.[12] Gift exchanges became his way of building networks both within and outside the Anglophone and Francophone imperial assemblage.

Sa'īd looked to Bombay for placing orders for any big ships he required to strengthen his flotilla.[13] His agents in Bombay supervised his ship purchases. In 1819, under their guidance, the Parsi shipbuilders of the city constructed a sturdy ship for his fleet made of teak wood—*The Shah Alum*. It could hold its own in a test of seaworthiness against European ships and would receive a benediction from a Muslim holy man before it set sail for Muscat.[14] *Caroline* was another purchase from Bombay made to order by the Parsi shipbuilders. The arrival of these ships from Bombay alarmed the British who, in this period, were still unsuccessful in monopolizing shipbuilding on the Indian coast. But they caused great excitement in Muscat, as their arrival inevitably coincided with an expedition the Sultan was leading: the battle against the Wahhabis at Ra's al-Khaimah in 1819 was the occasion for the purchase of both these Bombay ships.[15]

And of course, the Indian merchant community in Muscat offered the more enduring link between Oman and the Indian port towns. The Bombay government too had transactions when it suited its interest. For instance, it was always a ready supplier of pistols, guns, cannon and mortar to Sa'īd in his many battles with the Wahhabis in the interior.[16] The Sultan's artillery was armed in European fashion, and gunpowder was freely distributed by the Sultan from his magazines to people who required it.[17] Sa'īd slowly integrated Bombay into his new, more expansive, geography of the Indian Ocean.

In keeping his eye on a wider embrace of politics and commerce outside the Western assemblage, the Sultan developed vast stakes in Qajar Iran and established a foothold in both the Arab and Persian sides of the Persian Gulf. The connections between Persia and Oman go back a long way in history. Many of the Omani interior towns, such as Adam, with sophisticated water supply—*felejes*—have Persian settlements going back to antiquity. In the eighteenth century, the Persian warlords Nadir Shah (1747) and Karim Khan (1753) sent contingents to invade Oman and demand tribute. Nadir Shah tried his luck, not too successfully, in the interior towns of Nizwa and Al Rustaq as well. For some time, he held the port of Sohar in control.[18] But in the nineteenth century, the tables were turned: it was the Omani rulers who sought a foothold in Iran.

In 1798, Sayyid Saʿīd leased the port of Bandar Abbas from the Persians. The Sultan was willing to solve all issues over Bandar Abbas with the British because he had very high stakes in the port. It was of huge commercial importance to him. It was the place of deposit for exquisite fruit brought from the interiors of Persia and sent to Muscat. And dates from Burka and Al Rustaq in Oman were exported from here.[19] But most importantly, the slave trade between Oman and Persia was a source of huge profit. Bandar Abbas, Qishm, Lingah and other Persian ports, on lease to the Sultan, were critical to the flow of this traffic from Zanzibar via Persia to the Arab ports on the Al Batinah coast: Sohar and farther north to the kingdoms of Raʾs al-Khaimah. Omani Arab slavers and *nākhodās*, or the captain of the ship, used this route to escape British surveillance over Muscat. They used Persian vessels or Persian flags to exempt themselves from British checks.

The Sultan rarely stopped them from using such 'legal technologies' (the Persian flag, vessel and the pass). And they used these freely to negotiate the maritime legal culture that included many players: the Persian Qajars, the British and the French. The Omani Arabs picked the relevant flags, as it suited them to interrogate the many imperial legal repertoires that framed the ocean. This was their way of 'domesticating' imperial legal strictures to the local requirements.[20]

On the Persian Gulf, he already had a foothold in Makran in Baluchistan, where his father had managed to get the Gwadar port from Nasir Khan, the Khan of Kelat, in trust. The Omanis were expected to lend naval protection to the Makran coast as a consequence of this deal. Baluchistan became an enduring link with its military labour in the constant service of Sayyid Sa'īd. In 1828, more than 3000 Baluchi bodyguards were in his attendance. They manned his forts and palaces and were his trusted agents.[21]

The good relations with Persia always paid. In 1811, the Persian Shah was happy to send him troops under the command of Sadi Khan of the Qajar royal dynasty to fight the Wahhabis. The contingent arrived at Burka via Bandar Abbas, from where the Sultan picked them up on Omani vessels.[22] He also had Persian bombardiers to handle the artillery that he purchased from Bombay.[23] He held vast territories on the western shore of the Persian Gulf, possessing maritime rich parts of the Makran as far as Kutch, and the influential ports of Bandar Abbas, Gwadar, the island of Ormuz, Qishm and Larek.

But his most lucrative outpost was Zanzibar in East Africa. His personal wealth skyrocketed when he relocated his capital to the island in 1832. His sources of wealth on the island were royal monopolies, slave trade and clove plantations. He also collected cowries from Kilwa, Zanzibar and Lamu which he exported to Calcutta and the Persian Gulf on his own account. From the 1840s, he took advantage of the caravan trade in ivory and cloves. He collected an annual revenue of $75,000 from the slave trade. He was welcoming of foreign residents, flirted with the French and allowed the Americans to establish a trading consulate on the island in 1837. By the 1840s, he had his flag flying at most of the ports on the east coast.[24] This was despite the fact that his rule was riddled with often-violent resistance from the tribal chiefs of the east coast of Africa. He was involved in trouble with Mombasa, Makdisha and other clan chiefs.

The Sultan's clove plantations were run on slave labour.[25] He invested in clove cultivation, having passed penal regulations in 1828 that made it mandatory to put a certain fixed amount of land under clove plantation.[26] By 1854, half of the 7000 to 10,000 imported slaves in Zanzibar were employed on local clove estates. The anti-slave trade treaties that he signed with the British only increased slave labour in the island's plantations, as the export of slaves became difficult.[27] Later, when clove prices fell due to competition, he also experimented with sugar production and set up a factory with two experts to help him. He also tried his luck with indigo, but without much success.

Tapping into the British Private Firm Networks in Zanzibar

The Sultan was not only arbitraging between different political actors and their 'legal technologies' (the flag and the pass) but also 'forum shopping' on the commercial front. He did allow the Americans the favoured trading status before the British, who had helped him fight the Qasimis, and also formed alliances with the French. But this did not stop him from tapping into British networks in self-interest. His sugar plantations showcased the political practice he had perfected of tapping into British technology and private interests for his economic agendas.

Sayyid Saʿīd was always keen to invest and expand the sugar cane industry. He imported technology and personnel from Mascarenes and Britain and put them to his own use. By 1819, two sugar mills had been installed in Zanzibar. One of these was owned by Saleh—the wealthy Governor of the island, who had invested in clove plantations as well. In the 1840s, he encouraged many partnerships with the British, in which they provided the latest machinery and supervision, whereas the land and the slave labour came from Zanzibar. In 1847, 10,000 frasilas[28] of sugar was produced as a consequence of these partnerships and sent to Britain and America for refining.[29]

Sayyid Saʿīd had allowed British subjects and privateers to freely use slaves to work as agricultural labour on their estates. They paid a certain sum per slave to the dealer, with an understanding that the concerned slaves were to be the servants of and workforce of the Briton who bought them. The duration

of work was to be agreed upon between the contracting parties.
At the expiry of this designated period, the slaves were to be
released from slavery in the way the French had stipulated in
their contracts with the Sultan.

It was in Sa'īd's interest to allow slave labour in private
British plantations. He not only got money for the slaves but also
benefited from the plantations, as he often co-shared in these
private investments of British firms. Captain Cogan, who owned
a sugar mill and was in the business of sugar manufacture in
Zanzibar, was a particularly close business associate of the Sultan.
His firm, called Cogan & Company, was established at Zanzibar
in 1841 and functioned well until 1847, by which time many
employees belonging to the firm died and the business ceased.[30]
But in the brief years of its functioning, it worked in close tandem
with the Sultan. The latter supplied the sugar cane and the slaves,
a person to superintend the mill and an engineer. One half of the
sugar was to be the property of Cogan and the other half that of
the Sultan.[31]

Cogan used slave labour and camouflaged his omissions in the
narrative of liberal philanthropy: he offered them 'release' from slave
status after the work was complete. This triggered in-house tension
between private entrepreneurs like him and British officials. Consul
Hamerton, who was weary of this practice, declared that he 'will not
consider the business between God and my own conscience in any
other way than ordering and abetting the slave trade'. He was of the
view that the dealer who disposes of his slaves invariably buys others
to supply other places. He could procure slaves at the highest rate
from $6 to $10 per head and was most likely to make a profit on each
man made over to the British subject.[32] Hamerton was convinced
that Cogan, under the guise of free labour, was shipping slaves to
work in his sugar estates.

Hamerton was convinced that Cogan's claim of getting free
labour from Zanzibar to work for him on his estates at an island
was hollow. He was confident that even thirty free men did not
exist in Zanzibar who could go to the island or anywhere else.
Neither were there any sailors or free men or Indian-style lascars

available at Zanzibar. He pointed out that even the Sultan was rightly worried about the practice Cogan was adopting of taking natives of his dominions on board European vessels to act as ground labour or sailors. He feared that, soon, slaves would be shipped, as it was near to impossible to find free men in Zanzibar. Hamerton was so incensed with Cogan's affairs that he even resented the demand from the latter of twenty labourers to load the British ship *Guard of Liverpool*, which they had chartered to send to Britain. He refused his order, pointing out that only a Qazi could declare if a man is free or slave and that he could not provide him the freemen he required.[33] Cogan retorted pointing to the detrimental effects of this policy on trade and British merchants. He wanted to know if native sailors would be allowed to him if the vessel fell short of hands due to sickness or death. He also pointed out that his ship had a native interpreter on board and a reasonable number of natives to act as grooms at sea to animals taken as cargo.[34]

The Sultan walked the tightrope between British officials and private entrepreneurs. While he was happy to cooperate with privateers on the sugar plantations for profit, he was not too keen to allow them free play on their independent projects using slave labour in the garb of 'free men'. He was determined to stop this foul play by refusing permission and asking the Qazi not to grant certificates of free status to the men who were being shipped. He also threatened that if Cogan continued with this practice, then he would make similar concessions to merchants of other nations as well.[35]

Hamerton was angry at the numerous concessions that Cogan had obtained from the Sultan, including of course his business partnership with him. He felt Cogan had achieved this status because he gave the false impression in the island that he was close to Her Majesty and her ministers and that he possessed great powers in Europe. Hamerton was incensed that rumours of a decline in his own influence floated freely on the island ever since Cogan arrived in Zanzibar. He pointed out that the Sultan himself often expressed his concern over Cogan's business ventures as the Arabs laughed at them. At one point Cogan had asked him for Rs 20,000 for *wikalat-*agency—the pay of an agent.[36]

The Sultan was canny enough not to let British private merchants have a free hand in his commerce. He tried to control the markets, monopolize the trade of ivory and copal to Britain and Europe and threaten the margins of profits accrued by British private merchants and companies. In 1847, F.R. Peters and J. Pollock—the former being the resident partner in Zanzibar of the firm Robert Cogan & Company and the latter also a British merchant trading in Zanzibar—objected to the Sultan's trade to Europe. They argued that he had confined his trade to Britain alone for all these years. British merchants like them had been beneficiaries. Often produce from his own personal dominions alone was exported, and it was reciprocated by imports of the produce of the dominions of Her Majesty. These British merchants were alarmed at local gossip that the Sultan was intending to monopolize various articles of produce to load on his own ships bound for London. This control of the market was new and against the spirit of partnership that they had hitherto enjoyed with him.

Peters and Pollock who were also the petitioners of the foreign merchants, felt that the Sultan and his people would have an edge over them as they would be able to buy and sell merchandize cheaper and on more favourable terms at Zanzibar than the foreign merchants. They argued that the Sultan's merchants and producers would be content with lower profits and would therefore give larger credit than Europeans. They feared that this new competitive trend would drive the British, the Americans and the French to the Merima—the coast of Africa opposite to Zanzibar. But as per the articles of a treaty, they could not trade in ivory and copal there; also, the Sultan's authority there was imperfect. No Customs House existed there, and the likelihood of disputes with locals was very high.[37]

Making the Most of Imperial Rivalries

Of equal concern to the British was the arrival at Muscat of the American trader negotiator Mr Roberts, who had been appointed plenipotentiary to negotiate a treaty of amity and commerce with Oman. His arrival signalled the growing tilt towards America, as it began to view Muscat and Zanzibar as commercial depots. From the 1820s, the date trade from Muscat to America intensified. Ships from the American port of Salem sailed to Zanzibar and Muscat via Aden. They loaded dates from Muscat and coffee from Aden. Hamerton noted eleven Salem ships arriving in Muscat for dates between 1851 and 1852. They either paid in cash or through the American cloth—the merekani.[38]

A tightly knit community of American merchants from the port town of Salem trading in cotton (merekani) existed in Zanzibar as well. The improvements in the custom regulations soon became a necessity, as these were in the hands of Banias with whom the British had developed a relationship but the Americans had not. The Americans were subjected to harassment by the Customs House farmer, an Indian trader, and merchants who were jealous of interlopers. Their interferences compelled them to make a representation to their government, which sent Roberts to work out an arrangement for them in Oman for securing their commerce.[39]

The 1833 treaty that Roberts was sent to lay the ground for saw the appointment of the first American Consul in Zanzibar, R.P. Waters in 1837. Most of the American diplomats like him were non-career individuals working as merchants or as agents of commercial firms. Waters too came from the same stock, competed with the Indian Customs Master Shivji Topan and his son Jairam's firm and eventually made peace with them to survive. In 1840, he was working in partnership with them, and nine-tenths of his business was being carried out via this Indian firm. By 1842, he managed to diversify his clients and networks and worked relatively independently as a merchant.[40] He made contacts with eight Arab producers for the supply of cloves. And Swahilis such as Sadik B. Mbarak worked as his clerk.[41]

The internal Western and American tensions and rivalries for Zanzibar commerce only benefited the Sultan. As the Customs Master of the Sultan, Jairam made the most of the opening up of the ports to the Americans and foreign merchants. He used this moment to expand his business dealings and dig his heels deep into Omani political culture. His new business ventures in Zanzibar, which his father toyed with as well, included dabbling in the trade of cheap cotton cloth coming on American ships from Salem in New England in America. The American cotton cloth called merekani was made in Salem, and it flooded the East African market as it was cheap. But it was also popular because the American merchants advanced cloth on four to six months' credit. This attracted potential customers, as they got more time to collect the commodities the Americans wanted in return. Significantly, Jairam was the main business partner of the Americans. He conducted his business astutely and established great bonding with the American Consul in Zanzibar, Richard Waters, his business partner in the merekani trade.

All this only enhanced Jairam's capacity to offer cash to the rulers at short notice. His firm also lent credit at generous interest to American and European merchants, who leaned on him not just for the cash advance but also because that relationship brought them many advantages. Jairam being the influential Customs Master meant that dealings with him offered them a foothold in Omani bureaucracy and society. Their businesses were secure, and they got business partners with relative ease.

The American commerce injected competition and also a war of words with the British. The Sultan benefited, as he became the referee as the British alleged that the American Consul, Waters, was trying to create a wedge in the minds of the people as he distinguished between the East India Company and the Imperial Government, making them believe that the two were separate entities. He made people question the treaty of commerce between Britain and Sayyid Sa'īd on the grounds that it was not yet in force, being ratified by Captain Hennell, who was an officer of the East India Company, and did not represent the government. Waters even offered the help of the American government if required by Sayyid Sa'īd. Playfair, the British Resident, had to make a lot of effort to control the damage and make people think otherwise.[42] Indeed, Playfair alleged that the rumours were also directed against him, with the news that he had been acting without due authority of the Bombay government and he was in any case on his way out to Britain. Another rumour was that the British had failed in Afghanistan and China.

Playfair cosied up to the Sultan, trying to secure the British trading privileges guaranteed by their treaty. He continuously warned him not only about the nefarious designs of the American but also about other imperial powers such as the Ottomans. Playfair reported that holy spiritual men from Turkish Arabia were doing the rounds in Zanzibar, accusing the Sultan of having let down the Muslims by signing the commercial treaty with the British. He was relieved when the Sultan did not pay much attention to them.[43] As Sayyid Sa'īd grew to become a great agriculturist, he imported and exported far and wide and set up commercial agencies in Calcutta, Bombay, the Dutch Indies, Persia and China. He was contemplating direct trade relations with France just before he died in 1856.[44]

Coghlan was of the view that Sa'īd's son, Sayyid Majid, benefited from the political and commercial investments his father had made in the region, especially after he shifted his capital to Zanzibar. Majid could assert his independent sovereign status because he was riding the popularity wave, having cornered to his advantage the economic progress initiated by his late father. And this was indeed true, as in 1834, Commander H.M.S. Imogene had described Zanzibar as having 'little or no trade'. But in 1859, it possessed an aggregate trade estimated at pounds 16,64,577 sterling. The revenue also had increased at the same rate. Rigby noted that twenty-five years earlier, Sultan Sayyid Sa'īd did not receive more than 50,000 Crowns of annual revenue from the African possessions. But by 1847, this amount had increased to 1,45,000 Crowns, and in 1860 it was 2,06,000 Crowns. Coghlan reported that the African possessions had made such remarkable social and commercial progress that they were more extensive and far more fertile and valuable in every way than the Arabian territories. And their annual revenue exceeded the revenue of the latter to the amount of 77,000 Crowns or pounds 16,000 sterling.[45]

Continued Relevance of the Interior in Sustaining the Maritime Frontier

The Sultan ruled over a truly maritime empire, with commercial agencies stretched across Bombay and Calcutta in India, the Dutch Indies, Persia, China and the lake areas in Central Africa.[46] And yet, the tribal base and its economic assets remained important to his politics, as they were critical to the maintenance of his expanded maritime frontier. Sayyid Saʿīd kept his heels firmly dug in the tribal society—the traditional seat of the Imamate—even if he steered clear of its politics and himself preferred to live in Muscat. Even though not interested in the religious centre of power at Al Rustaq, he did realize the significance of the dates- and indigo-driven economy of the tribal interiors. Indeed, the export of dates from Muscat to America powered his economy in no small measure. Salem ships carted Arabian dates to American consumers through the long nineteenth century.[47]

More importantly, he realized the significance of military labour that the tribal interior could offer to help expand his maritime frontier. Indeed, his political sovereignty was derived from his careful balancing of the political economies of the tribal interior with the control of the more outward-looking Al Batinah coast. Sayyid Saʿīd's career exemplified the knitting together of the interior and the maritime coast even as it envisioned his larger role in the fast-globalizing ocean. The mutual dependence of the interior and the coast politics, and their collective balancing with imperial agendas, sustained his sovereign power.[48]

The tribal areas remained the key source of military labour that was needed to expand and protect the maritime frontier. This was particularly evident in the tribal military recruits that were brought in to protect his port towns of Sohar and Bandar Abbas, which faced Persian attacks. These recruits also came in handy in his fight with the Wahhabi reformists in the interior. In addition, he paid due attention to indigo manufacture, dyeing and cultivation, which was one of the major vocations in the interior towns. Sayyid Saʿīd encouraged it as he appreciated its economic value. Like his father Sultan bin Ahmad, he too realized the significance of the indigo revenues and the tribal economies that it sustained. He continued to reap the benefits of the investments his father had made in its promotion even if he did not add to them. He did try to introduce its cultivation in Zanzibar with the help of the French engineer Guillian, but with little success.[49] This combination of investments in the tribal interior alongside the expansion of the maritime exterior with tribal military recruits was new. It marked a break from the earlier times, when the port economies and that of the interior functioned separately.[50]

III

Governing in Arab Style: The Royal Household in Politics

The 'age of revolution' is characterized by the very Eurocentric feature of the separation of the private and the political spheres in political functioning. The Sultan's political practice reveals that this was certainly not the universal norm. He introduced a form of governance that was derived from the Islamic tradition—it marked a distinction between the 'inner' and the 'outer' spheres of functioning but did not see them as operating in isolation. Thus, the household—the inner domain—powered the politics of the outer sphere. This marked a definitive break from the European governance style, which separated the private and the public and viewed it as the universal political practice. In contrast, the Sultan's household became critical in pushing his political frontiers via his marriages and concubines. Significantly, he governed through his sons, the princes, whom he posted as Governors and overseers of his far-flung territories. But his women too remained extremely influential partners in politics and had a foot in governance. The friction between the Circassian and the Abyssinian women, from whom he sired sons, shaped his politics, as they lobbied for their respective sons to get plum postings.

Indeed, he located his politics at the cusp of the inner (private) and the outer (public) political spheres. He used his women to forge political and commercial ties with the world. His marriages to Iranian women, his aborted matrimonial offer to Ranavolena, the Queen of Madagascar, his string of favourite concubines ranging from Malabar in India to Circassia, Abyssinia and the Swahili coast and his hectic gift exchanges with Queen Victoria exemplify the critical role women played in his political projects.[51] This approach enabled him to forge wider alliances in the Western Indian Ocean and root himself in the port towns as diverse as Zanzibar, Bandar Abbas, Muscat and Sohar. His matrimonial alliances, in particular with Persian women of influence, reflected his new-found interest in maintaining a permanent foothold in Bandar Abbas to dent the increasingly aggressive moves of Britain to dominate the trade in the Persian Gulf.

However, the most integral to the household were his sons, the princes. He ruled through them, and they played a critical role in realizing his imperial ambitions. The fore-fronting of the princes in his imperial drive was based on the practice of open-ended succession that he upheld. He was clear that his heir would be from his immediate family, but it would be one who successfully competed within the familial domain. This made the imperial household the first important site for political training. The many wives and concubines of the Sultan jockeyed to lobby for the interests of their sons with the Sultan. Indeed, the success of princes to make it in politics depended a lot on the support they had from the household.[52] The Circassian, Abyssinian and Malabari mothers to his elder sons Thuwayni, Turki, Majid, Barghash and Khalid respectively prevailed. Many a time, their efforts determined the political success or failure of the princes. Others, like the older son Hilal, were less fortunate. His Abyssinian mother died early, and he fell out of favour as he had no one pushing his case from the household. After a brief stint as Governor of Burka (1838–41), he ended up in exile, with his family stranded in Mecca. In contrast, his brother Khalid, from a Malabari Indian concubine, rose in favour due to her influence. Thuwayni too had the backing of the Abyssinian lobby at the household, and he was himself close to an Abyssinian concubine.

Governorship offered the opportunity to forge alliances, cultivate friends across region and ethnicity and build diplomatic ties with the imperial powers to eventually create an independent niche if the prince so desired. It was the perfect arena also to create a social base in local society and form links with the mobile communities of bankers, financiers and merchants who dominated the wheels of finance in the Ocean. Governorship was the training ground to shore up resources and build social and military capital to sharpen individual competitive skills for succession battles within the family. But most importantly, it was critical also for the realization of the imperial aspirations of the Sultanate.

The Sultan's choice of princes for administrative and military positions at his key ports on the Al Batinah coast buttressed his imperial aspirations. At the same time, these postings helped him to train them in military warfare and diplomacy and initiate them into the art of body politic. The Governorships, in the tribal interior towns, such as Al Rustaq, as well as in the port regions of Muscat, Sohar and Zanzibar, were training stations that offered them the military, economic and political experience they needed to compete for the top position of the Sultanate after the Sultan's death. Saʿīd used the princes as his investment, posting them both in the tribal interiors and the port towns and making them in charge of critical military expeditions to combat the Wahhabis and retain control of ports on the Persian Gulf and the coast of Al Batinah.

The Princes and the Fight for Sohar on the Al Batinah Coast

Sultan Sayyid Saʿīd made the port town of Sohar on the Al Batinah a dependency of Muscat in 1851. But this was not before a long-drawn battle led by his third son, Prince Thuwayni. Thuwayni was born, as we saw above, from a Circassian concubine close to the Sultan and was therefore the chosen one for most of his important assignments. He was given the plum job of being the Regent of Muscat, which carried symbolic value, being the seat of the Sultan's power. Not surprisingly, he was personally trained by his father as he led the

campaign for the capture of the port of Sohar on the Al Batinah
and that of Bandar Abbas in the Persian Gulf. This was the perfect
training for the young prince in the art of military skills and body
politic, guided by none other than his father himself.

Thuwayni suffered many ups and downs in the Sohar mission.
He was guided by his father at every level. The port was shallow and
had little commercial importance. But its location made it attractive
as the gateway to the tribal interiors and its date plantations; it was
also strategically located to ward off external threats from the Gulf
and the northern kingdoms such as Ra's al-Khaimah, which were
mentors to the dreaded Wahhabis. Once Sohar was subordinated
with the active guidance of the Sultan himself, Prince Turki, who
was Thuwayni's brother, was made its Governor. Thuwayni went
back to look after the affairs of Muscat. Nonetheless, his fight for
Sohar became a useful exercise in learning the nuts and bolts of
military, politics and diplomacy in handling the imperial powers.

After the death of Sayyid Sa'īd, his sons Thuwayni, Turki, Majid
and Barghash spread out into the Ocean, consolidating their hold on
Muscat and Zanzibar, respectively, where they had trained in the art
of body politic as Governors. They used their experiences and, like
their father, they too consolidated their political public sphere by
putting together an eclectic and influential private household. They
sired children from concubines of diverse ethnic origins. Thuwayni,
as stated earlier, was close to an Abyssinian concubine with whom
he had a son.[53]

IV

The Quest for Global Visibility: Connoisseurship and
Entanglements with the Wahhabis

The archipelagic mindset of Sayyid Sa'īd yearned for global visibility
in an imperially crowded world. His household reflected his wide
embrace, with wives and concubines from a range of countries. And
even before he became a merchant prince, his ships brought home
fineries to cater to his culturally diverse household. They brought

toys and clocks from Europe, while silks, fine cloths, carpets, chinaware, perfumes and luxury items came from the East.[54]

Once he became the Sultan, he welcomed Europeans in Muscat and was eager to acquire information from them about those arts 'that his own countrymen cannot teach him'.[55] Shipbuilding technology and navigation techniques were some such knowledge clusters. He built his palace in European style, which smacked of his high aesthetic taste for luxuries. He often escaped to the mountains of Burka to avoid the June heat of Muscat.[56] Not surprisingly, the British community in Muscat felt safe with him, as he took a huge interest in the city and personally handled its municipal administration.

However, in the 'age of revolution', with Britain establishing its hegemony in the Persian Gulf, he wanted a larger participation in the Indian Ocean world. He looked for a space in the imperial drawing board to become a part of global deliberations on the pressing issues concerning the Wahhabis, slavery and the expansion of shipping and navigation technologies that defined the globalizing agendas of the time. These conversations gave him an entry into the imperial assemblage, where he leaned on Qajar Iran to offset Western manoeuvring on slaves. His household remained at the forefront of his forays into imperial politics. He married Persian princesses to consolidate his alliances and ensure the continuance of the slave trade even as he signed slave ban treaties with the British.

Milking the Wahhabi Threat

The Wahhabis were the principal revolutionary agents in the Indian Ocean world. In 1744, Shaykh Muhammad bin Abd al-Wahhab, a theologian who was committed to the doctrine of 'unity of God', formed a pact with Muhammad ibn Saud, the ruler of the Diriyah Oasis in the Nejd in Central Arabia. This combination of political, tribal and religious power in Arabia created ripples all over the Middle East. The Wahhabis were followers of this eighteenth-century reformist cleric, Abd al-Wahhab. They revolted very early in their history against ritual and the lack of proper religious observance

in the cities of Arabia, and also against Ottoman rule in the Hijaz
(1803–04). They rejected the Ottoman Caliphate. They had a
commitment to revolution, which meant an ideological righteous
justification of plundering the British, the Indians or the Omanis
who followed the Ibāḍī faith on grounds of political oppression and/
or religious observance.

Sayyid Saʻīd had a long history with the Wahhabis that informed
his relationship to them. His father, Sultan bin Ahmad, was killed in
skirmishes with Wahhabi pirates in 1805.[57] Sayyid Saʻīd grew up in
the care of his Regent, Badr bin Saif, who too allegedly succumbed
to the Wahhabis, becoming their tributary chief. Indeed, in his fight
against Badr to capture power at Muscat, he invoked his foe's links
with the Wahhabis to garner tribal support against him. Badr, who
relied on the Wahhabi cavalry, had marginalized the traditional
Baluchi soldiers of Oman. Sayyid Saʻīd used the discontented
Baluchis to consolidate his base in the tribal town of Burka. And
when Badr attacked Burka, this alliance paid off, as they repulsed
the attack. One of the slaves of Sayyid Saʻīd dealt the final blow that
killed Badr.

Sayyid Saʻīd took control of Muscat on an anti-Wahhabi and
pro-Baluchi and African slave plank. And yet, even as he became
Sultan, the Wahhabis continued to control Muscat, and he could
not stop their inroads. He marched against them in 1806, and the
treaty that followed made the Wahhabis publicly recognize him as
the Sultan of Muscat. But in return, he paid a tribute of $50,000
to them, hosted their envoy in Muscat, who ensured that Wahhabi
tradition and customs were followed and their cavalry was stationed
in Burka.[58]

The Wahhabis became a political nuisance as they supported the
tribal chiefs in the interior of Oman, who opposed the Sultan and
wanted to expand their influence in the region. They also indulged in
maritime violence, both within and outside the Muslim community,
and viewed it as perfectly legal to uphold their revolutionary cause.
But it was their acumen at sea that made them attractive to the Arab
kingdoms on the Persian Gulf. Not surprisingly, the Wahhabis found
ready mentors and patrons in the polities north of the Omani coast

of Al Batinah—Bahrain, Dubai and Raʾs al-Khaimah, all of whom used them to dip into the politics of the Omani coast. Indeed, the Muscat government was so overwhelmed by the Wahhabi presence at Al Batinah that, after 1845, it paid tribute to the string of their agents based in the Persian Gulf.[59]

The Wahhabis and their mentors in the Arab kingdoms of the Gulf posed a serious challenge to the British too, albeit for different reasons: they threatened their commerce in the Gulf. The British allied with the rulers of the Arab provinces of the Ottomans and with the Arab polities in the Gulf region to counter the Wahhabi threat. This shared concern regarding the Wahhabis brought the Sultan in close alliance with the British. By the early nineteenth century, the Wahhabis became an important fulcrum that brought together the Arab Sultans, the Ottoman pashas and the Western powers. They became the platform that enabled the entry of successive Omani rulers, such as Sayyid Saʿīd and Thuwayni, into the global canvas, where they became active participants and investors in the anti-Wahhabi deliberations.

The Wahhabi issues offered the Omani Sultans the opportunity to grab the international limelight in a world crowded by imperial powers. The shared global concern on the Wahhabis was evident when their 'pirate ports' were attacked both by the Bombay government as well as by the Ottoman pasha in Egypt. Between 1809 and 1820, the British launched two major operations against them, targeting their haven in Raʾs al-Khaimah. These attacks, coordinated from Bombay, used the rhetoric of crushing 'piracy'. In both these anti-Wahhabi campaigns, the Sultan pledged his full support to the Governor of Bombay.[60]

These campaigns marked the culmination of maritime violence that the Wahhabis had been accused of, and the British used all the Wahhabi tricks of sea warfare to destroy Raʾs al-Khaimah. The campaigns ended with a series of truces in 1820, declaring the coast as the Trucial Coast and heralding the consolidation of Britain's counter-revolutionary imperialism in the Ocean.[61] The period marked the commencement of a long process of the levelling of the plurality of definitions and meanings of violence; it saw the legalization of a certain kind of sea warfare and the beginnings of imposing norms of 'acceptable behaviour' on the ocean.

And yet, both the anti-Wahhabi alliance with the British as well as the counter-revolutionary clampdown were used by the Sultan to push his political aspirations. Indeed, his ingeniousness in milking the Wahhabi issue reflected the leaking ship of counter-revolutionary imperialism, in whose shadow Arab Sultans like him made careers. Allen James Fromherz views the Sultan's resistance to the Wahhabis, often with British support, as a useful tactic to justify the emergence of Oman as an important regional power.[62] But for the Sultan, it was more a foothold in the wider imperial canvas and global visibility that was at stake here.

Sohar, the Wahhabis and the Imperial Attention

The port of Sohar, as we saw above, became the flashpoint of the Sultan's Wahhabi politics when he tried to oust its tribal chief, who had the support of Shaykh Sagar of Ra's al-Khaimah, and get it in Omani control. His son, Prince Thuwayni, may have failed to deliver at Sohar, but there was no denying that his fight with the Wahhabis at the port town brought him instant imperial attention. It drew him into the larger British-led deliberations on the Wahhabis that were going on in Western diplomatic circles.

Entry into the imperial club over the Wahhabis was conditional on the continued protection of British commercial interests in the Gulf. Thuwayni, who was the Sultan's interlocutor, found that his seat was threatened each time his ambition appeared at cross purposes with this agenda. Major Hennell, Resident in the Persian Gulf, reminded Thuwayni that the maritime chiefs had entered into an engagement under the mediation and guarantee of the British government not to fight at sea but to refer all cases of maritime aggression to the Resident at Bushire for settlement.

Hennell did not want the Sultan to interfere with the Arab chiefs of the Gulf kingdoms, as that would unhinge the policy of maritime peace that the British had painstakingly maintained. He feared that Thuwayni's intervention would trigger a response from both Shaykh Sagar of Ra's al-Khaimah as well as the Dubai chief, Makhtoon. Thuwayni was warned that even though the superiority of the Sultan's ships was undoubted, hostilities would expose to danger the small trading boats of Muscat. This was because if the truce fell apart, the restrictions on the vessels of the Arab chiefs menacing around would be lifted. He was reminded that Muscat too was a beneficiary of the truce, as its trading boats were everywhere due to the varied and expanded nature of its commerce ensured by the truce. His request was dispatched to Thuwayni, whose fleet was suspected to be at the ports of Al Batinah.[63]

And yet the success of the Wahhabis and their expansion on the Al Batinah as a consequence of Thuwayni's failure at Sohar was disconcerting to Hennell. He was shocked at the 'imprudent conduct' of Thuwayni, which had made Sagar establish his control over large parts of the coast of Al Batinah. He feared that once the pearl fishing season was over, Sagar would return with a naval force and his ally Sayyid Giyās bin Azam of Sohar and make an overland attack on Soweik, Burka and Misna and take it over unless the British government intervened to help Thuwayni.[64]

The Wahhabis and the Call for the Sultan to Replace Prince Thuwayni

The British viewed the Sultan's fight for Sohar as an anti-Wahhabi crusade. They were watchful of his Sohar affairs and included him in their deliberations on the Wahhabis. Indeed, they blamed Thuwayni for the mess and wanted the Sultan to get involved personally in the British negotiations to deal with the Wahhabi threat.

Thus, Thuwayni, who militarily failed at Sohar, paved the way for the Sultan's entry into the imperial deliberations on the Wahhabis. The Bombay government directed Hennell to proceed to Muscat to act as a 'friendly mediator' between the two parties and get a settlement done that would be helpful to the family of the tribal chief Hammud and at the same time protect the interests of the Sultan, which he felt Thuwayni had jeopardized.[65] The government felt that the Sultan should not only return to Muscat from Zanzibar, as his possessions had so seriously been jeopardized, but that he should consider removing Thuwayni from the Muscat Regency. That would be the only way the Sohar family would be satisfied and drop their plans for aggression.

But the Sohar family wanted the Muscat agent to convey this advice to the Sultan in a way that Thuwayni's prestige remained intact.[66] The Government of India also approved the orders of Bombay to ask the Resident to mediate in a friendly way without any undue interference and not take on any definite course of action or responsibility were the mediation to fail. It felt that the Sultan would disapprove of the acts of his son; with Hamerton's influence and the cooperation of the Sultan, the friendly relations between the latter and the tribes would be restored.[67]

The Fall of Sohar and the Sultan's Entry into Imperial Circuits

The inclusion of the Sultan in any Wahhabi talk was evident when the Muscat Agent, A. Hamerton, suggested that the British should encourage a reconciliation between the Sultan and Sohar and establish a lasting peace. Hamerton was clear that the British government regarded the Sultan as an independent sovereign and did not wish to dictate to him on anything.[68] But they definitely wanted him to be at the centre of their Wahhabi strategy. Hamerton approved of the fact that the Sultan had deputed Sayyid Thuwayni to settle the dispute between him and Sayyid Gas bin Azan of Sohar and that he had the support of the tribes of Oman in doing so. He also appreciated that the Sultan was using force to get back from the chief of Sohar all the places that he had acquired from him. But Hamerton wanted him rather than his failed son to be at the centre of the Wahhabi deliberations.

The British government pledged neutrality when the Sultan decided to lead the Sohar campaign personally as an anti-Wahhabi drive. But it very much approved of his mission. In preparation of war with Sohar, the Sultan collected his forces at Burka and was confident of success, as his forces were superior. The Sultan had four ships all ready with stores and munitions of war. But he had no people capable of using either the ships or the munitions of war to advantage. Once he made all the arrangements, he commenced for Sohar.[69]

The Sultan, backed by the British, captured Sohar in 1851, and it continued as a dependency of Muscat until his death. This was a huge setback to the Wahhabis. It offered the Sultan the perfect foothold on the Al Batinah coast, located as it was north of Muscat and in close vicinity of important tribal-controlled spots—Sohan, Burka, Nakhil, Soweik and Seeb. And it of course brought him definitively into imperial circles. But more importantly, the Sohar campaign was viewed as an anti-Wahhabi campaign, and that brought the Sultan to the centre of imperial talks on what was a major political challenge. This position of strength in the imperially crowded world empowered the Sultan, who set about reordering his administration at Sohar with aplomb. He started by making his son, Sayyid Turki, the Wālī or Governor of Sohar.

The Sultan and the Sohar chief agreed mutually that all persons could hold and possess property in each other's territory and that rights and privileges were respectively guaranteed to all parties. They should retain status quo as if a regime change had not occurred. Hamerton wanted that, as a consequence of the change at Sohar, many subjects of Muscat would become subjects of Sohar and vice versa. He also believed that it would be proper to have an understanding of the rights of such people to retain their date groves and wells, houses and other property.[70]

The continued threat and losses that Sayyid Sa'īd suffered at the hands of the Wahhabis ensured his foothold in the British diplomatic war room. And yet, this position in the imperial club may have been his only permanent gain. Soon after Sayyid Sa'īd returned to Zanzibar thinking he had Sohar firmly in his control, other port towns such as Burka, south of Sohar, were up in arms. The tribal chief of Burka—Sayyid bin Ali—seized and confined the Sultan's son and incharge of the town, Hilal. The Wahhabi patron, Shaykh Sagar, was not one to lose this opportunity to hit

back. He seized from the Sultan's control Ghulla, Khor Fahan and
Dibba on the Al Batinah.

V

The Sultan in Imperial Circuits:
The Politics of the Slave Trade

Shaykh Sagar and the Slave Trade

Sultan Sayyid may have been an ally of the British in the anti-
Wahhabi campaigns, but he had his own very specific agendas to
meet when it came to the issue of slaves. His economy did depend
on the profits of the slave trade. The influential slave dealer of
Zanzibar, Sulaymān bin Hamad of the Bayt al-Wakil, was a great
support to his family. He lived for ninety years and when he died in
1873, he was noted to have been a presence in the Al Busaidi palace
and attended the durbar.[71]

A case in point of the Sultan's support to slave traffic was his
turning a blind eye to slave trade from his ports even when it involved
transactions of his foe and the Wahhabi mentor at Ra's al-Khaimah,
Shaykh Sagar. Indeed, his alliance with the British on the issue of the
Wahhabis and at the same time his tacit support for the slave trade
involving Shaykh Sagar revealed the leaking edifice of the British
counter-revolutionary endeavours. The Sultan's encouragement of
the slave trade continued even as the British clamped down on the
Wahhabis, taking him along in their politics.

The Sultan's political practice was characterized by allowing
slave trade from his ports even as he allied with the British in their
abolition campaign.[72] His appetite for slave profits intersected with
all his political moves, including the challenge from the Wahhabis
and their mentors, such as Shaykh Sagar of Ra's al-Khaimah. Thus,
even though he allied with the British to check the Wahhabis and
clip the wings of Shaykh Sagar, he remained invested in the slave
trade that this Wahhabi mentor carried on with impunity from

Omani ports. Indeed, the Sultan's clever politics on the issue of slave trade became his weapon against the waves of counter-imperialism as reflected in the British rhetoric on the slave ban.

Shaykh Sagar was heavily implicated in the slave trade at the port of Sohar. He used a string of vessels to dodge the British and carried on the trade with impunity. He used the port of Soor, far south of Sohar, that he controlled as the destination port for his slave traffic. The slaves were sourced from Zanzibar with the knowledge of Sayyid Saʿīd, who owned the island. The big vessels, buglas, of Shaykh Sagar reached Zanzibar via Muscat and were then sold off to escape British surveillance. Their commanders hired a house on the island and clandestinely collected slaves; having sold their own buglas, they loaded the slaves on smaller boats belonging to Soor. Some embarked on the *guncha* belonging to Shaykh Sagar. All these vessels dropped off slaves at Maculla and Shehr and then landed at Soor, where they offloaded most of their cargo without any hurdles, as Shaykh Sagar controlled the port.

The friction over Wahhabis notwithstanding, it was clear that Shaykh Sagar had the tacit support of the Sultan on the issue of slave trade. The Sultan was himself invested in it despite making noises to the contrary in imperial forums. Often, Sagar's slaves were offloaded at the Sultan's ports: Shinas, Ghulla and Khor Fakawan; some consignments were sent to Qishm and Bandar Abbas. Those intended for Ra's al-Khaimah were sent by the easier land route up the coast of Al Batinah from Muscat. Of course, when accosted by the British, Shaykh Sagar denied any involvement in this trade.[73] Indeed, he had it all nicely worked out. On their arrival, Sagar confined the crew and made the right noises. But finding their vessels empty, he released them, when he had privately agreed with them that he would get one-fourth of their cargo.

And yet, the slave trade bonhomie notwithstanding, Sayyid Saʿīd wanted his control over Sohar and the withdrawal of Sagar from its affairs. As we saw in the section above, he dabbled in intra-Wahhabi politics to capture Sohar and kept his son, Prince Thuwayni, at the forefront of the politics. Indeed, he trained Thuwayni in military strategy and politics while the fight against the Wahhabis drew him close to the British.

Slave Trade and Persia as the Gateway to the Imperial World

The Wahhabis connected the Sultan to the Western imperial politics. But the urgent need to clip the wings of the British control of the Persian Gulf necessitated equally strong ties with imperial Persia. Sayyid Sa'īd looked towards Persia for a foothold in the Persian Gulf, where Britain was establishing its hegemony to monopolize commerce. Even though of a religious Ibāḍī disposition, he got support from Shi'ite Persia. Persia leaned on him to firm up her position in the imperial assemblage, where a strong Perso-phobic current underlined Britain's ambition in the Persian Gulf. She allowed him to gain a foothold in Persian ports. This ensured his entry into the imperial drawing board and drew him into global deliberations on the safety of commerce in the Gulf. It put the imperial gaze on him.

Sayyid Sa'īd knew that the foothold in the Persian Gulf could be ensured only with a deep friendship with Persia. He strove to strengthen relations with it via matrimonial alliances. The strategy worked, as on many occasions, as a result of this personal link, he received military help from Persia in times of crisis. Help was particularly forthcoming in 1810 against the Wahhabis. A Muscati Shia, Mūsā al-Mūsawī negotiated the deal with Shiraz, and he got 1500 horsemen and a piece of artillery from them.[74]

But more importantly, this strengthened friendship that was cemented with marriage alliances became his signature style of politics, blurring the private and the public spheres of his rule. He used his foothold in the Persian circles to reroute the slave traffic to Bandar Abbas and other Persian ports, avoiding Muscat, where British surveillance was tight. And yet he continued to pay lip service to the abolition rhetoric of the British. Indeed, the Persia connect emboldened him to argue for the continuation of slavery in his territory and articulate to the imperial powers what it meant to him and his people.

Making Slavery Locally Legible: Persian Ports and the Slave Trade

The Sultan found the Persian ports particularly handy for the continuation of slave traffic as, unlike his own ports, they were not under British surveillance. Muscat, in particular, was on the British radar after the Sultan signed the slave ban treaty with the British in 1821. The treaty had earned him British recognition as the sovereign. It was indeed a big deal for an Arab ruler to be recognized as the head of a mercantile empire in a very imperial world. However, this did not stop the Sultan from dipping his hands in the lucrative slave trade that he diverted to the Persian ports to avoid the imperial scrutiny.[75]

Ports on the Persian side of the Gulf as well as on the Al Batinah coast were recipients of slaves from Muscat, Zanzibar and Ra's al-Khaimah. Most of these were under the control of the Sultan. Sohar and Soor on the Al Batinah coast, both under Muscat control, and Bandar Abbas and Qishm on the Persian Gulf, also on lease to the Sultan, were major slave depots. The Arab chiefs of Bahrain, Ra's al-Khaimah and Charrack up north on the Al Batinah coast were slave kingpins.[76] Even though many of them, as we saw in the section above, were involved in fighting Oman politically on the issue of Wahhabis, they indulged in slave trade with the tacit approval of the Sultan, who was also a beneficiary.

The Arab chiefs of Bahrain, Ra's al-Khaimah and Charrack brought back slaves from Zanzibar to the Omani-controlled ports of Sohar and Soor. Indeed, Soor was at the centre of this trade, being a major centre of manufacturing vessels involved in this traffic. Most of the vessels involved in the trade were from Soor. At Bandar Abbas, slaves were openly imported and bought and sold without restriction from the Sultan's officers and local authorities.[77] It was well known that the Arab chiefs along the Persian Gulf and the Al Batinah coast were in alliance with slave traders, even though they denied indulging in slave trade when accosted by the British.

Female Abyssinian slaves in substantial groups of twenty to thirty were continuously arriving at the Persian ports of Lingah, Bandar Abbas and Charrack from Zanzibar and elsewhere. British native agents reported these arrivals and sought the intervention of their government to stop the traffic.[78] The trade was of huge economic benefit to the Persians. Natives of Lingah owned vessels that brought slaves from the east coast of Africa to Lingah and Bandar Abbas. The bugla of Mohammad bin Sālih al-Kongī (of Congo) brought up to twenty slaves. Similarly, the bugla belonging to Barūk bin Mullāh Husayn, commanded by Ibrāhīm bin Husayn Alī, both inhabitants of Lingah, brought twenty Abyssinian slaves from Berberah. Half of these landed at Bandar Abbas for sale under the charge of a local person. The rest were sent to Lingah. Similarly, the bugla belonging to Ahmad Hussain Qazwīnī commanded by Muhammad bin Ahmad landed thirteen slaves in Bandar Abbas and Qishm and brought fourteen more to Lingah recently.[79] In another instance, the bugla of Muhammad bin Khamīs nākhodā brought a cargo of slaves that was sold at Bandar Abbas and Qishm, and the rest landed at Lingah.

The Persians allowed this traffic in the Gulf as they were equally active participants in the slave trade. In fact, slavery and the continuation of this trade established an enduring bond between them and the Omani Sultan. Apart from the Persian ports that were in control of the Sultan, slaves also arrived at the Persian-controlled ports of Congoon, Basra, Bushire and Al-Muhammerah. Several arrivals of slaves were reported in the port of Congoon, where they were openly sold in the bazaar. The customs duty on each slave was 17 Maria Theresa (MT) dollars. In 1850, as many as thirty-one slaves here were bought by a Lingah bugla and six by a Bushire merchant. Similarly, a bugla commanded by Abdullah bin Kulban belonging to Shaykh Jabir touched at Karak with twenty-two male and female slaves on board. A boat belonging to Haji Kasim, commanded by Pulad, bought five slaves from Congoon and landed them at Halilah. And a guncha (vessel) commanded by Shahin brought a cargo of thirty-two slaves from Muscat, which were taken to Basrah and Al-Muhammerah.[80]

Like the Sultan, the Persians too paid lip service to the British request to curtail this traffic. The corruption in Persian ports was so rampant that merchants involved in slave traffic managed to escape punishments taking advantage of local Persian support.

Merchants carted their slave cargo from one Persian port to another, looking for a favourable support base. For instance, a man called Shahin, owner of a gunchah and nākhodā of a boat from Al-Karak, unable to land at Bushire his thirty-two male and female slaves procured from Muscat, took them to Basrah and Al-Muhammerah. No action was taken against him, since he was a close associate of the Governor of Al-Karak.[81] In fact, he had taken these slaves on board from the boats of the Governor of Al-Karak, Haji Jabir. The arrangement was finalized by Ibrahim, the nākhodā of the Governor's vessel, on hearing that a ship of war was in need of slaves. The incident revealed that the orders of the government that banned importation of slaves into Persian ports were openly violated.[82] And yet, Hennell, the Resident in the Persian Gulf, felt that despite the corruption that diluted his efforts to curb slave traffic, he was still able to create an impression of overseeing that he hoped would not be without effect.[83]

The Persian vessels were exempt from British search and seizure. And this was cashed in on by the Arabs of the coast, who used them to cart slaves. Indeed, many non-Persian vessels involved in carting slaves used the Persian flag so as to escape the British arm of the law. This was, as we noted earlier, the perfect case where legal technologies (the flag and the pass) introduced by imperial powers to monitor the ocean through the norms of standardized international law were subverted by non-European stakeholders. Indeed, as Fahad Bishara shows for the case of Muscat dhows in the twentieth century, imperial law was 'domesticated' for local benefits. For instance, an Arab from Ghazālah called Sa'īd al-Ḥamūd hired a bugla from Ibrahim bin Hussain, an inhabitant of the Persian coast. This vessel brought up a cargo of male and female slaves from Zanzibar, who were landed partly in the Arabian coast and partly in the former port.[84]

The British were always keen to get the right to search and detain Persian vessels engaged in the slave trade. They urged the Persian government to allow them to seize all slaves found on board such vessels and convey them to a British colony to be freed. They proposed that the vessels in which they were carted and the crew that brought them would be handed over to the Persian government to deal with as they wished. This was urgently required, as they feared that if this was not done, then Persian vessels would carry slaves to the Turkish dominions as well as to Muscat, and also to the territories of the maritime chiefs of the Persian Gulf. On British pressure, the Persian government did respond by exercising a fine of 100 tomans for all vessels/merchants caught with slaves. But the Resident felt this was not enough. It would be effective in ports where the Persian hold was strong. But not in Congoon, Charrack and Lingah, where its hold was weak and slave traffic would go on unhindered.

Indeed, the British had a treaty with the Shah of Persia by which they cooperated in suppressing this trade and where penalties were to be levied by Persian authorities on dealers and merchants in case of deliveries. But both the British agents, as in the case of Mulla Ahmad in Lingah (a Persian port), and the Persian Shah's lower functionaries often connived to let the traffic go on and ignored it until they were investigated.

Both the Political Agent and the Shah alleged malpractices against each other, most notably the cuts and commissions involved to facilitate the trade. The case of Mulla Ahmad, who was complicit in this was significant, and he was accused by Felix Jones of moral misdemeanour.[85] Jones also complained often to the Persian Slave Commissioner for the suppression of the slave trade of his men breaching cordiality between them and British officers in their efforts to encourage slave traffic.[86] The latter dismissed this as idle banter of his low-ranking officers and reiterated his commitment to the treaty for suppression of this traffic.

In 1851, the British signed agreements with Persia and Turkey that empowered British cruisers on the sea to intercept slave vessels with Persian and Turkish flags and temporarily detain their cargo of human beings.[87] The inflicting of punishment to the dealers was in the hands of the Persian authorities. And in the case of the vessels of the Ottoman Empire, they could only liberate the slaves and deposit them to some Turkish port for adjudication.[88] Interestingly, while an Act of Parliament ensured that British naval officers profited financially from intercepting and liberating slaves from the ships of Oman, no such remuneration was forthcoming if they did the same job for Persian and Turkish vessels. Jones recommended remuneration for them to encourage them in their job.

Justifying Slave Trade

The Sultan justified the trade by clarifying to Hamerton, the British Consul at Zanzibar, that slavery had a very different meaning in local society. He pointed out that it had always been an integral part of his society. He called it an 'ancient institution' that was very profitable to both the Arabs and to the local society. He also continued to negotiate and bargain with Britain when the pressure for the ban intensified. In 1842, he sent one of his representatives to London, asking for Bahrain in exchange for abolition of slavery. But the British were firm that the traffic had to stop without any benefit, gifts or land.[89]

In 1849, Hennell complained to the Bombay government about the surreptitious way in which the Sultan continued to encourage the trade by ignoring slave traffic along the Persian coast. The shared understanding from the Persian and Arabian side of the Gulf was that both male and female slaves were bought from the African coast by the subjects of the Sultan. That the Sultan looked the other way, allowing slave traffic to continue, was evident when commanders of slave boats were told to carry on business without seeking any permissions from the Sultan. The commander of one of the boats from the Persian Gulf, who waited to take permission from the Sultan to embark his cargo, was told by people he 'was a fool for not managing his business without troubling His Highness on such a subject'.[90] But he was warned that in case of interception by the British cruisers, he should be ready to face the consequences. This incident proved that neither the Sultan nor his prince Sayyid Thuwayni were keen to take any active step to suppress the trade beyond giving the British a free hand to do so.[91]

In 1851, Britain and Oman signed a convention for the detention of Persian slavers by British cruisers. According to its

terms, the Persian government agreed that the ships of war of the
British government and the East India Company be permitted for
a period of eleven years to search Persian merchant vessels; Persian
government vessels that were not the property of merchants or
Persian subjects were exceptions. The Persian government gave an
assurance that in no manner whatever would any Negro slaves be
imported in the vessels of the Persian government. It also ensured
that the search of the private Persian vessels was to be in the
knowledge and with the cooperation of the Persian government,
with Persian officials on board the vessels of the British government.
If slaves were to be found in any of these vessels, the British
authorities were to take possession of them and cause no detention
or damage but deprive them of the slaves. The vessels were to be
delivered to the authorities of the Persian ports, who were to fine
and punish the owners of the vessels as they wished.[92] If the slaves
in Persia wished to go to Mecca for pilgrimage or to India, they
were to get passports, valid for eleven years, issued from the Persian
Passport Office in Bushire.

But these treaties notwithstanding, the Sultan had his
networks spread out in Persia, Africa and India to continue with
the slave trade with the tacit support of imperial networks and
people drawn to his enterprise for the lure of the lucrative profits
of this trade. The Sultan was always seen as turning a blind eye and
clearly gaining from this traffic from both his Persian ports and
the ones on the Al Batinah. The British agent at Muscat noted
that slave traffic passed under his nose. But, hinting at the possible
benefits of this trade to him, he attributed this not to the Sultan's
bad intention but rather to his lack of control on his officers. He
noted that despite the best intentions of the Sultan, 'every man in
his dominions of every rank and station stands out and almost may
be said to defy his authority'.[93]

This impression was not always unfounded, but more because
of the investment of so many diverse interests in the slave trade.
For instance, in a show of support to the British anti-slave
campaign, the Sultan and the Arab chiefs had given permission
to the vessels of the East India Company to search Omani ships

for slaves.[94] However, the profits of slave trade were so attractive that many across the board were invested in its continuance. This included the British. Indeed, their agents in Muscat reported that vessels carrying British flags also continued to cart slaves with impunity, violating British orders. The Bania Customs Master of Muscat reported that he had stopped one such ship from Bahrain, the *Fateh Al-Khayr*, with a European commander, who carried four female Abyssinian slaves. Three boarded from Jeddah on account of one Mr Musa and were to be delivered to Sayyid Ahmad in Bushire; the fourth belonged to a man from Kuwait named Khalif, and he embarked at Hodeida. The nākhodā, commander, was a foreigner and said he was clueless of treaties and was just doing his job. Khoja Haskeel, the agent at Muscat, reported that the British vessel refused to take these slaves to Bombay. Its sergeant Lt Fullerton said he was not authorized to do so.[95]

Bandar Abbas: The Sultan's Foothold in the Gulf

In 1798, Sayyid Sa'īd's father, Sultan bin Ahmad, conquered the Bandar Abbas port from one of the important Arab tribes, Banī Ma'īn, which was hugely influential in the area.[96] After the Omani conquest, the Persian government, its efforts to regain its influence at Bandar Abbas going in vain, farmed the port to the Sultan for 6000 tomans a year. By 1798, the authority of the Omani Sultan over Bandar Abbas appeared paramount. In a bold display of his hold on the port, he gave permission to the British to establish a fortified factory in return for a concession of offloading at Calcutta 5000 rather than the stipulated 1000 maunds of salt mined at Hormuz. The British were also allowed to mount guns at the factory and have forty or fifty British gentlemen reside there with 700–800 sepoys.[97] As a result of this concession, Bandar Abbas not only became useful for strategic reasons of controlling the Gulf traffic but also a source of revenue for the Sultan. By 1802, Bandar Abbas was providing a third of the Sultan's income: 1,00,000 MT dollars. Most of this was coming from the salt mined at Hormuz.[98] The port was of huge commercial importance, as it was the place of

deposit for exquisite fruit brought from the interiors of Persia and
sent to Muscat. And dates from Burka and Al Rustaq in Oman were
exported from here.[99]

In 1806, when Sayyid Sa'īd succeeded his father Sultan
bin Ahmad, Bandar Abbas proved to be an asset. It remained
an auxiliary port to Muscat on the northern shores. In times of
high winds, ships found it easy to dock there, and then re-export
merchandise to ports on the southern shores of the Gulf. Sayyid
Sa'īd also cornered a share of the Bandar Abbas trade with its
Persian hinterlands of Yazd and Kerman. He levied moderate
dues at Bandar Abbas so as to compete with other ports on the
northern Gulf like Bushier.[100] Sayyid Sa'īd was keen to hold on to
Bandar Abbas, even more as the control of piracy by the British
(1820 onwards) had adversely affected the trade of Muscat, and its
economy was showing a downward trend.[101]

The Persians did not lease the port to Oman in a fit of absent-
mindedness or weakness. The arrangement suited them, because the
port was difficult to administer, located as it was on the fringe of the
empire and locked between the sea and mountains and surrounded
by a 'barren' and 'unproductive' environment.[102] The port had a
'reasonable roadstead', as it was situated at the head of a bay that
was dotted with the three islands of Hormuz, Larek and Qishm. But
it was shallow, and the coast consisted of gentle shelving sand, which
made landing of big ships difficult. Steamships were anchored at a
distance from the port, and both cargo and passengers were taken
ashore in smaller boats or lighters of varying size.

Dealing with the ethnic and religious mix at the port was also
a challenge for Tehran. The population was largely Persian and
of the Shia sect, but they were hugely influenced in their dialects
and lifestyle by the Sunni Arab tribes who controlled the Persian
shore. And to make matters more difficult, Bandar Abbas had a hot
climate, with outbreaks of cholera occurring through the nineteenth
century. This made the Iranian nobility reluctant to live there and
administer the port. The Persians were anyway known to have a
weak naval force, and after the fall of the Safavid Empire, they had
found it difficult to control Bandar Abbas, which remained by and

large in the control of Arab tribal chiefs of the Gulf. The Persians left the matters of the port in the hands of the Governor of their nearby province of Fars. The renewal of the lease with the successive Sultans of Oman remained the chief forum for hectic bargaining between Oman and Persia for competitive political sovereignty, rights and privileges in the Bandar Abbas district.[103]

The Imperial Household in Bandar Abbas Politics

The Sultan was hugely invested in the management of Bandar Abbas, as it was his sure-shot access to slave profits. In order to dig his heels deep in the port society and strengthen his ties with Persia, he entered into several matrimonial alliances with Persian ladies. Indeed, these marriages became perfect examples to show the intimate connection between his inner private domain as represented by the household and the outer political sphere. As the women in the household powered his political shots, it became clear that the European-style separation of the private and the public spheres in governance had its limitations in the Indian Ocean world.

Sayyid Saʿīd was already married to Azza bint Seif, the granddaughter of the founder of his dynasty. And yet, in 1827, he married a second time a Persian princess, Sheharzāde, who was the granddaughter of the late King of Persia Fatḥ ʿAlī Shāh and the daughter of Ariz Mirza. And in 1847, he married another Persian lady, who was the daughter of Irich Mirza. This third marriage was short-lived, as she was a woman of extravagance and was hated in Zanzibari society.[104] The Sultan desired to marry into the Persian royal family and get the alliance publicly sanctioned by the Shah so as to confirm his position in Bandar Abbas. He did not succeed in his endeavour. However, the Princess agreed to the marriage because she and her mother were reported to be in 'very needy circumstances'.[105] Not surprisingly, she was brought to Muscat contrary to the desire and wishes of the Shah of Persia. The Sultan was reluctant to marry her once the diplomatic move around the marriage failed. But on her insistence, he eventually did so, but in his new capital, Zanzibar, away from the spotlight of his family and courtiers in Arab-dominated Muscat. His daughter, Salamch, by a Circassian concubine, was convinced that she married her father only for his status and wealth and was in love with someone else.[106]

Even though the marriage did not produce the desired diplomatic or political effect, it did drag the imperial household into politics. It made the Persian–Omani crevices in the assemblage more porous than ever before, as Iranian slave brokers, private merchants and agents moved effortlessly using Sheharzāde's influence in elite Arab circuits to further their commercial interests. Indeed, many of the treaties that the Sultan signed with the British to suppress slave and arms traffic were flouted with impunity.

In 1848, a number of slaves were shipped from the Persian port of Lingah in the Persian Gulf. They were not intercepted on Zanzibar roads as per the Sultan's treaty with the British. On investigation, it was revealed that this was no lapse but a deliberate move to help the slavers on the orders of the Sultan's new Persian Queen and her mother. The British Resident, Col Hamerton, reported that all the slaves were embarked by the order of 'an old lady, the mother of the Persian princess the Imam has married'. He added that this was done at the request of the 'Persian peddler who comes here frequently from Shiraz, and who calls himself the wazir'. The slaves belonged to the 'old woman' and the peddler. The Sultan's officers were afraid to carry out their duties and follow his instructions for 'fear of the mother of the Sultan's bride and the Persian Wazir'.[107] This incident created much apprehension in Zanzibar, as it was viewed by the people as having established the right of the Persian vessels to carry on with the slave trade when it was being denied to the Arabs.[108]

The fear that the Sultan's Persian wife instilled in the minds of his officers was not unwarranted. The Sultan was besotted with her beauty and indulged her to the extent of her extravagance becoming legendary in Zanzibar. She lived in Persian style, with 'a hundred and fifty Persian horsemen, who occupied the ground floor, and formed her modest suite'. And unlike the Arabian princesses, who were restricted to the house, she 'rode and hunted with them [Persian horsemen] in the open light of the day'. Her clothes were luxurious and stitched in Persian style, with 'genuine pearls from top to bottom'. It was known that if a servant found any pearl on the floor, he was allowed to keep it, as she always refused to take it back.[109]

But the marriage was short-lived. At one point, the Sultan was so distressed by her extramarital forays that he attempted to kill her, she being saved of this crime by the timely intervention of a faithful servant.[110] Sheharzāde was later divorced, and she went back to Persia. From her home turf she continued to meddle in the affairs of the Sultan, particularly in his strained relationship with Persia over the port of Bandar Abbas. Her familiarity with the Sultan's extended household gave her clout in Iranian circuits. She could identify and predict the actions of her adversaries during conflicts that often took sectarian colour in the form of Sunni–Shia disputes.

The Persian hold on the imperial household politics not only impacted the port culture but also lent colour to the politics over the slaves and arms trade in the Persian Gulf. The Sultan's divorce and the return of the Persian Queen to Shiraz by no means marginalized the imperial household's centrality in Bandar Abbas politics. In one of the battles for Bandar Abbas (1854) Sheharzāde was reported with the hostile Persian army aiming at members of the Sultan's family, whom she was very familiar with.[111] The imperial household was very much drawn to the centre of subsequent battles for Bandar Abbas.

Bandar Abbas and the Sultan's Imperial Connect

The British were always supportive of the Omani Sultan in his administration of Bandar Abbas. The fear from the 1820s that the Russians would move into Persia and break through the Indian Ocean, threatening British dominance, made them look for a friendly ally in the Persian Gulf. Sa'īd's friendship ensured the ease of traffic across the Persian Gulf. The British had an interest in his effective control of Bandar Abbas, as that ensured peace in the Gulf and security for their commerce.[112] The Sultan often cashed in on their weakness, threatening to block the ports of the Gulf in retaliation to Persian hostility. As the diplomatic games continued between the Sultan and the British, the latter downsized him by underplaying his threats. Col Hamerton, the British Consul in Zanzibar, was of the view that the British could take it easy as the Sultan was making empty threats. He had a 'number of fine empty ships', but no 'seamen whatever to man them'.[113] Similarly, he had not a single man in his service who had the least idea of working the guns or of handling a ship of war or conducting matters which would be necessary to blockade ports.

The Bandar Abbas Arab Governor of the Sultan lost no chance to take advantage of the crevices in the Omani–British relations. He requested that the rented territory be brought under the jurisdiction of the British Resident at the Persian Gulf. He was of the view that this would be a possible solution to the continuous strained relations between the Sultan and Persia.[114] But Hamerton was of the view that the Governor exaggerated the charge of demands and insults from the side of Shiraz. He pandered to the people in Muscat, who urged the Sultan to fight the Persians for all kinds of religious and other reasons and wanted him to damage its commerce by blockading the port of Bushire.[115]

Bandar Abbas placed the Sultan at the centre of the British effort to control the Gulf commerce. As an important participant in British deliberations on the Gulf, he pushed his own vested interests, which included safeguarding his profits from his rerouted slave trade that now avoided Muscat and centred on Bandar Abbas. Predictably, tensions persisted in the Omani-British interstice. The Bandar Abbas Customs Master was often accused of illegal exactions and detention of goods of British Indian subjects. Agents of Indian merchants, such as Mekji, the agent of Damodar Lodha of Bombay, at Muscat were paid $166 for losses he faced on certain goods by illegal detention by the Customs Master at Bandar Abbas. Similarly, the claim of Nansee Thakmsee of Bombay for duty taken in excess of 5 per cent from his agent Gulab Diwan by the Customs Master at Bandar Abbas was also settled by a bill. This was for 125 tomans, produced in the handwriting of the Sultan, payable to Seif bin Nathun, the Governor of Bandar Abbas. Hamerton, the British

Consul at Muscat, argued that he was able to resolve all disputes of claims made by the British subjects on the Sultan's subjects, with hardly any help from the native agent. Despite angry debates and discussion on the same, the issue was resolved.[116] The Sultan was willing to solve all issues over Bandar Abbas with the British because he had very high stakes in the port.

VI

The Sultan and His Legal Repertoire

Sayyid Saʿīd reflected his revolutionary spirit the best when he asserted his legal status on the waters by defining his legal authority and jurisdiction in particularistic ways. This was particularly true in the latter half of his reign, when the waves of counter-revolutionary imperialism began to lay out 'proper' codes of conduct at sea and attempted to level legal plurality by imposing imperial legal regimes. He countered this by introducing his own legal courts and asserting his political sovereign status based on his exceptional knowledge of the littoral and its people. He defined his jurisdictional limits on the basis of his sociological knowledge of the tribes rather than any abstract rule by law. Cases related to British Indian subjects involved in slave trade and trying to escape the British arm of the law often landed in his courts, only to be shifted between his and the Consular Courts, depending on the power play of vested interests.[117]

The Sultan's assertion of what the law on the water meant to him was clear when the British ship *Centaur* was wrecked off the coast of Muscat in dense fog and the discussions of recovery and reparation of its looted indigo cargo commenced. The *Centaur* had set sail from Calcutta in 1852 and was headed to Basrah in the Persian Gulf with its consignment of indigo. After the shipwreck, tribes from the Al Batinah coast looted the cargo and burnt down the ship.[118] These included those like the Banī Bū Ali tribe and the Arabs of the port of Soor, who were in the eye of the *Centaur* storm. Soor was the Sultan's port south of Muscat, from where allegedly the looted indigo was being distributed to markets in the Persian Gulf. And the Banī Bū Ali were the alleged carriers of the looted indigo.

The British insisted that since the shipwreck and loot were in the territorial jurisdiction of the Sultan, he should be held accountable. They alleged that the port of Ukkur, in his jurisdiction, had the *Centaur* indigo stacked in the storehouse that belonged to a Muscati called Muhammad. It was alleged that the people from Muscat had hired this godown for 20 Crowns. And the vessels used to cart the indigo belonged to Soor.[19] According to the underwriters and intelligence networks, Soor was the port with the maximum deposit of the *Centaur* indigo, and one whose boats were identified as the major carriers of the item for sale to other ports in the Persian Gulf, such as Ukkur.

The British wanted to hold the Sultan accountable for this misdemeanour, as the centre of this illegal activity and the tribes involved were well within his sovereign and jurisdictional ambit, measured territorially. The Sultan countered the argument by explaining his understanding of legal jurisdiction in the ocean. Indeed, his deliberations and understanding of law constituted the legal underpinning of his political sovereignty. The Sultan articulated his political sovereignty on the basis of his exceptional sociological understanding of the tribes that lived in his Sultanate.

He denied the involvement of the Banī Bū Ali tribe of Jalan and their Wahhabi Shaykhs in the loot and the carting of indigo to his port, Soor. He argued that his confidence stemmed from his deep knowledge of their behaviour. He offered a textured sociology of these tribes to prove their non-involvement. He was convinced that knowledge and the sociology of his subjects tempered and guided the limits of his legal jurisdiction.

He showcased his deep knowledge of the tribes to prove that they had not participated in the supply line to Soor. When the Muscat Agent, Atkins Hamerton, asked the Sultan to use his influence over the Shaykhs of the Banī Bū Ali tribe of Jalan and assist in the recovery, he said he had written to their head Shaykh Muhammad bin Alī bin Hamūdeh, urging him to ask his men to return the *Centaur* loot. But he did not do much; instead, he wrote back to say that he could not do much because everything was normally destroyed within four days.[120]

The Sultan revealed fascinating information on the sociology of the tribe. He revealed that as far as plunder, loot and its distribution were concerned, the chiefs of this tribe had little control on the members. And thus 'force alone would save the vessel and the cargo'. A force such as the British ship of war would help. But the Beddu (chief), didn't keep any loot for more than three to four days. They ruined and destroyed everything very quickly. So, by the time the ship reached, not much was left to salvage.

Given this trait of the tribe, the Sultan explained that the Beddu didn't collect and take care of the cargo they plundered from the vessels. They at once broke up and tore to pieces all and everything they got hold of. Thus, the underwriters and owners of the Centaur indigo were wrong to assume that the looted item was stored with a view to selling it at a future time. Instead, the Beddu threw the chests into the sea and into their boats. The moment they reached the shore, they broke the chests into pieces; they even broke the indigo cakes to divide them among themselves on the beach. In their society, he argued, men, boys and even women asserted their claim to a share of every article as it came ashore. This was the way they always behaved and were swift and quick to do the distribution before the Shaykhs arrived. His (the Shaykh's) portion was considered to be one-fifth of the whole plunder. This was what they had done to the Centaur cargo as well, using broadcloth pieces, which they obtained from a passenger to tie up their respective shares.[121]

He argued that the principle of division of everything was so etched into their lifestyle that it was difficult to believe that any of them would have enough indigo for sale. The Khoja merchants of Muscat and Muttrah made attempts to buy the indigo from these tribes but to no avail. Potential buyers were scared to go to the Beddu of the Banī Bū Ali to buy these small consignments that the tribals possessed individually. And the Beddu would not bring anything into Soor for fear of having it taken from them in consequence of the strict orders of the Sultan to his subjects, the Shaykhs of Soor.

Hamerton understood this sociology of the Banī Bū Ali tribe as offered by the Sultan and was of the view that the recovery based on the underwriters' understanding of the loot was difficult, if not impossible. Yet, he believed that a small quantity of the indigo might be brought into Soor by stealth, which would in all likelihood happen in a similar case under a much better organized government than that which existed in any part of the Sultan's territories. But many Arab merchants at Muscat with personal interests in the loss of the *Centaur*, and agents for merchants in Basrah and Bushire who were following the *Centaur* saga, did not agree. They believed that 'nothing like 1/3rd of the cargo has been obtained by the Beddu of the Banī Bū Ali' and that every article they got out of the vessel was ruined as a merchantable article. Others also told Hamerton that only a 'small quantity of the cargo has been procured from the vessel'. The rest was all destroyed as the Beddu broke the chests to pieces in the hold of the ship and cut up a silk cloth to use as a curtain to keep their act secret from neighbours. And thus, indigo in only very small quantities had been picked up along the shore.[122]

In defining his sovereign status, Sa'īd also highlighted its fragile fringe mainly because of the tenuous relations he had with some of his Arab tribes who were under the influence of the Arab Wahhabi leaders. The plunderers, he argued, were perhaps from this fringe lot and not in his control. They were of the Banī Bū Ali of Jalan, belonging to the camp that professed the Wahhabi tenet. Thus, touching them was explosive for the Sultan, as any interference from him would make him vulnerable to the wider Wahhabi onslaught.

Muscat was replete with rumours about the presence of the looted indigo in the town and other Omani ports, such as Muttrah and Soor. The Sultan was convinced that his enemies were circulating them so as to create ill feelings between him and his ally the British. Hamerton junked all reports of indigo being brought to Muscat and debunked all rumours of it being in Muttrah as well. In fact, he offered $1000 to anyone who would offer him any information of indigo in these two cities, but he got none. Rumours of the Persian merchant Muhammad Ali Banderi Kubabi having sent a man called Ali bin Ahmad to Soor to buy indigo with $1000 for himself and four other merchants were also found to be untrue. The merchant agent swore by the Koran that he had not gone to Soor, and others corroborated that he was at his date grove.[123]

Similarly, news that Bheeja, a notable Bania merchant of Muscat, who was an underwriter of native vessels and used to conduct business for the Sultan, had *Centaur* indigo stacked in carpets in his storehouse was also found false. The searches in the storehouses in Soor conducted by the Sultan's nephew Sayyid Hamid bin Salim and Khoja Haskīl similarly yielded no result.

The Sultan underlined his sovereign authority also by showcasing his exceptional understanding of the basic Soori character and nature to deflect attention away from the port being seen as the epicentre of the looted indigo. He underlined the basic goodness of the Sooris and their long tradition of helping ships in distress in their waters. Hamerton was happy that the Sultan always rewarded his Soor subjects for these good acts.[124] Clearly, for the Sultan, political sovereignty and jurisdiction were about knowledge of society and those who constituted it. It was not a hollow claim based on territorial demarcation alone and an abstract rule by the law as advocated by the British.

The Sultan's 'revolutionary spirit' did not end in the high period of counter-revolutionary imperialism when the rhetoric on abolition, codes of conduct at sea and imperial law began to define maritime social behaviour. As the subsequent chapters show, in this period of clampdown, his family's entanglements with imperial powers only intensified as he worked out his profitable political and commercial deals in tandem with British private firms, capitalists and slavers. The slave ban treaties he signed with the British, such as the Moresby Treaty of 1822, did not stop slave trade. They only enabled varied competitors—the British and the Omanis alike— to define jurisdiction. As jurisdictions became thick, they also got leaky. This porosity was tapped into its utmost by Sayyid Sa'īd for his commercial pursuits. Indeed, they remained the canvas for his sons as well to carve out their careers in the age of high imperialism.

Tippu Tib (1832–1905)

Oman: Sayyid bin Sultan Al-Saʿīd, Sultan
of Muscat and Oman (1804–56)

'East View of the Forts of Jellali and Merani, Muskat, Arabia, June 1793',
drawn by Thomas Daniell

Watercolour of Zanzibar waterfront in 1847 with a ship in harbour, possibly
the *Albrecht O'Swald* belonging to the German trading outfit O'Swald & Co.

View of Zanzibar waterfront showing the Palace Square and Harem

Portrait of a prosperous Indian merchant and his family in Zanzibar

2

Sayyid Majid: The Imperious Counter-Revolutionary

The Argument

On the death of Sayyid Saʿīd, the people of Zanzibar, as per his wishes, 'elected' his fourth son Sayyid Majid as their ruler. This was in keeping with the tribal tradition, where the ruler was chosen out of the most influential persons available. Sayyid Majid used this populous moment to assert his independent status. He made the most of the condolences the French and Americans sent him to bolster his political sovereignty and emerge as the counter-revolutionary Sultan in competition with brother Thuwayni whose claim to be the Sultan of Oman he resisted.

Majid displayed much loftier political aspirations than his brother Thuwayni, who was more rooted in the tribal bricolage, from where he bargained with the British. In contrast, Majid was drawn into imperial circles because, as the ruler of Zanzibar, he was surrounded by Western powers hungry for slaves. This specific context made it possible for him to expose the hypocrisy of the abolition narrative. He underlined his political sovereignty by defining his jurisdiction and his legal subjects, for whom he had obtained slave trade concessions from the British.[1] Indeed, he took advantage of the conjunctional moment when the British rhetoric on abolition, the imperial rivalries over the slave trade and the cholera pandemic created a rare political moment in the Western Indian Ocean.

Majid's temporal and spatial context lent him enormous confidence and global visibility, putting him a class apart from Thuwayni. His maritime Sultanate was based on the profits of the slave trade and the plantation economies that were dependent on slave labour. More importantly, it was marked by his bold decisions, such as laying the foundation of a new city—Dar as Salaam (Gateway of Peace)—in the middle of a raging cholera pandemic. He hoped to assert his independent sovereign status from this new spot and circumvent the British control of the slave traffic that intensified in the age of counter-revolutionary imperialism.

But most importantly, his calculated moves ensured that the Sultanate became an integral part of the wider imperial world: reaching out to imperial hotspots such as Bombay, pairing with Western private firms to invest in the slave labour-driven sugar cane plantations and being an active participant in the discussions on global issues, such as slavery. His imperial aspirations to be the independent ruler of Zanzibar were soon evident when he contended that the yearly grant that he remitted to Thuwayni was 'friendly subsidy' and not tribute in recognition of Thuwayni as the political sovereign of Oman.[2]

Profile: Sayyid Majid (1834–70)

Sayyid Majid was the fourth son of Sayyid Sa'īd, who was made overseer of his African dominions at Zanzibar on the death of his younger son Khalid (1854). He was the perfect choice, as he had spent most of his youth on the island·and was definitely not a Muscat man. Sayyid Majid, on account of his conduct and age, was declared 'of age' when he was eighteen years old. This meant that he left his father's Muscat house, where all his siblings reared from his father's various concubines lived, at a very young age. He was allotted a house and an establishment of his own in Zanzibar.[3] His house was called Bayt al-Wator, and he lived there with his favourite sister Salima and her Circassian mother.

He loved Salima and had his eunuch, Mesrur, give her horse riding lessons while he himself taught her how to use weapons and trained her in fencing and shooting.[4] He was a great lover of animals, and his house had white rabbits and rituals of cockfights for recreation. He was known to be very modest and of kind and gentle manner. His own house—as well as that of the Sultan, called *Bayt al-Sāḥil*—was always full of visitors from Oman, who came for help of all kinds, as Oman was economically poorer than Zanzibar.[5] It was while at *Bayt al-Wator* that he got married to a distant relative of his, Asche, who arrived from Oman. But she soon took a divorce and returned to Muscat to live with an aunt, as she was much troubled by Majid's sister Chadudj.[6] Once he became Sultan, his palaces remained very simply decorated, unlike those of his father. And he held very ascetic durbars, which were attended by clan chiefs who related to Majid as equals.[7]

Majid benefited from the political and commercial investments his father had made in Zanzibar, especially after he shifted his capital to the island in 1832. Coghlan was of the view that Majid could assert his independent sovereign status because he was riding the popularity wave, having cornered to his advantage the economic progress initiated by his late father.[8]

I

The Slave Trade Wars: Majid in the Imperial Circuit

The centrality of slave trade to Zanzibar made it the most popular destination for imperial powers who competed for its profits. This also brought Majid, as the island's ruler, into the imperial gaze. The global visibility was of political value to him, especially to deal with his rival Thuwayni at Muscat. Significantly, this sibling dispute intersected with imperial rivalries over the slave trade and offered the perfect entry point to both Britain and France for upmanship on the slave profits. The princes became pawns in these imperial rivalries. Majid took full advantage of the British leaning on him to ward off the French from the island. He used their help to fight out his case with Thuwayni. Indeed, sibling rivalries and imperial conflicts corresponded in interesting ways to launch Majid as one of the most sought-after Sultans in the imperial circles.

In 1859, Lord Elphinstone, the Governor of Bombay, justified British intervention in the conflict between Sultan Thuwayni and his brother Sayyid Majid on the following grounds: 'Sayyid Thoonee had been instigated by the French to attack his brother who has incurred their displeasure by his honest desire to act up to his engagements with us to suppress the slave trade.'[9] He suggested that Thuwayni be dissuaded from making the attack on Zanzibar and a steamer of the Indian Navy be placed at the island as a deterrent to the Sultan of Muscat. He urged that a British ship of war be dispatched to C.P. Rigby, the British agent at Zanzibar, if Sayyid Thuwayni succeeded in dethroning his brother. Elphinstone made British policy clear when he noted that 'Rigby should be told that Britains want to maintain neutrality [even] if they lend moral support to the peaceful ruler of Zanzibar'.[10]

Rigby justified his clampdown on Thuwayni on the grounds that he dabbled in the slave trade with full support of the French. He was convinced that from the time of the late Sultan Sayyid Saʿīd, the Omani ports of Muscat and Soor were slave depots under the watchful eye of Thuwayni. Arab dealers brought slaves into Muscat from Soor and made their onward journeys to India and the interiors of Oman. He identified the Joasmi tribe, from the Omani coast, as particularly involved in the traffic.

The treaty violations incensed the British who, on many occasions, referred specific cases for action to Thuwayni. For instance, they reported the case of the runaway slave Salim bin Muhammad, who had taken shelter in Aden after kidnapping and selling a woman slave to potential buyers. Thuwayni promised to take action when these runaways returned to Oman.[11]

Rigby maintained that not only was Thuwayni aided by the French, but that the latter were abusive and contemptuous of Sayyid Majid, who was sympathetic to the British anti-slave trade drive. Rigby viewed even the political challenge to Majid from his brother Barghash as a French conspiracy. He was convinced that Barghash 'was now under French protection and cannot be touched'. He wrote to the Bombay government that 'the question of the right of succession to the government in Zanzibar would have to be settled in Europe'. He observed that if Her Majesty Queen Victoria's ships had not been around, the French would have interfered more. 'They would have stirred up a revolution which would have been fatal to power of Sayyid Majid and injurious to British interest.'[12]

Elphinstone too backed Majid. He also pressured Sayyid Thuwayni to withdraw his troops from Zanzibar on grounds that, if his Arab subjects in Zanzibar got hostile, it would be disastrous to his morale. Commodore G. Jenkins, Commissioner in the Persian Gulf, offered to send a British Commissioner to broker peace. He travelled in Thuwayni's ship, *Caroline*, that carried a British flag and was accompanied by his relative Sayyid Hamid bin Halim bin Sultan, with the order to recall Sayyid Thuwayni's troops.[13] This was enough to indicate to the world that Sultan Thuwayni too was under the influence of the British government and that the latter was the chief mediator in the sibling feuds.

Majid quietly worked on his own agenda of carving his political sovereignty on the back of these imperial slave wars. The 1843 British treaty with Zanzibar had legalized local trade in slaves and banned export trade. But the latter continued under the cover of the former, with Majid turning a blind eye.

In 1862–66 the Customs House at Kilwa, south of Zanzibar, in Majid's territory, recorded the following slave exports to Zanzibar and other places:

Years	Zanzibar	Elsewhere
1862–63	13,000	5500
1863–64	14,900	3500
1864–65	13,821	3000
1865–66	18,344	4000

On each of the slaves shipped through the Customs House at Kilwa, averaging about 20,000 a year, the Sultan levied a tax of $2.5. And an additional tax of $2 was levied on every slave that landed at Zanzibar. Thus, the Sultan derived a sum of about $20,000 a year from this source, or about one-fourth of his entire revenue.[14] And many more slaves were shipped from other ports as well, thus increasing his revenue further.

The British suggested to the Sultan to make slave trade a government monopoly and indemnify himself with its profits so that a clampdown could be made on all other export trade. Other measures for narrowing down the trade and making it easily monitored were also suggested: he was asked to make it a private monopoly under his strict inspection and get an import duty. Or else, he could at least mark the dhows and European ships carrying slaves in a distinctive colour or using a mark so that some order or narrowing down be maintained in this traffic. Another alternative was to confine traffic to one port— Dar as Salaam or Zanzibar— and forbid intermediary traffic between ports and the mainland.[15]

Majid bargained hard. He was willing to mark the dhows but insisted they be brought to Zanzibar or the nearest port on capture. But more importantly, he feared the other restrictions suggested to him of confining traffic to single ports would be ruinous to his treasury. He underlined the need of a strong treasury because of the subsidy the British had forced him to pay to Muscat. Much to the chagrin of Commodore L.G. Heath of the Indian Navy, he cleverly linked the issue of slave traffic to the subsidy, arguing, 'with us the payment of a subsidy to the murderer of our brother is a question exceeding life and death, for it is contrary to the principles of our sacred book to give even bread to a parricide'. He said he 'appealed to Her Majesty's sense of justice in this matter'. In fact, he made the issue of subsidy central to the slave traffic suppression request, arguing forcefully, 'If we succeed we shall then be in a position to support the loss that this adoption of your proposals will necessitate.'[16]

Much of Majid's boldness derived from the fact that the British had their own fingers dipped into the profits of the slave trade. They needed Majid as an ally for their own profits even as the abolition rhetoric raged on the surface.[17] The complicity of local British officials in encouraging Majid to tap the profits of slave trade despite prohibition was not missed by H.A. Fraser, a long-time resident in Zanzibar and colleague of Bishop Tozer. He noted the continued presence of the trade in complete disregard to the recommendations to the British government of the Commission on the East African Slave Trade (1870).[18]

The British, in their political outbursts, never doubted Majid's good intentions as their ally in stopping the slave trade. They criticized him for lacking the logistics needed to stop this practice. Unlike their apprehensions about Thuwayni, they believed that Majid was not entirely indifferent but lacked the wherewithal to perform with competence. To Majid's benefit, they argued that he did try his best to intercept and recover abducted slaves. His vessels often returned with 300–400 recovered slaves from their Arab dealers. His Governor was ordered to give exemplary punishments to dealers, such as public flogging. For instance, the chief of the Soor Arabs was publicly flogged and imprisoned for such abductions. As a result of such measures and deterrents, the number of slaves exported from Zanzibar to the Persian Gulf showed some decline. Rigby pointed out that, as a consequence of Majid's efforts, the export of slaves to the Persian Gulf had decreased. And the tribes inland and along the coast had of 'late become slave owners themselves'.[19]

Rigby hinted at Majid turning a blind eye to slave exports at certain times. But like his colleagues, he too was more inclined to view it as a case of incompetence rather than ill intent. He accused Majid of being incapable of stopping the abduction of boys by the Arab slave dealers from his islands of Zanzibar, Pemba and Monfea on the east coast of Africa. He saw the geography of these islands and of the opposite mainland as ideal for the abduction of boys for slavery. The islands were covered to the water's edge with dense vegetation and had numerous creeks and small bays with many small islands in the vicinity where native boats could anchor, secure from detection and pursuit. He pointed out that the owners of buglas intended to abduct boys parked at these small bays on the pretext of obtaining food or water. The crew then descended on the plantations and carried away as many boys as they could find. Often their accomplice collected them at a spot for a speedy sale. Rigby was sure that the boys were kidnapped from the town of Zanzibar as well. So rampant was the kidnapping in the town that the Arab commander of one of the Sultan's ships of war was kidnapped. He was released soon when he was identified. Very often, slaves were just thrown overboard into the waters if the dealer suspected that he was being tracked or was going to be intercepted by a British cruiser.

Rigby also saw Majid's weak military as a disadvantage in stopping the traffic in slaves. He complained of the free way the piratical tribes of Jashamī Arabs had in the slave trade because of the 'pitiable state of weaknesses of Sayyid Majid's troops who were scared to interfere in their affairs'. In fact, the Jashamī were so belligerent that they extracted money from the Sultan as if 'it was a tribute rather than a charitable gift'. Sayyid Majid's contention that he had dissuaded them from these acts cut no ice. Rigby was of the view that these were useless requests as long as he continued to distribute money to them. He felt that the subjects of Sayyid Majid were involved in slave traffic with impunity and disregard to the treaties signed between Sa'īd and the British.[20]

Slave trade not only strengthened Majid's economic base but also pushed him to the imperial drawing board as an active participant in discussions of what was a truly global issue. F. Jones, Resident at the Persian Gulf, framed Majid in a wider imperial assemblage that moved beyond the French and included the Ottomans and Persia. He felt that Majid benefited from the Persian and Turkish vessels that carted slaves and were outside the legal purview of treaties on prohibition that he had signed with the British. Therefore, he endeavoured to include Majid in a reorganized slave convention that included the Turkish and Persian slave commissioners so that he became legally bound via treaties with these powers. Jones wanted the British slave convention to be assimilated with Persian and Turkish ones so that they could be allies in the anti-slave trade drive.[21] This was the best way to check Majid's use of their vessels for slave traffic.

The widening of the slave commission instantly pushed Majid into the canvas of the imperial world that stretched beyond the frame of the European empires. At the same time, it made him integral to the ongoing global discussions on slave traffic. And yet, apprehensions continued. Felix Jones, the political resident in the Persian Gulf, distrusted Sayyid Majid and advocated a harsh policy of naval surveillance along the Arab coastline. He saw Zanzibar as the 'hotbed' from where the 'seeds of the evil [slave trade] were annually disseminated'. He supported the establishment of a slave depot at the naval station at Bassedore, where captured slaves—men, women and children—and vessels could be kept. This was to be provided with adequate security. It was also equipped with a barrack, a doctor and hospital alongside huts and smaller buildings for the comfort of captured slaves. He proposed the appointment of a medical doctor, whose wife would take on the responsibility of looking after the females on the station. This station could be under the admiralty court in Bombay.[22]

He preferred a coal depot also to be established there to facilitate the swift movement of vessels to curb the trade. From the 1840s, Zanzibar, alongside Aden, was a coaling depot en route to the Suez. Steamships from Bombay needed refuelling before they reached Suez.[23] But the naval surveillance by the Indian Navy proved unsuccessful, as it was preoccupied with other important tasks and was not always available when needed.[24]

Nonetheless, the slave trade politics that centred on Zanzibar gave Majid a visibility in the imperial world that was exceptional. As Majid was a close ally of the British, they were mutually dependent. The British Consulate in Zanzibar had close relations with him. Majid was always anxious when there were gaps between the appointment of Consuls. His anxiety was evident when on the arrival of any vessel from India, en route to Aden, he would send merchants to ascertain if indeed a British Consul was on board. He was often seen pointing to the bare flag staff at the British Consulate, where, according to Rigby, he would remark, 'Oh! When shall I again see a Flag hoisted there.'[25] He was visibly relieved once the British Consul was permanently stationed on the island. Rigby reported that he

could 'scarce recognize him as the same individual' when he read
Her Majesty's letter that approved of his succeeding his father as
Sultan, and a ship of war arrived from the Indian government.[26]

Rigby was satisfied with his loyalty and good governance
and reported that 'all classes here the Europeans and American
merchants, the Indian traders and the Arabs . . . bear testimony to
the kind and amiable disposition of the Sultan, his justice and liberal
policies, they all consider him a worthy successor to his father'.[27] This
bonhomie based on mutual interests got Majid a souvenir of the
international exhibition held at London in 1862 from the Viceroy.
He had it made into an amulet. He hoped that the 'amulet which is
a mark of Her Majesty's favour and a token of your friendship will
prove auspicious for me'.[28]

Indeed, Majid reciprocated these gestures, indicating the close
ties he had established in British circles. In 1862, Playfair reported
that his predecessor Pelly had earmarked a house for purchase
for the purpose of a coal store. It was priced at 1000 pounds. By
the time he came to Zanzibar, its ownership had changed. It now
belonged to Sayyid Majid. But because he was not aware that the
British government was interested in buying it, he had leased it
for two years to a German merchant called Reike. The merchant
had spent a lot of money repairing the building and did not wish
to relinquish his lease. But Playfair managed to persuade him to
terminate the lease for a sum of 200 pounds. Majid was happy to
hand over the property to the British government for free, saying
he was gifting it to them as 'he had many obligations'. Playfair saw
this as 'oriental politeness' and offered to pay the money at once
to the Collector of his revenues, who in turn passed it on to the
Sultan. But Majid refused to take it, saying to the Collector, 'Let it
remain with you.'

Playfair therefore got no receipt for the deed of sale or
title deed. On his repeated requests for the sale document, he
was told that 'we have made it over to the exalted government
without price'.[29] Playfair regretted that all his efforts to induce
Majid to take 1000 pounds as purchase money failed and that
he had unnecessarily spent 200 pounds on Reike, who was now

unwilling to renew the lease. The 1000 pounds was returned, and Majid was determined not to accept money from the British. He said he would 'lock the house and let it decay but not permit it to be occupied'.

Playfair left it to the government to decide if they wanted the house as a gift from Sayyid Majid. If so, then a return present also had to be made. It is interesting that he suggested many options like a steamer or gunboats of 250 tonnes made of wood with a low-pressure engine. But this list also included a steam sugar machine and a sugar engine, as Majid was eager to introduce the manufacture of sugar in his dominions.[30]

Indeed, Majid was fully integrated to the gift exchange circuit that marked his entanglements with the imperial powers. In 1870, he gifted a diamond ring to Mr Churchill, the British Consul at Zanzibar, which was returned as the recipient was not permitted to receive gifts.[31]

The slave trade was not the only reason that brought Majid centre stage to the imperial world. He needed the British in his dealings with the interior tribes as well. In 1858, Rigby reported to the Bombay government the extreme satisfaction of Sultan Sayyid Majid on the presence of the British Consul on the island. He noted that the reason Majid leaned on British help was also because of the fear of internal opposition from the principal Arab tribe of Zanzibar, the Al Harth. They possessed large landed estates, had numerous slaves and furnished most slave merchants and brokers. They were the oldest Arab settlers on the island and aspired to acquiring its political sovereignty. Their chief, Abdulla bin Salim, had great wealth in ships and land and 1500 armed slaves. He was invariably at the vanguard of the opposition to Majid and never attended his durbar. But Majid always treated him with consideration, perhaps to soften the opposition. He allowed all his goods to pass the Customs House free of duty. He also gave him an annual allowance of 1200 government Crowns from his treasury. Rigby was of the view that this tribe wanted the brothers to fight so that they could install themselves in Zanzibar. And in this political adventure, they had Barghash as their chosen tool.[32]

Sayyid Majid and the Anglo-French Rivalries over the Slave Trade

Majid openly exploited British overtures to be their ally in the anti-slave trade campaign. He was particularly keen to make the most of their effort to ease out the French from this trade. Career advancement was possible, as the British aimed to dislodge the French from the slave trade and not to ban the trade per se. The pitch for a complete ban was articulated later in the 1860s, with the abolition declared in 1873. And then too the restrictions on slave traffic were largely on British subjects, such as the Indian Kutchi traders.[33] Jeremy Prestholdt argues that the slave traffic thrived, as Arab and British slave owners as well as the abolitionists, such as David Livingstone, were complicit in using the slaves as a clean slate on which to articulate their own identity and status. If the former used them as economic labour, the latter converted them to social capital. Even slaves had internalized the economic and social benefits of such ownership. Ironically, for slaves, freedom often meant becoming petty slave owners themselves.[34] Thus, the anti-slave campaign and the alliances against French participation in the trade did not end slave traffic. Nor were they meant to stop it. They merely shifted the use of slaves from mere economic labour to social capital, on whose bodies ideas of blackness, race and Africa were poised to emerge. They brought Arab and African slave owners in close alliance with both their British counterparts and the abolitionists. Reda Bhacker and Frederick Cooper also show that Rigby's abolition rhetoric was hollow, as slave labour was openly used in the private Arab and British plantations of Zanzibar.[35]

Sayyid Majid welcomed the anti-French alliance, fully aware that the British abolition rhetoric was about obtaining their monopoly on the slave trade and not ending it. The anti-French alliance proved useful for both Majid and the British. The latter benefited, as it diverted profits of the trade away from their French rival. And Majid gained, as driving away the French opened the markets to local Arab and African merchants and helped consolidate his social base. And in this venture, he had the full support of the

British Consuls and Officers in Bombay, who turned a blind eye to
the slave trade from Zanzibar even as they kept the anti-slave pitch
high. Their complicity was driven by the need for slaves to work in
plantations on the island, where British capital was invested. It was a
win situation for Majid, who emerged hugely emboldened. Even the
Kutchi traders looked to him for help when, as British subjects, the
going got tough for them. The additional bonus for Majid was the
return support that the British promised in his succession dispute
with his brother Thuwayni.

In 1870, the Earl of Clarendon Committee on the East African
Slave Trade reported that slave dealers, Arab subjects of Sultan
Majid, were conducting slave raids in the interior of Africa, the
neighbourhood of Lake Nyasa and beyond it, to obtain slaves. They
were all well-armed and provided with articles for the barter of slaves.
These included beads and cotton cloth. Their modus operandi was
to incite one tribe against the other and extend support to one of
them. Once their side won, the captives became their property or
were cheaply purchased by barter. Generally, a few yards of cotton
cloth was given in exchange for the slaves.

The members pointed out that the major hubs of this trade
were the territories of the Sultan of Zanzibar. By the treaty Majid
had signed with the British, slaves were legally trafficked for the
purpose of supplying slave labour in his and his subjects' plantations.
They were transported within the ports in his jurisdiction and over
specified periods only. The permissible limits were as far south as
Kilwa and up till Lamu to the north. The legal slave trade generally
commenced from Kilwa, and the caravans came to Zanzibar.
They often proceeded to Momfia, Mombasa, Pemba and Lamu.
Additionally, all export of slaves for sale to foreign countries was
prohibited and illegal. Slaves could be exported for domestic use
only. The committee reported that not all who were taken captive
survived. Only one in five or at times one in ten reached the coast
alive. And the fearful loss of life was accompanied by the miseries
that attended them.

The legal traffic was very lucrative and earned the Sultan and the
dealers huge profits. Slaves that cost next to nothing in the interior

were worth on an average $5 at Kilwa, $17 at Zanzibar and $60 on the coast of Arabia.[36] The committee pointed out that it was a common sight to see sick and feeble slaves lying for days before the Customs House at Zanzibar because their owners would not pay tax until they saw whether the slaves would live or die.

An illegal trade in slaves also thrived. This was in the hands of the northern Arabs, who arrived in Zanzibar with the north-east monsoon in the early part of the year. They purchased or kidnapped the slaves they required and exported them to Arabia, the shores of the Red Sea and the Persian Gulf. Majid, under pressure from the British, had issued a decree prohibiting the sale of slaves to the northern Arabs and imposing heavy penalties on those who broke the laws. This made it difficult for them to purchase in the open market. And yet they were undeterred. The Consuls considered them like a 'terror' to the local inhabitants. They reportedly pillaged and stole the 'negroes', who feared to move around Zanzibar in the season when the Arabs arrived. Within gunshot of the Sultan's palace, the British cruisers often intercepted dhows full of stolen slaves. Annually, about 3000 slaves were exported from Pemba and 5000 from Zanzibar by the northern Arabs.[37]

The British suspected Majid's complicity in the trade, even though he made all the correct gestures to distance himself from it. Henry Churchill, the Political Agent at Zanzibar, feared that this trade was carried out with the Sultan's full knowledge and in connivance with the French. He lamented that Sayyid Majid did not pay any heed to his warnings and was instead in constant touch with the French Consul on this matter.[38]

The foreign office suggested that Sayyid Majid be made to sign a treaty to confine slave traffic to a designated route within his territory. His freshly spruced up town of Dar as Salaam was marked as the exclusive port of entry for the shipment of slaves from the mainland and Zanzibar the sole recipient port for this consignment. From Zanzibar, slaves could be shipped to Pemba and Mombasa only. The foreign office wanted all slave traffic outside this designated route to be declared illegal and the slaves liable to seizure.

The Foreign Office was insistent that the slaves legally moved from Dar as Salaam to Zanzibar and thence to Pemba and Mombasa would be strictly limited to the actual requirements of the inhabitants of those places. The exact number was to be mutually determined by the Sultan and the Political Agent. And the number was to be gradually decreased so as to eventually cease all traffic. Each vessel carrying the slaves was liable to capture if it did not have a pass issued by the Sultan. The pass was to be valid for only one voyage, and the ship was to have distinctive marks on her hull and sails. A heavy penalty was to be attached to any piracy of these passes or marks. From the date of the said treaty, Sayyid Majid was expected to severely punish any of his subjects involved directly or indirectly in the slave trade, especially if involved in any attempt to molest or interfere with a liberated slave.[39] And no British subject, including the Kutchis, were to be allowed to dabble in its profits.

Sayyid Majid and the Play with the French

Majid's beneficial alliance with the British notwithstanding, he made the most of the French efforts to win him to their side. The French were determined to make the British ban on slave trade ineffective. They wanted to maximize their profits with Majid's help. In one instance, with his help, they dispersed congregations of slaves who were trafficked by the French private firms. They used the pretext of protecting British Indian subjects in Zanzibar from the attacks of these armed slaves. The fear and danger that these armed slaves triggered in Zanzibar were used by them to obtain permission from the Sultan to park their ships in Zanzibar to prevent the slaves' entry. The deal was that, in the eventuality of an attack by Muscat, these ships were to help Sayyid Majid's own five ships of war, which were equipped with armaments and had been readied for the Muscat attack: the *Shah Alam*, with forty-four guns, the *Piedmontese*, with thirty-six guns, the *Artemise*, with twenty-two guns, the *Setporna* and the *Africa*, both with four guns.[40]

Felix Jones, the British Political Resident in the Persian Gulf, was critical of this deal. He warned that slave dealers were getting increasingly active as a result of demand from southern Europe. According to him, the slave trade had assumed 'gigantic proportions' as a consequence of demand from the French colonies. Firms from southern Europe were not only contracted to supply many thousands of slaves, but they were also sending out large steamers for their transfer and transport to Bourbon and other French colonies. One such steamer was called *Engagees*. Jones was convinced that these contracts had the sanction of the French government and, as a result, trade 'at no period in history was ever carried out to the extent as at present all along the East Coast of Africa'.[41]

The French laid out a detailed plan to classify slaves for export as 'free labour' because Sayyid Majid was tied by treaty engagements with the British government, which forbade direct or indirect sale of slaves from the island. Captain Rigby reported with much concern the French effort to pressure Majid to permit the export of slaves from his territories to the French island of La Réunion or any other French colony as 'engaged labourers'. Rigby was alarmed that, even if this sly way of slave export had been tried in vain in the time of Sayyid Sa'īd, this time it was made with far more gusto.[42] Indeed, the French stationed 'war ships' in the Persian Gulf for the 'purpose of giving weight to these demands'.[43] Rigby was worried but happy that Majid was continuing his father's tradition of loyalty to and alliance with the British on the issue of slave exports to European nations.

Majid pointed out that his father, the late Sultan Sayyid Sa'īd, too had agreed to let slave dealers export 'free men' for labour to French colonies. But he refused permission for those slaves imported from Africa and who had no idea of their position, even when they were made free men. He had refused permission to dealers even when told that the French could procure 'freed slaves' from Zanzibar, and if unsuccessful, they would buy them from his territories on the coast of Africa by force of warships. He had replied that if 'you threaten to use force I cannot resist but I do not consent'. Sayyid Sa'īd openly declared his allegiance to the British when he said 'he was unable to resist the force of France but that the government with which he had a treaty for the prevention of the sale of slaves to Europeans would perhaps prevent France buying slaves in his territories'.[44] Sa'īd followed this up with a cry for help from the British Consul. Clearly, the pro-British slant of the Sultan of Muscat was a clever ploy to win over the support of not just the British, but his own Arab traders, dealers and brokers, who were 'averse to slaves being sold and taken away' by the French.[45]

Sayyid Majid carried forward his late father's policy. He resisted the French demands, hoping to win the support of the local Arab merchants and dealers. In 1857, he refused to yield to the continuous pressure from the French merchant Monsieur Reutone Rautony, of Bourbon, who wished to send his ships to Zanzibar ports to export 'free slaves' at a profit to Sayyid Majid. Rautony exhorted him to rebuff the British Consul if he created hurdles in the deal that he pitched as a 'high financial and moral winsome' for Majid. He argued that, morally, it was good, as the slaves were being freed to 'labor for wages in any country'. And financially, he made a compelling argument for the high profits it would bring, which he said would be shared between them. The deal was that the slaves would be transported in a fast-moving French ship called *Paikur*, and profits would be immense, as it would perform voyages with speed. Even the price of the slaves sent from Zanzibar would be equally divided between the two parties after taking care of the expenses of shipping, passage, etc. He made a demand of young and strong slaves. For every ninety male slaves, he wanted ten female slaves of fourteen to sixteen years of age.[46]

Monsieur Rautony, well aware of the Anglo-French competition over such profits, exhorted Majid to 'not pay attention to the words of the English Consul' and instead work in the interest of his own people. He reminded him that the British wanted to monopolize the slave trade because they needed them in their sugar plantations in Europe and India. They wanted to monopolize sugar manufacture and its sale and thus wanted to block slave labour to other countries. In contrast, France desired the 'happiness of all mankind'. He argued that slaves, on arrival at Bourbon and French colonies, would be 'taught labor' so that they may become 'wise and clever'.[47]

Sultan Majid was not attracted by the offer and was firm on his commitments to the British, which allowed slave traffic despite the shrill surface rhetoric. He remained concerned with the French merchants' activities in his ports. In 1858, he objected to the French vessels, loaded with slaves, carrying his flag to escape British surveillance. He threatened the French ship *Glamense* that he would deprive it of its flag and papers if it attempted to leave the port with 'negroes' on board. He gave similar warnings to all buglas belonging to the port.[18] The Sultan's strictures against slave trade were well known to his subjects. They communicated these to French ships like the *Glamense*, which arrived along with 'warships' at their first port of call Kisingia, a small port on the east coast of Africa within the Zanzibar dominion. The local people at this island, which was considered the destination of all 'slave caravans' coming from the interior and from the Lake Wanyassa, resisted the French purchases. They felt threatened by the warships that accompanied French merchant ships. These French 'brigades of war' came with the express purpose of protecting vessels involved in procuring slaves. And slaves were forcefully taken from here to be shipped to Zanzibar and other ports within its dominions. Sultan Majid was incensed at the violation of his orders and not only complained to the British Consul for help, but also dispatched his own yacht to the port Kilwa, ordering his Governor to stop this traffic.

Majid invariably had the support of locals, who were equally pained and concerned at the scale of this traffic that deprived them of profits and curtailed their participation in other trades. Majid was in continuous correspondence with the Arab and Indian merchants, warning them and forbidding them from participating in the slave trade to the benefit of the French. He sent a proclamation to the same effect addressed to the Banias and other Indian residents at his ports, urging them to exercise caution.[49] At Kilwa, his Governor Saif bin Ali assured him that he had proclaimed publicly through 'sound of horn' throughout the town that any of the subjects who disobeyed the order banning slave trade would be severely punished. He had also conveyed these commands to the chief of the Najoo tribe and to the chief of the Baluchis at Kilwa.[50]

But despite his proclamations and the support he received from the local trading communities and his subjects, French war brigades accompanying vessels with slaves were a common sight on his waters and ports: Kisingia, Kilwa, Pemba, Comron and from the east coast of Africa to the slave depots at Nosi-beh and Mayotte. French slave ships were also sighted at the west coast of Madagascar. Majid's obstacles merely forced the French to move slaves long distances by land from the opposite mainland of Africa to ports situated to the south of the island of Monfsa. This decreased the number of able-bodied slaves who arrived in Zanzibar, as most were taken to the new market that the French created in Monfsa.

Rigby noted that tribes found 'slave hunting' for the French more profitable than involvement in ivory or other trades.[51] Indeed, their participation adversely affected other trades, such as that of cloves and ivory, as Arab tribes preferred 'hunting slaves' for them.[52] Indeed, the high demand created by the French also increased the price of slaves. His firmness did not put an end to French efforts to procure slaves from the East African coast. But the restrictions he imposed did give a fillip to trade in ivory and copal.

Majid's restrictions on the French to please the British went to the advantage of the Arab traders. Majid became very popular by breaking the efforts of the French to establish their monopoly over the slave trade to the exclusion of the local dealers. Majid's cold shoulder to the French, whether it be in the trade in slaves or ivory, offered gains to the locals and helped consolidate his social base.

The Arabs from the north, who constituted the aristocracy and were referred to as Shirazi, benefited the most from Majid's crackdown on the French.[53] They were plantation owners and needed slaves for labour. They bought slaves cheaply—half a dollar a head, or ten slaves in exchange of one cow or bullock. They were too indolent and luxury-loving to bother about supervising the slaves, so the slaves had a relatively easy life at their plantations. They were provided with a hut and a garden around it. They got two days off a month and reportedly showed 'taste and cleanliness'. When hired out to labour by their master, they got 8 Indian pice per day. Out of this, the master took 5 pice, leaving them with 3 pice for their food and other needs. Many individual slaves were slave owners as well. Often even a servant who received $4–5 a month in wages owned a few slaves. Manumitting a slave was seen as a very laudable act, and the Arabs never defended slavery.[54] Rigby loathed the Arab slave dealers, even if he found the condition of slaves not so pathetic on Arab plantations. He called them a 'vile, base set of unfeeling wretches'.[55]

The suppression of French participation in the slave trade was a double whammy. It made Majid dig his heels into Zanzibar society and consolidate his hold over the Arab aristocracy, the Hadhrami Arabs who served as porters and menial labour on plantations and the Indian merchants and bankers who financed much of the local economy. Alongside this, it brought him in the good books of the British. Sayyid Majid's gains in rooting himself in local society were most evident when the local people resisted and opposed French merchants at his ports. On the west coast of Madagascar, there was a 'deadly feeling of hatred' against all white men among the population. Their opposition was most evident when, on one occasion, they burnt a French ship and killed its crew north of Monambo. This extreme step was triggered because a member of one of the Arab tribes had kidnapped members of the other tribe to sell to the French merchants. The French government, despite such local opposition and in defiance of the Sultan's authority and laws, sanctioned slave trade. Indeed, it legalized the trade by claiming that the exported men were 'freed slaves' or free labour, and thus the trade did not violate any injunction or law of the Sultan or the British.[56]

II

Majid and the Abolition Rhetoric: Slaves, Slavers and the British

Majid's political sovereignty was constituted through his ingenious entanglement with the British on the issue of the ban on slave trade and their shrill, if hollow, abolition rhetoric. He cleverly cashed in on the fact that, under the veneer of abolition, there was heavy British investment in continuing with this profitable trade. Rigby's measured responses to Majid's alleged violations on the prohibition of slave traffic reflected Majid's effective tapping into imperial politics and rivalries over the profits of this trade.

Majid's career remained rooted in imperial politics over the profits of slave trade. That the talk of ban on the trade was merely rhetorical and the gains were phenomenal was most evident when, in 1864, finding it difficult to collect the tax on cloves and coconut trees due to poor infrastructure, he decided to abolish these taxes and gain popularity. Not surprisingly, he substituted these with an increased tax on slaves. He hoped to increase his revenue from this source at a scale far bigger than what was possible from cloves and coconuts.

Significantly, he had the full backing of the British. He consulted Playfair before taking this step. Playfair diplomatically refused to intervene, even if in British circles, slave tax was viewed as a highly objectionable source of revenue. The British turned a blind eye to Majid's increased slave tax as they knew that this was his major source of income, a large part of which he devoted to the construction of public works likely to benefit his country.[57] The bonhomie between the British consuls and Majid over the slave trade politics was most evident when Playfair, having ignored Majid's increased slave tax, simultaneously praised him for his anti-slave trade measures.

Indeed, he was appreciative that Majid carried out these measures even though they made him very unpopular and his subjects complained incessantly about unnecessary searches. In one instance, they petitioned him about their dhows being searched unnecessarily and being unfairly treated. The master of one such dhow stated that his vessel was boarded by two boats while he was on his way to Zanzibar from Sharjah in the Persian Gulf. The dhow had neither slaves on board nor anything to suggest that he was employed in the slave trade. Even so, his boat was captured and burnt and the crew deprived of their arms and money worth $688.[58]

Clearly, the benefits were going to British dealers, merchants and plantation owners as well.[59] The tax structure of Majid was as follows: on every slave taken thence to another place, $4; on every slave exported from the island of Zanzibar to Maruna (maintained opposite the island), Mombasa or Lamu, $2; exportation of slaves to any other place was prohibited.[60] And yet, Majid was quick to establish his benevolent profile by his gestures of kindness towards slave children. On many occasions he rescued slave children from vessels headed to Zanzibar and sent them to be educated at Bishop Tozer's Mission.[61]

From British consuls and agents posted in Zanzibar to the officers such as Col Pelly in Bombay, all kept up the anti-slave trade rhetoric while at the same time ignoring or indeed offering tacit support to Majid's slave trade ventures. Indeed Pelly, the Secretary to the Bombay government, justified their inaction on Majid's ventures saying that his efforts to suppress slave trade would at once 'excite against him their [locals'] anger and disgust as well as that of the Arab slave dealers from the Asian coasts against whom his operation are directed'.[62] At the same time, he reassured the government that Majid was indeed with them in the prohibition drive. He was tightening up the northern Arabs engaged in the slave trade and had seized and imprisoned three sets of these Arabs, who were found in the act of shipping slaves from Zanzibar. He refused gifts to them and was ordering them back to their country, apart from confining them.

Pelly underlined the support he obtained from Majid in suppressing the trade. He argued that he relied more on the voluntary help of Majid rather than the dependence of Western cruisers to solve the slave menace. He was confident that, together, they could restrict this menace even if the local people were not courteous to him, as they thought that he was pressuring the Sultan to clamp down on them.[63]

Playfair, the Political Agent at Zanzibar, played along, reinforcing the impression that Majid was indeed hands-on in suppressing the slave traffic. He also recommended the presentation to Majid of two 12-pounders and a 24-pounder Howitzer, complete with carriages and limbers, as he had taken 'a most decided step towards abolition of slave trade, and one which causes a very serious loss to his treasury'.[64] By this, he meant the prohibition of the transport of slaves even from port to port in his dominion during the monsoon. Even though these could not be sanctioned, six mountain train guns with carriage were approved for delivery by the government instead.[65]

Playfair was so appreciative of Majid's efforts to cooperate that he reported that, when the Sultan was told that slave traffic had diverted to Kilwa because of his restrictions in Zanzibar, he took action. He ordered the Governor of Kilwa to not allow any boats to disembark slaves at that port without a special permit from the Zanzibar Customs House. He made sure that the permit was given only to the actual natives of his dominion. And the slaves who disembarked with permission were to be carried to Zanzibar.[66] He mandated that all his boats going port to port would have a Customs House manifesto stating the exact number on board. He gave full permission to British cruisers to seize all boats that contravened this order.[67]

Playfair batted with Majid, walking the tightrope between him and the British government. His fears that a curb on Majid's slave trade would be disastrous for Zanzibar's economy were based on his assessment of the island's dependence on this traffic. In 1866, it was reported that 72,000 or an annual average of 14,400 slaves passed through the Zanzibar Customs House during the last five years as imports. The majority of these slaves were exported to the Persian Gulf and the Red Sea. Every slave introduced into Zanzibar paid a certain duty to the Sultan and thus this was his major source of revenue.[68] Even though Majid was abiding by his treaty with the British and allowing their cruisers to hunt for slave vessels in his waters, there was no denying the fact that he needed slaves to cultivate his plantations and to supply to the labour market. He also was interested in their continued arrival in Zanzibar because he derived pecuniary benefits, as a considerable duty was levied on the importation of each slave into the island.

Playfair wanted the government to reconsider their pressure on Majid for the suppression of slave traffic. He feared that 'such a measure will cause the downfall of the Sultan'. He felt that Majid relied heavily on revenue from this trade and suggested that the only way he could be compensated for these losses was by encouraging entrepreneurship in agricultural products such as sugar cane. For this, he wanted the sinking of European capital to grow valuable crops like sugar and cotton.[69] He argued that this was the only option to increase revenues, as Majid had already increased the tax on cloves to 5 per cent ad valorem, to be paid by the owner of the cloves to the Director of the Customs House on receipt. If there was no receipt, then 5 per cent was to be deducted from the price to be paid to the seller, and the same amount was to be given to the Director of the Customs House. Similarly, each productive coconut tree was liable to a tax of 2 pice/annum. All those who had coconut trees in Zanzibar were required to inscribe the number of trees in the books of the Customs House. Whoever failed to do so was charged double duty. Sayyid Majid justified the internal taxation as necessary for the good government of his state.[70]

The tacit support of the British Consuls to Majid's slave trade hinted at their vested interest in the continuing traffic when the number of slaves in Zanzibar far exceeded the island's requirements. Arab dealers freely collected them and took them to the slave markets in the Persian Gulf, the Arabian coast and the Red Sea. Mr Seward, who briefly was Adjunct Political Agent at Zanzibar, observed the bonhomie between Majid and the local British officialdom when he noted that dealers found it easier to manage the vigilance of the British cruisers when they shipped their slaves from Zanzibar than from the coasts of the mainland.[71] He felt that the milder British naval restrictions were in place to avoid hurting Majid's economy and lose him as a critical ally in the Western Indian Ocean.

With all the informal British support network working for him, Majid was emboldened to protest if the boats of the British cruisers interfered with his vessels that were within his territorial waters from Lamu to Kilwa. Seward commented on Majid's political confidence, which he felt was derived from a firm economy that rested on his relationship with the British and which ensured profits from the slave trade. He was of the view that Majid was an 'independent prince' and included his kingdom 'among the civilized states'. Majid saw his rights 'as unequivocal and his sovereignty as complete as that of Her Majesty'.[72]

The advantages of this deft diplomacy were not missed by Majid's brother Sayyid Thuwayni. He, too, complained to the British Consul to curb this trade from his port of Kilwa. He drew their attention to the 'unprecedented amount of English coin' in which the payment for slaves was made to the French. Equally alarming for him was the 'greatly increased demand for gunpowder' for the sale to 'slave hunters' in the interior. This indicated the scale of the French slave trade.[73] He regretted that, despite the fact that the Governor General in the Portuguese territories of the east coast no longer levied a tax of $16 for his private advantage on each slave exported, as was the case earlier, and was serious about stopping their export, the trade continued.

The complicity of the British in the continuing surreptitious slave traffic was most evident in the reluctance to clamp down on Majid. In 1865, the American and European merchants appealed to Majid to assert himself and protect their interests as British officers clamped down on their slave vessels in his waters. They protested at a meeting in Zanzibar about the seizures by British Commanders of native vessels engaged in 'legal trade' within and without the dominions of the Sultan. They felt this was in contravention of existing treaties and contrary to the island's laws. Such seizures had 'greatly injured the trade' and sacrificed the interests of merchants and destroyed the confidence of the native traders. Most importantly, they were worried that it had exasperated the natives and shaken their confidence in the foreigners. They wanted the Sultan to intervene to uphold the treaty provisions that guaranteed that no vessel within certain limits of the Sultan's dominion should be liable to be condemned and destroyed on the sole authority of the Commander of any British 'Man of War'. They demanded that all native vessels seized while engaged in illegal traffic should be delivered to the Sultan for adjudication. This was the only way in which the waning commerce of the Sultan could be revived.[74]

It was no secret that, underneath the surface rhetoric of Abolition, a lucrative slave trade kept the wheels of British commerce in the region well greased. Majid was clearly integral to this British profiteering. In 1869, Churchill, the British Consul at Zanzibar,

gifted to Majid, who was at Dar as Salaam, a pair of Bombay couches
and four gilt mahogany chairs that he bought at a sale. He made this
present on the occasion of Ramadan. He reported that the gift was
to mark the 'friendly sentiments' of the British towards the Sultan,
'although his government was determined to put a stop to the slave
trade when carried out by the natives of India who were under his
protection'.[75] Churchill, clearly, wanted such trade to continue, as it
was legal carried out by British Indian subjects under the protection
of the Sultan.

Former Arab slave dealers who had worked for Majid, such as
Salim Jebram, were spotted as the 'zealous Arabs' in the service of
Rigby. Jebram was Rigby's most 'trustworthy informant', and his
timely information often led to the capture of slave dhows. When he
died, the British arranged to take financial care of his heirs.[76] It was
not for nothing that the British Resident in the Persian Gulf, Jones,
made a distinction between slavery in Muslim societies and that
in the Christian world. And despite his surface critique of Majid,
he explained what the specific case of slavery in a Muslim society
like Zanzibar meant. His particularistic articulation of slavery was
close to how Majid explained its local meaning. According to Jones,
slavery in Zanzibar implied little beyond loss of freedom and was
free of the atrocities that characterized it in the Western world.
Making a distinction between slaves and slave traffic and labour,
he naturalized the former, arguing that slavery was not something
opposed to the Islamic faith and nor was it considered unethical
to Muslims. Thus, he was against harsh measures for the 'arbitrary
suppression' of the traffic. Instead, he wanted the possessors of the
slaves to be pressured to step away from this traffic.

Jones believed that the treaties with the maritime chiefs
conceded to the British only the right to liberate newly recruited
slaves from the territories from which they were bought. It did not
give them the right over slaves already there or those fleeing and
taking refuge in British vessels of war. Naval officers had no right
to exercise authority over slaves of foreign powers who were at their
ports.[77] This particularistic explanation of slavery in Zanzibar was
critical to its justification by all Zanzibari Sultans, including Majid.

III

Slavery Spin-off: The Documenting of Legal Subjects

Slave traffic restrictions in Zanzibar helped Majid legally define and document his subjects. The documentation process was complex. But it became a great step forward in launching his 'paper raj', as legal registers listing his subjects became the recognizable meters of his political sovereignty. They offered an instant recognition of his sovereignty in imperial circles.

In 1860, the anguish of the Indian merchant diaspora in Zanzibar was most evident when Rigby commenced his trenchant measures for putting a stop to slave traffic and slave holdings. He made no distinction between British subjects and the subjects of native states in India when it came to offences related to slave traffic. He carried on with his tough measures with full authority for fifteen years. In this period, he deported a large number of Indians, who were convicted of offences against the slavery laws.

Majid supported him as he viewed himself as the major beneficiary of these drives. Rigby's measures diverted slave trade exclusively to his subjects. He issued a proclamation forbidding his subjects to sell or buy slaves from any native of India. Rigby was satisfied, as he felt that if the purchase of slaves was restricted to the subjects of the Zanzibar dominions, the demand for them would diminish, and their supply from the interiors would dry up.[78] His relentless drives ensured that in the course of a few months, over 6000 slaves were emancipated. Because of Rigby's policies, the jurisdiction of the Consul over natives of India, whether born in British territory or not, was sufficiently established by usage. And Sayyid Majid offered no opposition, either by protest or otherwise, to the Consul's proceedings and protectionism.[79]

Not surprisingly, Rigby's measures proved particularly harsh for the Bania merchants from India, who were deeply involved in the trade. They resisted in all kinds of ways, and Rigby complained that, despite the ban by Majid and the British government's order forbidding the purchase or sale of slaves by British subjects

in any part of the world, the Banias and other natives of India in
Zanzibar continued with slave dealing. He reported that although
all the slaves on the island of Zanzibar belonging to natives of
India, whether British subjects or natives of protected states, were
emancipated, there still remained about 2000–3000 slaves at
places on the opposite mainland held by natives of India resident
there. He declared a fine of $100 per person found in the possession
of slaves.[80]

In 1860, he highlighted the case of an Indian merchant, the
Bania Kanu Munji, who had been in Zanzibar for many years and
had exclusive dealings with Arabs and others at various places on
the African coast. He was a British subject and had been warned of
the heavy penalties he would incur if he involved himself in the slave
trade. But despite the warnings, he was found to possess sixty-nine
slaves (thirty-eight females and thirty-one males) on his plantation
6 miles outside the town of Zanzibar. Many of these were young
children. Munji was arrested and locked in the fort to be deported to
India. His slaves were emancipated by Rigby, and a Qazi was made
to issue legal certificates for the same to them. Munji was made to
pay a sum of $10 to each slave for his support. He was also made to
assign for a period of ten years two small plantations, each worth
about $600, for the support of the children not old enough to earn
their own living.[81]

Rigby's measures created a storm in the Indian trading diaspora.
This was expected, as the ownership of slaves was rampant in the
Indian trading community. Nearly three-fourths of the immovable
property on the islands of Pemba and Zanzibar, along with the
slaves living on it, was either owned or mortgaged to them by Arab
proprietors. Rigby ordered that when the mortgagee got possession,
he should emancipate the slaves and get them registered at the
British Consulate. No pawning or pledging in slaves was permitted
to them.[82]

The emancipation of slaves by Indian traders created all kinds
of economic hardships for them: it resulted in the fall in the value of
property; the heavy losses suffered by Indian subjects resulted in the
shaking of credit. At the same time, the fear of total prohibition of

slavery made no one give advance on security of any landed estate. Circulation of money was checked at the source, and commerce in general suffered, with land prices falling dramatically.[83] Not surprisingly, slave owners evaded compliance in all kinds of ways: they threatened to stop all trade if their slaves were emancipated; some denied they were British subjects; others disguised themselves as Arabs.[84]

Majid: The Beneficiary of Rigby's Measures

Majid emerged as the beneficiary of Rigby's strict measures. This was primarily because the beleaguered Banias looked towards Majid for help, as he had obtained trade concessions from Rigby for his subjects, who were exempted from the ban as long as they trafficked within the island's ports. Some Banias drifted towards him, willing to swap their British subject status with an Arab one so that they could continue to be slavers. Majid was quick to encourage them, as they were valuable social capital and of great value to his political aspirations.

Majid was able to lure them with relative ease because British officials and Consuls in Muscat had offered the choice to British Indian subjects to register as subjects of the Sultan or the British in freshly created registers. Predictably, this triggered a lively debate in British official circles on the definition and durability of subject status even as Indians made the most of the opportunity to become active agents in choosing their identity.

Not everyone in the British circles was pleased by this freedom of exercising choice offered to the Indian merchants. In 1862, the political agent at Bushire, Pelly, wanted the government to clarify if the Indians in Zanzibar were British or Zanzibar subjects, and if both the Hindu Banias and the Muslim Khojas could choose which government they belonged to. The Bombay government drew Pelly's attention to the case of Muscat, where this idea of choice had germinated with the Lotiya and Khoja merchants being given the option to register for life in a freshly created register that codified their subject identity and jurisdiction. The Government of India forwarded to him the relevant correspondence on the creation of such a register. It argued that the Muscat register had set the precedent in giving the choice to the individual merchant to give in writing whether they chose to be British subjects or not.

Pelly followed suit. He too created a register in which all British Indian subjects were directed to register their names. The Indian Muslim Khojas and the Hindus were asked to declare freely and in writing whether they claimed to be British subjects. Pelly's initiative resulted in sealing for life subject identities of the Indian diaspora in official ledgers.

Taking a leaf from Muscat's book, the Consul at Zanzibar, Playfair, also introduced the concept of 'choice' to British Indians in Zanzibar, enabling them to choose their subject status. In 1864, he initiated the process of 'registration' of Indians. His successor and critic of the registration process, W.I. Prideaux, called it the 'privilege of registration' that gave Indians in Zanzibar the choice of registering either as British subjects, in a register available at the Consulate, or as the Sultan's subjects by putting their names in his 'Book'.

All those who registered in Playfair's register and who were from the dominions of the British government were henceforth designated as British subjects. Those from provinces of Hindustan not under British protection, such as Kutch, were given the chance to register as British subjects by putting their names in the register if they so desired. All those who registered could claim British protection even if they were from provinces of Hindustan not under British control. Significantly, all the 'Hindee' or Banias from provinces of Hindustan not under British protection who did not register themselves at the Consulate Register were to be considered Arabs.[85]

Sayyid Majid was on board with this project. He was requested to issue a proclamation endorsing this arrangement, which was meant to restrict British subjects from carrying out slave trade. His proclamation said,

All Indians or Banians from the dominion of the British Government are British subjects, and those who are from the other provinces of Hindustan, and have registered themselves as under British protection, they are to be considered British subjects, and all their slaves who are formally freed are not to be interfered with. And any Hindu or Banian from other places except from British territory who may not have registered himself—they are to be considered as Arab.[86]

This continued until the order of 9 August 1866 of Her Majesty when, as a general rule, the Political Agent did not claim jurisdiction over unregistered natives of India.[87] And in 1868, it was decided that while the traffic of slaves by Indian natives would not be allowed, the possession of slaves for domestic purposes would for some time be tolerated provided no new purchases were made.

In 1869, as a consequence of these orders, Churchill prepared a list of Indians under the Sultan's protection who were permitted to possess domestic slaves. A similar list in Arabic was sent for record to Sayyid Majid. This was done on the understanding that, even though the Political Agent had no jurisdiction over unregistered Indians, it was expected of the Sultan that he would himself punish those Kutchis who trafficked in slaves and that no fresh arrivals from India would be added to his list of protectees. And by 1873, the Queen barred all natives of Indian states under British protection from possessing slaves and from acquiring any fresh ones.[88]

The registration process lent agency to Indians to choose their subject status, creating legally marked subjects whose identity was codified for good. This legal subject status was created by the individual's own volition and not as a consequence of any act of conquest, service, ethnicity or religion. Indians now had the option to identify themselves as Indians or Arabs depending on whether they registered at the Consulate Register or at the book of Sayyid Majid. The choice was theirs. They were designated as British subjects or the Sultan's subjects depending on whose register or book they preferred to register in. The registration process in Zanzibar gave agency to Indians to be the masters of their identity, but it also sealed their identity for good.

Majid emerged as an attractive sought-after sovereign because of the concession his subjects had to participate in the slave trade. The registration 'Book' for Indians helped him sharpen his sovereign status. This inventory of his subjects provided him with a legal document that confirmed for posterity his sovereign status as the temporal head of an ethnically diverse population. A bonus was that he had the stamp of legitimacy of the British government, at whose behest he had agreed to maintain the registration 'Book'.

Indeed, the registration option put Majid and the British as competitive sovereigns. This was a big boost to Majid's standing in the region, which was fast coming under British imperial control. It was clear that being Arab was good in the short run, but losing out on the British subject status for good would create fresh risks. Individuals tried to work themselves around both identity referents in all kinds of ways. Their claims and counterclaims offered a fresh canvas for Majid to define his own political sovereignty. Indians often entered into disputes on jurisdiction, interpreting their identity as codified in the register ingeniously. They questioned the jurisdiction of Consular Courts if it suited them.

Majid's 'Book' and the British 'Register' became competitive sites between which enterprising Banias tried to boost their business interests. The Advocate General at Calcutta was of the opinion that in the case of offences by British subjects relating to slave traffic in Zanzibar or any other foreign lands, all penalties legally incurred by their disobedience to the laws passed by the British Imperial Government for the suppression of slavery be imposed on them.[89] But given the straddling between the book and the register that Indians increasingly indulged in, the legal opinion from Calcutta remained a distant threat.

For instance, a British Indian subject disputed the jurisdiction of the Consular Court on the grounds of his having been born in Zanzibar. He argued that this made him a subject of the Sultan and exempt from the slave trade ban. This was not admitted, but it offered a chance to Sayyid Majid to indicate that all Indians whose names were written and registered in his book could rightfully claim to be under his jurisdiction and avail all the benefits thereof. There were fewer restrictions for those in Majid's care, and thus the option of registering as an Arab subject with Majid rather than a British subject became attractive for those with vested interests in slave traffic.

Majid consolidated his social base in the Bania community by asserting his jurisdiction over all the Indians registered with him. At the same time, he assured the British that he would not allow any of them to hold slaves more than what was written against their names. The competitive sovereignties that the registration process introduced in Zanzibar were most evident when Prideaux, being suspicious of Majid's 'Book' entries, requested permission to compare it with his own 'Register'. He occasionally satisfied himself that the entries had not been tampered with. From this list, it was clear that in February 1869, there were 350 Indians who claimed the Sultan's protection. Of these, seventy-six held 171 slaves, 270 held no slaves at all, and it seems, therefore, that their sole object was not to gratify their slave holding inclinations, as was sometimes asserted.[90]

At the bottom of this drive to codify subjecthood in a legal document—either the Consulate Register or the Sultan's Book— was the issue of effectively monitoring slave traffic from the island. British subjects were banned from exporting slaves, whereas there was no such ban on the Sultan's subjects, even though he was expected to dissuade them from indulging in slave trade. As Indian slavers and merchants swapped their identity for the Arab one, it meant they preferred to be Majid's subjects, abandoning their British status. Playfair's scheme, which offered them this choice, was clearly working. But in the long run, the fluidity of identities and subject status that characterized the Western Indian Ocean society was valued by all those who were invested in the slave trade. These included local consulate officials, Sayyid Majid and the British plantation owners and slavers and the Arab and Indian merchants.

Critique of the Register

The leeway that registration offered to carry on with slave trade was bound to invoke criticism from pro-abolitionists. Playfair's successor, Prideaux, protested the creation of the register. He was critical of Pelly raising the issue of choice again and triggering the possibility of trafficking, when two years back Rigby had settled the matter by a total ban on slave trade for all Indians. Prideaux couched his argument against a centralized system of identity codification by pointing to its disastrous effect on encouraging slave trade. He feared that this offer of choice to Indian merchants and slavers to swap identity gave them the agency to switch to Arab subject status so as to avoid the trade restrictions imposed on British subjects.

Prideaux feared that this would undo the work of Rigby in controlling the slave trade. He warned that the 'Indians would avail themselves of the privilege of registration just as it suited their purpose or not' and that 'they would speedily revert to their old practice of slave holding and slave trafficking'.[91] Prideaux was of the view that the codification of legal subjecthood was detrimental to the efforts of a blanket ban on slave traffic, which had been imposed by Rigby. 'Rigby's work was undone' by the 'privilege of registration', he thundered.[92]

The number of fresh Arab subjects in the Sultan's Book revealed how Indians opted for this identity to avail the slave trade privileges that Majid offered to his subjects. According to Prideaux, Indians 'had become more or less Arabized'. And very few, if any, intended to return to India, being mainly petty shopkeepers. In the Sultan's Book, the number of years their families had stayed are entered as follows: many for seventy years, few under forty years and one of them is listed as being there for 170 years. The number of these people was decreasing in the same manner as the old Arab families, and Prideaux believed that in a few years, they 'will have died out all together'.

Prideaux wanted greater clarity from his government if any Indian who opted to register in the Sultan's Book should be considered a 'naturalized citizen of Zanzibar'. He was equally curious about whether such an option of naturalization would be permitted in the future as well, and if so, under what condition. He argued that there was nothing wrong if Indians were 'recognized as Arab subjects' of the Sultan, provided that British principles on slave trade suppression were not compromised.

Prideaux went further to say that the registration process that defined the Sultan's sovereign status more sharply by making him the reference point of determining subjecthood should not be interfered with. He was confident that the government would not interfere with 'the profile provided the Sultan in addition to the concession already made will prevent them from purchasing any new slaves in the future'. In fact, he said this profiling by the Sultan 'will be good vis-à-vis us and the Sultan who regards them as his subjects'.[93] But he was always concerned that the only 'advantage a lately landed native of India would derive from becoming a subject of the Sultan . . . [would be] to have some slave dealing ventures in prospect'.

Critics of Playfair argued that this privilege of switching identities using the registration option gave the Indians the licence to indulge in slave traffic, as the restrictions were most strict on the British subjects; the Sultan's subjects, or those like the Kutchis, who were under his protection, were permitted to engage in slave trade for domestic purposes and indeed to own domestic slaves. In 1869, Churchill prepared a list of Indians under Sayyid Majid's protection who were permitted to have domestic slaves. A similar list in Arabic was drawn up and kept in the possession of the Sultan. Most of these were Kutchis, and he was expected to punish them and not add fresh arrivals from India to his list of the protected. But he did not always follow this willingly.[94]

Majid's successor Barghash was more stringent with following the rules of the game. The Kutchis who registered in the Sultan's Book as the 'Sultan's Hindees' and were under his protection he regarded as being under his jurisdiction. They disputed the Consular Court's attempt to bring them under its jurisdiction. Barghash supported them, but at the same time reiterated that he would never allow any of them to hold 'a great amount of slaves'. Prideaux, however, was suspicious of these claims and the entries in the Sultan's Book. But on comparing them to his own register, he was relieved that it had not been tampered with.

And yet, for Majid, the legalizing and documenting of his subjects was a hit, as he obtained for them attractive concessions for carrying on with the slave trade. This ensured a ready pool of slaves in his territory and made the island an attractive site for Europeans to invest in the sugar plantations using slave labour.

IV

Slavery and Foreign: Investments British Private Firms in Zanzibar

British and European private investors owned sugar plantations on the island, which worked with slave labour. They justified the use of slave labour in the narrative of philanthropy and liberal sensibility, insisting that those who worked for them were 'free labour'. They also claimed legal protection for their business enterprises by claiming to buy slaves for use strictly within Zanzibar and thus adhering to the treaty that banned their export. Majid welcomed their capital investments in agriculture and collaborated with them to his advantage. He supported their defence of the enterprise in the face of official criticism. This collaboration made him step into discussions in British circles on the expansion of private capital and the use of 'appropriate' labour on the plantations in East Africa.

Fraser and Company in Zanzibar

Majid invoked precedent and encouraged private British and European agricultural entrepreneurship on his island, as the profits from slave trade increasingly came under threat. He said he was only continuing with his father's tradition. He first experimented with a very liberal planter of Bourbon. He assigned him an estate to cultivate sugar cane and provided him with the labour on the condition that he got his own machinery and allowed him half the profit. He wanted to improve and expand this arrangement to other firms as well. A British and a Hamburg firm accepted his offer to invest capital in the island. Playfair, the Consul in Zanzibar, was not very enthusiastic about the entry of private firms in Zanzibar and their independent deals with Majid. He was of the view that, unless this alternate way of earning revenue was stopped, British efforts to 'effect a sudden revolution' in the institutions of the country would prove disastrous.[95]

In the 1860s, as Britain tightened its restrictions on slave trade and labour and banned the import of sugar from 'slave states', the Zanzibar industry suffered a setback. Sheriff shows that by the 1860s, only 20,000 kg of sugar was produced, and even this had difficulty finding a market.[96] Indian merchants found it tough to invest in this industry because of the prohibitions especially on them, as British subjects, to use slave labour.

And yet, both British subjects and the private British individuals had a way to work around the restrictions as the Sultan, the slavers, abolitionists and British administrators turned a blind eye to them, lured by the profits of this business. Majid used to his best the hypocrisy of the prohibition drive, which ignored the British and European firms who signed contracts with Arab dealers for slave labour to work on their plantations in Zanzibar. Indeed, the traffic of slaves went on in the garb of 'free labour'.

The former Indian Navy officer and Britisher, Francis Fraser, who had retired to Zanzibar, was an important case in point to show how plantations run on slave labour were of advantage to both Majid and the British. In the 1860s, Fraser obtained land from Sayyid Majid at Mkokotoni along with 500 slaves. He established sugar plantations by resurrecting the old formula of providing British machines and supervision and using local land and slave labour. In keeping with the economic practice of the island, he took credit from the British Indian subject, Ludda Damji, who was the agent of the well-known Indian banking firm of Jairam Sewji.[97] On the death of Ludda Damji, it was revealed that $1,00,000 of his capital was entangled with Fraser's firm. The slew of documents exchanged revealed large sums of money had been advanced by Damji to Fraser at different points of time. These were to the tune of $32,255, according to one particular receipt.[98]

Damji's replacement, Beniji Gopaldas, fought for the recovery of the money as, by then, Fraser had moved on to other contracts and deals in Zanzibar, including one involving bullock slaughter.[99]

Predictably, the bullock slaughter contract incensed the Sewji firm, as it hurt the religious sensibilities of his community. He, therefore, terminated all dealings with Fraser, withdrew his capital and asked for the return of his loans with interest. John Kirk, along with Taria Topan, the agent of Damji, got involved in sorting out the issue. Fraser was asked to give his entire sugar estate at Matichery, which was being cultivated by its current occupants, to Gopaldas. And in lieu of the interest on the capital, he was to give his adjoining private estate, as well as the machinery.[100]

Once Fraser's contract with Majid broke, under the pressure from British officers, he arranged another one with four Arab slave owners, who supplied him 400 'labourers'. The men were to be at his disposal for a period of five years and were to be freed thereafter.[101] The Arabs received money from Fraser for a year at the rate of MT$24 per labourer. Majid came under huge flak for allowing Fraser to operate with impunity on the island. The British Consul was insistent that he pay for and emancipate all the slaves on Fraser's plantation. In anticipation of his cooperation, he even gifted him his portrait made in appreciation.[102]

But Fraser was unrelenting. After retirement from the Indian Navy, he had become the head of a branch firm of Nicol and Company, Bombay, in which Smith Fleming and Company had a large interest.[103] The firm was the shipping agent of one Haji Fakīr Qadr Mohiyyuddin Rawshan of Tinnevelly and operated from No. 27 Leadenhall Street, London. It was also involved in the arms trade. It supplied large quantities of percussion caps to India in this man's name and was always suspect in the eyes of the British.[104]

However, its main business involved the dealings and contracts for slaves. And it needed slave contracts because it had sunk £70,000 in the island's agriculture. This represented a trading capital of three times that amount in the commercial branch of their establishment. Their commercial empire included a sugar factory in their estate at Kokotoni, about 20 miles from Zanzibar town. According to the British Consul of Zanzibar, R.L. Playfair, the factory, though still in its infancy, was the 'most important and hopeful of their numerous operations'.[105] He was not so optimistic about the estate being conducive to the growth of sugar cane or as a residence for the Europeans because it was one of the few places in the island 'with a deep sub-soil of stiff clay' that prevents percolation of water. Playfair thought the area was a marsh and was not sure if any amount of draining would make this soil productive.

Sayyid Majid and Fraser and Company had struck a profitable deal on this sugar manufacturing enterprise. Playfair, a staunch critic of private firms operating in Zanzibar, confirmed its operations. According to the contract, the houses for storage and manufacture as well as for residences were to be built by the money deducted from the sale of the sugar manufactured. They were to be considered the joint property of the two parties. Sayyid Majid agreed to give two *shambas* (estates), being the property of Sayyid Suleiman bin Sayyid, for the manufacture of sugar. He also offered all his manufacturing machinery, which was to be considered his property.

The agreement was a long-term one; no duty was to be levied for the first five years beginning from the day of manufacture. And once it was levied, it would not be more than 5 per cent. Fraser and Company had the responsibility of constructing and repairing roads, bridges and watercourses. The cost of these were to be shared, as were the profits of sugar manufacture, which were to be shared equally between the two parties. The Sultan was at liberty to withdraw from the agreement if there were no profits in the first ten years.[106]

The Foreign Office also approved of the contract, declaring it valid as per the law of their country because the slaves were not being exported and were well within Majid's territories. It said, 'the contract in question is not by the law of this country an illegal or invalid contract, and the British subjects entering into contracts with natives who may hold slaves in Zanzibar similar in tenor to the contract of 1864 will not infringe the law of the country'.[107]

They reiterated that there was nothing to prevent a British subject out of Her Majesty's dominion employing a slave as his servant or labourer so long as such an employment did not involve 'a dealing or trading in, purchase, else barter or transfer, carrying away, removing etc. any such slave'.[108]

Fraser and Company had also taken large sugar estates on lease from the Sultan and contracted a supply of slave labour from Arab slave owners. One of the contracts indicated that the contractors had promised to supply to the firm 400 male and female able-bodied labourers. These men were to be at the disposal of Fraser and Company for a period of five years. After this term the contractors bound themselves to guarantee the freedom of all the said labourers. The contractors revealed that these labourers would be slaves on the condition that Messrs H.A. Fraser and Company paid to them for every labourer a year's pay at the rate of $2 per month per labourer for the succeeding four years. The balance of wages, i.e., $1.5 per month, was payable to the labourers from whom they bound themselves not to exact or receive any portion of their pay on any pretext whatever. It was decided that for the first year the firm would clothe and maintain the labourers at their own expense and for the four succeeding years of the contract, they would not be called on to make any disbursement on this account. The contractors undertook to supply vacancies caused by death or desertion to the extent of 10 per cent per annum.[109]

Seward and the Critique of British Private Firms in Zanzibar

Not all in the administration approved of Majid's deals with private firms. In 1866, G.E. Seward, who was the Acting Political Agent at Zanzibar, wrote a memorandum on the issue of British cruisers targeting slave vessels in Sayyid Majid's waters. He reflected on the hypocrisy of the British slave suppression drive by pointing to the involvement of private British capital and entrepreneurship, totally dependent on slave labour, on the sugar plantations on the island.[110] Seward reported that the bazaar gossip noted the inconsistency in the British stand on slave suppression. The abolition rhetoric seemed hollow in the face of the dealings of private firms such as Francis and Company that operated with government patronage. He was of the view that the firm was connected to Nicol and Company of Bombay but was not sure on how much the latter was aware of its slave trafficking in Zanzibar.[111]

Seward was a huge critic of the firm of Francis and Company. He wanted to review its contract and sought legal opinion in this regard. He was wary of the current contract, which had a stipulation promising freedom for the slaves as the ultimate reward. But he cautioned that 'we should not be blinded by the illusory veil of philanthropy' thrown over the transaction. The firm, he argued, was 'animated by ordinary mercantile instincts'. He said it 'seeks the culture of sugar cane rather than of freedom'. He felt the firm was driven by concerns of profit as slave labour was more manageable, cheaper and easily attainable than free labour in Zanzibar.

And yet, the outspoken Seward was also not outright critical of the use of slave labour per se that the abolition rhetoric rejected. Instead, his critique was of the private firms benefiting from this labour and making profits. Like Majid, he too was convinced that slavery meant something different to the people on the island than what it meant to the Westerners. Like Majid, he too conceded that slave labour in Zanzibar was integral to its economy and thus the prosperity of the slaves had to be maintained as a priority. In this respect, the planters at the sugar cane plantations contributed hugely, as they used slave labour and kept them prosperous. He was happy that they educated the slaves by teaching them wholesale restraint, organization and discipline to understand and use well the freedom that awaited them. He approved of these efforts and hoped that the Arab slave owners would use this model too. He urged them to similarly educate them in restraint and eventually offer them freedom to eradicate and abandon slavery as an institution.

However, his appreciation of educating slaves did not mean his support for slave labour, and he remained critical of the firms that used it. He doubted their intentions and claims of benevolence. As he says,

I must confess to a strong unbelief in the existence of any motives of benevolence sufficiently strong to induce English capitalists to sink thousands upon thousands in the purchase of large estates, in the maintenance of skilled artisans, the erection of factories, the

introduction of machinery, in a climate proverbially un-adapted to
Europeans, in order that slaves may be made free.[112]

He was convinced that any representative of a capitalist knew that
sugar cane could be produced at a comparatively insignificant cost
and get high profits with slave labour. He pointed out that a 'glamour
of false benevolence is thrown over the speculations'.[113]

He was critical of the partiality shown by his government
towards the private firms using slave labour in Zanzibar. He wanted
to know from the government if it would let a British merchant
provide the impetus to enslave and encourage slave hunting in
Africa by its policies of slave contracts. According to him, in the
last five years 72,000 slaves passed as imports through Zanzibar
customs. He wanted to know what benefit Great Britain gained or
mankind from 'this commerce that can balance an evil so profound,
an injustice to Africa so flagrant'. He argued that the British position
in Zanzibar was embarrassing, as it was battling slavery elsewhere
and encouraging it on the island by allowing private capital to be
invested in the plantations run on slave labour.

He warned about the fall from grace that this policy had created
for British officials posted on the island. This contradiction was 'not
in the least comprehended by Arabs'. According to him, they 'charge
us with the commission of a tyrannous wrong by our interference'.
The Arabs found it 'hopelessly incomprehensible' when the agents
of a British capitalist pervaded the slave market and bought slaves
by the hundreds, ostensibly for their employment. He argued that
the association of the British with slave traffic was so complete
that he overheard an embarrassing comment in the slave market: 'is
this man an Englishman [angrezi] that slaves are brought for him';
'that those who were beggars have with his money grown rich in the
buying?'.[114] He asked the government to consider whether hundreds
should be enslaved so that a single British firm may gather wealth.
He concluded that the government should take a stand, as it was
the question of the nation's commerce versus the nation's honour.
Seward felt the latter was hugely compromised if commercial
interests prevailed.

No Legal Backing for Seward

Seward's critique emanated from his distrust of the private firms and not from any visceral dislike of slavery or use of slave labour. He investigated the legality of the firm's operations and brought to the notice of the government Fraser's viewpoint, who felt he was being unfairly treated. In backhanded support of Fraser, he referred to the planters' spirited defence, which argued that he had a contract for his dealings in full knowledge of Consul Playfair. This contract made Majid the owner of the slave labour, and he 'directed this labour'. He stressed that the Sultan's slaves on his estate worked 'for him [Sultan] were under his discipline his control and never for the labour supplier'. He stressed that the Sultan 'reared' the sugar cane crop, and his firm 'crushed' it into sugar. The profit or loss on the sugar plantations were shared by him and the Sultan who was a co-partner. In case the Sultan failed to supply labour, the firm stepped up in full knowledge of the Sultan. The slave labour was always paid.[115]

In his self-defence, he stressed that he had founded his contract on a 'Consular basis'. He hoped nothing 'sudden and ruinous would be done'. And he was willing to adopt any practicable suggestion.[116] He asked for a copy of the contract signed by Playfair to be studied by the government. He had worked in Zanzibar in accordance with it.[117] He pointed also to British subjects involved in farming revenues from the slave trade and British vessels and the crew dependent on slave labour. He wanted to know why no 'criminality' was attributed to such foreign residents engaged in business using slave labour.[118]

But the hollowness of the abolition drive was evident when even his backhanded critique of slavery did not get the desired legal approval of the government. L.H. Bayley, Advocate General at Bombay, was of the view that there was nothing in the treaties that the Sultan of Muscat signed with the British that related to the suppression of slavery within his own territories. He was of the view that slavery was legal in Zanzibar, and there was no ground on which the contract in question could be held illegal. He clarified that by the treaty of 31 May 1839, British subjects had the right to reside, purchase or hire lands or houses, etc., at Zanzibar. And Captain

Fraser's legal status was analogous to Britishers holding estates or of planters in the slave states of North America while slavery was allowed in those countries.

He concluded that Seward had no right to question Fraser's contract, given that slavery was legal in Zanzibar. And were he to do so, 'Fraser will have just ground for complaining of a clear violation of his liberty and rights as a British subject'.[119] He further underlined that Seward had in fact no right at all to interfere in the affairs of Fraser. They concluded that he was free to adjudicate if a dispute arose and was presented to him. But otherwise, he had no right to interfere in the private agreement which a British subject residing at Zanzibar entered into with a domestic there. And the British Political Agent, though residing in a slave country like Zanzibar, could not legally constitute himself a censor morum or contractum in regard to British subjects. And thus, British private enterprise dependent on slave labour continued unabashedly even as the abolition drive gathered steam on the surface. Indeed, the hollowness of the drive was evident as the slave market in Zanzibar got a boost because of contracts of private British capitalists like Fraser.

And yet, Fraser and Company, the favourable legal opinion notwithstanding, put the British government in a bind, as its operations with slave labour stood in an embarrassing contrast to its own shrill abolition campaign. Questions were continuously raised, even if for effect, by the government at Bombay and the Government of India on its dealings. The Bombay government asked what steps the firm had taken to ensure that the large demand that its contract generated in the native labour market would not act as a direct or dangerous stimulus to increased activity in the slave traffic within the interior of Zanzibar. They argued that it was imperative that they keep track of how Fraser's legal right to contract slave labour impacted slave trading. The government was of the view that the large slave contracts the firm signed with the Arab slavers offered an impetus to slave trade and defeated the entire purpose of the British campaign on suppression. Clearly, the suppliers could only meet the demand of the contract by 'buying or kidnapping their victims in the interior, and conveying them across from the mainland in a state of slavery'.[120] The government also wanted to know what were the guarantees of the firm's ability to enforce stipulation in these contracts, which provided that after five years as hired labour, their title to the privileges of free men and women would be respected in the Zanzibar dominions.

The Government of India supported the view from Bombay. It argued that, irrespective of the legal position, the private firm could not be allowed to operate in a manner that was so very inconsistent with the policy of the British government on the question of slave traffic in Zanzibar. It warned Fraser and Company that the government and its representatives would in 'no case support such contracts, or aid in respect of any difficulties which may arrive from them'.[121] The Foreign Office was firmly of the view that the labour contracts Fraser signed with Arab dealers violated the provisions of the Act 6 & 7 applicable to all British subjects. They warned him of penalties incurred and asked him to send his explanation in a representation.[122]

And not surprisingly, help for Fraser came from Majid, with whom Fraser had struck a mutually beneficial relationship. In the face of brickbats, Majid quickly freed 711 slaves working under the condemned contracts of the British sugar planter. Their freedom carried one obligation: they must work for whom they list. But they must work. Their wages were their own, their liberty and civil rights inalienable.[123] Seward applauded this 'laudable deed' and further requested the Sultan to make them agree that no slave freed under this act of grace would ever possess a slave. He was of the view that the 'freed man's ability to work vicariously through his slave is destructive of all the invigorating benefits that should spring from liberty'.

By his political acumen, Majid blunted the jibes of Fraser's critics, thereby ensuring that the mutually beneficial deal he had struck with private capitalists like him would continue unhindered. Seward was happy with Majid and wanted the government to accede to his request of receiving a portrait of Her Majesty. He felt this would 'encourage a Prince who should be encouraged to displace in his dominions slavery with freedom'.[124]

V

Sayyid Majid and the Indian Kutchi Capital

Sayyid Majid had no coinage of his own. He was dependent upon all the powers who had jurisdiction in Zanzibar for the money that circulated in his dominions.[125] His polity depended also on Indian capital invested by the Kutchis and Banias. He welcomed Kutchis, as they were critical to his slave-driven economy. The Kutchis, unlike the British Indian subjects, were exempt from the ban on slave trade as they technically came from the protected territory of Kutch ruled by their Rao. This was of huge benefit to Majid. He was compelled to emancipate slaves held by British Indian subjects when pressured by the Consul. But he was under no such compulsion with regard to the Kutchis.[126] In fact, he justified the Kutchi involvement in slave trade as legitimate and legal because of their legal exemption from the prohibition.

The Kutchis were subjects of the Rao of Kutch—an independent princely state in India. They were exempt from the provisions of anti-slave trade treaties that covered only British Indian subjects. This was good news for them, as their involvement with this trade went back to the 1830s. From this early period, a considerable amount of slave traffic was carried on between the dominions of the Sultan of Muscat, the Arab ports of the Persian Gulf and the ports of Kutch and Kathiawar. Most of this trade was of children slaves, both boys and girls. Measures adopted by the British agent failed to put a stop to this traffic.[127]

However, not being British subjects did not mean that they hesitated in leaning on British help when required. They borrowed money from each other to carry on their business in Zanzibar and, in case of any delay or backtracking of promises, they sought help from the Consulate office. For instance, in 1863, a Kutchi petitioner named Khakar Damodaran Devji, who traded in elephant ivory and European piece goods since 1851, had to close his business on the island as his credit was badly affected. He returned to Bombay, suffering a loss of $1000. One important reason for his return was that a fellow Kutchi, Mamula Mulji, pursued his claim for a certain sum of money that Devji owed him. Mulji applied to Pelly, the British Consul, for help in getting his money back. Not receiving too much help from Pelly, Mulji renewed his application to Mr Witt, a Dutch gentleman, who was placed at the embassy in the absence of Pelly. Witt came to Devji's warehouse and shop and, on not getting the payment, he threw his things on the street, saying he would auction them for the satisfaction of the debt.[128]

Devji petitioned to the Bombay government, arguing that his reputation and prestige as a merchant were damaged and that the extreme action was prejudicial to his credit. He argued that when he threatened Witt with a complaint to the Government of Britain, he was arrested. Devji alleged that he was confined for six hours on the request of Witt.[129] He was released only after paying $200 in satisfaction of the said debt. Devji urged the Bombay government to help him get back the $200 and the said security to be cancelled. Further, he wanted a payment of $1000 as cost of damage sustained by him in consequence of the actions of Mr Witt. His pleas went unanswered, as the Bombay government stood by Mr Witt.

The Kutchi dabbling in slaves was such a nuisance that the Bombay government invariably sought clarifications from the Government of India on the extent of their interference to curtail the practice. This was not easy, as the Kutchis were technically not British subjects. Indeed, their exclusion from British treaties banning slave trade was so handy for them that they did not opt to register themselves as British subjects in the Consulate Register. Not surprisingly, British Consuls in Zanzibar, such as Pelly and Churchill, accused Rigby of leaving them uncovered in the treaties he had signed on this issue with Majid. This lapse resulted in many Kutchis also opting to register themselves as Sayyid Majid's subjects when the choice was offered to them by the British Consul Playfair. As Majid's subjects, they were exempt from slave trade prohibitions. As we saw above, the restrictions of slave trafficking applied only to British subjects.[130]

Majid was quick to play on the Kutchi drift towards him. He always invoked the word of Consul Playfair, who emphasized that the law against trafficking of slaves was only applicable to those

British subjects documented in the Consular Register. All others were exempted. Majid further interpreted this to his advantage and argued that in accordance to this order, all Indians who had not opted to register as British subjects or avail protection by enlisting in the register were to be considered Arab. He reiterated Playfair's words, 'that all [Indian subjects] such as had not yet entered their names in the Consular register that he had sent us should be considered as Arabs, and that those alone who had caused their names to be written in the book were under British protection'.

Majid clarified further that such Arabs by default were also his subjects and under his legal jurisdiction. Offering himself as the patron and master of all the non-British subjects involved in slave traffic, he became a huge attraction for the Kutchi slave dealers, who looked to him for furthering their business. He regularly invoked Playfair, who said, 'all such who had not entered their names in the Consular register [be] as assimilated to that of the Arabs in reference to jurisdiction, and at liberty to buy slaves etc.'.[131] Majid underlined the fact that the status of all those Indians not in the Consular Register was 'assimilated by Col Playfair . . . to that of the Arabs, having being abandoned to our jurisdiction'.[132] He concluded that as per Playfair's orders, Kutchis had committed no crime in possessing slaves.

Majid used to his benefit the issue of choice in subject status, that the British had introduced, to further his political agenda and consolidate his social and economic base. Hugely dependent on Indian capital for his lucrative slave trade, he stretched his long arm farther to embrace other Indian merchants who were party to this traffic. They were attracted to him, as they could escape British restrictions on slave trade by availing of the option to switch subject status and come under his protection. He clarified that there were many other natives of India who were in his service, and many of them had been born in Zanzibar, some even fifty years back. He said, 'we look upon these and their children as our subjects the Arabs'.

Majid's claim over certain categories of Indians as his subjects was threatening to the British, as it cast his political sovereignty in an alarmingly embracive way. They soon came up with caveats to the option of subjecthood by choice. The Bombay government was resolute that British subjects residing in Zanzibar could not exempt themselves from British law by taking service with the Sultan or claiming his protection.[133] It asked the Government of India for its legal opinion. And the government stated in no uncertain terms that the Rao of Kutch in 1836 had entered into a treaty with the British, recognizing its paramount power, and that a British agent resided there. Thus Kutchis could not be exempt from British law and rules of slavery when in foreign lands only because they had not registered in the register of the Consul as British subjects. Both the Kutch traders, the Rao of Kutch and Sayyid Majid were informed that, 'though the retention by them of domestic slaves in their households may for a time be tolerated, all attempts at purchasing, selling or trafficking in slaves will be summarily put down, and that this Government will not entertain any claims for redress or compensation'.[134]

Churchill, the Agent at Zanzibar, conveyed the government's view to Sayyid Majid. Simultaneously, he warned his government that he wanted the number of domestic slaves also to be restricted to two to three, only as it was not always possible to distinguish between domestic slavery and slave trade for labour.[135] He kept the pressure on the Kutchis by punishing them for violations in slave prohibitions. For instance, he punished a Kutchi with a fine of $500 and imprisonment at the fort for taking advantage of the Sultan's protection and putting up one of his slaves for sale in the local market. His example set the tone. British Consulates began to extend their legal jurisdiction over Indian subjects, and many Kutchis came to surrender their slaves at the Consulate.[136]

Majid retaliated, as Indian Kutchis who had opted to be his subjects were the lifelines of his slave-run economy. He protested the arrest of the subject under his protection and threatened to not only not cooperate in such actions but complain to the Government of India.[137] Churchill reminded him that he had in the past agreed to cooperate in such matters and allow him jurisdiction over British subjects of all kinds in Zanzibar until the Government of India discussed the issue threadbare and got back to him. He had also promised non interference in the affairs of Kutchis in the Sultan's protection, provided they registered their slaves in the register and did not indulge in fresh transactions of buying or selling slaves.

In 1869, Majid bargained hard when Churchill asserted his claim over the fresh Kutchi arrivals in Zanzibar. Churchill was clear that all future arrivals of Kutchis to the island were deemed eligible to be covered under British law in every way and 'would have no excuse for their purchasing or holding slaves in your Highness's dominions'.[138] Majid agreed temporarily to their being under British law even if they were not registered in the Consular Register. But he made it clear that this was a temporary plan and that the matter would be resolved once the Government of India took a decision. He reminded Churchill that Kutch was not part of British India, and its subjects were different from those of Bombay and Surat.[139] The Government of India of course agreed with the views of the Bombay government, in perceiving as legitimate its control over all Kutchis and other Indian subjects in Zanzibar. But it did reiterate that domestic slavery or household slavery, when practised in Zanzibar by Kutchis or others, was to be ignored.[140]

The Rao of Kutch in the Defence of the British

The contest over the Kutchi capital investment in Zanzibar that lay at the bottom of these subjecthood and jurisdiction debates got even more complicated when the India office pointed out that the provisions of the Indian penal code could not be made applicable to the acts of the Kutchis at Zanzibar.[141] It was of the view that Kutchi dabbling in trade could be controlled only by putting pressure on the rao of Kutch. It underlined the proclamation of the rao of Kutch warning his subjects against trafficking in slaves, either at Zanzibar or any other place they visited. The Bombay government agreed and was keen that the rao should remind the Kutchis in Zanzibar about this proclamation.

At the same time, the Bombay government reminded Sayyid Majid that the new arrivals from Kutch would not be under his protection, and those that were at the moment should be monitored by him and not allowed to traffic in slaves. The British government would interfere if he was found remiss in his duties. By 1869, John Kirk, the Political Agent at Zanzibar, was convinced that bringing the Rao of Kutch's proclamation to the notice of Sayyid Majid had worked. The Sultan realized that his 'plans for gaining over the Indian community of Zanzibar for himself had failed'.[142]

The proclamation of the Rao of Kutch was published and pasted around the town and copies sent in Arabic and Gujarati to the various coastal stations where Kutchis were established. Kirk agreed to observe neutrality in the case of all Kutchis registered with Sayyid Majid. And the state of domestic slaves held by Kutchis was also not to be interfered with.[143] It was by and large agreed by the Bombay government that, as long as Kutchis in the protection of Sayyid Majid did not indulge in slave traffic, their slaves would not be interfered with and that Majid himself would take action if they indulged in slave traffic, failing which the British would intervene.

The proclamation of the Rao of Kutch stating that all his subjects were under British protection and amenable to British law in Zanzibar was to be upheld. Kirk was relieved that the proclamation of the Rao placed the most wealthy and enterprising mercantile community of the Kutchis under the sole protection and jurisdiction of the British and that the British influence was paramount in all matters concerning them.

Majid Questions Rao's Proclamation

Majid was not giving up so easily. He questioned the legality of the rao's proclamation, declaring he had signed no deal with him regarding the Kutchis on his island. More importantly, he used the Kutchi issue to define sharply his political sovereignty and jurisdictional limits. Unmindful of the rao's proclamation and the British legal position, he defined their subjecthood in terms of registry and documentation, service to him and birth in Zanzibar. Indeed, his contest for control over the Kutchis became a way of defining his own political self. His political entrepreneurship rested on his ingenious handling of Kutchi merchants by according to them the 'Arab status'.

Majid fiercely fought British efforts to deprive him of the benefits of Kutchi financial networks. Thus, it was no surprise that he asked each Kutchi to choose his protecting state. He argued that the Rao of Kutch had no right to issue the proclamation as he had no treaty with him. He insisted on viewing Kutchis as his subjects unless they had voluntarily registered in the Consulate Register and claimed British protection. Majid flaunted the 'Arab privilege' of buying and selling slaves to attract all Indian financiers and slavers to his camp and dissuade them from registering their names at the British Consulate. He hoped to secure every new arrival from Kutch for himself. He confidently looked forward to the time when British influence would be reduced to become at par with France and other foreign powers and have no major material stake in the country. Majid's success was evident when Kirk reported that registrations at the British embassy in the last few years had slumped.

In 1870, an order was issued by the Government of India for the regulation of all Consular jurisdiction in the dominions of the Sultan of Zanzibar. It made it mandatory for all British Indian subjects to register themselves in the Consular Register in Zanzibar within the specified period of their arrival. And anyone who refused to do so was not entitled to be recognized or protected as a British subject in regard to any suit, dispute or difficulty in which he may have been or may be engaged or involved within the dominions of the Sultan of Zanzibar.[144]

However, even after Majid died in 1870 and Barghash became the Sultan of Zanzibar, this issue of Kutchi slavers and their getting away using the issue of jurisdiction and the registration option continued. Barghash was of the view that he 'took no interest in this matter, and that if the Hindi under Arab protection persisted against his own and his predecessors' orders in the purchase of slaves, they should abide by the consequences'.[145]

VI

Majid's Household in the Imperial Assemblage

Very much in tune with the political practice of the Al Busaidi dynasts, Majid's household remained integral to his politics. The intersection of his household with imperial networks helped him tide over many supposedly scandalous events concerning the women in his family. The case of his sister Salima is particularly relevant in this respect.

Salima was born from his father's favourite Circassian concubine. In 1868, she contrived to quit Zanzibar on Her Majesty's ship *Highflyer* to Aden, where, after her baptism, she was married by the chaplain of the station to a Zanzibar-based German merchant, Ruete, with whom she was in a relationship. They proceeded after the nuptials to Hamburg via Marseilles.[146]

Salima's journey to Aden and her marriage to Ruete revealed Majid's handling of the domestic sphere that was marked by its fair share of scandal. Salima had made an earlier attempt to flee Zanzibar in the Hamburg barque named *Matilda* chartered by a Mr A. Young, a Hamburg merchant. But she was betrayed by one of her slaves and was arrested. The rumour in town about this particular escape was that she was allegedly pregnant and, by common consent, its paternity was assigned to Mr Young. The Arabs treated it lightly, and her brother Sayyid Majid failed to pursue the man.

However, Majid did consider it dishonourable of her to leave in this manner. He sent a lady confidante to Salima to report on her condition and avenge the wounded honour of the family. She did not report back correctly to the Sultan because of the tenderness of her heart and also as she wanted to avert catastrophe. She withheld the truth from the Sultan, who was relieved at what she conveyed even if he knew the report was a sheer evasion of truth.[147]

Nevertheless, Majid knew the truth and was keen that Salima physically disappear from the island in order to put a lid on this loss of honour to the royal family. Salima too wanted to leave, as she feared for her life if she remained with her countrymen. She petitioned to be allowed to leave on pilgrimage for Mecca. Majid agreed, and the bugla of the chief eunuch Johar was prepared to carry her. The Senior Naval Officer shared Salima's conviction and gave her the opportunity of flight, which his humanity could not deny.[148] Instead of Mecca, she landed in Aden and got married to her lover, Ruete, who was stationed there.

The government disapproved that the Commander of a British ship had got involved in the domestic quarrels of the Sultan's family.[149] But Captain Pasley defended his action on humanitarian grounds, as otherwise, the Princess would have been murdered in Zanzibar. He also implied that he had acted to help Majid, who was glad that she had left Zanzibar. He also pointed out that the 'pilgrimage to Mecca' was a mere excuse and that she was allowed that or the alternative of taking poison in Zanzibar. She left most of her property in the hands of Ruete, who promised to forward it to Aden. She brought with her besides her jewels only $1000; she never received the $12,000 as proceeds of an estate that she sold at Zanzibar.[150]

This domestic episode was a scandal. But the involvement of the British and the fact that Majid dropped a curtain over it ensured that nothing was said about it in Zanzibar. But the silence was taken as Majid's acquiescence. Predictably, Ruete felt emboldened to return to Zanzibar. Majid protested, asking the Consul of the House Town, who was the representative of German interests in Zanzibar, to deter him, as public opinion was against him. His life was at risk at Zanzibar and his presence would jeopardize the interests of other Europeans as well.[151]

The Government of India supported Majid and considered making a representation to the Prussian government with a view to prevent the return of Ruete.[152] At the same time, Princess Salima was kept in a kind of quarantine at Aden, where she lived in the house of a Spanish merchant, Mr Mass. The merchant was instructed by the British Consul not to withdraw his protection of her without the latter's permission. She was not allowed to proceed to Hamburg, or to have any intercourse or correspondence on any pretext with any European or English-speaking German visiting Aden. But she lived as a guest of the British, entitled to all their hospitality and aid. She was free to return to Zanzibar.[153] And while at Aden, she had a considerable sum in bullion, this being the proceeds of the sale of an estate. All her assets were in her possession. Her domestic slaves received no wages; her establishment at Zanzibar was modest and her expenditure trifling. It did not exceed Rs 200 or Rs 250 a month.[154]

Interestingly, L. Seward, the Acting Political Agent at Zanzibar, was as patriarchal in his views on Salima as her brother Majid. He attributed her rendezvous with the German lover to Majid's lack of restraint on her. And this especially when she was 'an ardent, handsome and intelligent woman'. He lamented Majid allowing her to live 'un-surrounded by any of the usual restraints which guard the honor of Arab ladies'. He regretted that, even though unmarried, she was allowed by her brother Majid to 'dwell all unprotected in the house adjoining that of her reputed seducer'[155] and that she was allowed to proceed on a pilgrimage to Mecca with her passport noting that, 'where so ever you desire, go'. She was supposed to set out on a bugla belonging to chief eunuch Johar. But with her passport entry entitling her to free travel anywhere and terrified that her actions would incite the anger of her brother Majid, she asked Captain Pasley of the British ship *Highflyer* for a ride.[156]

Seward wanted to suppress the news of this 'scandal' and was keen that the Bombay government use its force and influence on the editors of papers in Bombay and Poona to suppress any account of this incident that may be sent to them. He advised the Sultan not to have her back in Zanzibar as it would revive the memory of the scandal. He agreed to let her be in Aden, with the Bombay and Zanzibar government sending her money. She was left as a ward in the hands of the British government with the assurance that she would remain in their protection and that she would not be allowed to go to Hamburg.[157] Indeed, the agent at Aden was of the view that the American correspondents were not sensitive to the Sultan's feelings and had not refrained from publishing the details of the case with sedulous care. He wanted the family of Sayyid Saʿīd to be shielded from any further scandal.[158]

The news from the Aden agent was that despite his best efforts, Salima refused to shift from the Spanish merchant's house to a more secluded mode of life. Many influential Arab families of Aden were asked to persuade her, and many private apartments and establishments were offered to her but to no avail. The bibi was determined to renounce her former life entirely and become Europeanized, as she herself described it. She said she 'cannot after wearing the dress of Europeans revert to Arab costume nor will she quit Mr. Mass's house'.[159]

But the Government of India was clear that the Princess had 'no valid right to a maintenance from the British Government'. It not only asked them not to send her any pecuniary assistance unless she was in actual distress, and then too just the bare minimum for her bare necessities, but also reminded the Sultan that the British were not responsible for his sister's flight from Zanzibar. They therefore found it absurd to offer her maintenance. They urged the Sultan to provide for her as 'natural affection and regard for the dignity of his royal house may recommend to his judgement'. The government promised not to interfere in the way in which this bounty was transmitted.[160]

VII

Putting Together the Economic and Military Institutions

The Customs House was the centre of Majid's political and economic drives. The customs was farmed to an Indian Bania, Ledda, for the sum of 1,96,000 German Crowns per annum. As the Sultan levied no other taxes, the customs formed the whole amount of the public revenue, with the exception of an annual payment of 10,000 Crowns paid by the Mukhadim, a race of people who inhabited the more distant parts of the islands of Zanzibar and Pemba and who were the original inhabitants prior to their conquest by the Arabs.

Majid governed and carved his political sovereignty akin to a household. Ledda, his Customs House farmer, was integral to his household. In the words of Majid's sister Bibi Salima, even though a

Bania, he had shown great personal loyalty to the family. He 'never forgot to send us pretty and curious presents ordered from his Indian home which included, besides sweet meats, several baskets of fireworks'. She described how, in their palace in Zanzibar, she and other children would watch awestruck the 'effect of the beautiful Indian pyrotechnical constructions'.[161]

Militarizing Zanzibar

The military build-up to combat an aggressive Thuwayni became Majid's way of grounding his sovereignty in society and establishing his social base. He put a check on the spiralling Arab-Afro tension by recruiting 20,000 men that included Arabs, Baluchis, Makranis, natives of the Comoros Isles and Swahilis of the East African coast. They were commanded by Jamadars, who received $20–30 a month. This mix of Arabs, Africans and Baluchis were equipped with American muskets and carbines. The army was particularly popular with the East Africans. The Governor of Zanzibar, Sayyid Suleiman bin Ahmad, a confidential friend and adviser of the late Sultan Sayyid Sa'īd, doubled as the recruiting agent and middleman. He invoked the memory of the late Sultan and used his influence over the Arab tribes to keep this ethnic mix glued. He tried his best to contain the Arab-Afro identity tensions that threatened to rear their head.

African tribes from the interior of the mainland who had never approached the sea before flocked to Zanzibar, armed with bows and arrows. In fact, Sayyid bin Muhammad, the Sultan of the island of Mahilla, came with 150 of his followers and was given the command of the ship *Artemise*.[162] Majid distributed American muskets and carbines to the African tribes, Swahilis, the Comoro men and Negro slaves. These tribes detested the northern Arabs anyway and would have opposed Thuwayni. The Comoro men were hardy warriors comparable to the Baluchis and the Makranis, who were his best soldiers.[163]

Lt Col Rigby testified to the huge popularity of Majid among the Swahili population of East Africa. He noted:

When the invasion of the Zanzibar dominions by Sayyid Thoweynee
was expected the inhabitants of the Sowahil rose en-masse to
support Seyyed Majid. Many tribes under their own chiefs came
over to Zanzibar . . . and when some of the dhows which had Seyyid
Thoweynee's troops on board endeavoured to procure wood and
water, they were driven from every point at which they attempted
to land, and at length were obliged in consequence to surrender to
Seyyed Majid's ships of war.[164]

He added that, at Zanzibar, the Swahili population and the natives
of the Comoros Isles were all in arms to support Sayyid Majid
because they 'feared and hated' the northern Arabs, who they felt
came to Zanzibar only to 'kidnap their children and carry them away
as slaves'.[165]

According to Rigby, the mainstay of the army was 1400
irregulars, chiefly Baluchis, Makranis and Arabs from the coast
of Hadramaut, with a few Turkish and Albanian gunners. These
troops were garrisoned in Zanzibar, the forts of Kilwa, Mombasa,
Pemba, etc. They were armed with carbines and muskets. Their
salary ranged from $3–5 a month. Rigby did not think very highly
of them and commented on their lack of order and discipline. He
said, 'They wear no uniform and their arms are seldom or ever
cleaned.'[166] The Sultan, he argued, had the capacity to collect on
the spur of the moment 20,000 to 30,000 armed men from the
east coast of Africa even if he felt they 'have no proper leaders and
are contemptible as soldiers'.[167] The Sultan had a large number of
British guns but did not have ammunition or carriage for them. He
did have a sizeable naval fleet.

Majid maintained cordial relations with the British, and that
helped in his militarizing drives. In 1869, he gifted them free land
in Zanzibar for a jail and a cemetery. The land was formally owned
by the British Church Mission at Zanzibar. It was transferred to
Sayyid Majid and, on Churchill's persuasion, the house occupied by
Bishop Tozer was to be sold to him by the Sultan. But the grant of
the free gift of land made the grant of Rs 1000 for the site and all
the arrangements redundant.[168]

VIII

Upholding Law and Marking Jurisdiction

The treaty of 1847 had given the British the right to search vessels, on behalf of the Sultan, in Zanzibar waters. It allowed the seizure and confiscation of all vessels, including those of the Sultan's subjects involved in slave traffic. Exemptions were given only to those engaged in the transport of slaves from point to point within the Zanzibar dominions—between Delgado and Lamu. The British were keen to ascertain by inspection the legitimate and the contraband slavers, as thousands of slaves were stolen from Zanzibar dominions and embarked for ports in Arabia and the Persian Gulf. Up to 1850, the treaty was silent on the extent of interventions the British could make within the Sultan's jurisdiction. It secured to the British all but the privilege of entering rivers and landing on Zanzibar territory in the pursuit of slaves.

Majid inherited these provisions and demarcated his jurisdiction and defined his sovereignty accordingly. Both these rested on the exercise of his rights on the water. The British slave searches in his waters offered him the perfect opportunity to articulate sharply his sovereign status and jurisdictional claims. The treaties with the British allowed slave traffic strictly within its coastline and banned all slave exports. But the hollowness of their abolition drive meant that they interpreted the treaty in ways that gave them greater surveillance and control over this permissible slave traffic within Zanzibar's coastline. They used these powers to garner for themselves the profits of the trade. The contest with the British for slave profits became the perfect forum where Majid could define more sharply his jurisdiction and political sovereignty and underline his control of the waters.

He demarcated as his jurisdiction limits the length of the East African coast along the eastern shores of Pemba and Zanzibar islands up to Cape Delgado and Lamu. His sovereignty was derived from the exercise of his rights and power in this aquatic stretch. He protested the interference of British steamers and their slave searches in these waters. His sovereign status depended on his control of the waters, and he lost no opportunity to flex his muscles in that terrain. Indeed, he underlined his sovereign status in these waters each time he granted the British 'the privilege to act in his territorial waters'. The conditions on which these privileges were granted further highlighted his independent stature: every vessel seized under this order was to be brought to Zanzibar and was to be dealt with by him. He reserved the power to adjudicate and punish.[169]

And yet jurisdiction and sovereignty based on the right over stretches of water remained fluid and contested.[170] It remained a slippery terrain as it overlapped with international law and usage. The Political Agent, E. Seward, even if supportive of him, reminded him that this aquatic terrain was not his monopoly. Rather, it was regulated by an appeal to international usage. And, thus, to demand an end to the British search operations was an abandonment of the treaty of 1847. And yet Majid was unrelenting, insisting that his rights prevailed in the waters and that his sovereign status rested on the exercise of these rights.

Majid pleaded his case to the government on the grounds that the searches undermined in popular perception his status as an independent political sovereign who controlled these waters. He argued that British interference in his waters 'destroys the prestige of the ruler who in his own waters should in the eyes of his people be absolute'. He pointed out that their interference would be viewed dimly by his subjects, who would see it as an injustice to their Sultan and that this would unnecessarily spoil the trust they have reposed on the British. He said such acts 'are a chronic source of irritation, begetting hate amongst a people otherwise disposed to trust and attach themselves to the English beyond all other nations'.[171]

British interest in monitoring the contraband slave traffic for its own financial benefit lay at the bottom of these jurisdictional conflicts. They continued to tweak the treaty to get greater access to Majid's territories. Col Hamerton obtained a concession in the treaty to enter into the landed interiors of Majid's territories, hitherto exempted from the treaty, when he saw that the Sultan was using slaves on his plantations at huge financial benefit. Zanzibar's rivers, land and burn barracoons between Delgado and Songha Monara were now included within the ambit of the treaty where British surveillance extended. Hamerton inserted the words 'creeks, bays, harbors' in the treaty regulations so that he could enter Majid's internal local slave points and strike a blow at the southern slave traffic. He blatantly admitted that the practice of the past—i.e., search only in territorial waters—was founded on a wrongful assumption of privilege that made it possible for the Sultan himself or his successor to demand its discontinuance or apply it within the narrow limits described.[172]

In 1866, Majid objected to this concession to enter his landed territory that lay interwoven with the waters. He viewed it as an infringement of his sovereign status, which rested on the exercise of his undisputed rights across the waters and the land that lay between it. But the government viewed Majid's protests as unjustified. They claimed that this was no new concession and that his father, Sayyid Saʿīd, as an independent sovereign, had waived the right and had conceded to them the permission to enter creeks, bays and harbours to conduct search and detention. They insisted that for all purposes of search and detention, the interior landed territory and the aquatic zones were to be considered/defined as the 'high seas' and that, in practice, they had always had the right to conduct search and detention in the Zanzibar territorial waters so broadly defined. They reminded him that they had always operated in and about the ports and islands of Zanzibar and Pemba.

This contest over jurisdiction and boundaries of sovereignty exposed the British duplicity in the abolition drive. It also revealed their in-house differences on the issue of slave traffic. Majid made the most of these differences, looking for support in officers like H. Sanders, the Political Agent at Zanzibar, who exposed the double standards in the abolition campaign. Sanders was of the view that the presence of the British fleet in Zanzibar waters to suppress slave traffic was an anomaly when 'English capital, distributed by an English agent is busy in Zanzibar in setting on foot enterprises fully dependent on slave labor and to obtain this fresh, hundreds of Africans must be enslaved, new villages de-populated, new crimes committed'.[173]

Sanders pointed to the British hypocrisy, with their fleet leaving 'untouched the crowded dhow, and whose slave freight is destined perchance, for the estates of a British sugar planter in Zanzibar'; but at the same time, 'we confiscate that dhow without remorse if found in another latitude'. He ironically mocked the government policy, saying, 'We employ our fleet to limit enslavage; we employ our capital to encourage it.'[174] He made a strong plea to remove the British squadron from Zanzibar waters to a cruising ground where it could act with real efficacy and without provoking comment on the misapplication of British capital to the encouragement of slavery in Zanzibar.

Sanders wanted the Government of India to decide when and how this customary practice of the British having a wider jurisdiction of operation in the Zanzibar waters became a matter of right. As Sanders said, 'whether its customary exercise may have now gained for this practice the force of right, whether this right is inherent in the treaty, whether it shall be asserted as a right or relinquished as untenable are questions submitted for the consideration of the government'.[175] And once these 'time honored privileges/customs are dropped then [the] British will be left only with the treaty which is less liberal in its provisions'.

Majid got support from Sanders, but the Bombay government was clearly unsympathetic and more interested in curtailing his powers so that slave trade benefits went exclusively into British pockets. They defined jurisdiction not in mere physical terms stretching over water and land; rather, they viewed it in terms of Majid's juridical rights to dispense justice over any perceived infringement of his sovereign borders and powers. In that sense, L. Pelly, Resident in the Persian Gulf, did not see British entry into the interiors of the island as any infringement on Majid's jurisdiction as long as the vessel seized on suspicion was brought before the civil authorities of Zanzibar.[176] And that in itself proved that the Sultan's writ prevailed in the waters despite the presence of British cruisers.

Majid used to his benefit both Sanders's and Pelly's contentions about his sovereign status and defined his jurisdiction both physically as well as juridically by dispensing justice in his civil courts of any perceived violation of physical borders by vessels caught through British surveillance. At the same time, he turned a blind eye to British plantations in his territory using slave labour, as he too benefited economically from the investment of British capital in Zanzibar. While he looked to Sanders for support against undue British interventions in his territorial jurisdiction, he remained silent on his critique of the slave labour on British plantations in Zanzibar.

Majid's silence on Pelly's scathing critique of Sanders on the issue of the plantations run on slave labour was significant. He refuted Sanders' critique that the slavery suppression campaign was a farce, as British capital was creating and encouraging it for its own profits. In contrast, he emphasized that the conditions of slave employment rather than the practice of slavery per se determined whether the relations were exploitative or iniquitous. He argued that 'his experience made him conclude that employment of African labor on an Englishman estate at Zanzibar or elsewhere is susceptible of arrangements under which the employer shall receive fair labor and the laborer fair remuneration, without any injustice to either party'.[177]

Majid's careful carving out of his legal jurisdiction was most evident when he was expected to continue paying a subsidy to Salim, as the British recognized him as the ruler of Muscat.[178] John Lawrence, of the Government of India, explained to Majid that the Canning Award and the subsidy that it factored in was not a personal agreement between two Sultans but one between Zanzibar and Muscat, which made it binding for all of Thuwayni's successors on the island, as long as they were from his dynasty, to pay up.[179]

Majid took to moral grandstanding, refusing to pay subsidy to his nephew Salim, who had become Sultan of Muscat after the controversial death of his father, Thuwayni, in which he was allegedly a suspect. The more the Governor General of India urged him to pay because 'the people and Arab Chiefs and soldiers of Muscat had put Salim on the throne and exonerated him of murder charges', the more he got a chance to invoke the rule of law to underline his sovereign status independent of Muscat.[180]

Majid invoked the Muslim law to frame his sovereign status. He resolutely refused to pay the 40,000 Crowns subsidy to Salim because of the allegations floating about his hand in the death of his own father—Thuwayni. He argued that, according to Muslim law, he was not supposed to pay someone who was not cleared of such allegations. After long-drawn-out negotiations with the British, he compromised on making the payment to the Bombay government and not to Salim.[181] Indeed, he claimed that he was all prepared to attack Salim in revenge but was restrained by the friendship with the British and the hope that they did not approve of Salim's 'abominable deed'.[182]

Majid was able to sketch his juridical limits, underline jurisdiction and invoke Islamic law to assert his sovereign status because the foreign department was soft on him. The entanglement of British business interests in Zanzibar, the use of slave labour on their plantations and the huge profits of slave trade were enough reason to keep Majid in good humour. They feared that an unhappy Majid would be injurious to the commercial interests of a wide range of Britons and the British Indian merchants.

At the same time, they were concerned that non-payment would lead to the loss of revenue to Muscat. It would have a fallout effect on piracy and policing of the Persian Gulf. Their envoy— the missionary Bartle Frere—was of the view that the government should consider paying Zanzibar so that it could meet the subsidy payment; or it should pay the amount of the subsidy on Majid's behalf directly to Muscat. This would ensure his support on the island.[183] An unrelenting Majid looked to the queen for redress. His envoy went to London on the mission to meet the queen to get a favourable response to the issue of subsidy. The queen did not give him an appointment, and the envoy had to return only with a letter for Majid.[184]

Nonetheless, Majid's ingenious posturing revealed the extent of his outreach in an imperially crowded world that he accessed. He had the support of the foreign office, even if the Indian office rejected his demands. The former supported Majid's contention, as it needed his support for the suppression of the slave trade.

And the latter wanted him to pay the subsidy as per the Canning Agreement. The political Secretary feared that the loss of revenue to Muscat if the subsidy was not paid would open a Pandora's box: it would encourage Illegal ways of collecting revenue (piracy), of which Persia was already complaining; and Salim, after disturbing the peace on the Persian Gulf, already threatened to blockade the port of Bandar Abbas. Additionally, it would make it impossible for Muscat to pay rent to Persia for the Bandar Abbas lease, leading to the termination of the contract. It would also disrupt the compact between Omani chiefs that rested on Zanzibar paying the subsidy.[185]

IX

Urban Planning in the Age of Abolition and Cholera

The arrival of the cholera pandemic in Zanzibar offered fresh challenges to Majid. Col Hamerton reported its first instance in 1835, when 'hundreds were swept away by the epidemic'.[186] He said the local 'cholera pill' of opium, chalk and catechu proved fatal. Most importantly, it increased British interference in Majid's affairs, alongside of course cutting into his profits from the slave trade. Slave dhows with cholera-inflicted people became a liability on arrival at Zanzibar. In order to avoid paying customs duties on the sick and dying slaves, dealers cruelly dumped them into the ocean at their own peril. Such acts were a double whammy for Majid. It not only heightened the infection rates but also meant a reduction of slaves. Stationed at Zanzibar, Bishop Tozer quoted the *Lancet* journal to note, 'slave gangs drive through the streets in broad daylight, reduced to a skeleton state by starvation and disease . . . No estimate could be given of the ravages of the epidemic amongst these the most miserable of all God's creatures since man was created.'[187]

Later in 1870, he reported with horror that he saw a body, not a corpse, from a slave dhow being thrown into the water. He regretted that the political resident took no action on the owner and captain of the dhow even after he reported them. They denied the incident and no witnesses from members of his mission who had witnessed the outrage were ever asked for their evidence.[188]

Cholera also entangled Majid in land disputes, as the rising number of dead made the existing burial grounds insufficient and triggered the demand from communities for their expansion. Extending communitarian burial grounds led to conflicts over land, as those whose land was encroached upon protested. Such disputes became particularly difficult if the parties involved were influential. The demand of the Khojas, one of the most wealthy Indian merchant communities whose capital drove the wheels of his economy, for extending their burial ground landed him in trouble with the British, who viewed the encroachment with alarm. They opposed it on grounds of hygiene and infection spreading to the areas used by them for exercise and evening walks. Majid found himself at the centre of these disputes as cholera ravaged the island.

Majid, Cholera and Burial Ground Disputes

The cholera epidemic in Zanzibar only increased the tensions between Majid and the Consuls. Land usage, especially land earmarked for burial, became the site for these conflicts as the disease was associated with miasma or foul stench emanating from contaminated soil, air and water. Graveyards, where the infected dead came for burial, were viewed as the fountainhead of cholera. As the British Consuls stepped in to interfere in their proper usage, they stirred up fresh conflicts over property rights on the island. The cholera epidemic offered the perfect handle to the British Consuls to extract unique concessions related to land use and rights. But these also gave opportunities to Majid and his successors to assert their hold in sharper ways as the beleaguered communities, such as the Khojas, approached them for redress.

Khojas and Bohras from Kutch, Surat and Bombay were present in Zanzibar in large numbers. Along with the Hindu Banias, nearly all shops in Zanzibar bazaars were kept by these people, and all foreign trade passed through their hands. The Khojas and Bohras had settlements on the west coast of Madagascar and also at the

French colonies of Nosi-beh and Mayotte. Unlike the Banī Yās, they brought their families and became permanent settlers. Rigby found them as very 'thrifty and industrious people'. A new quarter of the town inhabited by them had sprung up in Zanzibar and was rapidly growing.[189]

Khoja merchants were important investors and entrepreneurs in Zanzibar's development. In 1873, on reports of thefts in the city, twenty-nine principal Khoja merchants signed a letter, binding themselves to supply the requisite funds to set up a team of watchmen under the Consulate to look after Indian property.[190] With the arrival of the mail service to Zanzibar, a lot of adventurers and high-class entrepreneurs as well as 'swindlers' descended there to set up cafes and casinos. A German, along with his wife, proposed the opening up of a 'café chantaut' and casino. He came from Bombay and Yokohama.[191]

The Khojas were at the centre of political discourse in 1870, when cholera spread in Zanzibar. The Khoja burial ground, lying at the south-west limit of the town, was viewed as being the epicentre of the disease due to its poor hygiene and sanitation conditions. Surrounded by a masonry wall to the north and filled with graves, it was its sea-facing south and south-west boundaries that were the bone of contention. This part of the grounds was seen to be gradually extending, with fresh graves coming up to fill it. The European and many Indian and native residents used the main road to its north to exercise. And from 4 p.m. to sunset, it was crowded with horses, carriages, bicycles and pedestrians. Games of cricket and golf were held on the grass, and a ridge that faced the sea was a favourite resting place for those who wished to escape for a short time from the stifling atmosphere of the town.

John Kirk, the British Consul, believed that the health and sanitary conditions of the town would be adversely affected if the burial ground extended over this ground. He referred to this open area as the 'lung of the town'.[192] He interfered on several occasions to prevent its being converted into building sites. He was opposed to it being used as a burial ground, as he said the 'seeds of disease and death would be carried by the wind directly into the streets and houses of the city'. At the time of the cholera epidemic, more than 400 burials a day took place at this extended open site at great peril to the health of people. Kirk warned that, if the ground was used for burials again, a similar dangerous situation would arise.

The Khojas defended their right to land use, invoking both history and customary usage. They claimed that the land was theirs, as the property had been purchased seventy years ago in the reign of Sayyid Saʿīd by Muhammad Meru, a Sunni Muslim from Surat. On Meru's death, he dedicated it to the service of the burials for all members of the Khojas. Since the deed was lost, there was a difference of opinion on how far their title extended. Evidence of the extent of land in their control was conflicting, and the argument on basis of usage was complicated because of this missing deed. Majid intervened and asserted himself: he did not dispute the Khojas' claim to land that was already in occupation, but denied their right to encroach any farther on the open ground.

The Khojas never took the matter to court, fearing that an adverse judgment would close any chance they had of arriving at a settlement by other means. The matter was further complicated because of the divisions within the Khoja community: the Ismāʿīlīs, Sunnīs, Bhagats and the Shiʿa Ithnā ʿAsharī. Each sect offered different usage claims. The British had been asked to intervene in the disputes on different occasions—at one point to prevent the dis-internment of two American sailors from the burial ground, and at another point to prevent Majid's brother, Sayyid Barghash, from seizing and converting the land into building sites. The Aga Khan, on a visit to the city, was asked to intervene by the British Consul. His intervention ensured a solution by which the present ground was to be extended and enclosed for a distance of about 90 yards along the ridge. And when this was fully occupied by graves, a fresh piece of land was to be provided farther away from the town at the expense of the Zanzibar government. On these conditions, the Khojas renounced all their claims to the remainder of the land, which reverted to the local administration on the express understanding that it was not to be built over or enclosed but to remain as a public recreation ground in perpetuity.[193] As the spiritual and religious head of the Khojas, the Aga Khan played an influential role in solving the dispute.

And once again, in 1873, the issue of acquisition of land from the Khojas for a European cemetery in Zanzibar remained an ongoing issue of conversation between the British and the Khoja leadership. The neck land connecting the town to the mainland of the island of Zanzibar, which was a freehold of the Khoja head stationed in Bombay, was identified for the European cemetery, as during the cholera epidemic a number of Europeans were buried there. Even though the Khojas did not bury their dead there, they did not want to give any permanent rights to the Europeans and wanted fresh applications for each internment. Edward Steere, the missionary bishop, urged the Zanzibar Acting Consul, E. Smith, to ensure that the Khojas gave them the aforesaid land so that Europeans could 'bury their dead without fear of their remains being disturbed and their memorials destroyed by Arabs and Hindis'.[194] Majid continued to protect the rights of the Khojas, and the issue remained unresolved and left to his successor Barghash to deal with.

The issue of land rights that the burial ground controversy triggered in the cholera decade continued after Majid died. Barghash, who abandoned Dar as Salaam and reoriented his energy to the development of Zanzibar, remained entangled in these issues. He too negotiated with the Khojas and sharpened his political career, hemmed in as it was within the imperial assemblage. In this case too the Khojas never took the matter to court, fearing an adverse judgment.

Dar as Salaam: The Escape from Pandemic Politics?

In 1866, when Reverend Dr Livingstone, the Protestant missionary doctor, visited Majid in Zanzibar, he referred to the island as 'Stinkibar' because of the foul stench from the beach, which was the main depository of the town's filth. He commented that 'no one can enjoy good health here'.[195] Majid too was ill and unable to meet him. But he was sick with a 'tooth ache and gum boil'. Later, when he did meet him at the time of his departure, Dr Livingstone commented that Majid 'looked very ill'.[196]

Disease, illness and environmental contamination that affected air, soil and water remained lingering tropes in the descriptions of Zanzibar. The stench in the island was overbearing, and much of it was attributed to the poor sanitation system. The island had been in the grip of both the 1865 and the 1869–70 cholera pandemic.

Zanzibar was reported to have very poor drinking water. In the interior, the wells, though deep, were said to be dry during the hot season, and people flocked to rivulets. But even when the wells were not dry, they collected drainage as a result of the seaward slope of land and the porosity of coral rock. At some places, Sultan Sayyid Sa'īd had constructed stone tanks to store river water. Richard Burton, who travelled through Zanzibar in Majid's reign, reported that the 'city owes much fatality to want of drainage, and it might readily be drained into comparative healthiness'.[197]

The death and destruction it caused made it imperative for Majid to act. He was concerned with managing the cholera outbreak, especially after his own brother, Sayyid Ghalib bin Sa'īd, died of the disease. Even though Ghalib was politically inconsequential, never attended the durbar and was uninterested in state affairs, the death of a royal brought the urgency to control the pandemic close to home. Ghalib's funeral was attended by Barghash and not by Majid, yet the control of the contagion became a pressing issue for the latter.[198]

Cholera had been rampant on the mainland and was widely believed to have been transported to the island via slave dhows, which landed there full of slaves ill with the disease. Many times, slaves who were believed to not survive cholera were thrown into the waters to escape paying the customs duty unnecessarily. Majid was pressured by the British to provide food and water to the slaves on such dhows, and he was held responsible for their overcrowding.[199] And yet, there was no certainty about the source of infection.

J.N. Radcliffe, the medical officer who wrote a report on the East African cholera in 1865, was convinced that it was an import from India.[200] The distance between Bombay and Zanzibar by dhow could be covered in a mere eighteen days. And thus this was the most likely route of the epidemic in Zanzibar. James Christie, the physician to Majid, was not so convinced of the Indian origin and the diffusion route of the pandemic. The Indian merchants on the island, the Banias, denied any link with the Indian strain of the cholera. Instead, they attributed to it Somalian origins and thus its relatively lower impact on the Somalian immune system. But the mortality rates remained high, drawing attention to the air and water contamination and the poor sanitation system in Zanzibar.[201]

The Indian link with cholera was dismissed, but the sanitation drives and urban planning that the epidemic had triggered in Indian cities made them an attractive model to emulate. It was no surprise that the pandemic decade saw Majid visit Bombay several times. The British Consul, Lewis Pelly, urged him to visit the city, as he considered it the model 'modern city'; he also wanted him to meet with the Public Works Department of the city and bring back home ideas of urban planning. His successor Playfair was equally impressed by the roads and carriages of the city and wanted Majid to hire surveyors and road builders for Zanzibar. Playfair used his contacts with a Parsi businessman in the city, who loaned a private rail car to Majid to see both Bombay and the nearby city of Poona. Majid spent three months in Bombay interacting with a range of people and imbibing the ideas of urban planning.[202]

Bombay's urban planning was heavily shaped by the management of cholera. The city was riveted with debates on sanitation and public health that focused on the miasmic theory of cholera, which identified foul odours in the environment emanating from open drains, soil, filth and congestion as the cause of disease. Urban planners paid attention to these issues; by the end of the century, attention focused on sanitation measures and clean water supply as cholera came to be increasingly identified with dirty water. Soon, adequate waterworks, sanitation and congestion control in the city became critical to cholera management.[203]

Majid brought these urban planning lessons home from his visits to Bombay. Convinced of the link between sanitation drives and the control of cholera, Majid focused on the sanitation of Zanzibar. Playfair pitched in by urging the Indian merchants who owned nine-tenths of the shops in the town to pave all their principal streets with coral and chunam. This was intended to set an example and encourage similar investments in the rest of the town. But Playfair soon realized that Majid had no revenue to devote to municipal purposes. He thus urged him to make financial arrangements by imposing a tax on the Arab clove and coconut producers to increase his revenues for sanitary developments. Predictably, this tax met with tough resistance from the Arab landowners, who refused to pay, citing no precedence. Majid, as a way out, converted the clove and coconut tax to an export tax on the European and American shippers dealing in export trade; he increased the export tax on slaves in particular.[204] This created a furore in imperial circles, and John Kirk complained that Majid had imposed this export tax for sanitary improvements on the suggestion of Playfair.[205] Playfair of course denied the allegation, and the government, after going through the relevant correspondence, believed him. They informed the British merchants that they were not liable to the tax.[206]

Majid was convinced that he needed urban development to urgently handle the cholera pandemic. The ravages of cholera were cutting into slave profits and placing him in difficult confrontations with the British. The undue British interference in his functioning that the epidemic introduced became the trigger for not just sanitary efforts in Zanzibar but for laying the foundation of his new city centre, Dar as Salaam. He planned the dream city as the deadly cholera epidemic devastated slave dhows headed to Zanzibar and his slave profits plummeted. The fear of illness and infection brought the British intervention and critique of his rule at an unprecedented high. It was to offset these hurdles and ensure a safe haven free from British interventions for the slave trade that Dar as Salaam was chosen as the preferred alternate port. With its vast stretches of land and relatively better air, water supply and natural environment, the town was less prone to disease and thus relatively protected from the epidemic, and thus from British interference in his management of cholera.

The original Swahili name of Dar as Salaam was 'Mzizima', meaning 'healthy town'.[207] This itself indicated that it was Majid's chosen escape town that stood in contrast to Zanzibar, which was being ravaged with infections related to the cholera pandemic and its related political fallout. He projected it as the 'healthy' town in sharp contrast to Zanzibar, which had become notorious for its foul smell and unhealthy climate.

Dar as Salaam was built on the pattern of Bombay. After having bought the land by money, gifts and *bakshish* to the tribal elders called Jumbe, he sent Indian merchants, workers who could build with stone, painters timber fellers and slave labour to build.[208] The neatly drawn new town remained a mosaic of ethnic communities involved in commerce and construction (Indian, Arab and African) until the later German and British colonial rule began to redraw its map in racially segregated ways.[209]

Bagamoyo, the old port town close to Dar as Salaam, was traditionally the destination point of the slave and ivory trade from the interiors carried by local traders called the Nyamwezi. Over the nineteenth century, these traditional traders faced tough competition from wealthy Arab Omani merchants from the coast, who marginalized them with their Indian credit supply and clout in the Zanzibari Sultanate. By the 1850s, Omani Arabs had excluded the traditional traders of the interior, the Nyamwezi, as well as the coastal Shirazis and peasants who dominated this trade.[210]

Majid hoped that the new city of Dar as Salaam on the mainland would attract such Omani ivory and slave traders and help them consolidate their hold over the trade as they settled in the new town. In return, he geared to benefit from their investments in the city's development. He thought this would be a sought-after destination for the Omani Arab merchants in the foreseeable contingency of a British clampdown on the maritime slave and ivory route to Zanzibar. It would attract wealthy Arabs of Pemba and Zanzibar invested in this trade, who would reroute the traffic from the interior Lake Tanganyika region to Dar as Salaam to avoid British restrictions at Zanzibar. Edward Seward, the British Consul in Zanzibar, observed that Majid hoped to 'form the nucleus of a trading port, whence caravan routes shall radiate into the interior, and which bye and bye roads along the coast will connect with Keelwa and Lamoo'.[211]

Majid hoped that the shift of the wealthy Arabs to the new city would kick-start agriculture and commerce and increase the demand of slaves. He was of the view that Dar as Salaam would soon replace Kilwa as the nucleus on the east coast, supplying slaves to Mombasa, Lamu and Brava.[212] He was convinced that its significance as a commercial hub alongside the availability of cheap slave labour and vast fertile lands would attract rich Arab settlers from the disturbed regions of Arabia. Their investments and contributions would energize the city and ensure that land traffic in slaves continued despite the restrictions on maritime trade.

Historian of the Swahili coast, Steven Fabian, has argued that Majid focused on Dar as Salaam as he did not have absolute power and control over Bagamoyo, an established commercial town on the mainland, where a strong local leadership prevailed.[213] Instead, Dar as Salaam was to be his own city, where he would avail full profits of trade and independent management. This new commercial hub was also meant to circumvent the commercial power of Indian traders and creditors in Bagamoyo.[214] Scholars of the east coast of Africa, J.R. Brennan and Andrew Burton, have viewed the shift to Dar as Salaam also as a kind of refuge from the overbearing presence of British Consuls in Zanzibar.[215]

The cholera epidemic certainly offered a greater opportunity for consular interference in his governance. Indeed, the British were using cholera management to intervene in the governance of Indian cities with stringent laws on sanitation and hygiene that touched religious tradition and social life. Zanzibar was no exception, where too cholera management became a handy ploy to interfere in Majid's governance.

Majid decided to lay its foundations on the mainland to provide for himself a refuge from the interference of British Consuls posted in Zanzibar.[216] Cholera was indeed the excuse for too much British interference in the administration of Zanzibar. It was touching issues of land rights, property ownership and religious observances such as burials. In this decade of cholera, it was very clear that Majid could not have a 'secure dominion' in Zanzibar.[217] He felt he could avoid consular interference by shifting to Dar as Salaam. He chose to move to the new site despite opposition from the merchants, who saw it as relatively of less value in profits of trade and doubted its suitability for the use of slave labour.

The British Consuls always interfered with Majid's plans of urban developments in Zanzibar to ensure good health and commerce. They posed a string of hindrances. Their ego clashes and their internal feuds sabotaged Majid's urban planning. The British Consul suggested the making of a sea wall, which would have improved the commercial facilities of the port, given better access to the suburbs and recovered much valuable ground from the sea. But the project was stopped because of a protest from another Consul, mainly because it had originated with his rival British colleague. This Consul suggested that the same end could be achieved by opening a new street through the crowded huts and lanes between the palace and the outskirts. But this was again opposed by another Consul, who said he would take in his protection some properties to be crossed in whatever direction the road might be aligned.[218] The shift to a new city Dar as Salaam in the midst of a raging cholera epidemic and financial strain thus made perfect sense.

Cholera and Urban Planning of Dar as Salaam

Yet, the concern for controlling the spread of cholera remained; so did the need for having a new urban administrative site planned to keep the environmental contamination, the miasma and water-borne infections at bay. Majid's desire for a planned city that would keep both the cholera and the British intervention at a safe distance made the shift to Dar as Salaam his perfect refuge. According to Edward Seward, the British Consul at Zanzibar, the question of its 'healthfulness' remained a serious one as 'affecting the future of Dar as Salam'.[219]

In contrast to Zanzibar, this new urban site was known for being 'cool and refreshing' and a sought-after place for the ailing and sick. Bishop Tozer, inflicted with a severe fever, was advised to visit Dar as Salaam for a 'change of air'. The new city was recommended to him as 'cool and refreshing' as compared to the 'low, marshy, fever and dysentery producing isle of Zanzibar'. J.M. Gray, traveller and scholar, noted that 'he returned with us at the end of a week quite another man'.[220] And Dar as Salaam notably retained the tag of a 'health spot' even after the reign of Majid, when his successor Sultan Barghash withdrew all support from his development projects.[221] It continued to be viewed as a town where the 'climate is healthy, the air clear and fevers uncommon and easily shaken off'. The site was reported to be 'beautiful and the surrounding country green and well wooded'.[222]

Significantly, Majid's lessons from Bombay about urban planning that focused on availability of good clean water, uncontaminated soil and clean environment to ward off cholera influenced his choice of the site for the planned city of Dar as Salaam. He preferred the site for building his new city as it was reported to have 'hale and robust' air and 'sufficient and good water supply'.[223] It had 'many streams' that emptied into the harbour and 'shallow lakes frequented by water foul [fowl]' that made it stand in stark contrast to the stench and filth that characterized the Zanzibar beaches, making it cholera prone. Dar as Salaam was known for its 'numerous little hills of beautifully sweet water percolating'. Similarly, the soil was not contaminated. Rather, it was sandy and full of humus and capable of growing sugar cane or cotton. Its grain-producing quality was doubtful, and Majid offered incentives to people to keep it in cultivation.[224] Alongside, to attract cultivators, he offered land in any reasonable measure to those who were willing to undertake the agriculture of the neighbourhood. The sole condition attached to the gift was that the land be made to yield produce of some sort and be kept under cultivation.[225]

Soon after his return from Bombay, he began to work on Dar as Salaam. He planned this capital city in 1862 and began construction in 1865–66. He spent large sums of money in transporting building material to Dar as Salaam for the construction of his palace, a government centre and dwellings for his officials.[226]

Majid preferred the site, as it was relatively unoccupied as compared to the other coastal towns, such as Bagamoyo, which boasted bustling commerce and strong local tribal control. Dar as Salaam was 40 miles south of Bagamoyo, surrounded by unsettled area with no strong tribal hold. It offered no political challenge as it was riveted by tribal conflict. Unlike the settlements of Lamu and

Mombasa, this was a safe place for the fugitive slaves as there were no tribal groups raiding the area. It stood on the margins of the long-distance commerce in slaves and ivory being peripheral to the caravan trade. But Majid hoped to make it the 'nucleus of a Trading Point' from where the caravan routes would radiate into the interior. The harbour was narrow, fed by rivers and not the best for shipping. Majid was aware of this drawback and worked on it with suggestions from his contacts in Europe.[227]

Economically, he visualized the town to be powered by coconut plantations, and the diversion towards it of the long-distance caravan trade. Trade was directed towards Dar as Salaam to the prejudice of other ports, further north, which had before enjoyed the monopoly of caravans from the interior.[228]

At that time, caravans headed by flags and men firing guns swaggered through the streets to receive royal presents, and men of high estate from Zanzibar spent their revenues open-handedly.

Majid encouraged Hadhrami Arabs and Indian traders to relocate there in order to develop coconut plantations and trading houses. He sent seeds of coconut trees from Zanzibar and asked them to plant them in Dar as Salaam. The support of the merchant community was less than enthusiastic. The idea of relocation to assist in the building of a brand-new town in the middle of a raging cholera epidemic must have been a deterrent for the merchants. Yet a decade later, J.M. Gray reported that his plantations contained 36,000 trees, of which three-fifths were bearing fruit. Some 2000–3000 seedlings were also planted alongside these trees.[229]

The merchants feared that a new town would mean increased competition and decline of profits. So prevailing was Majid's trope of 'healthfulness' of Dar as Salaam that they invoked it in the reverse to resist the shift to the new mainland town. The Banias, reluctant to leave their locations where they were economically well entrenched, declared it a 'fever stricken' place that was completely uninhabitable in the rainy season.[230] The Arabs also called it 'unhealthy', even if they were less vocal in their opposition for fear of repercussions. One of their peers had been flogged for his opposition to set an example. And their opposition also derived from the fact that it had no terrain for the maintenance of slaves. They feared that their slaves would flee.[231] Majid did in fact experience the loss of forty slaves from there. Seward was also of the view that unlike Lamu and Mombasa, which were flanked by tribes who would make it difficult for the fugitive slaves, Dar as Salaam had 'no such flight restraining territories'. Thus, getting a supply of slave labour was a genuine hindrance in this choice of urban settlement.[232] Seward also pointed to its narrow harbour making it inaccessible to dhows and that a steam tug would have to be ordered from Hamburg for moving on its narrow trading channel, which was supplied with water by a string of rivers that never ran dry.

But Majid's resolve was undeterred. He went ahead with building his new capital despite opposition from the merchant community. Significantly, he allocated a lot of money on the project in a decade when the entire east coast of Africa was ravaged by the cholera epidemic. His representative Suleiman bin Ahmad, the cousin of Sayyid Saʿīd and Wazir of Zanzibar, visited the adjacent village of Mzizima to negotiate with the local majumbe (chief) and gifted him, clothes, rice and a lot of money until he agreed to let the Sultan settle there.[233] Suleiman had many contacts with the pagan chiefs of the coast. He was very influential in making local inhabitants make grants of land to Majid. Original acquisitions included areas of Gerizani and Kichwele. Later, Majid acquired areas of land at Kurasini and Upanga. He put this land to the cultivation of rice and coconuts.[234]

Building work in the city began only in the later part of 1865. The town was built on the north side of the Dar as Salaam river that spread into a landlocked basin, where vessels of large size could anchor with perfect safety. The Sultan's residence was built at the inland extremity of the basin at the far right of the town. From this point, a line of stone houses formed a crescent facing the anchorage with a broad road and a flight of steps communicating with the sandy beaches. Wells affording a good supply of fresh water were located along the inner line.[235]

In 1866, the Zanzibar Consul reported to the Naval Officer posted on the east coast that he had issued a pass to sixteen slaves belonging to Majid to proceed to Dar as Salaam to work in the building work. The stone for most of the buildings came from the islands which form the eastern breakwater protecting the entrance to the Dar as Salaam harbour.[236] He structured the city in three concentric zones. At its centre were the stone buildings of the administration and business, close to the harbour. Beyond this were the shamba fields—coconut plantations—owned by the Sultan or his Arab allies and worked by slave labour. And finally came the outlying Zaramo and Shomvi villages.[237]

The building works may have been slow at Dar as Salaam, but the excitement it generated in the Sultan and the elite merchants and bankers who accompanied him to the site was phenomenal. In 1868, when the iconic East African slave baron Tippu Tib arrived in Dar as Salaam with his entourage, he was royally treated by Majid. Tippu's biographer reported that, 'for [the] time being things were lively in Dar as Salam. All who belonged to society had proceeded with the Sultan's court to the new capital.' He noted that the Sultan's escorts also included all non-trading Consuls and a number of Europeans. The upper-class Arabs from Zanzibar, Pemba. Mombasa and Lamu as well as a great body of Indians had also accompanied him. Indeed, the Indian merchants were Tippu's main creditors. And seeing his cartloads of ivory, they were hopeful of getting back the money that they had credited to the slave merchant.[238]

Majid ensured that religion did not cause any dissensions in Dar as Salaam district. Indeed the Shāfīs, Bohras and the Khojas lived their own lives peacefully, the Shāfīs and the Bohras often liaising on issues. The Indian community was involved in the copal trade, grain speculation and money lending. They lent money to small traders at the rate of 8 per cent. Lower down, in the KiWālī district, there was more copal and ivory. People felt very secure there under the Sultan's authority. The slave caravans moved from Dar as Salaam crossing the river and passing through the Sultan's plantations. Elephants were found in large numbers, and gum and mang trees abounded.[239]

The visible decline of Dar as Salaam after Majid's reign was matched by a steady growth in its economy, as the trade and agricultural activities that Majid had initiated continued to pay dividends, even if his public works, such as the construction of his palace, fort, houses, roads received a setback. Dar as Salaam remained the principal supplier of rice to Zanzibar in the period of Barghash and until it was handed over to the Germans by him in 1887.

Sayyid Majid, Sultan of Zanzibar (r. 1856–70), with (on the right)
one of his brothers, 1865

Town Hall, Bombay, from *Views at Bombay, taken and drawn on stone by
J.M. Gonsalves* (Bombay, 1833)

Zanzibar Slave Market, after a drawing by Edwin Stocqueler, 1860

Sir Lewis Pelly (1825–92)

Credit: The Rijksmuseum

Enslaved labourers in Zanzibar, c. 1870–80

Credit: Herskovits Library of African Studies, Northwestern University Libraries

Studio portrait of Tippu Tib seated between a Zanzibari and a European official, c. 1880–90

3

Sayyid Thuwayni:
The Counter-Revolutionary Sultan

The Argument

Majid's brother Thuwayni nurtured even loftier imperial ambitions. He was the favourite son of the Sultan and was left to look after the Muscat affairs by his dead father. His location brought him imperial attention at a time when the waves of counter-revolutionary imperialism were gaining momentum. The significance of the Muscat port was never lost to the British. It was a premier distribution point of imported slaves and was well equipped with a telegraph line connecting it to Aden, Persia and Karachi.[1] Thuwayni was crucial on both counts.

Thuwayni made the most of the imperial gathering at Muscat and used its rivalries and networks to emerge as the Sultan of Muscat. The port was a meeting point of Asian and European powers. The Germans, the French and the Americans were all keen on having a foothold in Muscat. Iran had leased its port of Bandar Abbas to the Sultan, and it too kept an eager political eye on Muscat.

Thuwayni reached out to the imperial powers to consolidate his position at home and assert his sovereign status globally. He used his ties with Asian imperial powers, like Qajar Iran, to balance the growing influence of Britain in the Gulf. Playing on the Russophobia in the British circles, he became their conduit to Qajar Iran. At the same time, he engaged with Western powers to handle the Wahhabis and the slave trade issues.

He agreed to British arbitration in his dispute with Zanzibar but milked it most judiciously. He tapped into the Anglo-French rivalries to bolster his claim to be Sultan. His talks with the British on the issue of the Wahhabis and the telegraph line earned him instant global visibility in a world still crowded by imperial powers. Ironically, his entanglements with the imperial powers only intensified in the age of counter-revolutionary imperialism, launching him as the counter-revolutionary Sultan in his own right.

Profile: Sayyid Thuwayni (1820–66)

Thuwayni was born in Muscat in 1820 and was the third son of Sayyid Sa'īd. He was placed in charge of Oman affairs in 1833 at the young age of thirteen. Very early in his career, he dealt with tribal unrest in the important port town of Sohar and the ancient seats of Al Busaidi power at Al Rustaq and Nakhil. He liked educated people and had a *diwan* written for him. Penned by Amir bin Humayed bin Muhammad bin Ruzayq, it was called *Diwān Silk al-Farīd fi Madḥ-i al-Sayyid Al-Ḥamīd Thwaynī bin Sa'īd.*

Thuwayni remained based at Muscat, came very seldom to Zanzibar and looked down upon his brothers and sisters, who were born on the island. He remained a perfect stranger to his Zanzibar siblings, who themselves had never been to Muscat. He was known as an able warrior and his soldiers idolized him. Like his father, he loved warfare and was the most accomplished of all his brothers in the art of warfare. He had one legitimate wife, Ralie, and several children.[2]

Thuwayni was assassinated in the fort of Sohar, allegedly by his son Sayyid Salim, who then proceeded to Muscat and seized the throne. His tomb exists on the second floor of the citadel in the old town, which is a lofty square plain building surrounded by a moat and the residence of the Sohar Governor.[3] Salim ruled until 1868,

when he was attacked and deposed by Azzan bin Qais, who occupied
Muscat and forced Salim to fly to Bandar Abbas.[4]

I

The Sibling Dispute: Thuwayni and the Fight for the Political Sovereignty of a United Oman

Sayyid Sa'īd had placed Thuwayni in charge of Muscat and Oman
affairs from the age of thirteen. This convinced Thuwayni that he
needed to step into the shoes of his dead father as the rightful ruler
of both Oman and Zanzibar. He wanted to firm up his political
sovereignty over Oman's fluid and often contested geographical
topography, which stretched from Arab-dominated Muscat to
Zanzibar in East Africa. Indeed, he wanted to stretch it farther
towards Iran, where his father had a foothold in the Iranian port of
Bandar Abbas in the Persian Gulf. But there were many obstacles in
the way.

Thuwayni's claim to be the sole inheritor of his late father's
political sovereign status, which extended over the Arab as well
as African possessions, was always challenged by his siblings. This
was due to the fact that Sa'īd had not designated his successor
at the time of his death. When Sa'īd shifted base from Muscat
to Zanzibar in the 1830s, he made Thuwayni, as his eldest son,
incharge of Muscat (1846). On the death of his younger son
Khalid (1854), his fourth son Sayyid Majid was made overseer of
his African dominions at Zanzibar.

On the Sultan's death, which happened at sea as he was en route
to Zanzibar from Muscat, the people 'elected' Majid as their ruler
as per his wishes. This was in keeping with tribal tradition, where
the ruler was chosen out of the most influential and popular persons
available. Sayyid Majid used this occasion to assert his independent
status as ruler of Oman. In the absence of any documents to prove
his succession, he used the condolences of the French and Americans
sent to him on his father's death to bolster his claim. He contended
that the yearly grant that he remitted to Thuwayni was 'friendly

subsidy' and not tribute in recognition of the political sovereignty of Thuwayni at Muscat.[5]

Sparks flew between the siblings on the non-adherence to the agreed division of spoils of their late father: Majid was to pay his brother Thuwayni a yearly sum of 4000 Crowns. Likewise, Thuwayni had agreed to divide the horses that belonged to the royal stables of their father with Majid. The latter sent for his share of the horses without sending his annual payment of 4000 Crowns and was generally irregular in that payment.

Thuwayni was insistent on his dues from Zanzibar, as he was in dire financial straits. His near-bankruptcy due to the informal division of Oman's Arab and African dominions between him and Majid had deprived him of the profits of the lucrative slave trade. The British agent at Bushier, Felix Jones, also reported to the Bombay government that, even though Thuwayni's expenses, such as the payment to the Wahhabis and the dependants and relatives of his late father, remained unchanged, his revenues had decreased ever since Majid claimed independent sovereignty of Zanzibar. He pointed to Thuwayni's leanings on the tribal interior to balance his losses. He further observed that Thuwayni had decided to double the imposts on produce from the interior and was contemplating raising the duty paid by British dependants from 5 per cent to 7 per cent. Jones believed that the bleak economy was because of the practice of 'monopoly and contracts'. If this was abandoned, the economy would flourish. Jones found Thuwayni 'apathetic and culpably indulgent' in financial matters. And thus, he was not too hopeful of improvement unless the British government intervened on his behalf in East Africa.[6]

The Tribal Base and the War Sound with Zanzibar

In 1858–59, Thuwayni declared war on his brother Majid at Zanzibar. Determined to get his financial dues, he put together an army, leaning on the tribal chiefs and Bedouin elders to recruit troops from their villages for his Zanzibar campaign. He was not a great seafarer. Nonetheless, being stationed at Muscat, he had inherited

his father's fleet. His preparations for a military confrontation at
Zanzibar were complete, he embarking in his own ships while the
troops following him in hired vessels. Merchant vessels had been
asked to curtail their voyages to Zanzibar to make way for Thuwayni.[7]
In 1859, he left for Zanzibar with a large contingent consisting of a
frigate, a large corvette, a brig, a troop ship and about a dozen buglas
with troops.

Lt Col Russell was dispatched to Muscat to mediate in the
princely feud. He met Thuwayni at Ras-al-Had on board his
vessel, and the latter immediately agreed to British arbitration and
recalled his ships of war.[8] Thuwayni agreed to abandon his voyage
to Zanzibar on condition that the British compel Majid to comply
with his demand of a united Oman, with Zanzibar recognizing his
political sovereignty.

Thuwayni was clear that this was his primary condition for
agreeing to British arbitration. He said he wanted the recognition
by all of a 'consolidated state, without any division; Zanzibar being
subordinate to Muscat'. He was insistent that 'the interests of the
one shall be identified with those of the other', as he said had been
the case during the time of his father and forefathers.[9] In addition, he
demanded an annual payment of 40,000 French dollars; and as had
been the case in the time of his father, he wanted the continuation
of a promise of assistance in case of any hostility involving Oman.
He demanded that the property of all the orphans be handed over
by Majid to the charge of a trustworthy person in whose custody
all parties would feel satisfied that it would be safe. He also wanted
Majid to indemnify him for all the expenses entailed on account of
dispatching an army as a consequence of his opposition. He made
it clear to Lord Elphinstone, the Governor of Bombay, that he had
abandoned the voyage on his plea and hoped that his arbitration
would bring the desired results.[10]

British Arbitration and Thuwayni's Careering

Lord Elphinstone preferred arbitration and truce over war. This was
best for British commerce. But it also suited his political interest

to generate documentation on the Sultanate, access the legal documents related to the dead Sultan and intervene accordingly to legitimize his intrusions in the region. He was most interested in the will of Sayyid Saʿīd. Alongside, he intensified the hunt for precedent and the knowledge of local practice and custom. The latter was crucial for him, as it became the bedrock to 'create' the Omani legal tradition that would legitimize his intrusions.

Both Thuwayni and Majid were no unsuspecting victims of British political design. The British hunt for the Sultan's will, precedent, claims and invocation of Arab tradition offered them a canvas to perfect their political career even if it made them complicit in the production of a reinvented Omani legal tradition. They pushed themselves willingly into the arbitration wrangles to derive maximum benefits to their careers. Arbitration became a welcome forum, whose legalities they were happy to cannibalize for their self-interest.[11]

The imperial assemblage comprising the French, the Germans and the Americans who framed their lives made arbitration even more attractive as they 'forum shopped', dragging in imperial powers to complicate its legal wrangles to their best advantage. Not surprisingly, Majid expressed his keenness on arbitration as he said 'the hostilities with his brother had greatly afflicted him'. He wanted to pursue agriculture and commerce and be cordial to all relatives, as his father desired. He did not mince words in conveying to Lt Col Rigby, the British Consul in Zanzibar, that 'respecting any claims Sayyid Thuwene might make against him he would entirely abide by the just decision of the British Government'.[12]

Rigby, Arbitration and the Production of Omani Tradition

British arbitration produced the Omani legal tradition. This reinvented tradition was temporally and spatially contingent on the royal sibling dispute over succession and inheritance, and it lay entangled with the imperial assemblage. Rigby, its principal architect, claimed that this invented tradition derived from Omani custom and practice as collected by him from the locals and family members of the Sultan and as documented in the Sultan's revenue, trade and other documents.

Rigby, who was soft on Majid as they were allies in the anti-slavery campaign, always suspected Thuwayni's commitment to British arbitration. His worst fears were confirmed when the French Consul in Zanzibar told him that Thuwayni 'is acting a double part, and has been in communication with him [the French Consul] on this subject [arbitration]'. When reminded of his commitment to the arbitration of the Governor General of India, he backtracked with his hasty reply, 'It is not so. Sayyid Thuwayni is sending Hamid bin Salem here, and we are going to arrange everything on his arrival.'[13]

Rigby and the Hunt for Oman's Written Past: Manufacturing a Favourable Tradition

Rigby wanted a good deal for Majid. He increasingly invoked precedent to produce a tradition that favoured his ally in the anti-slave trade campaign. In the absence of written documents, he relied on elders and notables of the royal family for information on past practice. The only documents that he could locate pertained to the dead Sultan's domestic affairs, the payment to legatees, distribution of alms, etc.

In his hunt for precedent, his most trustworthy informant was Saʿīd's cousin and brother-in-law, Sayyid Hilal. Rigby was willing to go by what Hilal said as he was 'the eldest member living of the Imam's family', the brother-in-law of the late Imam, and a man who was for 'many years the intimate friend of the late Imam'. Rigby said he was 'cognizant with everything that has taken place at Muscat and Zanzibar for the last forty years'.[14]

Hilal confirmed that there was no written will that the Sultan left behind. Rigby concluded that this was clearly a society where declarations in open durbar and word of mouth—the oral—prevailed in politics. Indeed, Hilal emerged as Rigby's most reliable source of the Omani past. His interpretations of history and precedent opened the perfect way of legitimizing, justly or unjustly, the claims of Majid.

Rigby submitted a report to the Bombay government, detailing the information and knowledge he collected on the Omani past. He elaborated on three points of inquiry as far as the dead Sultan was concerned. First, whether the Sultan possessed the power to divide his dominions or to bequeath them, to whichever of his sons he pleased as per Arab custom or precedent. Second, even if he had such powers, whether it was his will and intention that Sayyid Majid inherit his African dominions. Third, whether he wanted that after his death his African dominions should form a separate state altogether independent of the ruler of Muscat.[15]

Rigby concluded that his inquiries with Hilal revealed that 'the rights of primogeniture have never been recognized among the Imams of Oman'.[16] This meant that there was no set line of succession to be followed. There existed many precedents in the dead patriarch's family of dividing his dominions as he pleased and assigning any part he wished to whichever son he wanted in his own life. On the death of a chief, his sons invariably disputed the succession. The one with most influence and might with the tribe, or who gave the greatest hopes of being an efficient leader, was elected. Indeed, Sayyid Sa'īd himself had been elected ruler of Oman on this principle to the exclusion of his elder brother Sayyid Salim. Even his father became ruler, superseding two elder brothers. And his grandfather had divided his dominions between his two sons in his lifetime.

Rigby used this manufactured 'tradition' to reconstruct Sayyid Sa'īd's inheritance for his sons. He argued that Sa'īd, in the absence of the practice of primogeniture, divided his territory in his lifetime between his three sons. In this division, each son was the independent sovereign of his share of territory. He said as per the tradition he pieced together, the Sultan never intended to make Zanzibar a tributary of Muscat. He wanted the two to be independent of each other. This was evident soon after he disinherited his eldest son, Sayyid Hilal, possibly for violating his harem.

Rigby noted that his information revealed that the Sultan divided his Arab and African dominions as follows: he appointed his third son, Thuwayni, to succeed at his death to the government of his Arabian possessions and sent his second son, Khalid, to that of his African dominions. Khalid was installed as the ruler of Zanzibar in the absence of his father, who was at Muscat. After Khalid died in 1854, Saʿīd passed over two of his sons and appointed his fourth son Majid to succeed his deceased brother in Zanzibar. In an open durbar, the Sultan publicly proclaimed to all the Arab chiefs that Sayyid Majid was their political sovereign.[17]

Rigby concluded that his informant was clear that Saʿīd hoped that each of his sons stationed at Muscat, Zanzibar and Sohar respectively would succeed to full sovereignty of each of their dominions on his death. He considered this so plainly settled that he did not consider any written will on this necessary. He had notified this to the foreign governments who were his allies. And the fact that neither his eldest son, Sayyid Hilal, nor the two elder sons of his brother Salim bin Sultan had ever disputed the succession proved that they too considered the late Imam well within his right to appoint his own successor.

Rigby's manufactured 'tradition' relied hugely on his informant Sayyid Hilal. Rigby did not dispute this version, as it suited him in that it recognized Majid as an independent political sovereign. Hilal proved even more helpful when he went further to elaborate that, as per his understanding of 'tradition', it was Muscat that became subordinate to Zanzibar after Saʿīd shifted to the island and made it his new administrative centre. Rigby reiterated Hilal's view that in Arab custom, wherever the chief resided became the centre of government. By this logic, the Sultan's shift of his political base to Zanzibar made Muscat a dependency of the latter. From this perspective of custom, there was no question of Zanzibar being subordinate or dependent in any way to Muscat. The fact that he had appointed his eldest and favourite son Khalid to Zanzibar and his younger brother Thuwayni to Muscat proved that he did not in any way want Zanzibar to be subordinated to Muscat.

The search for precedent and history also made Rigby lean on written accounts of the history of the east coast of Africa to show that, historically, the dead Sultan never alluded to any payment from Zanzibar, whether verbally or in written form. Rigby concluded that his findings confirmed that there existed no history of any tribute linking the two states. The Sultan had acquired the greater part of the African east coast. And while he was alive, he willingly parcelled the full sovereignty of Zanzibar to Majid.

Rigby was of the view that neither 'tradition' nor custom and precedent supported Thuwayni's claim for subsidy from Zanzibar. It was perhaps based on a verbal promise made by Majid to continue his father's practice to remit to the Muscat treasury 40,000 Crowns annually, as the income of Muscat was less than that of Zanzibar. Majid had agreed to check this fiscal imbalance in the way his father did but on the condition that Thuwayni would not attack his brother Sayyid Turki, who was based in Sohar, north of Muscat. Rigby noted that Majid broke his commitment after Muscat attacked Sayyid Turki. Thus, the money flow to Muscat stopped.

Tradition Contested: The Ingenious Thuwayni

Rigby's manufactured 'tradition' rejected the practice of primogeniture. He argued that Thuwayni too agreed with him and claimed that the eldest son had never succeeded the throne from the time of his grandfather. And from whatever he had gathered, each Sultan, including Sayyid Saʿīd, passed on political sovereignty and territory as they wished.

However, the canny Thuwayni gave his own spin to this version of tradition. He welcomed Rigby's rejection of primogeniture but extended the argument to buttress his political claim of being the ruler of a united Oman even though he was the third son of the dead Sultan. This posed difficulties for Rigby, as it meant Thuwayni's assertion of his sovereign status over Zanzibar as well.

Thuwayni argued that his father had allocated to him the charge of Muscat, the original seat of his power. This choice of the Sultan in itself indicated that he was his preferred successor. He was steadfast in his claims of being the political sovereign of a united Oman, with Zanzibar as his tributary. He invoked custom, tradition and history to reinforce his claim. As he said, 'I speak no new thing, for it is patent to the universe, tradition, history, usage, public recognition, all acknowledge this.' He argued that even Majid recognized this 'tradition' before he turned refractory. He accused him of having negated 'tradition' for his political ambitions, which were emboldened because of British support.[18] He continuously alleged that Majid was intriguing against him and 'sending money, guns and munitions of war' to their brother Sayyid Turki to use against him.[19]

Thuwayni, also made attempts to step out of Rigby's arbitration frame and reach out to Majid independently to get his support for his claim to be the sovereign of a united Oman. He used informal channels to strike a deal with Majid. For instance, he sent his cousin Sayyid Salim bin Ahmed, the second son of his father's brother, to ostensibly settle all disputes with Sayyid Majid. Sayyid Majid pledged peace with Muscat but reiterated that if his mission was to make claims against his sovereignty on the island, then it should be declared openly in the presence of the British Consul.[20] He offered to present Sayyid Salim to Rigby because, as per the agreement on the arbitration, everything had to be settled through the mediation of the Governor General of India. Salim's motive as a private emissary of Thuwayni was clearly to strike a private deal with Majid. He was grateful for the British offer to arbitrate and diplomatically left after promising to meet Rigby alone at a later date. Clearly this was an excuse. His private secretary later reported to Rigby that he had been sent by Thuwayni to press Majid for his payment of 40,000 Crowns annually.

Thuwayni, Imperial Rivalries and the Play with 'Tradition'

Arbitration and the making of Thuwayni's career were powered by the politics of the imperial assemblage comprising the French, Germans and the Americans, who offered alternate forums for the warring siblings to further their case. This 'forum shopping' presented by the imperial assemblage offered the perfect canvas for careering to both Thuwayni and Majid as the British arbitration proceeded.

Clearly, arbitration was shaped in no small measure by the imperial politics for the control of the Western Indian Ocean. It was particularly entangled with the Anglo-French rivalries for supremacy in the region. Both the imperial powers desired a friendly foothold in Zanzibar to benefit from the lucrative slave trade. The French, finding Majid inaccessible as he was a devoted ally of the British, were willing to ratify any 'tradition' that supported Thuwayni's claim of sovereignty over Zanzibar.

Rigby observed that French interest also drew from the fact that Zanzibar was rapidly becoming the emporium of the trade in slaves and ivory of all the east coast. Even the produce of the Portuguese settlement was brought here for shipment to avoid heavy duties levied at Portuguese ports. He was hopeful that before long the whole coast, as far as Delagoa Bay, would form part of the Zanzibar dominions. The Arabs were forming settlements along the Mozambique channel and expressed the desire to become the feudatories of Majid.

Rigby feared that the French were interested in supporting Thuwayni because they hoped to get in return a port on the African coast in their control. They also aspired to obtain a footing on the mainland because of their recently acquired knowledge that the interior was fine, healthy country producing abundantly cotton, sugar, coffee, etc. Their settlements at Mayotte were very unhealthy and had failed to attract commerce to their ports.

Lord Elphinstone, the Bombay Governor, agreed with Rigby and felt that the French support had emboldened Thuwayni to go to war with Zanzibar in order to uphold his version of Omani tradition. In 1859, he observed that, 'Sayyid Thoonee had been instigated by the French to attack his brother who has incurred their displeasure by his honest desire to act up to his engagements with us to suppress the slave trade.' Elphinstone suggested that Thuwayni be dissuaded from making this attack, and a steamer of the Indian Navy be placed at Zanzibar as a deterrent to the Sultan of Muscat. He urged that a British ship of war be dispatched to C.P. Rigby, the British agent at Zanzibar, if Thuwayni did indeed dethrone his brother. Elphinstone made British policy clear when he noted that 'Rigby should be told that Britains want to maintain neutrality if they lend moral support to the peaceful ruler of Zanzibar'.[21]

Both Rigby and Elphinstone pressured Thuwayni to withdraw his troops from Zanzibar on grounds that, in the event of hostility, if his Arab subjects in Zanzibar also became hostile, it would be disastrous to his morale. Commodore G. Jenkins, Commissioner in the Persian Gulf, offered to send a British Commissioner to broker peace. He travelled in Thuwayni's ship *Caroline*, which carried a British flag and was accompanied by his relative Sayyid Hamid bin Halim bin Sultan with the order to recall Thuwayni's troops.[22] This was enough to indicate to the world that the Sultan was guided by the British government and that the latter was the chief mediator in the sibling feuds.

Rigby complained of the French effort to derail arbitration in favour of Thuwayni and to the detriment of Majid's interests, as he was their ally in the anti-slave trade campaign. He alleged that the French 'had taken Sayyid Barghash, the rebel brother of Sayyid Majid under their protection' and 'he cannot be touched'. He alerted the Bombay government to the problems arising from working with the Omani siblings within the politics of the imperial assemblage that framed their lives. The extent of entanglement with the imperial rivalries was evident when he wrote that 'The question of the right of succession to the government in Zanzibar would have to be settled in Europe'. Rigby warned that if Her Majesty Queen Victoria's ships were not here, the French would have interfered more. 'They would have stirred up a revolution which would have been fatal to [the] power of Sayyid Majid and injurious to British interest.'[23]

II

Thuwayni and the Quest to Be Sultan

The Al Batinah Tribal Frontier

While the political tug of war across the waters to Zanzibar continued, the tribal societies of the coast were also tapped into by Thuwayni to further his political aspirations. The Al Batinah coast of Oman had important ports whose hinterlands were under the control of

Arab tribes, including the Wahhabis. These included Sohar, Soham and Soor respectively; in the interior there existed formidable tribal hotspots—Burka, Nakhil and the old capital of Al Rustaq, which were under Wahhabi influence. But most importantly, the coast had Thuwayni's rival brother, Sayyid Turki, as the Wālī or Governor of Sohar. And he too nurtured political aspirations to occupy Muscat. Turki needed to be tamed also because he galvanized the Wahhabis in his support. The Wahhabis were a menace, but the political challenge they posed to the British as well was useful, as it swung the British to Thuwayni's support because he was seen as a key ally in their anti-Wahhabi campaigns.

The Al Batinah coast launched Thuwayni as the premier warrior prince in the Al Busaidi stock. The conquest of the Al Batinah coast, with its important ports, inland tribal societies and date plantations, was critical for Thuwayni's political ambition of heading a vast maritime Sultanate with a stable landed interior.

Indeed, the Al Batinah political project became the forum to carve out his political sovereignty. He used it to put on display his friendly ties with the British. This friendship empowered him to dig his heels into tribal society. But more importantly, he used the spectacle of the very pronounced march of his army to Sohar and the equally public display of the demolition of urban spaces en route to the port to underline his sovereign power.

Thuwayni and the Attack on Sohar, 1858

It was important for Thuwayni to have a hold on Sohar if the imperial ambition of a united Oman with the tribal interior and coastal port towns intact was to be realized. Sohar remained a site of contest between Thuwayni and his brother and Wālī or Governor of Sohar, Turki. Turki's claim that he was the independent sovereign of Sohar was therefore always questioned by not just Thuwayni but also his brother Majid.[24]

Thuwayni began to plan the conquest of Sohar to oust Turki once the Bombay Governor, Elphinstone, brokered the Muscat-Zanzibar truce. Thuwayni's foothold in Bandar Abbas made it easy for him to access Sohar. It also helped that the bulk of the population of Sohar was of Persian or Baluchi descent. Thuwayni had inherited the goodwill his father Sayyid Saʿīd had carefully cultivated in both these constituencies. Thuwayni also hoped for help from the British as Turki was not in their good books: reports of his active involvement in the slave trade, his protection of tribes who looted and pillaged ships in the Persian Gulf and his influence in the Wahhabi-influenced tribes of the interior made him a sore point in his dealings with the British as well.

In 1858, Thuwayni launched his attack on Sohar from Bandar Abbas. His guns, mortars, 1000 casks of gunpowder and other provisions came from Muscat in his ship *Caroline*. He was confident that he would be joined by the Persian Army on the march to Sohar.[25] He was determined to snatch back Sohar from Turki and had his eyes on two other important towns: Khābūrah and Sukham situated on the sea coast.

Following the attack from Bandar Abbas, Thuwayni began his march to Sohar from Muscat. He stitched a range of alliances in the tribal society as he moved from Muscat up north to Sohar. These alliances ensured his control over the date cultivations and other fiscal profits from the tribal interior.[26] He collected his followers, an army of Arab tribes of Hazar and Badavine of Al-Sharqiyyah.

His army arrived at Khābūrah, where he had an encounter with Turki. The city surrendered to him after violent clashes. The city of Soham was taken without any fighting as its garrison was too weak to hold out for long. Thuwayni then marched to Sohar, where his army and that of Turki clashed, and he besieged the town.[27] He subsequently conquered the ports of Khābūrah and Sohar, and matters were amicably settled between the brothers with the mediation of Rashid bin Hamidul Ghāfirī.

According to the settlement, Sayyid Turki was initially left in possession of Sohar and other adjacent places, and he was to receive from Thuwayni 300 French dollars per month. Thuwayni was always wary of Arab chiefs loyal to Turki creating strife for him. Their revolt was always like a sword of Damocles over his head. The British advised him to maintain a 'liberal and just' policy with them like his father and sort out issues with Turki to resolve the matter.[28] But matters improved once Turki was booted out of Sohar and other places which were in the possession of the tribe of Ghāfiriyyah, particularly the Banī Jābir.

Asserting His Political Sovereignty in the Tribal Interiors

Thuwayni cultivated his social base in the tribes of Al Batinah and could garner a big army from his Arab tribal support base at short notice. These soldiers were recruited ad hoc and were dispersed once their job was done.

In 1860, he marched close to Burka to quell a rebellion with a force of 12,000 men. Seven thousand of these were under his command. The chief initially seemed to surrender but soon turned hostile and said his men were not willing to give away Suwayq or Khābūrah. But Thuwayni had already allowed most of his army to disperse and go back home and was left with only 6000 men at his command. He got help from Sayyid Salim from Sohar, who sent troops. He also asked for help from Pengally, the British agent at Muscat, who sent letters threatening punishment to the rebels for their treachery.

Pengally blamed Thuwayni for this event, as the Arab army was, he said, 'little better than an armed mob', its discipline being 'foreign to both master and man'. It could only be kept together by the 'men being paid and fed with regularity'.

Since Thuwayni's exchequer was in a strained condition, he had been in a hurry to disperse the men. Pengally was of the view that if he had not dispersed them, they would all have deserted, as an 'Arab merely fights in the capacity of a mercenary ready to serve under the leader who will treat him best and oblivious to the cause he may be defending'. Pengally was convinced that they did not fight ever for any 'patriotic motive'.[29]

Thuwayni turned towards the city of Nakhil where, given the news of his military successes, the tribal people reached out to him to sort out their problems. He was happy to mediate, as that was a way to underline his political clout in the interior. He made a political practice of marching through the interiors from Sohar to Nakhil and interacting with the tribal society. He negotiated deals with tribal factions to consolidate his social base. For instance, he stopped at Burka en route from Sohar to Nakhil and interfered in tribal factional politics, exercising his military prowess.

Thuwayni had a history of interactions with Nakhil tribals. As far back as the year 1772, the Muscat Sultan imprisoned six of the Alyen Aribah tribe and sent them to Zanzibar, where they were left free to settle. When the Imam died, these six returned to Muscat and joined their own tribe. The head of their tribe, Jabir, who was residing in Serjah, resolved to settle in Nakhil. Initially only 100 followed him. They established themselves on a hilltop, constructed bastions, as also connecting curtain walls and a mosque. They repaired a fort that was in ruins and established two villages. This tribe was said to have entered into a confederacy with Sayyid Turki, who supplied them with troops, arms and provisions.[30] They were assisted by the Ghāfiriyyah, who had the support of Sayyid Thuwayni.

Thuwayni's interventions in the Nakhil disputes enabled him to insinuate himself as the arbiter and sovereign who could resolve issues that Turki was unable to do. Thus, he stopped at the town of Moshima, at war with Nakhil, and summoned Nakhil elders to appear before him. Thunriyan, the Shaykh of Moshima, met him along with three other men whom Turki had imprisoned earlier in the city of Sumail for their alleged role in murdering the ruler of Nakhil. Thuwayni pardoned them after assurances from the Shaykh that they would follow his orders and accept him as their ruler. They were fined $800 for the murder. They paid the amount and stated that the murder was done without their knowledge.

While on his way to Nakhil, Thuwayni put to death Ḥamūd bin Khulfān bin Surḥān al-Jābirībin Serham al Jabir, the person left in charge of Khābūrah by Turki. He summoned the people of Nakhil on his arrival at Mustenat. Three people who had been imprisoned by the Mujtahid for the murder of a former Governor of the place appeared and were pardoned by Thuwayni at the intercession of seven of the elders of the tribe of Hināwī. But they had to pay on demand: $800 as blood money of the murdered Governor, 200 swords, 200 daggers and 200 guns. They were allowed to go back to Nakhil.

Thuwayni's success as a mediator earned him political dividends. The people of Nakhil 'entertained' him and he in turn demanded from them 200 swords, 200 daggers and 200 muskets. They presented these to him as a mark of acceptance of his rule. After being adequately satisfied with their overtures, he 'declared peace and tranquility with the people of Nakhil'.[31]

Milking the Wahhabi Threat to Attack Sohar

Thuwayni's dealings with the dreaded Wahhabis in the tribal interior brought him the maximum political dividends. It brought him in close alliance with the British, who had their own axe to grind in the face of this political challenge. Indeed, he got the British on his side in his fight with brother Turki, as the former disliked Turki because of the influence he wielded over the Wahhabis.

The British agreed with Thuwayni that he was a 'dangerous intriguer and a most extortionate ruler'.[32] In 1860, Brigadier W.M. Coghlan, in charge of the Muscat and Zanzibar Commission, insisted in his report that Thuwayni should be officially informed of his recognition by the Government of India as the paramount sovereign of Sohar and the claim of Turki to be independent of the Sultan of Muscat be disallowed.

The imperial entanglements of Thuwayni lent him huge credibility in tribal society. Local people began to approach him to complain against Turki. In 1861, delegations of Muslims and Jews from Sohar arrived in Muscat and complained about his misadministration. They urged Sultan Thuwayni to protect them from his own brother. These delegates included many British Indian subjects, who warned of rebellion and anarchy if Thuwayni did not intervene to quell the discontent.[33] And the involvement of the British Indian subjects drew the attention of the Bombay government as well to the affairs in Sohar.

Lt W.M. Pengally, British agent at Muscat, mediated a meeting between the two brothers at Muscat, even as Thuwayni prepared to launch an attack on Sohar.[34] He assured a safe passage to Turki to visit Muscat.[35] Turki arrived at Seeb, near Muscat, and met Pengally. But he deferred his meeting with Thuwayni for the morning. Pengally suspected foul play and went back on his promise of safe passage and got Turki arrested while he was in Muscat territory.[36]

III

Thuwayni and the Making of a Political Sovereign

The Public Spectacle: Marching Victorious to Sohar

The defeat of Turki encouraged Thuwayni to consolidate his gains at Sohar militarily. He sent his son Salim to replace Turki and dispatched vessels of war carrying seventy guns to Sohar to bolster his position. This was necessary, as many of Turki's soldiers and the disaffected people of the port town geared up in opposition, even if the tribals in the interior supported Thuwayni.

Indeed, accustomed to his march northwards on the Al Batinah, up the coast from Muscat, he himself arrived via Seeb to Burka en route to Sohar. He used British mediation and their apparent show of support to him because of the Wahhabi fear to his political advantage. He used this incident to mobilize around him his ethnically and religiously diverse subjects.

Thuwayni used the British fear of the Wahhabis to his advantage. He marched to Sohar via Seeb and Burka and was confident that the British support for his rule in Sohar would help him establish 'peace and prosperity throughout the portion of his hitherto misgoverned territory [Sohar]'. [37]

Thuwayni made a spectacle of his army's march northwards from Muscat, up the coast of Al Batinah, to Sohar. All along the way, he demonstrated his social clout in the tribal areas to underline his exalted status, both to the British as well as to the tribal societies of the interior. In keeping with projecting himself as the sovereign, he himself sailed to Sohar on the corvette *Rahmany* in the company of his squadron. But in a well-choreographed move, his contingent of about 1000 men comprising infantry and cavalry, marched from Burka for the purpose of cooperating with the vessels of war.

The deserted town of Sohar still had its forts manned and guns loaded. But on the order of Thuwayni, the gates were thrown open and his troops assumed possession. The takeover was peaceful. He left his son, Sayyid Salim, all of twenty-two years of age, in charge of Sohar.[38]

The British imperial frame in which he had successfully made an entry helped him gain credibility at Sohar. His friendship with Pengally came in very handy. Pengally continued to mediate between Sohar and Muscat, urging the people 'in the name of British government to refrain from rebellion and remain loyal subjects for future mild and impartial rule of Sayyid Thoonee'.[39] He intended to play a neutral mediator, egging on Thuwayni on the one hand and on the other urging the Bombay government to pressure him to pay as 'subsistence money' a suitable monthly allowance, to the tune of $400–500, to his brother Turki for his entire life on condition of his loyalty to the British government.[40]

The fall of Sohar had its desired effect on the materialization of Thuwayni's political dream. He began to be accepted as a political sovereign of not just Muscat but entire Oman. This encouraged Thuwayni to exercise his might and consolidate his hold on the Arab tribes in the interior.

The Public Demolition of Urban Structures

On his victory at Nakhil, Sayyid Thuwayni destroyed all the dwellings there. He ordered the place to be razed to the ground and the principal tower to be blown up. The people of Nakhil reminded him of the pardon he had granted, but he was unrelenting and insisted on all the towers and buildings being blown up. This was accordingly done.[41]

Once he was assured of his social acceptance in Nakhil, he asserted his presence in the tribal interior by announcing the transfer of power in the region through wide-ranging and public acts of demolition. He ordered the demolition of all the new fortifications at Nakhil and secretly ordered the people of Al-Ma'awil, Banī Ruwaha and Sureera to enter Nakhil in the morning with shovels and other implements and carry on demolitions as per his orders.

Soon after, he decided to destroy the towers of the old street called Ahjumeinee. Ignoring the pleas of the local people asking for forgiveness and pardon for their support to Sayyid Turki, he ordered major demolitions of urban spaces such as streets and towers.[42]

Pengally proved a loyal supporter of Thuwayni, his chief conduit to the imperial assemblage who hoped to get Thuwayni's support in the anti-Wahhabi plans of the British. Pengally always expressed utmost satisfaction at the improved state of law and order in Sohar after the installation of Thuwayni's son, Prince Salim. He reported that the desolate and ransacked state of the town was improving and that all Arab tribal chiefs who earlier collected money from Sohar using threat and intimidation were now referred to Muscat in the event of their demands.[43] British mediation lent the much-needed confidence to Thuwayni and enabled him to dig his roots deep into Muscat society. He went about controlling the inland tribes and managing the date cultivation and other fiscal matters.

At the end of the day, the Turki incident benefited him more than it did Pengally, who lost his job because he was not seen to be neutral enough as a mediator between the brothers. He was accused of partiality towards Thuwayni, who arrested and locked up his brother in Muscat because of Pengally abruptly cancelling the security that he had promised Turki.[44]

Imperial Checks on Thuwayni's Political Ambition: The Axe Falls on Pengally

And yet, political sovereignty carved out by entangling in imperial networks was bound to be fragile. Thuwayni's help in dealing with the Wahhabis made the British support his political moves. But this did not mean that there was no serious concern at the public expression of his political ambitions. Pengally was often pulled up by the administration for his unabashed support to Thuwayni.

For instance, the honourable board disapproved of Pengally's incitement and threats to the rebels at Suwayq and Burka as he prepared to assist Thuwayni in handling the revolt. The board felt that he had overstretched his brief. He was also accused of interfering on behalf of the Sultan with the chiefs of Abu Dhabi and Ra's al-Khaimah, which should have been left to the charge of the British Resident there. He was reminded that his task was the protection of British interests in the Gulf, for which the Resident was willing to liaise and help. Also, his role at Muscat was limited to offering advice to Thuwayni keeping British interests in mind and urging him to 'judicious and engaged action'. It was not in any way to pledge himself or the British government to 'assist him in measures of coercion'.[45]

Thuwayni was told that he had to depend on his own measures and not lean on British help in handling his internal affairs and that the British were there only to offer the best advice to a 'just administration' so as to ensure 'welfare of the Chief's dominions . . . and security and progress of trade in general on their coast'.[46] In fact, the board threatened to withdraw the agent if dissensions in the neighbourhood of Muscat increased.

IV

Thuwayni, British Indian Subjects and the Strengthening of Sovereignty

The Sohar success emboldened Thuwayni. It successfully entangled him in imperial networks and embedded him in tribal society. He turned his attention to the British Indian subjects in his territory to sharpen his sovereign status. As we have seen, British Indian merchants and bankers oiled the financial wheels of the Sultanate. Thuwayni too was dependent on their capital and services.

Like his father, he too contracted the customs to British Indian subjects. He contracted the customs for a lump sum of about $1,20,000 per annum to a British Indian subject. The contractor levied various rates of dues according to the description of the articles. European nations paid 5 per cent ad valorem duty under treaty. But he also received an income of 10 per cent in kind on certain date plantations in Batinah and his own estates.[47]

Many British Indian slavers also flourished under Thuwayni's protection. As the global demand for dates from the interior swelled, so did the dependence on slave labour to work on the date plantations at the Al Batinah.[48] Indeed, he was always suspect in British eyes because of his protection of Arab and Indian slavers. In 1857, Lt Col A. Hamerton, consul and agent at Muscat, reported the case of Azim Khan Cashmere, active in Muscat since at least 1850. He described him as a 'notorious' slaver who sought his help in getting a pass for his bugla and claimed his entitlement to British protection. He was reported to have a Persian Register, a Turkish Register and the Imam of Muscat's Register. This entitled him to use the flags of these powers as required. The access to this range of flags facilitated the flow of his buglas along the slave coast. Hamerton had information about one of his cargo buglas, sailing with an Arab flag, being engaged in the transportation of slaves from various places in the African coast to Madagascar, where the slaves were collected for the European slave ships. The cargo ship with slaves was destroyed by the British ships, causing a great sensation in the Red Sea area.[49]

Alongside, Thuwayni encouraged private traders both Arab and Indian Kutchi as well as the private British and European trading companies to operate from Muscat.[50] Kutchi Indian traders based in Muscat noted the decline of the port city from the 1840s, when Thuwayni's father, Sultan Sayyid Sa'īd, moved his base to Zanzibar. But its significance as a premier market for arms slumped drastically when the British clamped down on the private trade of slaves and arms post 1857.[51] Arms for even the personal use of Thuwayni were difficult to get. In 1858, Messrs Wallace and Company sought and obtained special permission from the Bombay government for selling thirty muskets with bayonets for the personal use of Thuwayni in Muscat.[52]

But the enterprising Thuwayni was unrelenting. The port town attracted wealthy Kutchi merchants, such as Ratansi Pushottam, who migrated to the city to take advantage of the new opportunities. In 1857, his uncle, already based in Muscat, welcomed him and mentored him in his ancestral firm Natha Mekhan.[53] His firm, dealing in arms in Muscat, flourished, as it leveraged itself to the interests of Thuwayni and the private European and British trading firms. And he was not the only one. The firm of another well-known Kutchi trader, Gopalji Walji, also had a meteoric rise in this period.

Thuwayni was encouraged by British Residents, such as Felix Jones, to bring such British subjects who had lived for long in his territory under his protection. The government was clear that British subjects who lived in Thuwayni's territory were under his protection as long as they lived there. However, the British subject's 'allegiance to his own sovereign and to the laws which govern him in that capacity he cannot denationalize himself by any act or will of his own'.[54]

Jones explained that this was similar to Arabs and others in British India, who had obtained documents certifying them as British subjects during the course of their Indian stint. Such documents were valid and entitled them to British protection only in British territory. They did not have a 'wide world signification'. This meant that none of these men could ask for British protection when under a foreign power. The same rule applied to children of aliens born on British soil. Women under British law had the nationality of their husbands and had no independent right to property; the same should have been in international law.

These rules were most problematic for the Indian Banias in the Oman and Persian Gulf, as they had a long history of trade ties with the region. They were to be under the protection of the Sultan as long as they were in his territory. Many of them had settled on Arab shores for a very long period, without having returned to India for many years. Many were settlers in Arab ports even before the British conquest of India. More importantly, they used both the British and the Sultan to further their commercial interests and ground themselves in Arab society. They owned land, temples, houses and mosques and were completely mingled with the sons of the soil.[55] Jones was of the view that this was unacceptable and that as per the residency rules, he suggested that they were not entitled to British protection once they were in Arab territory.

The Khojas

Thuwayni used Jones's injunctions on British subjects residing in his territory to his advantage. He was most invested in the case of the British Indian Muslim subjects, the Khojas, as they had hugely contributed to his economy. Interventions in their affairs offered him the perfect forum to underline his sovereign status. In 1859, Muhammad Jafar Khan, nephew of the spiritual leader Aga Khan, reported from Muscat that the Khojas who had migrated from Kutch, Kathiawar, Bombay and Sindh in India were major investors in the growth of Muscat. They were a key component in the social base of the Sultans of Muscat from the eighteenth century. However, Thuwayni forefronted them more than ever because intervention in their disputes brought him legitimacy in the eyes of the British and also proximity to their officials. These were more relevant than ever as he contested with his brothers to step into the space vacated by his father's sudden death. The British encouraged his flirtations with them—as shaken by the 1857 Mutiny in India—they preferred to handle Indian Muslim subjects in Muscat via him. This was the only safe way to keep tabs on Muslim subjects abroad.

Muslim Khojas, also known as Lotias in Muscat, settled in large numbers in Oman for trade but also because they felt they were closer to Persia, which they could access with relative ease for pilgrimage to the Aga Khan. They had made considerable investments in the city guided by their religious belief, which made each Khoja give one-fifth of their property annually for the Prophet and his descendants. Offerings and presents poured in from the Khojas in every town and city and were collected systematically by two supervisors of the Aga Khan. As per Indian custom, one of the supervisors was called 'Mukhiya' and the other 'Camria'. The offerings were collected in all the towns in a prayer and guest house called the '*Mehmān Khānah*'.

The property and money of the Khojas with no heirs also went into the Aga Khan's kitty. But many with legal heirs also opted to bequeath their assets to the spiritual leader on their death. Many houses, shops and gardens were acquired by the Aga Khan in this manner, not just in India and Oman, but in Kabul, Kandahar, Balkh, Bokhara, Badakshan and Persia, where his disciples were scattered. His supervisors often sold this property and deposited the money in the Mehmān Khānah.

In 1859, Thuwayni got the opportunity he was looking for when 'refractory' Khojas in the Muttrah village of Muscat plundered the place of worship and depository, Mehmān Khānah.[56] The supervisors took the matter to the British agent Khoja Haskīl and asked him to be a witness. But the Aga Khan asked his nephew, Muhammad Jafar Khan, to take the matter to Sultan Thuwayni to obtain redress. Thuwayni, despite opposition from the rebel Khojas to allow Jafar Khan to reside in the Mehmān Khānah, ordered his son Sayyid Salim to ensure his residence there. He was welcoming to him and negotiated with the rebel Khojas. Jafar Khan waited for Thuwayni to return from his planned trip to Bandar Abbas and Sohar and solve his dispute.[57]

Jafar Khan, in the knowledge of Sayyid Thuwayni, submitted a petition to the British Resident. He in turn asked his agent, Khoja Haskīl, to bring the matter to the urgent notice of Thuwayni. The Sultan referred the matter for complete investigation to Haskīl, who submitted his duly researched report to him. Satisfied with the British report on the case, Thuwayni handed over the Mehmān Khānah and the house to Jafar Khan and promised a written order for the same.

On the question of return of the property plundered from the house, he promised intervention and resolution of the dispute on his return from Zanzibar.[58] It is significant that despite relying on and taking in the loop the British agent in addressing the grievance, he refused to have the agent countersign any order he issued. He also refused any request to invite the agent to resolve the issue of plundered property, or even inform him that this matter of property plunder remained unresolved even if the dwelling house and Mehmān Khānah had been handed over to Jafar Khan. On his part, Khan was dissatisfied and considered the matter unresolved. But Thuwayni had milked it to his advantage.

The Seedis were traditionally also viewed as the servants of the
Khojas. They lived in the Khoja quarters in Muttrah, away from the
quarters of the Baluchis. There was a riot once in the town, when
the Baluchis allegedly attacked the Seedis at a dance party. They
then attacked the Khoja fort in the town, and the latter asked for
British protection. The Sultan also wished to consult the British on
the necessary steps to be taken. The Seedis too attacked back with
sticks and stones. One Seedi got a sword to attack, and about fifteen
to twenty Baluchis were injured. The Political Resident put a guard
at the Khoja fort. But as far as the Seedis were concerned, they were
regarded as Arab subjects, as were the Baluchis. So the matter was
referred to the Sultan.[59] He intervened and projected his sovereign
status in the process.

The protection that the Aga Khan and the Khojas received
from Thuwayni was suddenly lifted when the Sultan died. Sultan
Azzan bin Qais threatened to sell the Khoja Jamā'at Khānah (house of
assembly) and the building around it belonging to the community. A
distressed Aga Khan wrote to the Political Agent in Muscat for help,
to no avail. He stressed that the British should intervene in Khoja
affairs as they were British subjects who had moved to Muscat from
the British territory of Kutch, Sindh and Kathiawar in India. He also
complained that a faction of the Khojas at Muscat claimed a share
of the community's property as they refused to accept his spiritual
leadership. They disowned the Aga Khan, claiming themselves to be
the 'true Khojas'.[60]

Even after the death of Thuwayni, the issue of the British Indian
subjects and their use by the successive Sultans to bolster their
interests continued. In 1870, a dispute arose between the Seedis
and the Khojas over a Jamā'at Khānah located in Muttrah that had
been used as a public guest house set apart for the Khojas travelling
between Karbala, India and Africa. The Seedis who had splintered
from the orthodox Khojas were deprived of this building's use.
The Aga Khan was angry that the then Sultan of Muscat, 'Azzān
bin Ghayr, handed over to the Seedis, for considerations of money,
one of his buildings. He was incensed that he had contravened the
arrangements he had made with his predecessor Thuwayni.

The Seedis questioned if the building had been set apart for Khojas as a public guest house. They claimed that they had purchased it from the ruler of the country and used it as a mosque. Thus, they claimed the building as their bona fide property, inalienable and incapable of desecration by conversion into a guest house. The current Sultan agreed with them that it was a mosque and said he would not interfere with it. He denied the claims of the Aga Khan on the building. Pelly felt the Aga Khan's argument had weight and doubted the claims of the Sultan, who he said was a 'despotic prince' not even acknowledged by the British. He needed more time to investigate before the government interfered.[61]

V

Thuwayni's Global Visibility: Dealing with the Wahhabis

The Wahhabis, as we saw in Chapter 1, posed a challenge to Sultan Sayyid Sa'īd. They continued to be a political threat to Thuwayni despite their taming in the 1819 Wahhabi battle led by the British and the Oman ruler, when they retreated to the mountainous regions of Nejd.

However, they reared their head again in the 1860s. They took advantage of the conjunctional moment when Sayyid Sa'īd was dead and his Sultanate was riveted with succession feuds, and the Ottoman Pashas in the Arab provinces less hostile to them as a consequence of their Sultan nurturing aspirations to be the Caliph of global Muslims. Their resurgence was helped also with the British being completely involved in dealing with the 1857 Indian revolt against their occupation. From 1865, they appeared to be on the ascendant both as an aggressive temporal power in the interiors of Arabia as well as leaders of 'fanatical' revival in India.

Clearly, their new generation had not experienced the power of the Egyptian Pasha, the late Sultan of Muscat and the British naval and military expeditionary forces. Their resurgence was visible in the increase in piracy from vessels coming from the Wahhabi ports. And their aggressive overtures were evident over land, as they streamed in from the north into the territories of the Sultan of Muscat. The Wahhabis, in this period of resurgence, were led by formidable warriors such as Amir Faisal and his son Abdullah. Indeed, their clout in the tribal interiors of Oman and India increased so much that, in the words of the Bushire Resident, 'we began even in India to speak of the wahabees as of a powerful body of fanatics'.[62]

Sayyid Thuwayni, Wahhabis and the Entry into the Imperial Assemblage

Thuwayni's career as the political sovereign of Muscat coincided with this period of Wahhabi revival. This proved to be a huge challenge as well as an opportunity. He used the imperial politics around them to his advantage and very successfully balanced his politics with Western powers to acquire global visibility in the imperially framed world.

Very much like the Mongol Chingez Khan in medieval times, who viewed the Ottomans as his subordinates even when he established his empire, the Wahhabis too considered the Muscat Sultan as their Wālī. Indeed, incensed by Thuwayni crushing the revolt at Soor that they supported, the Wahhabi Amir Abdullah bin Faisal insulted Thuwayni by repeatedly referring to the Sultan of Muscat as his Wālī. He considered him his subject and repeated that he did not want him in Oman and that he would 'eject him and nominate someone in his stead'.[63] The Wahhabis always demanded tribute from Thuwayni to underline Muscat's subordination to them.

Thuwayni's political sovereignty was questioned by the seventy-five-year-old Amir Faisal, based at B'ir al-'Ayn. He was convinced that God had given him 'all Arabia from Kuwait, through Amman to Raisel Hadud and beyond that to Makullah'. He treated Thuwayni as his subject and never failed to remind him that the British could not mediate in his affairs, as they 'have no right to mediate between a Chief and his subjects'. This was seen as a clear indicator that 'Sayyid Suwaynee [Thuwayni] is his subject and not an independent chief'.

Faisal demanded that Thuwayni raise his tribute four times more and instigated the tribes at Al Rustaq to rebel against him. The mounting pressure of the Wahhabis drew the British closer to Thuwayni, as they too geared to fight against this major political challenge to their commerce in the Gulf. They warmed up to Thuwayni, fearing that, 'unless the government upheld Sayyid Thuwayni he must purchase Ameer Fysul's good will with a long purse and much humiliation'.[64]

Thuwayni, emboldened with the friendly British overtures, rejected the Wahhabi claim of his subordination to them and underlined his status as an independent sovereign. He also used the Wahhabi challenge to cosy up to the Western powers and gain status and legitimacy in his society. He repeatedly flaunted his ties with the European powers and Americans, who he emphasized always treated him as an independent sovereign and allocated him a space in the imperial assemblage for discussing the Wahhabi issues.

Indeed, the Wahhabis enabled his entry into the imperial club and made him strike personal friendships with British officers. Residents in the Persian Gulf, such as Lt Col L. Pelly in particular, were convinced that Thuwayni's exhausted exchequer because of poor management of his revenue and the political challenges from within his family circuits made the Wahhabi threat very real and tough for him.[65] Indeed, Pelly's concerns, even if triggered by protecting British maritime interests, became the beginning of an enduring personal friendship with Thuwayni.

Pelly leaned on Thuwayni as his local ally, as he feared that the Wahhabis would urge the Arab tribes north of Muscat to revolt. This would be disastrous, as it would break the maritime peace and stability that the Canning Award had introduced in the region. Pelly urged the Bombay government to intervene and help Thuwayni in his fight against the Wahhabis. He argued that the division of Oman had so weakened Thuwayni that he was incapable of handling the Wahhabis with his own resources alone. But the government chose neutrality and let Thuwayni face the music of his mismanagement.[66] Yet, Pelly's friendly overtures to Thuwayni continued. There existed a very cordial relationship between the two.

This was indeed the ideal moment to strike personal friendships with British officers, as they leaned on him to rally against a common enemy. And predictably, Pelly was not his only friend. Such friendships were innumerable and remained Thuwayni's asset during his entire career. Bartle Frere, the former Bombay Governor and the British missionary interlocutor, was equally soft on Thuwayni over the Wahhabi issue. But unlike Pelly, who wanted full British support for an 'incapacitated' Thuwayni, he was more in favour of encouraging him to garner his own resources. He wanted him to behave like his father, who had met the Wahhabi challenge on his own.

At the same time, Frere was quick to promise him British support when he was in trouble. He was of the view that the Government of India had to get proactive, as the renewed Wahhabi threat would not only adversely impact the Persian Gulf commerce by the revival of piracy but also interfere with the telegraph project. The Wahhabis could snap the telegraph lines and disrupt communication with Europe. Frere reminded the administration of their treaty ties with Muscat and urged them not to be passive in their support to Thuwayni.[67] He cautioned that even though the Wahhabi support base was in the interior tribes, if they trounced Muscat, the maritime tribes would swing towards them. Both the Sultanate and the littoral chieftainships would then have to accept their dominance. This would be detrimental to British commercial interests.

Thuwayni had friendly assurances from Felix Jones, the Political Resident at Bushire, as well. He assured him of British help against the Wahhabis. At the same time, Jones advised Thuwayni to go solo and sharpen his attack on the Wahhabis, as that would gain him legitimacy and underline his authority on the global canvas. Indeed, Frere coaxed him to follow his late father's policy of consolidating his finances, conciliate and revive the spirit of his fanatical tribes, reorganize his military and naval forces and to repel by force if negotiations failed with the Wahhabis. He was warned that 'tame acquiescence' and constantly increasing the tribute that he paid to them would fail to protect both his as well as British subjects from their attacks.[68]

The Wahhabi issue had forced the British to strike a friendship with Thuwayni and include him in their imperial drawing board. Thuwayni saw this imperial entanglement as a huge political investment, even if there was no consensus on the British side regarding how much he could be trusted in this fight. The Bombay government remained suspicious of him—they believed that he had fractured his father's carefully crafted ethnic and religious equilibrium and reduced Muscat to 'disorder', 'bankruptcy' and lack of 'justice'.[69] Jews, Indian merchants and a range of Arab tribes were said to have complained about him. The lack of law and order had led to many Jews leaving Muscat.[70] Thuwayni's requests for increased subsidies and financial help were seldom entertained.

Even Felix Jones, who was soft on Thuwayni in the interest of protecting commerce, was not so forthcoming on the issue of bolstering his political authority and relieving his economic hardships. Indeed, he 'distrusted the professions of the whole race [Arab], particularly those of new claimants to power'.[71] He felt that the newcomers turned out to be most ungrateful of what he said was a 'singularly ungrateful family of mankind'.[72] He believed that reticence would be culpable and lead to complications and possible claims of indemnity against them.

Thuwayni's Wahhabi Offensive: Marching into the Imperially Crowded World to Fight In-House Battles?

Thuwayni milked the Wahhabi issue to the utmost despite the British apprehensions about him being a trustworthy ally. He used it to balance his politics with imperial interests. Needless to add that he used it as his entry to the imperial drawing board. This was also useful in strengthening his political games with his brothers Turki and Majid, who contested his claim to succeed their father as the Sultan of a united Oman and Zanzibar.

Each time Thuwayni hit out at the Wahhabis, he leveraged with the British to get their help in his fight with his brothers. As he prepared his march from Sohar to the Wahhabi stronghold at B'ir al-'Ayn, he alerted the British to the fact that Turki was allying with the enemy and stirring strife and trouble for him. He pleaded to them to reconfine him to prison, from where he had been released on their request.[73] At the same time, with the British on his side, he used the occasion to pressure Majid to hike the subsidy he paid to Muscat. He demanded this increase ostensibly to meet the military expenses incurred in the march against the Wahhabis.

And yet, this balancing with imperial politics was riddled with tensions. There was no way in which the British were ready to support him as an independent sovereign of Oman and Zanzibar in the way they treated his father. It was in British interests that Omani political sovereignty lay divided and contested between him and his brothers. This situation increased their importance as the principal arbitrators. Thus, Pelly was supportive of his anti-Wahhabi stance, but disapproved of both his aggression and the political bargaining. He underlined the conclusions of the British arbitration, which had decided on the terms and conditions of the relationship between him and his brothers. He rejected outright his claims for an increased subsidy from Majid as the Customs House revenues of Zanzibar had increased. He was very clear that all demands of Thuwayni had to conform to the arbitration terms.[74]

In a similar vein, he responded to Thuwayni's apprehensions on Turki by involving the latter as well in the fight against the Wahhabis. Indeed, he diluted the clout Thuwayni hoped to gain in imperial circuits by his war against the Wahhabis by roping in Turki as well. He deputed Turki to lead the fleet to the Wahhabi ports. He felt this was a good ploy, as he was an 'enterprising warrior' and 'might prove dangerous if left in Muscat'.[75]

Pelly's friend, Frere, too promised British help on the condition that Thuwayni take the lead and showcase himself as a formidable ruler. He pressured the British government to assure him of all material and moral support once he had set his own house in order. Naval ships and munitions would be provided to him to re-establish himself at Soor or wherever he was ousted from. He wanted Pelly to be dispatched to Muscat to get active with British plans and advised the blocking of Wahhabi ports by British cruisers. The Resident at Bushire seconded his views. And in 1865, the Bombay government sanctioned a loan of 2 lakh rupees to the Sultan at the rate of 5 per cent on the security of the customs of Gowadur. The sanction of the Government of India was sought.[76]

The Rustaq Revolt and the Imperial Dilemmas: Thuwayni Digs His Heels in Wahhabi-impacted Tribal Areas

Thuwayni looked to the tribal interiors as well to consolidate his position and take on the Wahhabi challenge. He was convinced that his Wahhabi success in the interiors would earn him a comfortable seat in the imperial club. He got the opportunity he was looking for when one of his relatives led a revolt against him at the interior town of Al Rustaq, the old capital of Oman and the seat of the Ibāḍī sect. The revolt had the support of the Wahhabis.

Thuwayni then commenced on his march to Al Rustaq. The tribal regions that he covered were not necessarily revenue-bearing territory. The bulk of his revenue was primarily derived from sea customs. He collected only a small revenue on dates, at 10 per cent upon the produce, from some of the tribes located in the interior. He had little authority in these Arab frontier tribes. That was the reason why small groups of Wahhabis from Nejd came down the passes to this seaboard and used their religious opinion and dissensions within the Arab tribes of Muscat to mislead the latter.[77]

Thuwayni used the Wahhabi political challenge to change his precarious position in the tribal areas. He began to forge alliances with a range of Arab tribes in the interior of Muscat. He needed to control the tribal region, as it was the most fertile ground tapped into by the Wahhabis to destabilize him. The modus operandi of the Wahhabis was best reflected in the details of their attack at Soor, the shipbuilding port town south of Muscat.

The detachment of Wahhabis passed along the Muscat frontier from B'ir al-'Ayn and became the guests of their co-religionists, the Banī Bū 'Alī tribe, whose haunts were in the uplands immediately behind Soor. They had a subdivision named the Al-Janabah of the highlands, and these in turn had clansmen settled at Soor, who were long known as the most notorious slavers and pirates along

the east coast of Africa. They united and invited the Wahhabis
to invade.[78]

Thuwayni cashed in on the Al Rustaq revolt by soliciting British
help and hoping for his entry, as an equal, into their anti-Wahhabi
imperial club. He used his friendship with Pelly as the conduit. When
Pelly arrived in Muscat in 1865, Thuwayni complained to him about
the revolt. He alleged that the recalcitrant relative was encouraged
by several Bedouin Arab tribes who were under the influence of a
Wahhabi chief, Turki, who resided as the deputy of the Wahhabi
amir at B'ir al-'Ayn, near the frontier of Muscat. Showcasing his
preparedness, he was quick to tap into the Bombay government for
help to deal with the Wahhabis. He was successful to the extent that
the British Resident at Muscat facilitated his march to Al Rustaq.

Thuwayni hoped to use this Wahhabi-inspired tribal revolt to
negotiate the terms of the Canning Award that had administratively
separated Oman and Zanzibar as independent polities and made the
British the sole arbiters and caretakers in the Gulf. Thuwayni argued
that the division of Oman post-Canning Award had weakened him
and he, therefore, needed the British to support him against tribal
unrest and Wahhabi infiltration in his territories.[79] He hyped up the
instances of the Wahhabi indoctrination in his territory. He argued
that this was detrimental to political stability in Muscat and that he
be allowed to blockade some of the ports in the Gulf, strike alliances
with Arab chiefs favourable to him, and the British restrain Arab
chiefs favourable to the Wahhabis from breaking truce.[80]

Help was not as forthcoming as he hoped. But the revolt
precipitated conversations on the issue in which he was a key
participant. This, in itself, was an achievement, as it lent him huge
global visibility in what clearly was an issue of grave imperial concern.
Significantly, the British dilemma in interfering in the tribal areas
of the Al Batinah to fight the Wahhabis alongside Thuwayni
derived from the nature of agreements they had allegedly entered
into with various stakeholders, including the Wahhabis, to guard
their maritime interests in the region. Each time they protested the
attacks on British subjects as a result of the Wahhabi rampaging
in Thuwayni's backyard, they were reminded of these maritime

agreements by the Wahhabi Amir, Faisal. He never failed to remind them that this was in keeping with the agreement that the Wahhabis had with them from the time of Sayyid Saʿīd, whereby they were not to oppose the British government at sea and not oppress their subjects. But the people on the land and the coast would be their subjects, and the British government would not oppose this or injure any of these people.[81]

However, on many occasions, the Government of India denied the existence of any such agreement.[82] The British were in a bind over the terms of the treaty they had signed with the late Sultan Sayyid Saʿīd of Muscat, which restricted their role to the development of commerce and lines of communication, the maintenance of peace at sea and to the protection of British Indian subjects. Cooperation over political challenges on land, such as that posed by the Wahhabis, was not on the cards.

Indeed, Thuwayni was always advised by his British friends Pelly and Frere to consolidate his position in the interior so as to fight the Wahhabis over land on his own. Thuwayni was reminded that this was how his father, the late Sultan Sayyid Saʿīd, had handled the issue. Indeed, the reluctance of the British to invest in Thuwayni's land-based disputes that did not pose serious threats to their maritime commerce became the trigger for the beleaguered Thuwayni to strike his roots in tribal society to combat the Wahhabis. Even though Pelly was keen on hearing and extending his cooperation to Thuwayni, the Bombay government disagreed. It wanted Thuwayni to handle the tribal unrest on his own. Governor Elphinstone instructed Col Disbrowe to 'adopt a somewhat indifferent tone to Imam of Muscat'.

Elphinstone used the occasion to critique the Sultan and attributed the Wahhabi-inspired revolt to his failure as a ruler. He invoked his late father and argued that the crisis in the empire could be averted if 'he [Sayyid Thuwayni] imitate the example of his illustrious father, to set his finances in order and conciliate and revive the spirit of his feudatory tribes, to re-organise his military and naval forces and to repel by force, if negotiations fail, the insolent aggression of wahabi neighbours'.[83] And in 1865, the Government of India reiterated that, even if they supplied Thuwayni with arms and ammunitions of war to a moderated extent, they expected him to take effective measures to organize the means of resistance against the Wahhabis. They said, 'The Imam must not entertain the expectation that the government of India is prepared to fight his battles for him.'[84]

Ironically, their reluctance to help Thuwayni deal with the Wahhabis even though they shared his concern and extended moral support earned him many dividends. He dug his heels into tribal society and obtained global visibility by being part of the Wahhabi-centric international conversations with the imperial powers.

Thuwayni's Global Presence: The Wahhabi Attack on Muscat and the British Financial Crisis

The year 1865 was momentous for Thuwayni. It saw the coming together of the entry of the Wahhabis into Muscat and the simultaneous precipitation of the banking financial crisis in Britain. This conjunctional moment offered Thuwayni the perfect global attention he had been waiting for. The Wahhabis destabilized Muscat and added to his financial burden, as commerce was disrupted, and he had to increase his defence budget. But they increased Britain's financial woes as well.

Their disturbances made Muscat unsafe in British eyes. British subjects rethought their financial investments in the city, and many began to flee with their savings. The British avoided the delivery of coal to Muscat, which was economically disastrous, as the port was a key coal depot and refuelling station for British steamships, given that it was on the India route. But in 1866, Pelly did not allow the offloading of 1500 tonnes of coal in Muscat because of its political instability. He directed that coal cargo ships should avoid Muscat until he confirmed that the port was safe for trade. In fact, fearing long-term disturbances, he suggested that the ideal plan would be to have a direct line for coal from Bombay to Basrah, touching only at the ports on the Persian Gulf, which were under British control and peaceful after the maritime truce. He wanted a coal station at Bushire or some other point to the south of the Gulf.[85]

To add to the British and Thuwayni's woes, the Wahhabi disturbances coincided with the economic crisis and panic generated in Britain with the collapse of London's premier bankers, Overend, Gurney & Company. The panic reflected in the run on the bank, with clients withdrawing their money en masse; it only ebbed with the government indicating through legislation that the Bank of England was its bank and had its backing. This panic had a global impact, with merchants refusing to invest and transact with anyone except a government bank. Bombay too was impacted—despite this being a boom time for cotton export in the city, exports were adversely affected consequent to the American Civil War, which disrupted supplies from America. Pelly was worried about the impact of this on the fortunes of Muscat. No cotton was being shipped from Bombay because the merchants were doubtful of everybody unless it was a government bank.[86] Pelly was worried about the severity of the financial crisis in both Bombay as well as London, because of which dividends from the government bank of Bombay were not expected.[87] This financial difficulty was only exacerbated by the loot and plunder of British subjects in Muscat triggered by the Wahhabi unrest. The maritime truce tied his hands and frustrated him to the extent that he wished to be relieved of this 'special career' opportunity in the Gulf and be posted within the Indian frontier.[88]

These developments put the imperial gaze on Thuwayni, their key point of contact, via whom the situation in Muscat could be salvaged. And Thuwayni weighed in, trying to cash in on this moment. In a show of support to the British, he toyed with the idea of blockading the Wahhabi ports, but mostly restricted his interference to the demand for reparation for losses incurred to British subjects.[89] This again brought him in conversation with the imperial powers.

Pelly was asked by his government to negotiate between Thuwayni and the Wahhabis on more helpful terms than in the past. Indeed, the Governor General was sure that he did not want an abrupt withdrawal of Britain from the affairs of Muscat, as that might lead to the entry of the French influence on the Sultan. He was, however, of the view that a native agent be appointed to supply local news so that the extent of British intervention could be regulated, given the changed context.[90] Indeed, the Resident and Consular Agent at Muscat were designated as lines of communication with the Bombay government, and as always, the protection of British subjects in the region was to remain paramount.[91]

The conjunctional moment of crisis that put British subjects at risk made the Bombay government also go soft on Thuwayni. It agreed with Pelly's plan of encouraging and assisting the Sultan in combating the Wahhabis by land and taking hold of their key headquarters at B'ir al-'Ayn. It continued to disapprove of any seaborne help to Thuwayni. This was because any conflict at sea would adversely impact British commerce. The government agreed to aid him by using their influence over the maritime Arabs of the pirate coast and support him in blockading Wahhabi ports in the Persian Gulf. But it disapproved of Pelly's open mediation and his attack on Wahhabi ports using British vessels and officers. The attack in particular on the ports of Hatif and Damam by British vessels, accompanied by a competent officer Mr Pasley, was condemned.[92]

However, the increasing Wahhabi challenge to British commerce made them bend to the Sultan with military assistance. The leaning on Thuwayni to combat the Wahhabis seemed desirable, and yet caution was maintained with an eye on protecting British commerce. In 1866, the Government of India sanctioned the grant of two eighteen-pounder guns and ammunition to the Sultan. But it refused Pelly's request for the loan of 2 lakh rupees to him. They offered to give this loan later if required without interest, but made the customs receipts of Gwadar a guarantee for it. Gwadar was a telegraph station and needed to be protected at all costs.[93]

Thuwayni's friendship with Pelly proved handy. He constantly strove to broker a good deal for him with the British. He encouraged Thuwayni to deal with the Wahhabis on land and promised help even if he was constrained by his government's orders prohibiting any sea combat. Pelly always praised Thuwayni's warrior qualities and persuaded him to undertake land combat, as that was what his government desired so as to protect the hard-earned peace in the

Persian Gulf for their commerce. He turned down Thuwayni's request that the British warships blockade the Wahhabi ports, saying it was difficult to agree to as it would adversely affect British commerce.

Thuwayni prepared to strike a blow at the Wahhabi sea ports. But Pelly urged him to simultaneously strike their headquarters, B'ir al-'Ayn, by land and hoped he would obtain possession of it. Egging him on, he advised him to show his strength and talent, reminding him that 'while kindness and gentleness are admirable in private individuals, yet that in a ruler firmness, boldness, justice and rigour of character are the essentials'. He assured him that these qualities would ensure 'you greater obedience, more respect, and more success than any quality of scattering money'.[94]

Pelly's emphasis on land combat made it even more imperative for Thuwayni to consolidate his hold in the tribal areas. He used his clout in the interior to help Pelly obtain money owed to the British subjects, the Banias, and helped Pelly approach the Arab tribes for its recovery. And thus, even if the Bombay government refused to directly assist him, having Pelly on his side helped him showcase the position of significance he held in the imperial circles. This lent him authority locally and made it easy to strike alliances with a range of Arab tribal chiefs. They were critical for the collection of taxes, revenue and indeed for his political survival.

Pelly too navigated a delicate path, as he balanced his friendship with imperial interests and the restrictions these imposed on him. Pelly was warned not to pull in the government as a third party in any agreement he worked out between Muscat and the Wahhabis. In fact, the government was clear that it did not want any treaty signed with the Wahhabis regarding tribute payment by Muscat or any other matter that involved the British in any way.[95] Pelly was authorized, however, to use his personal office to negotiate a deal between Thuwayni and the Wahhabi Amir, especially with regard to tribute payment. He was also asked for reasons of commercial interest and protection of British property in Muscat to let the Resident return and take charge of the residency there.[96]

Thuwayni's friendship with Pelly went a long way in creating the impression locally that he was engaged in imperial conversations on the Wahhabis. It became key to his visibility in the larger imperial front against the Wahhabis. Pelly continued to help Thuwayni, despite the restraining effects of his government regarding seaborne combat. He often entered into independent negotiations with the Wahhabis on the issue of attacks on the British subjects and kept Thuwayni out of the negotiations to avoid the charge of excessive mediation on behalf of Thuwayni.[97]

In a show of support for Thuwayni, Pelly even offered to approach the Ottoman Sultan to pressure the Wahhabis to stop their attacks on Muscat. This gesture conveyed the message that Thuwayni was very much caught in the politics of the imperial assemblage, whose networks he could tap for his self-interest.

Pelly tapped into the Ottoman connection when, through his interviews with the Wahhabi envoys, he learnt that they considered themselves as subjects of the Ottomans. And Pelly was of the view that the Ottoman Sultan be approached with the request to stop their attacks on Muscat territory.[98] The Government of India clarified that Amir Faisal had remained tributary to Turkish authorities at Mecca. However, his tribute was regarded as an offering to the Ottoman Caliph in his capacity as the global spiritual head of the Muslims. This did not amount to the Wahhabis accepting him as their temporal Sultan. The Ottoman Sultan never exercised any authority or jurisdiction over the Wahhabi country. The government clarified that the Ottoman government was in no position administratively to control and restrain the Wahhabis and their dependants from the piratical practices in violation of international law. It said that if indeed that was the case, it would have been less burdensome for the British government to control them and get into maritime surveillance.[99] Nonetheless, by drawing in the Ottomans into Thuwayni's anti-Wahhabi drives, Pelly firmly placed him as an active participant in the global politics and discussions on the issue.

The death of the Wahhabi Amir Faisal in 1866 and the feuds between his son Abdullah and brother Saud offered an opportunity to Thuwayni to strike at them and defend his Sultanate. Pelly's back-door negotiations with British officials showed results when the British bombarded Wahhabi fortifications on the pirate coast. This destruction of Wahhabi fortifications on the pirate coast and the destruction of their crafts by Captain Pasley encouraged Thuwayni.[100] As Damam and other ports were bombarded by British guns aiming at Wahhabi forts along the coast, Haji Yaqub emerged as the local agent and pilot who assisted Pasley.[101] Even though Damam did not fall, the Wahhabis were certainly checked. The Banī Yās entered into a treaty with the Sultan and were to move from Sohar towards B'ir al-'Ayn. The Janebeh tribe, which had rebelled at Sohar, were adequately punished by Captain Pasley, who bombarded the port.

Not surprisingly, Pelly's proactive role in the Wahhabi woes of Thuwayni and his bombardment of Damam in particular was criticized by the Government of India. So were his efforts to negotiate between Thuwayni and the Wahhabi Amir.[102] In fact, Pelly so disapproved of the Government of India's foreign policy that he even offered to resign, saying that it was a tough choice, as 'it was disappointing for an officer to give up a special career which he has long cherished and in which he hoped that he might ultimately obtain some recognition from his Government'.[103]

VI

Bandar Abbas: The Foothold in Qajar Iran

Thuwayni was equally keen on a foothold in Qajar Iran as marking his presence there was useful in balancing his politics with the Western imperial powers. His father, as we saw in Chapter 1, had maintained a long relationship with Persia with similar intent and held Bandar Abbas on a long-term lease. Thuwayni worked to renew it and keep the Omani control of the port intact. He made many more economic and political investments in the port city than his father.

A foothold in Bandar Abbas was more important to Thuwayni than it had been for his father. It was attractive, as it was his overland gateway to Central Asia and gave him the avenue to dabble militarily with the Arab chiefs of the Gulf. Additionally, it was close to Sohar, where his rebel brother Turki posed a political challenge with his mobilization of the Arab tribes. But most importantly, both the anti-slave trade campaign and the telegraph projects of the British centred on Bandar Abbas. Thuwayni's foothold there was ideal for balancing his politics with imperial interests.

In 1856, the Shah of Iran sent Imam Quli Khan as his ambassador to Thuwayni to offer his condolences on his father's death. Khan also carried presents from the Shah. Thuwayni, quick to cement the cordiality, made him a return present of a horse, 4500 Mahmud-shahi keronis[104], a pair of pistols in a case, a watch and a shawl. He also gifted him three horses: one as a present for the Mushīr al-Mulk and two for the Shahzadahs.[105] These gifts were no idle presents. Qajar Iran, especially its port city Bandar Abbas, had to be an ally in the development of Muscat and in the realization of Thuwayni's imperial dream.

Thuwayni was quick to use this bonhomie to his advantage. In 1863, he appointed Haji Mohammad Bankir as his agent in Bandar Abbas. Bankir was given full powers to renew his contract with the Persian government relative to Bandar Abbas and its dependencies.[106] Once Thuwayni renewed the lease of Bandar Abbas, its administration was handed over to his trusted Vizir Muhammad Alī Kebābī of Minab. He made Kebābī's son, Haji Ahmad Khan, the Deputy Governor of the port city. Later, when the latter succeeded his father as Vizir of Muscat, he was replaced by Shaykh Sayyid, who was made the Governor of Bandar Abbas.[107]

The results of Thuwayni's interest in Bandar Abbas were soon evident. Until the early nineteenth century, Bushire rather than Bandar Abbas remained the chief port of call in the Gulf. But this began to change in favour of Bandar Abbas. Thuwayni got increasingly involved in the British political and commercial interest in the region. He exploited to his advantage the Anglo-Persian tensions over the fear of Russians entering the Gulf. This became his means to insert himself into the imperial drawing board. He entered into an agreement with the British for the service of mail steamers (1864) that passed through Bandar Abbas en route to Muscat; he also signed up with them for the expansion of the telegraph line across Makran and Muscat.

These agreements adversely impacted Bushire. The telegraph line made it lose its significance as the collection centre of news. And the movement of the steamship in the riverine traffic of Iran increased the significance of Bandar Abbas as a trading port, soon making it the entry point of arms and goods from Europe. Moreover, its shallow waters and the practice of using small boats to ferry goods to the harbour made it a perfect port for the illegal clandestine arms trade to India avoiding Muscat, where the British controls were excessive. This trade flourished as it suited all the involved parties: the British, Europeans, Arabs and Indians.

Thuwayni and the Perso-British Rivalries

Thuwayni's control of Bandar Abbas was ideal for balancing his politics with imperial interests. The British viewed the Persian Gulf as the critical conduit for maintaining their Indian empire. Not just arms and equipment, but cotton and indigo also passed through its waters to Europe. It was equally important for maintaining communication between India and Britain. It was on the route for British Indian steamships that carried subsidized mail from India to the Persian Gulf. Many private steamers operated on this high-priority route, which was under constant vigilance for fear of both Persian and Russian threats. And by the 1860s, the heavy-investment telegraph line was being laid along its coastline.

The British were convinced that Thuwayni was ideal for checking the politically expansionist Persia that was often the obstacle in the smooth flow of imperial projects: the telegraph, the mail service steamships and commerce. Thuwayni could also help dilute for them the Russian threat through his foothold in Persia. Thuwayni was quick to cash in on the Perso-British rivalries to his advantage.

Thuwayni kept the British in the loop of Persia's political expansion: its military operation in Bahrain; its purchase of four warships from Europe to defend her coastline from Bandar Abbas to Jashk, which included the islands of Ormuz and Qishm; and its encroachment into Central Asia gnawing into the territories of the Baluchi chiefs such as Nusserabad, Candahar, Kedge—the capital of the Khan of Khelat's Makran territories.[108]

Thuwayni's warnings were confirmed by newsletters from Makran, which informed the British about Persian military build-up and expansion in the region. He played the perfect intermediary in the Anglo-Persian relations, keeping the British on tenterhooks by his commitment to assist Persia with his navy, as per the lease, in the defence of its coastline. He also allowed the passage of Persian troops through Bandar Abbas towards Makran, Baluchistan and even Kutch.

The British scared him with 'reliable' information about a Persian offensive in Bandar Abbas and Herat to oust him and decentre British projects in the region. The news was of concern also because it suggested Russian help to Persia.[109] News from merchants in Sindh indicated that Persians were entering into western Baluchistan via the east coast of Makran, where the telegraph cable was being laid. They needed to be stopped at Herat. The Sindh Commissioner regretted that the British were not proactive in its affairs so that the Persian takeover could be averted.[110] He regretted this more, as the natives of Sindh looked to the British for help. They attached a lot of significance to Bandar Abbas as the gateway to the world of trade and opportunities.

James Outram was dispatched to Bushire to figure out the political and commercial implications of Persia's Bandar Abbas expansion and its impact on British interests.[111] Thuwayni's constant inputs from the ground put the British in a quandary over Persia's expansion. They increasingly viewed Thuwayni as the counterpoise to this aggression—he was someone whose help was paramount in particular in the laying of the telegraph line that stretched across the Persian coastline.

Thuwayni and the Telegraph Politics at Bandar Abbas

The telegraph line that stretched from Bandar Abbas to Basra, Baghdad and Karachi moved along the Persian Gulf coast, making communication to British India easy. Its critical importance in handling Britain's Indian empire made it imperative that it be protected along its long route that passed through much of the territory controlled by Thuwayni.

However, the British stepped into the domain of contested jurisdictions and sovereignties between Persia and Oman at Bandar Abbas, the point of origin of the cable line. They deftly handled the contestations with an eye to further their own interests. If it suited their interests, they happily drew in the interior Baluchi chieftains as mediators in these Perso-Omani conflicts.

Thuwayni was no unsuspecting victim either. He benefited the most from the telegraph line-driven imperial politics. He rooted himself firmly at Bandar Abbas and dealt with the contested nature of his sovereignty and jurisdiction, which stretched from the port along the Makran coast and spilt into its dependencies Angaun and Larrack. He milked to his benefit the British overtures to him as well as to Persia and to the Baluchi chiefs to facilitate the laying of the telegraph line.[112]

Thuwayni, the Baluchi Chiefs and the Telegraph

The British used the Baluchi chiefs to assist in the telegraph project. The chiefs traditionally held the land along the Persian Gulf and nurtured aspirations for independence even if they were subordinated to either Muscat or Persia. They were well acquainted with the social and political conditions of the intermediate countries and were the best source of information about possible political alliances that enabled the expansion of the telegraph line.

The British used them as mediators between Muscat and Persia to open up land for the telegraph line. The British leaning on the chiefs benefited Thuwayni, as many of them were subordinated to him. But more importantly, many of the ports that lay on the route of the telegraph were firmly under his control. This entangled him in the telegraph-driven imperial politics in the region.

The British tapped into the Baluchi chiefs located along the Persian coast as well to soften the ground for the telegraph line.

This was specifically important for the line that was to stretch between Karachi and Bandar Abbas.[113] Traditionally, these chiefs swayed in allegiance between Thuwayni and Persia. Thuwayni used the telegraph line to instigate them against Persia. Indeed, British efforts to draw them into the telegraph project gave Thuwayni the opportunity to use them as the site to define his political sovereignty.

The Baluchi chiefs, such as Meer Abdullah bin Murad Muhammad, who were powerful and had become tributaries of Persia twelve years back, were tapped into by the British for support. They indicated their willingness and capability to protect the telegraph line, seeing in it a means to assert their independent power and resist the sovereignty of the Persian Shah.[114] Thuwayni encouraged this sentiment.

The British considered it important to lean on independent chiefs of less influence as well. The close-by small town of Gwetur, which belonged to Deen Muhammad, a petty independent chief of the Zidgal tribe, and the neighbouring coast under the Baluchi chief, Lalla Midyan, was viewed as a poor area. A small subsidy could be used to obtain the trust and support needed for the protection of the telegraph line. Clipping Persia's wings even at the cost of consolidating the political sovereign status of Thuwayni in the Gulf was essential at a time when it was aggressively expanding towards Makran and Baluchistan.

The British considered Thuwayni as their ally in the telegraph project. The ports he held were viewed as safe havens for the installation of the telegraph. Political Agents at Muscat, such as H. Disbrowe, often warned the Resident at the Persian Gulf to guard against Vizirs of the Sultan, such as Haji Ahmad, while laying out the telegraph project.[115]

But these fears notwithstanding, the dependence of the British on the support of Thuwayni for the telegraph line was of great use and value to him. It went in his favour in the ongoing contest with Persia about the nature of his sovereignty and jurisdiction in Bandar Abbas and its neighbourhood. It ensured that his interests remained protected and the contestations between him and Persia were resolved in his favour.

The territory between Bandar Abbas and Sudrej—a place on the coast about 60 miles east of the small town of Jashk—was chosen for the telegraph line. This was under Thuwayni's jurisdiction. He had obtained it from Persia in 1856 as part of the treaty signed by his father Sayyid Sa'īd at the time of the renewal of the lease of Bandar Abbas. Meer Hussain, the Governor of Jashk, saw the inhabitants as peaceful and quiet and saw no difficulty in establishing the telegraph line, provided Thuwayni undertook to protect it and the Persian government sanctioned the enterprise. The land, particularly between Jashk and Bandar Abbas, was well cultivated and afforded extensive pasturage ground for the numerous flocks kept by the Baluchis.

Thuwayni used the British zeal for the telegraph line to push the boundaries of his sovereignty outside the port of Bandar Abbas and lay his claim to areas contested by Persia. He reassured the British of his wide ambit of sovereignty each time they feared that, despite his best intentions, he would not be able to grant them an absolute permission for the electric telegraph between Bandar Abbas and Sudrej. Thuwayni reiterated that the Persian Shah had no right to interfere with any concessions that he may make within the limits of his contract or farming of Bandar Abbas.[116] He urged the British government to carry on with their plans. But his enthusiasm brought under scrutiny the terms of the treaty under which he held Bandar Abbas. Persia claimed that the treaty clearly stated that the coastline around Bandar Abbas was under Persian sovereignty and Persia had banned Muscat from allowing any foreign government to set up any base there.

Nonetheless, the British felt safe leaving the telegraph line in the protection of Thuwayni. He of course saw it as God-sent in the materialization of his political aspirations. Several of his ports were preferred sites for the cable line. Chabahār, a small town on the coast, under his jurisdiction, was chosen as a safe site for the telegraph. Again, the port of Gwadel was also seen as secure for similar reasons. It traditionally belonged to the Khan of Khelat, a Baluchi chief, whose ancestors had given it to Muscat after supporting Sayyid Sa'īd in his accession to the throne on condition that they would always defend it against the enemies of Khelat.

Needless to add, Thuwayni's claim over the area was contested by the Khan. But he refrained from attacking or openly defying him because his Baluchi followers favoured Thuwayni for levying no tax on them and building a wall around Gwadel for their protection against his attacks.[117] The safest stretch for the telegraph of course was between Bushire and Bandar Abbas. This was uncontested Persian territory, with what the British saw as a 'civilized population engaged in trade' and not an area of contested sovereignties.

The entanglement of Thuwayni in the telegraph politics to further his political aspirations continued to face challenges from Persia. In 1866, the port of Gwadar, on the Makran coast, was chosen as a safe haven to set up a big telegraph station after Thuwayni claimed it as his territory. But soon after the line was laid, a Persian prince with his rabble-rousers arrived at Bandar Abbas and threatened an attack by 3000 men if the plan went ahead. He asserted that Thuwayni had no right over Gwadar and could not give permission for any kind of construction. The Sindh Commissioner had to send a police force to support Thuwayni. The latter had signed a convention to protect the British telegraph line and stations passing through his territory. This was now being questioned in Gwadar. The British were in a quandary—if they did go by the convention, then they had to protect Thuwayni as well from Persian high-handedness.[118]

Bandar Abbas and Thuwayni's Political Economy

By the time Thuwayni became Sultan of Muscat (1857), a considerable portion of the Indian trade had already been diverted to Bandar Abbas, where customs duties were low and the roads were considered safe.[119] Thuwayni further encouraged this economic diversion. In 1864, Lt Pelly was of the view that Bandar Abbas was at the most favourable commercial position. Its trade had considerably increased in the last two or three years. He attributed its prosperity to the administrative and commercial acumen of the Sultan's Arab Shaykh, who was the Deputy Governor at Bandar Abbas. He thought he was an 'intelligent man, favorable to commercial interests'. Pelly felt that even though the Arabs were in 'civilization inferior to Persians', they were preferred by foreigners as 'protectors and encouragers of trade'.[120]

The port was also thriving because the Sultan had worked out a foolproof system of revenue collection. He had the port on contract for 16,000 tomans. But he in turn sublet the revenue and customs to a British Indian subject of the Khoja caste for 25,000 tomans a year, plus the expenses of administration, which amounted to another 4000 tomans. The revenue from dates collected at Minao amounted to 16,000 tomans, which he paid to the Shah. And the remaining 13,000 tomans plus profits of the contractor were covered by the customs.[121]

Thuwayni levied 5 per cent duty on all goods that passed through the port, out of which 1.5 per cent went to the Yezd authorities and 3.5 per cent to the Sultan. The British Indian merchants at Bandar Abbas were few: sixty Khojas, thirty to forty Shikarpuri Banias and four or five Kutch Bhatias. They were all *gomashtas* or agents of Sindh or Bombay firms. They always complained of corruption of the Governors and local officials in the interior of Persia. The corrupt officials made it difficult for them to get goods, such as cotton, safely from the interior of Persia to Bandar Abbas. The Kirman Governor refused to have goods passed unless merchants consented to his taking away half of them at prices they had advanced to the producers. They complained that this practice deprived them of profits. British Indian merchants avoided the interior because of these difficulties and restricted themselves to Bandar Abbas itself or at the most to Yezd and Kerman, where they had commissioning agents. Hardly any trade was done between Bandar Abbas and Shiraz, or between them and Persian subjects in Tehran or Isphahan.[122]

Thuwayni benefited also from the fact that the Government of India was very keen on the continued prosperity of the port. It was on the route for British Indian steamships that carried subsidized mail from India to the Persian Gulf. Many of these private shipping enterprises that had been given permission to operate between India and the Persian Gulf for mail diversified to carrying cargo and pilgrims, thereby increasing the port's significance. Many paired with partners to get into the export and import trade between India, the Persian Gulf and Britain. Imports from Britain were mainly cotton piece goods and rifles, and from India indigo, rice, tea, copper and iron.[123]

British private enterprise—the British Indian steamer companies—operated in the Persian Gulf with a view to both profits as well as establishing British political influence in the Persian Gulf. Henry Bartle Frere, Governor of Bombay (1862–67) had got permission to subsidize mail service into the Gulf and given contract to the British India Steamship Company Gray Mackenzie and its partner Grey Paul Ltd. They operated from the Persian ports of Lingah, Bushire and Bandar Abbas, importing primarily rifles, guns, arms and cotton piece goods into these ports. Imported guns and arms smuggled into Bushire and Bandar Abbas circulated along the Persian Gulf via these private British Indian companies. Persian companies in the arms trade were warned by the British to stop such traffic.

These were empty threats, as they worked in close collaboration with British Indian companies to supply arms illegally to British enemies. Thus, a Persian-Armenian company, A. & T.S. Malcolm, worked closely at Bushire with the British Grey Paul Co. even as it supplied imported British arms to its enemies. It was reported that 3,00,000 rifles landed in Bushire, for which the local Governor received a 10 per cent commission.[124] Bandar Abbas too was at the centre of the gun import trade from Britain and Europe. It was also the centre for the export of Persian opium to Britain and Hong Kong.[125]

A clandestine slave trade also operated alongside from Bandar Abbas and oiled Thuwayni's commercial wheels. From the time of Sayyid Sa'īd, Bandar Abbas and Qishm, both under the control of Muscat, were entrepôt for slaves from East Africa. This was despite the royal orders against the traffic that the Sultan had agreed to abide by.[126] Thuwayni, who was then in charge of Muscat affairs and the overseer of Bandar Abbas, was witness to the slave traffic at these ports.

Female Abyssinian slaves in substantial groups of twenty to thirty were arriving in Lingah, Bandar Abbas and Charrack from Zanzibar and elsewhere. The British were extremely keen on having the right to search and detain Persian vessels engaged in the slave trade. Indeed, their intervention was much desired by native agents posted at Lingah.[127] This was because the people of Lingah owned vessels that brought slaves from the east coast of Africa to their port as well as to Bandar Abbas. For instance, the bugla of Mohammad Sālih al-Konghī (of Congo) brought up to twenty slaves. Similarly the bugla belonging to Barūk bin Mullāh Husayn, commanded by Ibrāhīm bin Husayn Alī, both inhabitants of Lingah, brought twenty Abyssinian slaves from Berbera. Half of these landed at Bandar Abbas for sale and under the charge of a person deputed for this job. The rest were sent to Lingah. Similarly, the bugla belonging to Ahmad Hussain Kasweni, commanded by Muhammad bin Ahmad, landed thirteen slaves in Bandar Abbas and Qishm, and brought fourteen more to Lingah.[128] In another instance, the bugla of Muhammad bin Khamīs Nākhodā and that of Nākhodā Hussain carried slaves. Part of the cargo was sold at Bandar Abbas and Qishm, and the rest were taken to Lingah.[129] Thuwayni also reported that of the six Abyssinian and African slaves sold at Qishm, one male was purchased by the mother of Shaykh Sagar at Ra's al-Khaimah and one female by the wife of Muhammad Abdullah. They were imported into Qishm in the vessel of Yusuf Murad of Lingah. The remaining slaves were taken to Bandar Abbas in Sagar's boat.[130] Indian children were being imported into Shiraz in Persia by Persian subjects. And the local Governor was told by Fars authorities to report the matter to the British agent there for further inquiries.[131]

Thuwayni always extended support to the British against piracy or slave trade with an eye on profits for himself. He was always quick to respond to any transgressions by his subjects in Bandar Abbas or elsewhere that agitated the British. In 1860, when the Shaykh of the port of Khoomzar (virtually independent, though in name under the Imam of Muscat) was accused of piratical acts in carrying away six men from the port of Shaam (a port under the precarious hold of Shaykh Sultan bin Sagar), he not only dispatched his warship *Curlew* to Bandar Abbas with instructions to the chief of that port to punish the Shaykh of Khoomzar, but also ordered him to listen to the advice of the Resident and act accordingly for the release of the men.[132]

His strategy was to liaise with local officers rather than get orders from Bushire by the Political Resident at the Persian Gulf. Clearly, beneath the surface anti-slave trade rhetoric, what prevailed were private British interests. And Thuwayni had his fingers dipped in these with collaborations at the local level.

The same strategy worked in his dealings with the Persians. Much of the slave traffic around Bandar Abbas was carried on with Persian support. The Arab traffickers needed Persian help, as the latter's ships were exempted from seizure and search for slaves. As a result, Arab chiefs carried on slave traffic on ships flying Persian flags. An Arab from Cazblah called Sayyid al Humud hired a bugla from Ibrahim bin Hussain, an inhabitant of Nego on the Persian coast. This vessel brought up a cargo of male and female slaves from Zanzibar, who were landed partly in the Arabian coast and partly in the former port.[133]

Thuwayni benefited from this trade and cashed in on the fact that Britain was weary of clamping down on Persia, as it needed it as an ally in its anti-slave campaign; Persia was also dealt with cautiously because of the fear that the Russians could use it as their conduit into the Gulf. Persia, fully aware of this predicament, was flexing its political ambitions and expanding into Central Asia and the Persian coastline.

The Indian Merchants at Bandar Abbas: Thuwayni's Leveraging with Imperial Powers

Thuwayni's investments in Bandar Abbas transformed the port town. In 1866, Lt Pelly, Resident at Bushire, described Bandar Abbas as a 'walled township with suburbs along an open sea beach, back grounded by a range of lofty and apparently desolate mountains'.[134] He reported on the increased prosperity of the Persian Gulf in general. He of course attributed this to the maritime peace, steamship communication, good prices and sale of cotton and the comforts that the peasantry could import as a result of the profits of cotton. But he also made a special observation on Bandar Abbas that he felt had 'principally thriven'.[135] This he did not attribute only to the British effort to maintain peace in the Gulf. Rather, he underlined the participation of a range of Indian merchants active in the port: Khojas, Multanis and Banias.

These British Indian merchants flourished under Thuwayni's patronage. They carried out their lucrative businesses secure in the friendship that Thuwayni had struck with Pelly. More than their economic importance, they were valuable as his political capital, as he used them to create a niche for himself in the imperial assemblage. He used them and the British fear of their exodus from the port to bargain hard in the assemblage.

His modus operandi was most evident when, in 1866, the Bandar Abbas lease was abruptly truncated by Persia and was put up for renewal on more stringent terms. The lease had been renewed in 1856 for a period of twenty years at the rate of 16,000 tomans per annum to Iran. But after the first ten years, the Persian authorities seemed to pretend that it was only for ten years and wanted the port vacated by the Arabs or else have the lease renewed on terms more favourable to them. They warned that if this was not complied with, they would lease it to another contractor. The Governor of Kerman was the likely contender, as he had offered 6,00,000 tomans instead of the 16,000 paid by Thuwayni. The Governor of Fars, viewed as an able administrator by Europeans, had deputed a Persian prince to sort out these matters with the Arab Shaykh.

Pelly was worried that in the event of the issue escalating to a war situation, the British Indian traders in Bandar Abbas would flee the port and probably never return if it came under the administration of Iran.[136] Thuwayni took advantage of these fears. The Indian merchants became his bargaining counter with Persia. Pelly took up Thuwayni's cause because of his interest in the continued residence of the merchants at Bandar Abbas.

Pelly created a hype about the port's prosperity being under threat as the British Indian subjects there lived in terror of Persian invasion. He pointed out that they were removing their treasure to the island of Qishm and were thinking of moving away. Khoja merchants at Bandar Abbas, such as Ibrahim Lalji, asked for British protection as rumours floated of an attack by the Kerman Governor, who was reported to be arriving with 700 military men. The Governor had seventeen charges against the Sultan and was reported to have sent an ambassador to Muscat asking him to pay a fine of 2,50,000 qiran or evacuate Bandar Abbas. Rumour had it that if Thuwayni did not concede, there would be a war. Multani merchants were also sending their treasure to the safe custody of Qishm. They had held a meeting at the town and come to this decision.[137] This was true of all other merchants, as reported by the Bania Nabandas from Bandar Abbas.[138]

The situation in Bandar Abbas was so unsettling for the British subjects that Pelly feared that, if the Persians continued to hold it, their treasury too would suffer.[139] Indeed, tensions were so ripe that the Arab Shaykh of Bandar Abbas, a man who had always fostered trade, returned to Muscat. But the weight of the British behind Thuwayni made Persia blink. The Arab Shaykh received a communication from a Persian authority asking him to return immediately to solve some matters in dispute between Arabs and Persians. The Shaykh agreed to return but bring with him a vessel of war from the Sultan as a contingency measure.

Indeed, the British Indian merchants offered the perfect forum for Thuwayni to negotiate the imperial rivalries and burrow his way through the imperial assemblage. The protection of the telegraph line that ran from Bandar Abbas to Karachi softened the British towards Thuwayni. With a compliant Thuwayni, they established their Consulate in the port town and felt entitled to certain legal rights over the British subjects who came there for redress. Bandar Abbas became the site of jurisdictional contests between Britain and Persia as the merchants petitioned for redress.

Thuwayni watched, waiting to make the right move for digging his heels into the imperial assemblage, which was riveted with tensions. It was in his interest to have a weakened Persia if Bandar Abbas was to become a permanent acquisition— the quintessential Omani port. He was not disappointed, as it was imperative for the British to plead Thuwayni's case, as too much was at stake at Bandar Abbas and the Persian coast that he controlled: the telegraph line, coal depots and the investments of the British Indian merchants.

Pelly underlined his commitment to Thuwayni and lamented that the Sultan had been treated harshly by Persia, which had restored him in Bandar Abbas on stricter terms of an annual subsidy and the hoisting of the Persian flag. Urging the government to step in for Thuwayni, he wanted to know if they should reconsider their arrangements with Muscat and not have an independent free port in an insular position where 'we may concentrate our merchants, coal and telegraphic stations'.[140]

The Indian merchants at other Persian ports too took advantage of these imperial conflicts. In 1866, they petitioned to Pelly that they were being subject to huge exactions by the tax farmer of the port of Lingah. They threatened to leave if the situation did not improve for them.[141]

Haji Ahmad Khan, the Persian-origin Arab in Bandar Abbas

The long Muscat presence in Bandar Abbas as its revenue farmer ensured that its Arab Governors and revenue contractors struck local roots in society. These Arabs created a sub-political culture, as they were rooted deep in Bandar Abbas society. Their long histories as influential Arabs in a Persian port city outlived the vicissitudes of lease politics. Very often, Muscat had to intervene to clip the wings of its officials in Bandar Abbas to secure its own interests. And needless to add, Persia left no opportunity to get itself the best deal from the port revenues, taking advantage of such friction.

The life of Haji Ahmad Khan, the Omani Arab Governor at the port, is a case in point of the careering opportunities that Bandar Abbas offered to Arab entrepreneurs. Haji Ahmad was born in Minab, which is an agriculturally fertile Persian fishing city, located between Makran and Bandar Abbas. He was Persian by birth, although his father had migrated to Oman and the family were very much part of the Arab elite of Oman. Both he and his father had been the Vizirs with the Omani rulers Sayyid Saʻīd and Thuwayni. They were sent to Bandar Abbas as Governors. His Arab profile and Persian origins became an asset as he slipped seamlessly across the imperial assemblage, invoking his multiple identities to his benefit.

As the Vizir of Thuwayni, Haji Ahmad had bought considerable landed property in Bandar Abbas. The tales of his corruption were legendary in the Persian Gulf. In the summer heat of 1864, when there was the routine exodus of the Sultan as well as a range of Persian, Arab and Baluchi elites to the cooler climes of Burka on the Al Batinah, there was a rumour that Haji Ahmad, along with his possessions, wives and family too migrated to Meenao near Bandar Abbas. And in his case, this was not just a summer stint, but for good, though he left his houses behind. The heat was on Haji Ahmad, as the $35,000 subsidy he received from Zanzibar went missing. Since he received the money on behalf of the Sultan, he was held accountable. He confessed on interrogation that he had spent the money. Thuwayni was incensed and stopped the practice of Haji Ahmad receiving any future money on his behalf. Disbrowe, the Political Agent at Muscat, feared that the 'ease loving' Thuwayni may find it difficult to get a replacement for him. More importantly, being of Persian origin, Haji Ahmad could use his influence, once located at Meenao, to create trouble for the Sultan on the Persian coast.[142]

In 1864, Thuwayni was upset, as he could not account for 40,000 German Crowns that pertained to his exchequer and had been entrusted to Haji Ahmad. Haji Ahmad was removed from the Vizarat, and he relocated at Meenao, close to Bandar Abbas. But he connected with the Shiraz authorities and created trouble, as a result of which he was reinstated as Vizir by Thuwayni. Such was the fear of his clout to create disorder on the Persian coast.[143]

By 1866, Haji Ahmad was so entrenched in the port society that he embarked on an independent career when the lease was ended, and he lost his clout following the murder of his mentor Thuwayni. He enjoyed British protection and, much to their chagrin, he was reported to have seized vessels of a Muscat subject, carrying 700 bags of dates, causing alarm.[144] The vessel belonged to Nākhodā

Muhammad bin Ahmad and was valued at $800.[145] Haji Muhammad was threatened by the Muscat authorities of confiscation of his property if he did not return the vessel.[146]

The Persians kept him busy in the business of bidding for the revenue of Bandar Abbas as an independent contractor. This marked the beginning of his career independent of Omani court politics. The Persians encouraged competition among such Arab privateers to get them hungry for wealth and power independent of Muscat. Haji Ahmad too was asked to outbid Shaykh Sa'īd, the Arab Governor of Bandar Abbas, who was sent by Thuwayni's son and successor Sultan Sayyid Salim to renegotiate the lease.

Thus in 1866, when Shaykh Sa'īd, the Arab Governor of Bandar Abbas, came to Shiraz to renew his lease, the Persian authorities asked the ousted Vizir of Muscat, Haji Ahmad, to outbid him. Both Shaykh Sa'īd and Haji Ahmad had grown roots in Bandar Abbas in the course of their postings and were keen to continue their profitable careers in the area, unmindful of the political change in Muscat.

Fearing competition on the arrival of Haji Ahmad, Shaykh Sa'īd made a present of 14,000 tomans to the Mushīr al-Mulk Mulk Mirza Muhammad Ali Khan and also paid him one-third of the revenue of Bandar Abbas. This prevented Haji Ahmad from carrying forward his plans. But Haji Ahmad was not in the mood of going back empty-handed. He thus made a present of 5000 tomans and farmed the port of Lingah. This did not please Shaykh Sa'īd, who felt that he had paid 14,000 tomans and one-third of the revenue of Bandar Abbas for nothing; two-thirds were yet to be paid. He therefore refused to pay the balance to Persia.

The Shah of Persia was incensed and wondered why Mushīr al-Mulk had given the province to someone who could not pay the money to the government. He sent the Prince Governor of Fars to Bandar Abbas to recover the revenue. And even as the aspirations and competition between these two Arab officials for the revenue farming of Bandar Abbas were being used by the Persian government to get the best deal for itself, a dramatic turn of events in Muscat spoilt the show for both the Arab contenders. Sayyid Salim, who became the ruler of Muscat after allegedly murdering Thuwayni, reappointed Haji Ahmad as Vizir and, on his request, summoned Shaykh Saʿīd to Muscat to quiz him about the independent deals he had attempted to strike with Persia.[147]

Shaykh Saʿīd was removed from the Governorship of Bandar Abbas. But this did not stop him from meddling in the revenue farming politics of the region. He got the lease renewed at 20,000 tomans instead of 16,000 tomans in his personal capacity as a direct dependant of Persia. He underplayed his identity as the representative of Muscat. This was at about the same time when the port of Lingah was leased to Haji Ahmad in his personal capacity as a dependant of Persia.[148] He continued with this assignment even after he was reappointed Vizir in Muscat by Sayyid Salim. The latter was so involved in stabilizing his rule that he did not pay attention to the Persian side of his former dependencies. But Shaykh Saʿīd proved to be not a very submissive lessee. He rejected demands for the balance tribute, and the Governor of Fars had to march to Bandar Abbas to coerce him to pay.

The British role as mediators and maintainers of the maritime truce was clearly threatened with the Persian effort to strike independent private deals with Muscat Arabs. Such Arabs, like Shaykh Saʿīd and Haji Ahmad, became very important entities in the region. Lt Col Pelly, the Resident in the Persian Gulf, resented this indirect control of Bandar Abbas by Persia via Omani Arab privateers. He was of the view that it was detrimental to British trade and commitment to peace on the coast, as it would result in Arabs descending there for making fortunes, create instability and result in loss of revenue for Persia as well.

The Persian effort to create and work with Arab privateers was so intense that once, when Pelly persuaded the Omani minister to accompany him to Shiraz as his guest, the hosts zeroed in on him. The Persians remained focused on the possibility of striking an independent deal with the Muscat minister. In their effort to prop him as their Arab contact who they could wean away, they agreed to renew the lease to Sayyid Salim on condition that only the said minister be appointed Governor of Bandar Abbas.[149]

Thus in 1868, when a Muscat minister arrived in Bandar Abbas as an emissary of Sayyid Salim to renew the lease of the port, he was categorically told that this could not be done. Significantly, he was offered the lease of these districts in his personal capacity on condition of his settling in Bandar Abbas with his family and declaring himself to be a Persian subject.[150] The minister was due to travel with Pelly to meet the Prince Governor of Shiraz to negotiate on behalf of his Sultan. But when it was clear that the Shiraz Governor wanted him to come alone and negotiate for himself in his private capacity, he was non-committal and threatened to return to Muscat, leaving the message that Sayyid Salim was keen to blockade the port if the lease was not renewed.[151]

The minister lamented that in the past too his trips to Tehran and Shiraz had been in vain and he feared that he had 'sacrificed the Sultan's opportunity to idle negotiations'.[152] He was convinced that, as the winter approached, the Persians would reinforce Bandar Abbas. And he was surprised that this interest in the port was new, as all these years it had neither Persian troops, nor a single gun afloat to defend her coast or islands.

Clearly, by the end of the nineteenth century, Omani Arabs loomed large in their individual capacity as influential and wealthy privateers in Bandar Abbas. They came in all colours: able sought-after revenue contractors, wealthy entrepreneurs, influential notables and interlocutors between Britain, Oman and Persia. They had made spectacular careers straddling the imperial assemblage that framed Bandar Abbas.

Not surprisingly, their entrenchment was a source of concern to the Omani Sultans. Sayyid Salim's naval demonstration along the coast of Bandar Abbas to put pressure on the Shah and thus divert to him for talks rather than rely on private Arab individuals was revealing. It made the Persian government consider taking over the direct management of Bandar Abbas. They wished to make a nephew of the Governor of Fars the Governor of Bandar Abbas. But they were very keen on British help, which they considered critical in keeping Bandar Abbas in their own hands.[153]

VII

Muscat Post Thuwayni

After the mysterious death of Thuwayni and the installation of Salim as the new Sultan, the city was taken over by the Wahhabis. Significantly, the Wahhabi hotspots of Muttrah, Rustaq and Nakhil, which Thuwayni had successfully tamed, were energized again by the influx of the Wahhabis, whom Salim welcomed. A Mullah named Gariber, who was from Suwayq and was held to be the highest spiritual authority in the territories, entered Muscat. He left a following of some 800 mullahs and others a mile or so outside Muttrah. Simultaneously, the chief of Rustaq, who had been rebelling against Thuwayni for more than a year and was connected closely to Salim by marriage, appeared on the scene with a strong following. Another mullah called Khaleelu was already in Muscat and was being advised by Salim's relatives to 'fanatical and ultra measure'.[154]

The British recognized Salim as Thuwayni's successor. Thuwayni's terrified family, consisting of some thirty-nine people, including ladies, children and slaves, left for Zanzibar. Thuwayni's son Sayyid Muhammad had been invited to relocate to the island by Sayyid Majid. Muhammad waited for the invite to be extended to the entire family. Eventually he left for Zanzibar with all family members. Atchinson, the Political Agent at Muscat, emphasized that they left on their own accord without any force or coercion on his part and that the parties in power had been 'kind and courteous' throughout with the family.[155]

Thuwayni's murder and the family's exodus made the future of Bandar Abbas uncertain. It triggered panic in the British Indian subjects in Muscat. Many had trade investments in the Persian port. But they began to flee to the Persian port of Gwadar across the Gulf of Oman. The British did not want any move by which the Bandar Abbas lease would be terminated and Sayyid Salim left vulnerable. A financially stable Muscat was in their interest, both from the security point of view as well as from the commerce angle.

In fact, this was the reason why they recognized Sayyid Salim as the de facto ruler of Muscat and were clear that if they so dealt with him, they would have the right to exact from him a strict adherence to the engagements of the Muscat state with them.[156] They agreed to the fact that the significance of Persia was only because of its relevance to the Indian empire. They felt that this was the only reason on which the annual payment for the Persian mission from the Indian revenues could be justified.[157]

The Wahhabi incursion loosened the foothold in Persia that Thuwayni had carefully cultivated. But unlike the British, the Persians were reluctant to recognize Salim. Although they did deal with him as the head of Muscat, they were reluctant to renew the lease of Bandar Abbas to him. The issue of the renewal of the lease of Bandar Abbas became a moot point after the murder. The treaty with Sayyid Sa'īd limited the renewal of the lease only to the sons of the Sayyid and not his grandsons. The engagement provided that it would not be binding on the Shah of Persia should a usurper at any time obtain possession of Muscat.

The Persians saw Salim as a defaulter. There was no doubt that Salim was in financial distress. He was reported to have sold one of the four ships that Thuwayni possessed, the *Prince of Wales*, for $8000 to Haji Ahmad. Soon Haji Ahmad sold it to a Bania called Bhimji Gopaldas.[158]

It was widely believed that Salim was financially dependent on the Zanzibar subsidy for payments to Persia. So, the Persian Governor terminated the lease of Bandar Abbas on non-payment of the rent. The Persian government feared that Salim, emboldened after his recognition from the British government, might begin retaliatory raids on the Persian Gulf as he had already threatened to block the port of Bandar Abbas. All this would be detrimental to commerce, and the Shah wanted to place some ships of war made and commanded by British officers in the Gulf. He agreed to pay for them in instalments from his treasury.[159]

The Persians refused renewal to Salim on the grounds that the terms of the treaty were valid only for Sayyid Sa'īd and his sons. They used the treaty renewal to bargain with him on the revenues from

the port: the revenues of Bandar Abbas had risen to 60,000 tomans
and that he was willing to increase payment from 16,000 to 25,000
tomans only. This was inclusive of all demands, such as douceurs
and irregular payments to Persian officials. Further, renewal would
exclude the islands of Angaun and Larrack, which Salim said were
his and not included in the original lease.

The matter got further complicated when the Muscat agent in
Persia used threatening language and indirectly raised questions
about the sovereignty of Angaun, triggering suspicion in Persian
circuits. The British wanted to avoid conflict in the region. While
they reiterated that they were in favour of the renewal of the lease,
they recognized the authority of Persia in Angaun and the entire
territory covered in the lease.[160] Salim threatened to blockade
Bandar Abbas if the lease were not renewed.

Pelly was not against the blockade of the port by the Sultan, but
he and the Government of India were against any hostile operations
against Persia. He was asked to mediate and prevent a collision for
the interest of British commerce. He was asked to make the Sultan
agree to British mediation.[161]

Finally, with his intervention, the lease was renewed for seven
years at 25,000 tomans.[162] The Sultan was not willing to include in
it the islands of Angaun and Larrack, as he said they were part of
his hereditary possessions and never part of Persia and thus not in
the original lease.[163] And he had the support of the Resident of the
Persian Gulf in this claim over these islands.[164] The conditions of
the lease were that it was restricted to Salim and his descendants.
Article 12 provided that if any conqueror took possession of Oman
and Muscat, then the Persian government would not be bound by
any of these conditions in regard to that conqueror.[165]

4

Sayyid Turki: The Sultan in the Age of the Nation State

The Argument

The politically tumultuous period at Muscat after the death of Thuwayni was lifted with the installation of his rival brother Sayyid Turki as Sultan. Turki had a brief stint as Sultan from 1871–88. Unlike his brothers Majid and Thuwayni, he faced the challenge of maintaining the Sultanate in the age of the nation state. This made him refurbish his monarchy in sync with the political practices of his time even as he dug his heels into the tribal interiors to strengthen his traditional roots.

He strove to create a 'modern monarchy' at Muscat, but one that was heeled in the tribal bricolage and more engaged with Asian imperial strands in Qajar Iran, even if it derived from aspects of Western imperial practice. His fight for the defence of the port town of Sohar, his foothold in the Persian port of Bandar Abbas and his successful conquest of Muscat reveal how he leaned more on the inland tribes and the non-European resources to build his Sultanate.

His Sultanate remained more inward-looking, based on the agricultural revenues from date plantations. The Wahhabis remained his strong support base in the interiors. They ensured that, unlike Barghash, his mobility remained more overland into the tribal interiors, where they were a potent force. His close association with them made him a suspicious character in British eyes. They deported him to Bombay as well. But the Wahhabis posed a grave political challenge to the imperial powers, and this perforce drew the British also in conversation with him.

He derived from the British politics of exile and used it to firefight recalcitrance within his household. The Bombay stint fired his imaginary and left an indelible impression on him. He saw British imperial cities, such as Bombay, as integral to his political geography and consolidated his household by using them as sites to offload inconvenient siblings. Turki's new, refurbished Sultanate was based on a resurgent household that shaped his politics and blurred the private–public divide.

Profile: Sayyid Turki (1832–88)

Turki was born in Zanzibar in 1832. He lived on the island until 1854, when his father took him to Oman and made him the Governor of the port town of Sohar on the Al Batinah coast. After the death of his father, he contested with his brother Thuwayni for the Muscat throne. Thuwayni viewed Turki's location at Al Batinah as an eyesore. As we saw in Chapter 2, he valued Sohar as it was the principal gateway to the tribal interiors that he had successfully integrated to the maritime coast. Thuwayni, along with his brother Majid, questioned Turki's independent sovereignty at Sohar on grounds that 'no proof existed' to establish his claim.[1]

Turki was determined to keep his control over Sohar, as he too realized its significance as the gateway to the interior, in which he was hugely invested. But more importantly, he had his eyes on Muscat as well and the dream to be Sultan in the shoes of his late father. The fight for Sohar was his gateway to Muscat. Both these port towns became the sites where he invested to refurbish the Sultanate as a 'modern monarchy'.

I

Turki at Sohar: Tribal Bricolage and the Oceanic Predicaments

Sohar on the Al Batinah coast was an important international port for Oman since antiquity. Its commercial fortunes waxed and waned with Portuguese rule and later under the various Omani dynasts. In 1803, it came briefly under Wahhabi control, much to the chagrin of the Sultan. It remained a principal exporter of lime, lemon and dates to India, Southeast Asia and the Americas. Politically, despite several attempts by the Omani Sultan to capture the port, it remained an independent state whose chief, Sayf bin Hamūd, entered into an agreement with the British government in 1849 for banning the slave trade. An Act of the British Parliament (1853) was passed to give effect to this engagement.

In 1851, Sultan Sayyid Saʻīd captured Sohar, and it continued until his death as a dependency of Muscat. It offered him the perfect foothold on the Al Batinah coast, located as it was north of Muscat and in close vicinity of important tribal-controlled spots—Sohan, Burka, Nakhil, Suwayq and Seeb. Its waters were shallow, and it was not a very useful port for the steamer-driven traffic of the nineteenth century. But it offered an entry into the interior date plantations and was a good base for participation in the inland politics.

The Fight for Sohar: The Limitation of the Bricolage

Thuwayni, with the British on his side, picked up cudgels to oust Turki from Sohar. Turki's fight for Sohar revealed that the 'political wilderness' of the tribal interior was a critical, even if slippery, space for careering. Alliances with tribal factions were temporally contingent, loose and flexible. Neither state building nor careering was ideologically driven but rather shaped by spur-of-the-moment contingencies. And yet this bricolage of alliances remained the nuts and bolts of Turki's career.

The contingent nature of tribal alliances was best revealed in
1857, when Thuwayni blockaded the Sohar port by both sea and land
with the assistance of some of his tribal allies: the tribes of Shaykh
Ahmad bin Sudayrī with his Bedouin dependants. He was successful,
because when he approached Sohar to blockade the port, Turki's
tribal allies—the Jashamī chiefs and the troops of the Ali Saad Ali
Bu Rushid and Hawāsinah tribes—backtracked. Significantly,
they argued that they were with him only to fight the forces of the
Wahhabi, Bin Saud, and that they would not interfere in the fight
between the two brothers.² The blockade was temporarily lifted,
only to be reimposed in 1859.

Thuwayni insisted on drawing Turki into maritime conflicts
that exposed the limitations of his power, which was based on tribal
support. Thuwayni focused on the maritime coast as the site for the
display of valour against Turki. At Thuwayni's insistence, as soon
as the blockade of Sohar was lifted, a truce was worked out at sea.
It was brokered by the nephews of the late Sultan Sayyid Saʿīd—
Muhammad bin Salim and his brother Sayyid Ahmed. Suleiman,
who arrived from Zanzibar, ended the stalemate.

Thuwayni insisted that the meeting with Turki be held not
on land but in a vessel with him on board. Interestingly, Suleiman
took Turki's men in his vessel, and they boarded Thuwayni's vessel,
where negotiations for truce began. Thuwayni restored to Turki all
the possessions he had taken from him in the Al Batinah. Thuwayni
then sailed back to Muscat.³ It was agreed that they would be in
alliance, control their tribal followers and not go on any operation
without consultation.

This imagery of the truce, worked out on vessels at sea, best
exemplified that the tribal bricolage that Turki had painstakingly
built was tempered by the politics of the maritime coast. Thuwayni's
insistence on a vessel-based truce was his way of drawing Turki to
the waters that he hoped would rock his carefully crafted bricolage.

Not surprisingly, the truce was short-lived, riveted as it was by
the bricolage of tribal politics. Thuwayni had to start an operation
against Turki, as he rebelled against Muscat with the help of the
Jashamī tribe. On his part, Thuwayni claimed to have the support of

all the maritime chiefs of Oman. Turki claimed he had the promise of help from the Ra's al-Khaimah chief, Sultan bin Sagar.

The maritime politics-driven bricolage that powered Turki had the potential to disrupt commerce. This drew the British into his small world. Tribal factions intersected with imperial politics, drawing Turki reluctantly to the centre of the larger oceanic world framed by Western powers.

Felix Jones was furious when the fight between the two brothers and their tribal supporters created outrage as well as a murder on the sea. He reiterated that the British policy on the sea had been one of vigilance, as people are so prone to bloodshed, slaughter and revenge at the slightest occasion on the high seas.[4] He underlined the position of the Resident as the arbiter for the mutual good of the warring factions. And he took the help of Commander Jenkins to obtain from Turki adequate reparation for the outrage. He wanted both the brothers, specially Thuwayni, as the supreme ruler, to rectify the aggressions of their followers. Jones said that, even though he did not have specific treaties with these two warring brothers, the word of the Resident was generally agreed to for all practical purposes.

Jones was clear that the 'landward' fights were best ignored and the sea outrages should be focused on, as the latter 'give insecurity to general commerce and if overlooked occasion perturbation in all the adjoining tracts for rancor and desire for revenge with individual Arab families outlasts by a long period the signatures of their Chiefs to compacts which restore general peace and tranquility for a time'.[5]

Turki's Revolt at Sohar: Tapping into Family Politics

Turki tapped into family and household networks when the tribal bricolage proved slippery, and maritime conflict was not his favoured option. He exploited the sibling rivalries, specially between brothers Thuwayni and Majid, and cosied up to the latter, via whom he hoped to access the imperial networks. On the Al Batinah coastline, he had the support of the Arab chief of Sharjah, Turki bin Ahmad.[6] He declared open revolt against Thuwayni.

Thuwayni was weary of Turki's warm ties with Majid. He alleged that Majid was deliberately picking a fight with Muscat so that the distraction could give Turki a free way into the port city. Jones confirmed that Sayyid Turki had asked for the 'necessary things' from Sayyid Majid if the latter wanted him to attack Muscat in the event of Thuwayni sailing to Zanzibar to battle him.[7] At the time of the impending war between Majid and Thuwayni, Turki was hopeful of getting arms and ammunition from the former so that he could attack Muscat while the latter was away in Zanzibar.[8]

Thuwayni's response was to build a strong military base and remain alert, even if that increased the economic pressures on him. He had to maintain, at great expense, a number of irregular Bedouin in the field.[9] Jones was with Thuwayni even as he tried his best to avert conflict between the brothers in the interest of British commerce. He minced no words in saying that he and the government disapproved of the ongoing hostilities that were 'detrimental to the security of trade by sea'.[10] He noted with concern that Majid 'encouraged and abetted' Turki to oppose Thuwayni and also offered him material aid to go on the offensive.[11]

Majid as His Conduit to Imperial Networks

On his part Turki saw in brother Majid, who was the British ally in the anti-slave campaign, the perfect route to be introduced to imperial politics. At one point, in a mark of conviviality, he asked Jones to take care of his territories on the Al Batinah coast so that he could embark to Zanzibar to meet Majid for 'sundry purposes'.[12] Jones agreed to keep an eye on his property but advised him to abandon the trip and was willing to offer his friendly mediation to sort out his differences with Thuwayni.

That Turki was actively tapping into imperial rivalries for his revolt against Thuwayni was clear when his agent used a French ship, *Girende*, that sailed from Zanzibar laden with arms and gunpowder, to turn to Sohar. The ship had come to Zanzibar from Bombay; it had started its journey with sugar from the French island of Réunion, was cleared by the British subject Sudali Damlia, the customs agent, and was cleaned and then loaded with cloves for Bombay, from where it had returned with cargo. Turki's agent offered the ship $500 to touch at Sohar. Significantly, the ship contained goods that Majid had dispatched for Turki: six guns for the defence of the fort of Sohar and 200 kegs of gunpowder, imported from the USA, each containing about 80 pounds.

Rigby, the British Resident at Zanzibar, reassured the government that the commander of the ship, who had since returned to Zanzibar with a cargo of rice from Madagascar, had declared before the Customs Master that he took nothing more than this to Sohar. Not wanting to upset the balance he had maintained in British relations with Majid, Rigby underplayed the role of Zanzibar in the revolt and tried to cover up the overtures of Majid to a recalcitrant Turki. He did not see any nefarious intent in the gunpowder that was loaded on the ship. He argued that there was no reason for alarm, as Zanzibar was a natural depot of the item: more than 10,000 kegs of it were annually imported there from the USA, and it was very cheap there, while it was expensive at Sohar.

Rigby further reassured his government about Majid's trustworthiness by pointing out that the ship *Girende* was the only one sailing to Sohar. There was no other suspicious movement along this route and thus, the charge of Majid conspiring with Turki to attack Muscat must not be taken seriously.[13] Instead, he accused Thuwayni of being in constant touch with the French Consul at Zanzibar. He alleged that letters from Thuwayni for the Arabs of Zanzibar arrived via American cargo ships from Muscat.[14]

II

The Wahhabis as Political Capital

The Wahhabi-mediated Truce at Sohar

Turki's revolt against Muscat brought together the tribal societies of the interior, the ports of Sohar and Zanzibar and the Anglo-

French rivalries in close coordination. But it forefronted also the jurisdictional overlaps and contested sovereignties in the region. The flexible jurisdictions and myriad claims of sovereignty made territorial borders porous, enabling the Wahhabis from the interiors of northern Muscat to enter as mediators and referees. The Wahhabi agent, Sadeyrer, brokered truce and brought about a reconciliation between Thuwayni and Turki.

According to its terms, Sohar, Lewa and some districts of these areas were to remain with Sayyid Turki. He was to get $300 from Thuwayni. In lieu of this, Turki was to expel, with Thuwayni's cooperation, several identifiable tribes who had supported his revolt from Sohar and other places under him. This included the Ghāfirī tribe, especially Beni Jabir.[15]

The Wahhabis Draw Turki into Imperial Circles

The Wahhabi-mediated truce alarmed the British. It compelled them to pay serious attention to Turki's ambition to occupy Muscat. And this was while Jones, in particular, had avoided interference as he saw the sibling friction as a land-confined conflict not appropriate to interfere beyond 'warning all parties against extending their feuds to the sea'.[16] But the truce changed this attitude. Bartle Frere was of the view that the Government of India had to get proactive, as the renewed Wahhabi threat would not only adversely impact the Persian Gulf commerce by the revival of piracy but also interfere with the British telegraphic communication with Europe. The telegraph line was being laid along the Gulf with Muscat as the hub, and a passive attitude to the Wahhabi expansion was risky.[17]

Brigadier W.M. Coghlan, in charge of the Muscat and Zanzibar Commission, insisted in his report that Thuwayni should be officially informed of his recognition by the Government of India as the paramount sovereign of Sohar and the claim of Turki to be independent of the Sultan of Muscat be disallowed.

The mediation of the Wahhabis to end the Turki revolt convinced the British that he was heavily influenced by them and dependent on their support. It was not for nothing that they considered the Sultans of Muscat as their subordinate Governor, Wālī, and extracted tribute. They viewed Turki as encouraging their infiltration into the interiors north of Muscat to radicalize the tribes.

Turki and His Wahhabi Base

The Wahhabis of Central Arabia were a challenge to both the Omani Sultans and the British. They were not only active inland but also on the ports of the Persian Gulf, where the British viewed them as the 'chief instigator of Arab piracy', whose activities had seriously affected the commerce in the region.[18] In the early nineteenth century the Wahhabi activities and expansion was severely curtailed by the Egyptian Pasha, Muscat's Sayyid Sa'īd and the British naval and military expeditionary forces.

But the Wahhabis, as we saw in Chapter 3, reared their head with a vengeance from 1856 because of the death of the Sultan of Muscat and the weakening of the Egyptian Pasha. Their revival was visible in the increase in piracy from vessels coming from the Wahhabi ports and their aggression by land on the territories of the Sultan.

After the death of the Sultan, the Wahhabis became an important social base for Turki, who was the Wālī of Sohar. He reached out to them in the tribal interiors of Al Batinah. As he claimed independent control of the coast, he dug his heels into its tribal society, which was heavily infested with Wahhabis, and belligerently attacked any interlopers.

In 1858, his men attacked a cargo of dates at Al Batinah that was homeward bound when it arrived just off the port of Sohar. The cargo belonged to a *bateel* (a dhow or ship used for pearling) pertaining to members of the Shahriyar who were under the authority of Shaykh Muhammad bin Ali. The Turki followers came in two buglas and attacked the bateel and killed three people, carrying the bateel and her cargo to Sohar.[19] Ali lodged a complaint with the British agent, who began to collect details of the case.

Thuwayni viewed Turki's social embedding in the tribal areas of the Al Batinah as an eyesore. Both he and Majid questioned

Turki's independent sovereignty of Sohar on grounds that 'no proof existed' to establish his claim.[20] They had the support of the British, who loathed him for his closeness to the Wahhabis. Like Thuwayni, they were convinced that Turki was fanning the Wahhabis from the tribal interiors to attack the port town of Muscat and become the Sultan. Thuwayni was assisted by several maritime tribes of Oman in his contest with his brother and the rebellious subjects at Al Batinah.[21]

Turki loathed Thuwayni also because he refused to pay him a set amount from the Zanzibar subsidy. This made it difficult for him to pay tribute to the Wahhabis, who were clearly an influential constituent in his tribal base. In not paying Turki, Thuwayni was in violation of the deal he had struck with Majid, who sent him 40,000 Crowns as subsidy on the condition that he not attack him and part with the said amount to Turki. Muhammad bin Salim, Thuwayni's nephew, had brokered the deal and had brought with him the initial 20,000 Crowns as the first instalment of the money. Out of these, 5000 Crowns were for Turki to pay the tribute due to the Wahhabi chief. But Thuwayni did not pass this on to Turki and instead started his hostilities to him. In consequence, the latter sent an agent to their sister, who resided at Zanzibar, to collect 10,000 Crowns that was in her charge. This money was the balance of the patrimony bequeathed to her from their father, the late Sayyid Sa'īd. The agent was afraid to carry this money in a vessel with an Arab flag, as rumours of Thuwayni's invasion were doing the rounds.

Turki's encouragement and friendship with the Wahhabi radicals made the British agree with Thuwayni that he was a 'dangerous intriguer and a most extortionate ruler'.[22] And this made it all the more important to take notice of him. This emboldened Thuwayni, who felt further strengthened with the arrival at Muscat of a delegation of Muslims and Jews from Sohar to complain of Turki's maladministration. This underlined his sovereign status in the Al Batinah coast, as they urged him to protect them against his own brother. These delegates included many British Indian subjects, who warned of rebellion and anarchy if Thuwayni did not intervene to quell the discontent.[23]

The threat faced by the British Indian subjects made it all the more urgent both for Thuwayni and the British to engage with Turki. The British countered the Wahhabi mediation and influence by dispatching their agent at Muscat, Lt W.M. Pengally, to mediate truce between Turki and Thuwayni. Pengally was clear that Thuwayni should attack Sohar in case the mediation failed.[24] Turki, on Pengally's assurance of a safe return, agreed to visit Muscat via the issue of an *aman*, or pledge of security.[25] He arrived at Seeb, near Muscat, and met Pengally. But he deferred his meeting with Sayyid Thuwayni for the morning. A peeved Pengally suspected foul play: he cancelled the aman and gave permission to Thuwayni to arrest his brother while he was in Muscat territory.[26] This marked the fall of Sohar via imperial machinations.

The fall of Sohar was marked by Thuwayni's son Sayyid Salim being appointed ruler of Sohar and Turki being carried as a prisoner to Muscat and lodged in a fort there. Thuwayni sent a force and took possession of the town. Salim was promised the support of the British if he continued to support Thuwayni.

And yet, Turki's clout was revealed with the people of Sohar expressing outrage at his arrest. They protested against his removal to Muscat as a prisoner. They were critical of Pengally's way of handling the situation, for which he was criticized by the Bombay government as well.[27] Thuwayni's rule notwithstanding, Sohar remained Turki territory. He had a firm social base there, with the Arab tribes and Wahhabi leaders supporting him. His deep roots in the Al Batinah society were too formidable to crush despite the treachery of Pengally that led to the fall of Sohar. His physical presence on the coast was enough to threaten the paper-thin rule of Thuwayni, propped as it was with British help.

The Wahhabis Remain His Social Capital

The fall of Sohar and the captive Turki did not mean that his enviable clout with the Al Batinah tribes reduced and his close relations with the Wahhabis were severed. Indeed, the link remained intact and became his critical social capital, making him a sought-after figure in his family circles. This valuable social asset ensured that sibling rivalries remained transient and temporally contingent. The household leaned on him for help if any member felt the political heat. Thus, despite the bad blood at the fall of Sohar, Thuwayni leaned on him when Soor, the Wahhabi hotspot south of Sohar, challenged Muscat's control.

Turki was quick to respond, as it offered him the perfect opportunity to display his clout. Indeed, Thuwayni looking towards him, cut short the British plan to deport him to Bombay as punishment for the Sohar resistance. Before the deportation plan could materialize, the brothers worked out a deal and Turki was dispatched by Thuwayni on a military mission to capture Soor where an insurrection had begun against him.

The temporally and spatially contingent nature of sibling relationships were at their best display when Turki left for Soor on a ship with 550 soldiers from various tribes. It was as though the Sohar incident had never happened. Some of the tribes, like the Banī Janbeh Ra'īs and Siyabinis were soldiers; others were superannuated, ill-armed and ill-equipped in every sense. Banī Bū Hasan and other tribes friendly to the Sultan were expected to flock to Turki's standard on his arrival at Soor.

Turki anchored off Soor and sent word to Rashid bin Salim to surrender the fort. He did so even though the Wahhabi leader, Abdul Aziz, resisted, saying that Soor belonged to the Wahhabis and not to Muscat. Turki asked Thuwayni to arrive in Soor as he had circumvented it and the Wahhabi Abdul Aziz had no one on his side. Thuwayni proceeded by land to crush the rebellion at Soor.

The combined sea and land assault planned by the two siblings was a great success. Abdul Aziz ran away from Soor to Jalan and was finally ejected from there as well. Soor was taken by Thuwayni. The rebellious Junabee tribe were brought back to Soor as prisoners. Twenty-six of their elders who returned as prisoners remained so until such time as the tribe had paid into the Sultan's exchequer the full amount of the expenses incurred by the Sultan in crushing the rebellion. This included also the losses incurred by British subjects on the occasion of the plunder of Soor.

III

Forced Mobility: The Exile to Muscat and Bombay

Turki's embedding in tribal society of the interior and his clout with the Wahhabis was both an asset as well as a liability. It made him an attractive go-to man when help was needed. But it also made both the British and Thuwayni suspicious of his moves. This mistrust imposed forced mobility on him.

In 1861, the Bombay government was concerned that a compact had been signed between Turki and the Amir of the Wahhabis for the cession of Sohar to the latter.[28] This was surprising, since in 1859, Thuwayni had assured them of Sohar's security and expressed 'no further anxiety on the transfer of his port of Sohar to the Wahhabis'.[29] Reports of the Wahhabi presence at Al Batinah and in Sohar in particular continued to pour in.

In 1865, the British feared Turki's clout in the area. They forcefully shifted him to Muscat under the vigil of Thuwayni. But this physical transportation to Muscat did not end his social capital and investments in the Arab tribes and the Wahhabis. Indeed, the Wahhabis became the lifeline for Turki, his main social and political capital, offering him the promise of a political comeback.

In 1866, some Banias complained to the British that about twenty-eight days earlier, a Wahhabi detachment had come down from the port of Soham, which was only a few hours away from Sohar, and had driven them into the seas. One Bania drowned on reaching Sohar. It was clear that the Wahhabis had come down the passes and reached the seaboard at various points along the Muscat coast from Soor in the south to Sohar in the north.[30] Thuwayni repeatedly alerted the British to the fact that Turki was allying with his enemies (the Wahhabis) and stirring strife and trouble for him. He pleaded that he be re-confined in prison, from where he had been released on their request.[31]

The Wahhabi fear was sure to get Thuwayni the support of the British. They warned Turki, threatening to not help him out in case Thuwayni took action against him for the safety and good order of his territories threatened by the Wahhabis. They agreed that he was no doubt of 'excitable temperament . . . constantly fretting and chafing over his captivity in Muscat'. And it was quite likely that he would not hesitate to harm Thuwayni if he got an opportunity. Lt Col Disbrowe alleged further that Turki was a nuisance also because of his 'nocturnal peregrinations and forcible or uninvited entry into respectable people's houses'. He was particularly keen on the women inmates of these houses, in particular a specific courtesan of the town.[32]

Thuwayni was very keen to put him back in prison. But the British, realizing his deep tentacles in the Al Batinah coast and the harm he could bring via his relations with the Wahhabis, preferred his physical removal from the region itself. They suggested that he be removed far away to Bombay in India, where their government would keep him under their vigil.

Disbrowe felt that his removal from Muscat to India on condition that he would never return without the permission of the Sultan would make Thuwayni most satisfied. The Government of India approved this plan of sending Turki to India on any allowance the Sultan sanctioned. He was told to accept this offer, or else the government would not interfere between him and Thuwayni.[33] As luck would have it, while these negotiations were on, Thuwayni died and his son Salim installed himself as Sultan. He put Turki in prison.

In the given circumstances, Turki agreed to go to Bombay rather than remain imprisoned at Muscat. In fact, Pelly intervened to save him from a violent death and arrange for his shift to India. By 1868, Turki was in Bombay. He gave no cause to the British to be alarmed by his antics. And he was always careful to remind them of his good conduct. He wrote to the Governor, sensing his return to Muscat, 'I have always taken the greatest care not to give cause for any suspicion whatever and thought that nobody could give any evidence against me of my doing anything wrong or writing any suspicious letters.'[34] He hoped that the government would not consider him guilty of acts that he had not committed without any clear proof.

Turki's Return to Muscat

The Bombay stint brought Turki close to the British. He was seen as a possible ally to get out of the instability that followed Thuwayni's murder and Salim's installation as Sultan. By 1869, the Government of India looked towards Turki. The eventual takeover of power by Salim's relative Qais as the Sultan made them nervous. They turned to Turki as a possible way out of the mess at Muscat. They considered getting him back to Muscat if Pelly, with his ear to the ground, felt that the 'people of Muscat want him back'.[35]

The Bombay Governor also agreed as, according to him, this was advantageous for several reasons. First Salim's rule was unstable, and Qais, who had ousted him briefly, was also very unpopular. In contrast to both these contenders, Turki was viewed as having a far greater personal following as he belonged directly to the ruling family's lineage. People viewed him as their 'best soldier'. Second, the British believed that he was a 'gentleman attached to our interest and aware of our power'. Third, his accession to power was also useful in that the question of Zanzibar's subsidy, which the British had settled in the context of succession remaining with the sons of Sayyid Sa'īd, would not be up for review. Finally, he was suited also to keep the Bandar Abbas lease intact, as that too was conditional on power remaining with the sons of the late Sayyid Sa'īd.

The Bombay government supported Turki's return to Muscat and his succession as Sultan also because it felt that a strong ruler there would keep Persia in check and clip its ambitions towards other ports like Gwadar.[36] The Government of India granted the permission for Turki's return but wished to project its neutrality by stating that no government ship or steamer be used to transport him. Nor should anyone accompany him, it declared. No pledge, protection or assistance was to be given to him in any attempt that he may make to establish his authority over Muscat. So even if the government made his return to Muscat administratively smooth, it reiterated that it would acknowledge him as a ruler only 'if his rule is acceptable to Muscat people'.[37]

IV

Turki's Bid to Be Sultan: The Attack on Muscat

Ironically, the forced mobility of Turki became his political asset. The exile at Bombay fired his imaginary. It made him view British Indian cities as integral to his political geography, and the politics of exile attracted him as a useful political practice to emulate. The wide exposure to British society at Bombay charged his dream of becoming the Sultan.

Soon after his return from Bombay, emboldened by British support, he attacked Muscat to avenge Thuwayni's death. He was confident of the support networks he had established in the tribal society of the Al Batinah as well as the contacts he now had with the British society of Bombay. He made a dramatic entry at Muscat with about forty followers coasting along the Persian Gulf from nowhere less than the British stronghold at Bushire. This was a testimony to his friendship with Pelly, the British agent in the Gulf.

Pelly was indeed tricked by him, as he may not have approved of this random show of strength in the Gulf. Turki took permission from Pelly to go to Kuwait to live with the Arab Sunnis rather than be with the Shias in the Persian Gulf. But instead, he hired a native craft and headed to Muscat. On the way, he picked up about forty idle desperados and one or two native crafts at sea. He was confident that the Baluchi Governor of the principal Muscat fort would surrender to him. But that did not happen, so he took possession of another fort that commanded the town and commenced firing on Sultan Salim's house.

Salim put a barricade immediately of rice and date bags below the fort, but Turki removed them. The Baluchi Governor of a second fort on the other flank of the town refused to act against him, so he ended up taking that fort. But this was not the ideal situation, as he was in there with little provisions, scarce following and surrounded by the sea. One of Salim's cruisers kept a watchful eye on him.[38] Pelly, as expected, played a helpful role. He advised the native agent at Muscat not to interfere. He felt that even if Salim escaped this time, the threat to him from his uncles would continue.[39] But in this instance, he offered no direct support to Turki's bid for Muscat.

Turki retreated on not getting any British aid. But if the imperial networks failed him, the tribal connections helped. He took shelter with the Banī Yās tribe on the pirate coast. But they refused to help him attack Muscat without British consent. They asked Pelly for permission to assist Turki by sea.[40]

The entanglement of the imperial and the tribal networks in defining his political entrepreneurship was most evident when Turki asked Pelly to help in getting his cash deposits transferred to him. He needed these to attack Muscat by land using the money to lure and keep intact his tribal supporters.

Drawing from the Tribal Context

Turki leaned on his tribal base, with not much help coming from the imperial context. He focused on a land march into Muscat rather than the sea route. The reports of Turki's march from the tribal interior to Muscat made the British less wary of him, as this did not disrupt sea commerce. In a sudden change of stance, their support was now forthcoming.

Turki's clout with the tribal society made him very attractive to the British. The tribal support base with which he planned to march into Muscat from the interiors of Oman was good enough reason for them to stop viewing him as a rebel. He was increasingly perceived as an acceptable ruler. The British resolved that they would support him, as he was making his political bid from his tribal support base, which in no way threatened their maritime commerce. He was definitely more acceptable to them than Salim.

Turki's tribal context brought the imperial networks on his side. The British, impressed by his support in the tribal society and assured of no disruption to their commerce, rejected any suggestion to bombard Muscat or attack Turki to prevent his march to Muscat. They argued that it was not only advantageous to have Turki as Sultan but also that the British were to be seen as not interfering in palace successions. They were to be guided only by the principle of maritime truce that guarded its trade and traders. Salim was seen as a sinking ship, whom both the Arab tribes and Persia had rejected.[41]

Turki benefited from this turn in the imperial assemblage in his favour. He was emboldened when the support to him continued despite local officers warning against it. The Political Resident at Muscat continued to report the panic in the city on news of Turki's arrival and the disappointment of the locals, who looked to the indifferent British administration with hope.[42]

The chiefs of Abu Dhabi and the Dubai state intervened to avert the attack on Muscat. The Abu Dhabi chief said that, as per his talks with Sultan Salim, he was trying to negotiate a truce between him and Turki by restoring to the latter the districts of Batinah and granting him a pension of $3000/annum. He feared that his influence in Muscat would lessen with Turki as the Sultan.

Salim was influenced by the Wahhabis and recognized Abu Dhabi's mentorship of this radical group. But this would lessen by the restoration of Turki to power in the Al Batinah. The British government, however, was steadfast. Since Turki was planning to move by land and not sea, the British felt there could be no objection of a son of Sayyid Saʿīd being in Muscat territory.[43]

Tapping into the British Imperial Networks

Pelly supported Turki against Salim but was disapproving of his out-of-the-blue hostile moves, which he saw as detrimental to British commercial interests. He declined any pecuniary aid to him. In fact, the native agent at Muscat was warned not to interfere in this affair and alert the British subjects of danger to their assets. Many of them had already begun to leave Muscat, and others left their valuables at the agency for safe custody.[44] At the same time, Pelly was told by the Bombay government to use his local relations with all the chiefs on the pirate coast to deter them against affording Turki any assistance in his attempts to attack Muscat.

Turki's connections with the Wahhabis also came in the way of getting full-fledged British help in his fight for Muscat. He posed the classic dilemma for the British. He was needed to oust

Salim from Muscat. And yet the multiple contexts from where Turki derived his sustenance were problematic. Of these, his deep connections with the Wahhabis were the most troublesome. And of course, any conflict via the sea route was repulsive, as it jeopardized their commerce.

The government hoped that its disinterest would dissuade Turki from taking the sea route and launching the attack via land, which would be of less consequence to British commercial interests.[45] The maintenance of the maritime truce was critical to the level of support the British were willing to offer Muscat. Pelly was told to act on Turki's attack on Muscat, as it was viewed as an 'infraction of the maritime truce'.[46]

Salim, Turki and the Fight for Muscat

Both Turki and Salim were careering at the intersection of the imperial, the tribal and the family networks. They were a tough competition for each other using the same social and political capital. Later that year, unsuccessful in his designs on Muscat, Turki decided to retreat. Salim lent him a boat and supplied him with provisions and money. Turki was reported to have taken refuge in the Persian Gulf with one of the Arab chiefs.[47]

Salim oscillated between the imperial, the tribal and the family networks to protect his career in Muscat. He leaned on the Soor tribes for help, only to be warned by the British against the move, as they were supporters of Turki. Caught in this conundrum of his making, he went for advice to his mother as well. 'Do you come to consult me now?' she is reported to have said. She said she understood Turki's intentions, as he must be 'wanting to take his father's territories and revenge his brother's blood'. She was angry and advised him to apologize to Turki. After being shunned by her, Salim reportedly came out of the house crying.[48]

Like Turki, Salim was quick to tap imperial politics when nothing else worked. He emphasized to the British that Turki's aggression against Muscat violated the maritime truce, as he attacked his fort by sea. And yet he had forgiven him even though he had the power and ability to 'kill him'.[49] He alleged that Turki managed entry into a fort in Muscat because of the treachery of the man in charge of it. He reminded the British that his arrival via sea was in violation of the terms of the maritime truce and thus demanded penalties.

He urged the British to act against him, stating that he had released him from prison on their request. He argued that 'you liberated him knowing that he is prone to do mischief'. So, it was 'incumbent on you to turn him out of this place and punish him for his having acted contrary to your established order at sea'.[50] Salim also invoked the interests of the Bania merchants to solicit British support. He reported that due to the crossfire, the British subjects—Banias—were alarmed. He wanted them to sell him some shots.

But the native agent was reluctant to intervene except when it came to protection of British subjects. Thus, when Turki's shots aimed at the houses of merchants Messrs McGill and Rozario, he stepped in and told Turki to refrain from firing. Turki pleaded ignorance that these houses belonged to Britishers and asked that the flag be hoisted there to enable him to identify such houses.[51] Salim sent boats with guns to keep up the attack on Turki's bugla at sea. Pelly supported the diatribe against Turki, demanding that if it was proved that Turki had indeed attacked Muscat, the salary of Rs 300/month that the government gave him would be withdrawn.[52] The Government of India decided not to extend any countenance or protection to Turki after his attack on Muscat.[53]

In 1868, Salim was finally ousted from Muscat but by a relative, Qais, and not by Turki. He took refuge in Bandar Abbas,[54] but was always eager to re-enter Muscat. But the British put their money on Turki. They informed Salim that there would be no negotiations with him. If he came to Karachi or Gwadar and gave himself up unconditionally, he would be granted the same provisions as Qais. But if he did not comply within the given time period, the terms would not be renewed. Rather, he would be made prisoner wherever found and would then receive only such terms as may be thought fit and which would be not as favourable as these ones.[55]

V

Turki Installed as the Sultan in Muscat: Refurbishing the Sultanate as the 'Modern Monarchy'

In 1871, Turki was installed as the Sultan of Muscat with the full recognition of the British. His rise to power was contingent on the particular conflation of imperial and tribal support networks. His family's carefully crafted foothold in Bandar Abbas proved particularly handy in the conquest of Muscat.

Turki invaded Muscat from the southern port of Soor. Both the British and the tribal chiefs sent recruits to help his army. The Banī Bū Hasan tribes joined Turki. Some 400 men of the neighbouring tribes also arrived in his support. Some of them abandoned his mission due to desertions caused by low salary or else their dismissal by him. But he did have more than 100 or 150 men at the time of his attack. He provisioned the forts for three months. He alerted the British subjects at Muscat and Muttrah to remove their valuables and prepare to leave at a moment's warning.[56]

In the battle for Muscat, Turki drew support also from the Omani power broker in Bandar Abbas, Haji Ahmad Khan. As we saw in Chapter 3, he was initially Thuwayni's appointee there, but had over the years struck an independent career in the port and rooted himself in local society. He felt hugely empowered and emboldened to lend his weight to the succession wars in Muscat after the murder of Thuwayni. In 1869, he sent his Arab clerk, Haji Saleh Bahraini, and Muallim Sayyid Arab of Muscat to Turki with the purpose of borrowing money when Mustafa Quli Khan, chief guard of Zil al-Sultān, came to collect from him 18,000 tomans. After initial refusal, this money was finally obtained from Turki. But this was not without a return price: Haji Ahmad Khan had to dispatch 200–300 riflemen to Muscat to assist Turki in his attempt to become Sultan at Muscat.[57]

Turki's refurbished Sultanate had at its core a resurgent household and a tribal base: its outer shell was constituted by his entanglement with Asian and Western imperial powers. The forging

of matrimonial alliances, the tribal bricolage politics in the rural
areas and the conquest of ancient Omani towns strengthened the
core. The exterior was defined by the use of the imperial politics of
exile and the dabbling in the politics of Qajar Iran at Bandar Abbas.

VI

Strengthening the Inner Core of the Sultanate

Royal Marriages and the Welding of Family Ties

Turki cemented the royal family ties by matrimony. His children
married their cousins—i.e., the children of his brother Thuwayni.
In 1878, Turki's daughter was married to her cousin Hareb, the son
of Thuwayni in Muscat. Turki stayed away at Muttrah to be out
of the way during the ceremony in accordance with Arab etiquette.
The bride was the widow of Hareb's younger brother Mohammad,
who died in 1877.[58] And in the same year, his eldest son Muhammad,
who he had made Governor of Sohar, was married to Thuwayni's
daughter at Muscat, Lady Zowaneh bint Thuwayni bin Said.[59]
    Turki bonded well with his brother Barghash in Zanzibar, as
he saw him as someone with no imperial ambition for Muscat. The
cordiality between them resulted in many gift exchanges that proved
particularly useful for the cash-starved Turki.
    Turki mediated matrimonial alliances within tribal factions
as well so as to strengthen himself in the interior. In 1873, Shaykh
Saleh bin Ali Al-Harithī was endeavouring to strengthen himself by
seeking marriage with the daughter of Munsoor bin Nasir, who was
the Shaykh of the Al Wahhabi Bedouins. Turki played the broker
and extracted a deal. He invited Saleh to Muscat for a meeting.
On his arrival, he wanted a solemn assurance from him, in concert
with other Shaykhs of the tribes, that in return for this matrimonial
alliance he would remain quiet in future and refrain from hostile
demonstrations against the Sultan. Both Saleh and Munsoor agreed
to this. The Al Wahhabis are Hināwīs and a very powerful tribe.

To get them to a favourable relationship with Muscat was a great feat for Turki. It held promise to their intention to join Turki and yield to his authority.[60]

Turki himself was happy to enter into matrimonial alliances with daughters of tribal chiefs to dig his heels into Omani society. In 1872, he married the daughter of Sayyid Hamad bin Salim. The British ships the *Rifleman* and the *Columbine* fired salutes and were dressed with flags in honour of the occasion.[61]

Rooting Himself in the Tribal Bricolage

Turki doled out favours to tribal factions to embed himself in the interior. He could not please all the tribal groups. But he balanced them out, offering favours to some to the exclusion of others. Turki was wary of the Bedouins and favoured the Hināwis and the Baluchis. Indeed, he continued to use the Baluchi guards who manned the Muscat fort from the time of Sayyid Sa'īd and Thuwayni. He refused to surrender the forts to the command of the Bedouins because the Baluchi Commandant Rajub was formidable and was much sought after by the Bedouins. Aziz, his younger brother, had been instigated by the Bedouins to demand Rajub's dismissal simply to get him in their service.[62] Turki's sovereignty, entrenched primarily in the tribal bricolage of the interiors, continued to be contested by his brother Aziz, who was similarly rooted in tribal politics. Needless to add that the diabolic nature of tribal politics made his sovereignty rocky.

Rocky Bricolage: The Revolt of Aziz

In 1873, Turki's younger brother Sayyid Abdul Aziz revolted against him. Like Turki, he too was embedded in tribal support networks, in particular the Bedouins, and he continuously incited them against Turki, rocking his tribal bricolage.

Indeed, Aziz had been exiled to Bombay by the British because of his turbulent politics with the tribes. He made many unsuccessful attempts to return to Muscat. In 1873, in one such attempt, he got stranded in Makran and made an attempt to recover his old position of Wālī or Governor of Gwadar. And once he was not successful, he decided to continue his march to Oman, only to be intercepted by one of His Majesty's vessels of war. He was accused of returning to Muscat to foment trouble for Turki. And since he crossed the sea in violation of the maritime truce, he was arrested near Soor by British cruisers.

The government ordered him to remain in residence in Karachi provided he refrained from interfering in Oman and did not leave the port without their permission. He resentfully agreed to stay put in Karachi. Quarters were prepared for him in a suitable place in the port town, and he prepared to occupy them at the earliest.[63] He was sanctioned $300 per month from the date of his capture, which was to be adjusted to the Zanzibar subsidy paid by the British government to Turki. He was warned that if he intrigued, then the warrant under Regulation III of 1818 would be enforced.[64] But Aziz was unrelenting. He refused to accept $300 from Turki. He agreed to abide by the orders of the British government but reiterated that $300–400 were inadequate for his position. He refused to remain in India for such a paltry amount, as he was convinced that he had a right to a proper provision being made for him by his brother Turki.[65]

From Karachi, Aziz continued to fan the Bedouin against Turki. In 1875, a large number of Bedouins collected outside the walls of Muscat, and their Shaykhs informed Turki that if he did not surrender the forts of Jelali and Merani, they would consider themselves in opposition to him and plunder the town without further delay. He ultimately yielded, because his tribal support base shifted. The Hināwī tribe discovered some breach of faith on the part of Turki. The Baluchi fort guards also played foul. Turki asked all the tribes of Oman to reach Muscat and join him in resisting the opposition to him. This made the Hināwīs feel threatened. They asked him to adhere to the engagements he had made to them. As the Hināwīs put up a tough stance, Turki decided to move to Gwadar with his family and left Muscat to his brother Aziz.[66]

The Bedouin unrest disrupted trade. But once Aziz took over and Turki moved to Gwadar, the traders resumed their business.

Aziz claimed widespread support for himself in Oman, based mainly on the Arab tribes of the interior. He presented a list of grievances against his brother to the British. He insisted that airing them did not amount to any rebellion or threat of an attack on Muscat. He argued that the British desire that the Omani people should have prosperity, peace, justice and tranquillity was impossible under Turki's rule. He accused him of having become 'neglectful' of his subjects. He argued that the 'whole of Oman is full of rebellion, sedition, oppression and disturbance'. The country, he said, was 'without a ruling hand . . . without justice and without tranquillity'. He referred to the people as 'sheep without a shepherd'.[67]

He took the British in the loop by reminding them that, for two and a half years, he had remained quiet, hoping that his brother would get out of the lap of the seditious and establish peace and tranquillity to the land. But that was not to be. In fact, he found the British too prejudiced against him. But when he saw that the whole of Oman was one in their opposition to Turki and asked him for the leadership to march towards Muscat, he agreed to join them.

He explained that they would have aligned with someone else if he had declined. And making his own career plans clear, he said he 'considered it advisable to join them not seeing any other way to gain my ends'.[68] He used the card of the British subjects in Oman to ensure the neutrality of the British government in this conflict, saying that 'there is no fear for them'. He advised the British government to 'cause them to ship themselves and all their property, and remain on the sea until everything is settled and quiet'.[69]

Ross, the Political Agent in the Persian Gulf, was keen on this mediation. But at the same time, he downplayed his threat. He was wary of his tribal social base and considered it untrustworthy. He felt that the Bedouins in this case were propping rival brothers for their own gain. He felt the Bedouins supporting Aziz were doing so to distract Turki and consolidate their own hold on the region. They did not have his political aspirations in mind. And Aziz himself was convinced that even if he were to succeed in his revolt, the local people would not accept him, as they were aware of his temperamental character and did not trust him.[70]

The British wanted Turki to return to Muscat, and they feared that Aziz would become friends with the religious party and surround himself with *mutawaas* (religious compliance officer) who had already made their appearance in town. But Aziz was constrained for lack of funds. In fact, he asked the British to help with $5000, which they refused.[71] They were keen to support Turki to prevent Aziz digging his heels in at Muscat.

In 1878, Lt Col Miles, Political Agent at the Persian Gulf and Consul at Muscat, reported that Turki wanted the help of the British against Aziz, who was heading the turbulent Bedouin tribes of El Sharhiyeh in rebellion against him. He pointed out that the brothers had been sparring since 1875 and that Turki's offer to Aziz to accept a pension of $500–600 and retire from Oman to settle in India had been rejected by him. Aziz was willing to relocate in India only if the British government would mediate and guarantee him the regular payment of the pension from Turki.[72]

Bricolage and Imperial Politics: Suppressing the Revolt

Turki returned to Muscat with British assurances of help. Aziz was still belligerent and the tribal bricolage replete with tension. Taking no chances, Turki pulled up the defence of Muscat. The ditch around the city was re-dug and the walls repaired at an expenditure of several thousand dollars. The city was made a garrison with more than 500 Nejdian soldiers—tribals of the Wahhabi disposition from Nedj in the north of Arabia. And he had made repeated pleas to the British to help in case of an attack by his brother. Miles commended Turki for his investments in Muscat and highly recommended his request for continued British help in his affairs in Muscat.[73] And indeed, when the impending attack on Muscat by Aziz seemed real, on the request of Turki, he did warn him of British retaliation were he to attack Muscat. He hoped that this would have the approval of Lt Col Ross, as it also involved his effort to protect the interests of the British subjects in Muscat.[74]

Turki and Aziz fought with their respective tribal support base. At the time of the revolt, Aziz had the support of the Beni

Rumeylah and Beni Jabir tribes, who were his main loyalists. Aziz had reached up to the Sumail Valley with a force of 300 men and had the support of these two tribes. The diabolic nature of the bricolage and its transitory nature of support was revealed when it was clear that the tribes supporting Aziz were those who had been collected by the Governor of Sumail, at the request of Turki, to oppose his movement.

Turki was in full preparedness for war. The Governor of Sumail assured him that he was fully in control and 'watching them [enemies] with open eyes; and that all the tribes, the Sultan's slaves and his subject people were fully alert and had surrounded the fort'. The Governor asked for more ammunition, gunpowder, caps, coffee and rice supply for the defence of the town. The impending attack had increased the price of rice to $6 per gunny bag. And even at that high price, it was not easily available. He also complained that he had been repeatedly requesting for a gun, which he had not received yet. He regretted the non-supply of a gun and capping machine, stating, 'If I had written for greater things I would have received it much earlier.'[75]

Turki leaned mainly on British help. He urged Lt Col Miles to write more emphatically to Sayyid Aziz about the British support for Muscat. But Miles did not write again, as Turki was confident that his brother would not be able to move beyond Sumail. He waited for the rebellion to get more serious before reiterating his stand in a second letter.

But the panic and terror in Muscat and Muttrah of this rebellion was 'ten times worse than last year' because of the 'wanton murder and cruelties committed by the Bedouins then in their disappointment'. Miles reported that the suburbs of both towns were deserted. No man could be seen. And a large number of women and children were still living on board ship. Trade was at a standstill for over a month. He said people looked demoralized and appeared to have no confidence in the local government.[76]

The conflict between the brothers shook the tribal bricolage. If Aziz leaned on the Bedouins for help, Turki tapped into the Ghāfirīs for support. He dispatched his son Sayyid Faisal with 300

Ghāfirī men from Burka to oppose Aziz. Sayyid Faisal, while on
the job, assured him of their support. In order to ground himself
firmly in this tribal faction, he obtained Turki's assurance that
their subsistence money was paid regularly. He reported that
the $300, rice and the ammunitions he had sent were partly
distributed among them. But there were still murmurs that their
subsidy money was due. He was of the view that the best way to
ensure the continued support of Ghāfirīs was the maintenance of
a good supply of money, ammunition and rice. Faisal also made an
urgent request for a gun carriage to be sent as guns were useless
without it.[77]

Aziz relied on the tribes Runeyah and Ḥabūs alongside the
Bedouins. His supplies were provided by the villages through which
he moved. The people of the village of Alleya, tortured by the rebels,
offered help. But the tribal support base was slippery, scattered
as it was with spies from rival camps, forcing the tribes to switch
alliances. The people of Alleya reported that Faisal's spies mingled
with them, not only to get information but also to seduce them to
become obedient to Turki.

The people of Alleya expressed the transient nature of the
bricolage culture the best. They reported that they were at first
oppressed by the Aziz rebels and tried to get rid of them. And now
they were at the target line of Faisal. As the rebels became dispirited,
the people of Alleya sent word that they wished that he would refrain
from attacking them.

In return for their support, it was decided that their lives and
property would be safe until the rebels retired 'discomforted and
shame faced'.[78] It was widely believed that even though Faisal's
forces, the Ghāfirī tribes, outnumbered those of Aziz one to ten, they
were 'Hadhi', or settled Arabs. They always had a dis-inclination to
face Bedouins no matter how numerically superior they may be. But
despite this, the people of Alleya and Sumail by and large supported
Faisal and opposed the rebels.

Village societies continued to bargain with rival factions to
get them off their territory and buy peace. There was a rumour
doing the rounds in the bazaar that the people of Alleya offered

Abdul Aziz a sum of $1100 to retire from their country. But he demanded $2000 to do so. Even though this was not confirmed, Lt Col Miles reported that 'confidence has been to a great extent restored in Muscat'. As he said, 'Merchants have re-landed their goods and trade has been resumed.'[79] And Sayyid Faisal continued to be confident that his guns continued to kill the rebels and the 'tops of their houses fall on them by our guns'. This was after the breaking of the house of their chief.

The people of Alleya, he stated, were with him and were making their own efforts as well to get the rebels out. On one occasion, they asked him to stop the assault for two days while they tried to negotiate with the rebels to leave. They promised that if the rebels did not leave, they would enrol themselves under Faisal and allow them free access in their area and cooperation to chase the rebels. Sayyid Faisal, in consultation with the elders of the Ghāfirī, agreed to this proposal. But they resumed firing and appealed for continued supplies and money from Turki to keep the fight on.[80] Finally, the people of Alleya paid $1000 to Aziz and ensured his withdrawal from their area. This marked the end of his rebellion, and Alleya submitted to Turki.

Aziz was deserted by his supporters. Yet, he did not agree to reside in India on a pension, as desired by Turki. Following the suppression of his rebellion, the people of Alleya joined hands with the Ghāfirīs and pledged support to Turki. Faisal's spies always followed Aziz to track his further plans and movements.[81] They revealed that the money that the people of Alleya had given him and which his ally Ḥamūd al Jahafee had received had never been passed on to him. Jahafee did not share it even with his Shaykhs of Banī Bū Hassan. This caused dissension and the two Shaykhs were unlikely to join in any future collaborations with Aziz. Aziz himself managed to get via extortion a mere $100 from an Arab in the course of his retreat from Alleya–Sumail.[82] However, disorders and turbulence continued in the region. Turki had to send officers to establish tranquillity in his freshly occupied domains post the rebellion of Sayyid Aziz.[83]

Putting Down Roots in Tribal Towns: The Fight for Burka

The rocky bricolage politics notwithstanding, Turki had sensed the political benefits of using tribal conflicts to dig his heels in society, garner economic gains and negotiate with the British. He remained forever on the move in the tribal areas of Al Batinah. His political entrepreneurship involved negotiating his way through the tribal conflicts and laying his control over the date-bearing areas of the Al Batinah coast.

Soon after he quelled Aziz's rebellion, he sailed northwards from Muscat in his yacht the *Dar el-Salam*, to occupy the ancient tribal town of Burka. Before he left, he ordered the Beni Rasih and Hishm, two Ghāfirī tribes of Jailan south of Muscat, to join him. They had assisted Sayyid Faisal also at Sumail. The people of Nakhil were also asked to send a force to Burka to cooperate with him in the attack on one of the strongest fortresses in Oman, the El Hazm in Burka, under the command of Sayyid Ibrahim.

Turki mastered the art of fighting in the tribal areas where the control of sources of water, the trade routes and the maintenance of the date trees were key to success. Striking the interior towns keeping the date plantation vicissitudes in mind was key to his military strategy. He told his men, en route to Burka, to destroy all the trees and water resources around the town, even if they were unsuccessful in damaging the fortress.[84] He also attempted to intercept the town's trade with Rustaq, inland south of Burka, close to Muscat. He prohibited dates and other produce of that district being brought down to the coast.[85] He often abandoned the march to Burka if the date harvest season was over and the produce had been collected. There was no point destroying fruitless trees.

In 1878, E.C. Ross, Political Agent in the Persian Gulf, was much relieved when Turki abandoned the attack on the fortress of Burka because the harvest from date trees in the neighbourhood had all been gathered. He paid and dismissed the Beni Rasib and other Arabs tribes and urged them to go back home. An alarmed Ross was of the view that perhaps he had embarked on this expedition to release his two Indian slaves in the possession of Sayyid Ibrahim.

These were released by Ibrahim on his arrival.[86] Or perhaps he abandoned his march as the enemy had a bigger force than he had managed to collect.

This strategy was well thought out to make the most of the hardship the tribes and the date plantation owners were facing during the unprecedented economic crisis of 1878. In this year, heavy rains and flooding had destroyed the date crop in the whole of Oman, causing severe hardship, as this was the main produce of the country and the staple food of the people. There was fear of famine as also of tribal disturbances triggered by this economic stress.[87] Indeed, the hardships intensified because the previous year (1877) had seen low harvest. Also, the import of rice was less because of the famine in Madras.

Turki not only cashed in on the economic distress to establish his control on the Al Batinah agricultural and trade hotspots but also made the most of the local fears that the laying of the telegraph and British expansion of the steamship were creating in the area. He was determined to use all this to his advantage and leverage it to the tribal conflict, on the back of which he was set to establish his career.

Turki handled the tribal politics by using a carrot-and-stick policy. He struck financial deals with some of the tribes and at other times indulged in an open offensive against others. This was most evident when, close on the heels of the Aziz rebellion, rumours of the rising of the Sharhiyeh tribe were heard. But both Sayyid Ibrahim and Abdul Aziz did not join in because of the low possibility of its success. But those who did gang up against him were dealt with through money deals or outright aggression. For instance, when the Mutawaa tribe gathered strength against him and their leader Shaykh Saleh bin Ali raised the banner of revolt, Turki sent him enormous amounts of money via his servant to quell the revolt. Indeed, he tried to use his services to dissolve the tribal coalition. He initially agreed and got his allowance increased as well. But the truce lasted for only a month.

The negotiation with the tribes via both striking deals and aggression was the stuff that characterized Turki's efforts to consolidate himself in the Al Batinah coast. Such dealings and fluid alliances remained integral to his career building project. Thus, soon after he had sorted matters with the Mutawaa, the tribes of the Sumail Valley, the Ghāfirīs and the Hināwīs had to be dealt with. Turki sent his Vizir, Sayyid Sa'īd, to negotiate truce with them. He successfully organized one that lasted for six months.[88]

Again, soon after the Mutawaas left Muscat, Shaykh Ḥamūd of Al Wahibeh, who was part of the rebel force, seized upon the date groves at Boshir and threatened to destroy them unless Turki paid them $2500. This demand was complied with. And on the heels of this came the news of Shaykh Saleh's impending march to Muscat. Soon he and his tribal followers of about 1500 men arrived and occupied Muttrah without opposition. Turki was taken by surprise and relied only on his party of Wahhabi and Baluchi soldiers. Sayyid Abdul Aziz could not work out an alliance for this attack, but Sayyid Ibrahim bin Kais had arrived at Muttrah in support.[89]

Blood feuds were continuously reported from the region, and rumours of Sayyid Abdul Aziz intervening and using them to hit out at his brother Turki floated around, keeping the atmosphere of internecine warfare ripe. But this is exactly the stuff that Turki walked on for his political entrepreneurship.

Turki's military strategy in the tribal interiors worked wonders. From 1878, there was an increase of trade from the Muscat port. This was because of his effective control of the date plantations enabled by his control of tribal towns such as Burka. He also relieved the economic distress by replacing the square-rigged vessels that sailed between India and Muscat with country crafts, the buglas. They performed the voyage to Calcutta and back as easily and quickly as ships. Several successful voyages made in 1878 contributed to a rise in trade. Again, he sold the customs farm during the year for $1,06,000.[90]

And yet even if things improved, they were no match for the prosperity of Zanzibar, which was perceived as being more economically alive. A steady emigration of Arabs to this African kingdom was in place: 1000 Arabs left their mother country during the year to permanently settle there.[91]

Emboldened by his strength in the tribal interior, Turki got his eldest son Muhammad installed as the Governor of Sohar. He imprisoned its serving Governor, Sayyid Badr, whom he invited to Muscat as part of his political strategy. Badr was subsequently sent off to Zanzibar.[92]

VII

Consolidating the Sultanate Exterior

Adopting the Imperial Political Practice of Exile

Turki's exile at Bombay early in his career exposed him to the world of British India. It fired his political imagination, and he began to view Indian port towns as integral to his political geography. He too used these ports as sites of exile for his rival siblings to keep them away from his machinations, just as he had been removed by the British before he became Sultan. British imperial networks were extremely useful to firefight household politics.

His younger brother Aziz as well as nephew Salim had to be tamed. Turki wanted to snatch away the control of important Persian ports such as the Chabahar from his rival brother Aziz. And Salim of course was his arch-rival at Muscat. Both these siblings were handled by tapping into British support and drawing from their political strategy of exile, which they had perfected in the Western Indian Ocean.

Turki freely tapped into imperial networks for the control of these ports. In 1871, he complained to the British that the people of the Persian Chabahar port, in the Gulf of Oman, complained of Aziz and wanted him to free them from Aziz's control and to receive them under his own protection. They wanted to become dependants of Muscat as in former times. Deen Muhammad, of Chabahar, wrote to say that he had taken Chabahar and would hold it on Turki's account if he accepted him and his people as his own subjects. Turki sent his Wālī to negotiate. But he was convinced that as long as Aziz remained at Gwadar, he would always be up to mischief, not only there, but also in Oman. Turki wanted the British to remove Aziz from that port and hand it over to him for future peace and stability.[93]

One of the advantages of tapping into and straddling the Eurasian imperial assemblage was the easy access it offered to British cities in India and elsewhere, where his rivals could be exiled. British Indian cities became perfect sites of exile for rebel princes and the Sultan's foes. Turki certainly benefited from this expansion of his political canvas into British India.

Thus, Aziz, who had come to Bombay for the treatment of his eyes in 1872, was asked by the British, by way of help to Turki, to remain there permanently on a pension. His repeated requests to the Governor of Bombay to return remained unheeded. There was no attention paid to his turning down of the Sultan's proposal to stay permanently in India or Zanzibar on a monthly stipend of $200.[94] Aziz continued to challenge Turki and threatened a return to Muscat.

The British openly sided with Turki and denied all allegations made by Aziz. In 1873, the Bombay government inquired on an allegation that the Aga Khan had aided Aziz with $500. The Aga Khan denied this and, as proof, pointed out the assistance of $5000 that he had given to Turki. He said he could not possibly aid both sides.[95] Aziz continued to be in exile at Bombay.

In 1873, Aziz was told that Turki agreed to give him $300 per month allowance provided he reside in British territory and not interfere in his territory or in his rule, either in Oman or Makran. He was asked to present himself to the British at Gwadar within ten days of this letter and was warned that if he refused to come, this offer would not be renewed. If he threatened Gwadar, he would be arrested and disposed of according to the pleasures of the Viceroy. He was further told he would be arrested and made prisoner if he ventured to sea to enter Oman or the Persian Gulf.[96]

Aziz was summoned to Karachi, from where the *Columbine* ship was ready to take him to Bombay for detention in India. Turki sanctioned the allowance for him.[97] The Commissioner at Sindh was told to detain him in 'honorable surveillance', with a warning of being taken into custody if he intrigued or attempted to escape. A pension of $300 was sanctioned for him, and this was to be deducted from the subsidy payable to Turki.[98]

The Commissioner reported that Aziz argued that he made plans very much like Turki: leaving Bombay and returning to Oman. But due to bad weather, he landed in Makran and attempted to recover his old position of Wālī or Governor of Gwadar. Once he failed, he decided to march to Oman, only to be intercepted by one of Her Majesty's vessels of war. Clearly, he had landed in Muscat to foment trouble for Turki. And since he crossed the sea in violation of the maritime truce, he was accordingly arrested at sea near Soor by British cruisers and lodged at Karachi in quarters specially prepared for him.[99]

He was sanctioned $300 per month that was to be paid by Turki; and warned that if he intrigues then warrant under regulation III of 1818 will be enforced.[100] But Aziz turned down the money offer on grounds that it was inadequate for his position. He refused to remain in India in lieu of such a small amount as he was convinced that he had a right to a proper provision being made for him by his brother Turki.[101]

The interactions with the British helped Turki ward off political challenges from his nephew Salim as well, who was still hopeful of his reinstallation as Sultan of Muscat. Salim was a wanderer on the Omani littoral and had taken refuge in Bandar Abbas after being ousted from Muscat by his relative Qais. In order to end his nuisance value, Turki was willing to grant his nephew a monthly allowance of $300 per month on condition that he would reside in British territory and abstain from interference in Muscat affairs. But Salim refused the offer, claiming a larger allowance and the unrestricted right to certain property in Muscat.[102] He used the ports of the Persian Gulf on the other side of Muscat as his base; he intended to leave Dustyari for Jashk and Qishm on the Persian Gulf to keep watch on Muscat events.

The Salim threat revealed how useful his forced exile to Bombay had been in firing his imaginary about a world beyond Oman that had become integral to his politics. Turki pressed his British imperial networks to deal with Salim's challenge. In 1873, the Government of India asked the Commissioner in Sindh to inform Salim that if he surrendered unconditionally, he would be granted the pension provision offered by Turki. But if he did not comply, then the offer would be withdrawn and he would be made a prisoner wherever found. He would then receive only such terms as he considered fit.

But Salim refused to accept these terms and claimed the Muscat throne as his right. In 1873, he captured Gwadar, on the Persian side of the Gulf of Oman, escaped to the island of Qishm in the Persian Gulf and continued from there to intervene in the affairs of Oman.[103] He hopped around the Persian and British port towns, straddling the imperial assemblage and never losing an opportunity to use its networks, as so many of his siblings were doing. He arrived in Bombay in 1873 and asked for British support, playing the victim: he had been ousted from Muscat by Qais in 1868.

He alleged that his palace had been plundered and the estimated loot was of 20 lakh rupees, together with many heirlooms of the dynasty. He was forced to flee Muscat with his mother, brother and sisters and remain in hiding in foreign lands. Later, he sent his mother and sisters to Zanzibar in the hope that they would get aid there. Not only did his plan not materialize, but their belongings were destroyed by the hurricane that hit the island. They were stranded there, looking to him for assistance.[104]

In 1875, the British government arrested Salim while he was making an attempt to revisit Oman with a band of armed followers and with the aim to cause disturbances against Turki. Turki was very pleased to know of the arrest of Salim. He was keen that he be deported to British India on a stipend of $100, which he was willing to pay. In fact, he demanded that Salim be handed over to him.[105]

Salim was not handed over to Turki but was trotted around the prisons of British Indian cities, which were by now integral to the connected world of the Western Indian Ocean. He was captured and removed to Karachi and later to the fortress of Hyderabad in Sindh, where he was detained by a warrant issued under Regulation III of 1818. While at Hyderabad, Turki consented to allow Salim a monthly allowance of $100 for his maintenance. He also ordered that the prisoner was to be subjected to such a degree of restraint as would 'prevent his escaping or carrying on intrigues'.[106]

Along with Salim, his brother, Sayyid Harib bin Thuwayni, was also captured. But since there was no ground for his detention, he was permitted to return to Muscat.[107] He was sent to Qishm via Bandar Abbas en route to Muscat.[108]

The financial aspect of the deal also revealed how integral British Indian cities were to the Omani political ambit. It was decided that the allowance of $100 payable to Salim would commence from the date of his arrest. The advance was to be drawn from the Hyderabad treasury. Also, the expenditure incurred in connection with his removal from Karachi to the fort at Hyderabad, and the cost of removing Sayyid Harib to Muscat, would also be charged to the Hyderabad treasury. It was decided that in case Salim refused to sell the assets he owned in Karachi, then the cost of their maintenance would be deducted from his allowance.[109]

But since Salim was in a pitiable state with not even a change of clothes, the magistrate of Hyderabad suggested that advances be made to him to such an amount as he deemed necessary until such time as his first stipend was due.[110] And yet, typical of the complicated jockeying for power of the feuding Busaidi siblings, the British did not consider Salim a spent force. They treated him as a royal. At the fort of Hyderabad, he had quarters assigned to him, three attendants and his horse, all being looked after by the Karachi police.[111] The British were not going to take any chances, now that the frontiers of the Western Indian Ocean touched British Indian cities.

VIII

Tapping into the Western Imperial Networks to Support the Sultanate

Turki's successful straddling of the tribal and the British imperial networks consolidated his career to the extent that it alarmed Lt Col Ross, the Political Resident at Bushire. He tried to underplay its success, calling it a 'sign of weakness'. He was of the view that 'his feeble tenure of power and inability to take the field in person do not make it prudent for him to initiate hostilities against his most powerful rival'.[112]

But there was no doubt that the imperial networks were as important for Turki as the tribal ones. The issue of the losses suffered by the British Indian traders during the many political turbulences on the Al Batinah coast offered the perfect entry point to Turki to connect favourably with the British. For instance, he used the card of the British subjects in Muttrah to draw attention to the conflicts in his territory. The tribal threat to their subjects in Muscat and Muttrah was enough to make the British step in to help him. They fired a few shots at Muscat and Muttrah to dislodge the enemy and discourage their attack on the town. Dissensions broke out in the enemy ranks. Shaykh Saleh made a demand of $20,000 and the restoration of his and Sayyid Ibrahim's allowance. This was rejected. The loss to British subjects at their hands was estimated at $15,173.

Handling the challenges faced by the British subjects became a way of digging his heels in the Al Batinah and also establishing connections with the British. As the Sultan regained control of the Al Batinah with the help of the British, he gave them permission to press for the reparation of damages to British subjects. Thus, a sum of $3600 as reparation was obtained from Soor from the Janebeh tribe for the plunder of a Bania at that town two years before.[113]

Again, in 1877, the Government of India sanctioned that $1000 from each quarterly payment of the Muscat–Zanzibar subsidy was to be deducted to make good the losses incurred by British Indian traders at Muttrah in January 1874.[114] Further, the losses incurred by Turki and the balance outstanding against him on account of the traders of Mesnāh in consequence of an attack made by Ibrahim bin Kais in 1874 were to be duly investigated and Turki to be reimbursed accordingly.[115] This was a large sum of $12,717.[116] Significantly, these arrangements were made after due consultation with Turki and the merchant community involved. The payment was ascertained after a panchayat of merchants was assembled at Muscat to assist in the inquiry; all the evidence that could be produced by the Mesnāh traders on behalf of their claims was taken. Indeed, many of them had lost everything, including their books and accounts, and none of them were able to give a rigidly accurate statement of their affairs.[117] But even beyond this wider consultative process, Turki was always happy to pay for the losses incurred by British subjects in his territories. Thus in 1874, he paid $450 to traders as full value of the goods stolen at Seeb.[118]

In return, Turki was also keen that the British detain at their Indian ports vessels that came from Omani ports without clearing their full customs dues. He was anxious about the loss of customs also from vessels that sailed from Oman to Persian and Turkish ports without clearing customs in Oman. He ignored the latter, as he had no relations with these powers. But he wanted the Government of India to recover from them the just dues of British and other traders and check the defraud faced by the customs farmer.[119]

In an act of generosity and in return for his help to British Indian subjects, his request was favourably attended. The Government of India agreed to assist him in recovering his unpaid customs duties by seizing and detaining all crafts that may enter Indian ports from Oman except those that could produce a certificate from Turki's customs authorities.[120]

Zanzibar Subsidy and Slave Ban: Quid Pro Quo?

Turki tapped into British help when Barghash, his rival brother at Zanzibar, refused to pay him the subsidy as decided by the British-sponsored Canning Award agreement, which had divided the Sultanate into Muscat and Zanzibar.

Barghash's refusal alarmed the British, as it encouraged Turki to take up arms. The British feared that if Turki tried this route, then arbitration would be in shreds and their commerce adversely affected. They were particularly worried about the effects of 'Arab filibustering', in which they feared the Indian subjects, through whose hands the entire trade passed, would be the chief sufferers.

The British made an offer to Turki to prevent him from taking to arms and in the interest of peace in the Persian Gulf and East Africa. They offered him a subsidy regularly from Her Majesty's treasury at Bombay. At the suggestion of Bartle Frere, special envoy to Muscat, he was permitted to draw $40,000 from the Consulate for arrears of last year, with $20,000 being half the subsidy for the current year.

Bartle Frere, who was also the chief interlocutor with Barghash for the suppression of the slave trade, was keen to lure Turki for similar reasons. He needed his support for the ban on slave traffic from the port of Muscat, where he was currently stationed. In a visible warming up to him, Frere said 'he had not seen a ruler more friendly to British interests'. He was of the view that the Muscat port being strategically positioned so close to India and so easy for fortification was critical to British interests. It was, therefore, very essential for them to see that a ruler favourable to them was there.[121] He was also aware that Turki was desperate for money from Zanzibar, as he inherited a depleted treasury at Muscat.

Frere was convinced that this helpful move would draw Turki away from Persia and entangle him with British interests, such as abolition. He was concerned that both Turkey and Persia invoked a history with Oman to draw the Sultan into their affairs. This was worrisome, as the prospect of a Sultan who looked to 'Persian capitol and its legations for orders or inspiration' was not good for the British supremacy in the region. Frere was equally concerned about the takeover of the Wahhabis in Muscat as a backlash to Turki's entanglements with Persia.

Frere recommended payment of subsidy on condition that Turki paid the pension to his younger brother Aziz and nephew Salim, who were both in Bombay. These pensions were to be paid from the British treasury by deducting the amount from the Zanzibar subsidy before it was paid to Muscat. The Sultan was also to be clearly told that the British would not allow 'British territory which affords them a secure refuge in exile a basis for intriguing against the peace either of Muscat or Zanzibar'.[122]

On the recommendation of Frere, the British government undertook to pay him the whole Zanzibar subsidy subject to his good behaviour, with arrears from the date of succession. They hoped to eventually make Zanzibar pay the entire amount. And whatever future remission was granted was to be shared between the Indian and British governments.[123] Turki was insistent that he get the arrears of the subsidy and continue to receive it annually. He argued that if this was not to be, the British should permit him to seize Zanzibar. But the British reminded him of the Canning Award as a deterrent to his plans.[124]

Prohibiting Slave Traffic from Omani Ports

Frere's overtures paid off when Turki signed a treaty wherein he committed himself, his heirs and successors to prohibit the import or export of slaves within his territories. He also agreed to abolish all public slave markets and finally free all slaves as soon as they set foot in his territory. This last item was particularly heartening to the British, as it discouraged slave traders from bringing their human wares to a country where the latter at once ceased to be available property.[125]

Turki was instantly compared to Sultan Barghash in Zanzibar, who was bargaining hard with Frere on the issue of abolition. His praiseworthy, bold move earned him instant visibility in imperial circles. S.B. Miles, Consul General at Zanzibar, praised Turki, saying that he had taken this step even when his income was one-third of the Zanzibar revenue, and he had to rule a kingdom as large as Britain that contained nearly a million turbulent and warlike subjects.

He added that Turki's gesture was particularly commendable as his finances did not admit of his maintaining either a fleet or an army. His many rivals made his tenure precarious as well. Comparing him to Barghash, he said that:

[L]ooking at their respective positions, the one blessed with a large revenue, with undisputed power and without an enemy, the other

financially embarrassed and surrounded by foes and rivals it would
appear that Turki's bold attitude against slave trade and his faithful
adherence to his engagements compare not unfavourably with the
conduct of his younger and more fortunate brother.[126]

IX

Tapping into Asian Imperial Powers: The Fight
for Bandar Abbas

Turki's refurbished Sultanate relied more on Persian imperial
politics than Western power play. Unlike his brothers Majid and
Thuwayni, he had no great desire to be seen as part of the Western
imperial club. Instead, he kept his options open with the Persian
imperial networks and used them as a counterfoil to Western
imperial dominance. Turki used the renewal of the lease for the
Omani rights over the port of Bandar Abbas to assert his power and
entangle himself in Persian imperial politics.

Dealing with the Omani Legacy in Bandar Abbas

Turki's father Sayyid Saʿīd, we saw in Chapter 1, had leased the port
of Bandar Abbas from the Persians. And his brother Thuwayni
fought to maintain his foothold there by extending the lease. Turki
too remained embedded in the port's politics. In fact, he invested
in it much more than his family members. This was expected as,
over the years, the Arab Governors of Bandar Abbas had become
power brokers commanding clout in Persian society and were in a
position to back him as the Sultan in Muscat. Turki leaned on them
more than he did on Western powers in his jockeying for the top
job at Muscat.

In 1868, the lease of Bandar Abbas ended when Azan bin Qais
deposed Thuwayni's son, Salim, at Muscat. The Persians argued that
it stood valid only for Sayyid Saʿīd's sons and not his grandson. They
were wary of Salim anyway. For similar reasons, Zanzibar too was
unwilling to pay Salim the subsidy.[127] This meant that Salim had little

money to pay the Persians for the Bandar Abbas lease. The Persians terminated the lease in his lifetime itself for non-payment.[128] ·

Salim commenced retaliatory raids on the Persian Gulf, viewed as piracy, as tensions brewed between him and the Persians. Paradoxically, he fled to Bandar Abbas and later, feeling insecure, he moved to the Persian port of Qishm, where he lived off the revenues collected from Bandar Abbas. As he threatened to blockade the Bandar Abbas port, Persia asked for British help as it had no resources of its own to meet these acts of aggression.

British officers had to tread with caution. They assisted the Persians so that peace could be maintained in the Gulf and commerce run smoothly. At the same time, they encouraged the Persians not to break the lease on grounds of Salim being a usurper. The British had recognized him as Thuwayni's successor. Again, a Persian flotilla in the Gulf was to be 'deprecated', as it would send confusing signals about the maritime truce and control of the Gulf they had painstakingly acquired. But at the same time, it was not to be openly discouraged either, since Salim threatened piratical attacks. The issue was further complicated by the fact that Muscat, Zanzibar and Persia were not under one undivided authority. It was suggested that they all be kept under the India office.[129]

The British wanted to avoid conflict in the region. While it reiterated that it was in favour of the renewal of the lease, it recognized the authority of Persia in Angaun and the entire territory covered in the lease.[130] Pelly was not against the blockade of the port by the Sultan, but he and the Government of India were against any hostile operations against Persia. He was asked to mediate and prevent a collision in the interest of British commerce. He was asked to make the Sultan agree to British mediation.[131]

Finally, with Pelly's intervention, the lease was renewed for seven years at 25,000 tomans.[132] The Sultan was not willing to include in it the islands of Angaun and Larrack.[133] And he had the support of the Resident of the Persian Gulf in this claim over these islands.[134] The conditions of the lease were that it was restricted to Salim and his descendants. Article 12 provided that if any conqueror took possession of Oman and Muscat, then the Persian government would not be bound by any of these conditions in regard to that conqueror.[135]

Turki and the Bandar Abbas Lease: Omani Arabs as Brokers

Turki, as the new Sultan of Muscat, brought the lease negotiation once again back on the table. He was keen to build on the Omani foothold in Bandar Abbas and renew the lease favourably. Persia was reluctant to deal with Turki in view of his past misdemeanours, such as inciting rioters during the food riots. It conveyed the message that it was fully capable of maintaining its affairs in Bandar Abbas and averse to leasing it to Turki, who had heaped indignities on it in the past. In fact, when Sayyid Turki became Sultan, the Persians were keen to deal with independent Arab entrepreneurs of Persian origin, such as Haji Ahmad, rather than renew the lease with Turki.

Turki knew Haji Ahmad well from the time of his brother Thuwayni. Indeed, he had been helped by him in his conquest of Muscat. In 1869, he sent his emissaries, the Arab clerk, Haji Saleh Bahraini and Muallim Sayyid Arab of Muscat to Sayyid Turki with the purpose of borrowing money that he needed to pay off 1,80,000 tomans to Mustafa Quli Khan, chief guard of Zil al-Sultān. After initial wrangling, he got the money and a bargain was struck: Haji Ahmad had to dispatch 200–300 riflemen to Muscat to assist Turki in his attempt to become Sultan at Muscat.[136] This arrangement had ensured his foothold in Omani politics even if he had dug in his heels at Bandar Abbas.

Turki packed off Haji Ahmad to Bandar Abbas to handle the affairs at the port. But typical to the Arab Governors who had taken root in the port society, Haji Ahmad used the opportunity to pursue his private interests with the Fars Governor General.[137] The Persians were keen to play ball. Soon they appointed Haji Ahmad as the Governor of Bandar Abbas under their own control. He became a Persian subject as well.

Haji Ahmad's tenure rocked the port with disturbances. By 1871, he had become so big for his boots that the inhabitants of Bandar Abbas complained about his oppression to the Shiraz agent.

The agent reported that he collected part of the revenues but paid nothing of it to the Persian government. There was also a deficit of 20,000 tomans on account of arrears of the revenue of the previous year. He was consequently summoned to Shiraz.[138] His misdemeanours compelled the Persian government to pursue the renewal of the Bandar Abbas lease directly with Turki.

Turki was asked to depute an agent for these negotiations.[139] Typical of the commercialized political culture of Bandar Abbas, Agha Mahumad Ali, the malik al-tujjar (chief of merchants), offered his services to broker the deal. He offered to negotiate if Turki sent a petition and some presents and articles for the Shiraz authorities. But Turki would rather do the deal by himself.[140] The Persian government was keen to farm Bandar Abbas to Turki even if it had doubts about his stability and solvency.[141]

Indeed, it was not in the interest of independent contractors such as Haji Ahmad to let the lease go through by passing them away. Haji Ahmad reminded the Persians that in 1870, Turki had landed in Bandar Abbas during the period of riots in Persia over wheat shortage with about 400 followers in two large buglas. They wanted to plunder wheat that was being transferred in Bandar Abbas and then raid Muscat from Bandar Abbas.[142]

His influence no doubt created apprehensions in the Persian circuits against Turki. The British watched the developments apprehensively as the lease renewal negotiations failed.[143] The Persians also rejected most of Turki's requests for a foothold in the port city. Turki argued that Omani subjects in southern Persia engaged in trade were not adequately protected by the government and that he needed to install his agent there.[144] But even that was not allowed. The Persian government was in no mood to relent. It was widely believed that subordinate officers might use this opportunity to extract money from Turki.[145]

Turki was unrelenting. He strove to eliminate independent contractors such as Haji Ahmad and establish direct dealings with Persia. This was easier said than done. Allegations and counter allegations between Haji Ahmad and Turki continued as the latter tried to oust him from Bandar Abbas and take control of it. In 1875,

Haji Ahmad complained to the Persian authorities that his houses
and landed property in Oman and Muscat had been confiscated
by Turki. The furniture and other items therein had been sold by
auction to the value of $4000, which he had kept with him. And
also, all valuable property from his house had disappeared.

Persia took up his cause. The minister at Tehran wanted the
houses and landed property to be restored to Haji Ahmad, and
urged Turki to reimburse him in kind or cash for whatever had
been destroyed. Turki was warned that Persian authorities would
retaliate if Arab Muscatis living in Persia were so shoddily treated
in future.[146]

Sayyid Turki of course denied these allegations. He maintained
that when in 1868, after the coup by Azan, Haji Ahmad fled from
Muscat, he removed all his personal property to Bandar Abbas in
a vessel called *Fateh Manah* that belonged to one Haji Baqar. Two
years later (1870), when Turki acceded to the throne, he found
that no personal property of Haji Ahmad remained in Muscat.
And thus, these accusations were without foundation. Haji Ahmad
did, however, have two houses in Muscat, and a share along with
his brothers and sisters in his father's inheritance, which included
a house in Muscat and certain land property in Oman. These, he
stated, were intact.[147]

Tapping into the British Networks to Entrench Himself in Bandar Abbas

Turki was not giving up on Bandar Abbas so quickly. In order to
embed himself in the Persian port, he played on the Anglo-Persian
rivalry to further his interests. He raised with the British several
instances of popular dissatisfaction with the Persian rule in Bandar
Abbas and pleaded with them to help him establish his hold on the
port town. Thus, Turki's Vizir reported to the British that he had
received a petition from a Sayyid at Bandar Abbas stating that the
people were dissatisfied with the Persian government and wished
for a return of Arab rule. The Sayyid wanted Turki to be in touch
with the petitioner and do the needful. But E.C. Ross, the Resident,

convinced Turki that he could not intervene, as the matter rested with the Shah of Persia.[148] Again, in 1879, he sought the permission of the British Political Agent at Bandar Abbas to establish an agency at the port town to look into the interests of his subjects who traded there and felt unprotected and vulnerable. Even this was declined. The Vizir was asked to place the request to the Persian government. But the Political Agent warned him to not be too hopeful as, during the negotiations for the lease renewal, the Persians had said that if the Muscat Sultan sent his agent to that port, he would not be officially recognized.[149] Finally, a dejected Turki had to let the matter drop. This meant the end of formal Omani interest in Bandar Abbas.

Persian Assertion and Turki's Losing Hold over Bandar Abbas

Turki lost control of Bandar Abbas as, by 1882, Persia established firmer centralized control over the port. They also removed the port from the control of the Fars Governor, who had acted as their agent in the frontier and to whom the port belonged. The ports of Bandar Abbas and Lingah were detached from that province and given to the Amin al-Sulṭān, who was the Accountant General and had considerable influence at court. He in turn gave the two towns to one of his agents, who handed them over to a merchant at Bandar Abbas with supreme authority in that place. The British found this shift very unsatisfactory and prejudicial to their commercial interests. But they could do little about it.[150]

In 1883, the increasing centralized control of the Shah on Bandar Abbas was evident when the Amin al-Sulṭān appointed his brother Muhammad Hasan Khan as Governor of Bandar Abbas and Lingah. He in turn farmed its revenues and customs directly from the Shah, bypassing the Fars government. These ports, therefore, continued to be separate from the Government of Fars.[151] Significantly, Muhammad Hasan Khan's appointment was referred to as the appointment of the sadr-i-mulk, and he was declared the Governor of Bushire, Bandar Abbas and islands on the coast of Fars.[152]

These new Persian farmers or contractors of customs continued with many of the taxation practices of their Arab predecessors that had made these ports different from other Persian ports. One of them was the custom of charging 3.5 per cent duty on all goods imported rather than the 5 per cent charged at other ports. Further, no internal transit passes were issued for free transit of goods into the interior. In fact, as goods moved into the interior, the merchants paid *rahdari* (road tax) and other taxes as appropriate. All Indian traders vouched for paying this duty and asking for no further transit passes as they moved to the interior of Iran with their goods.[153]

Under the centralized control of the Persian revenue contractors who were dependent on the Qajar government in Persia, the centrality of the merchants in the political culture of the port only increased. In 1888, the Persian government proposed that, like in most other large towns of Persia, in Lingah and Bandar Abbas too commercial transactions were to be regulated by a body of traders called *Majlis al-Tujjar*. British Indian traders were to be encouraged to join these bodies. The British were worried that this might enhance their privileges as protected subjects.[154]

The Hindu community and the British Indian subjects at Bandar Abbas revealed that the committee of merchants was to consist of six Persians and four British Indians. Of the latter, two were to be Hindus and two Khoja Hyderabadis. Their principal point of concern was that they had to declare and promise in writing that there would be no objection to any decision of the committee regarding any cases, even in those where British subjects were concerned. The decision would not be liable to revision, and there would be no necessity to refer the matter to the Resident or the Foreign Office Agent. The British Indian subjects were reluctant to give such a promise, as they wanted to remain under the protection of the Foreign Office Agent and the British residency.[155] Soon, other non-Arabs were allowed to set up shop in Bandar Abbas. Notable among the new entrants were the Russians. The Russian firm Messrs Boghaoff of Marseilles appointed an agent in Bandar Abbas. He was an Armenian from Tehran named Makertich Khelantharian.[156] These developments alarmed the British and made them go soft on Turki and his Arab agents. For all these reasons, the Arab influence via private interests such as

Haji Ahmad Khan lingered in Bandar Abbas. They had developed a dynamic of their own that outlived the political vicissitudes of the period.

Beyond the Lease Politics: Haji Ahmad Khan

Turki soon realized that the Arab Omani presence in Bandar Abbas had a life beyond the lease politics. As we saw in Chapter 3, Omani Arab Vizirs of Persian origin, such as Haji Ahmad, had created private careers during their postings as Governors in the port. Their private interests and the enclaves of influence they crafted continued even if the lease of the port went through a rocky ride. Indeed, such individuals created the more enduring bonds between Oman and the Asian imperial powers such as Qajar Iran, irrespective of the installation of new Sultans at Muscat.

At one level, these privateers strengthened the Omani foothold in Bandar Abbas. At another level, they posed a political challenge because of the clout they wielded in Persian circuits. Haji Ahmad was a perfect case in point. Turki wanted to both use his influence to tap into Persian imperial networks as well as clip his wings and call the shots himself.

Haji Ahmad, as we know from Thuwayni's period, had a long experience of being a Vizir of the Omani Sultans. He had also formed strong networks in Bandar Abbas in Thuwayni's reign, when he was appointed as the Arab Governor of the port. He had used the official stint to carve out a private career for himself as a revenue contractor of the port.

After losing his post as Vizir on the murder and subsequent takeover of Sayyid Salim, the jobless Haji Ahmad kept his eye more firmly than ever on his Bandar Abbas career. He wanted to become its revenue contractor again. But he had competition from the Arab Governor of Bandar Abbas, who was itching for an independent career at the port after the murder of Thuwayni.

Even when the new Sultan Sayyid Salim called Haji Ahmad back to Muscat and reappointed him as his Vizir, his ambition in Bandar Abbas did not cease. Indeed, in 1868, he was so keen on his career as revenue contractor in the port, which he saw as more profitable and permanent than the Vizarat, that he made a private proposal for the Governorship of Bandar Abbas to the Persian government. He offered to pay 30,000 tomans instead of the earlier 20,000 and was willing to shift his family from Muscat to Bandar Abbas.

He was noticed in Persian and British circles as an efficient administrator and ingenious manipulator. He used his clout as Salim's Vizir to urge Oman to improve Bandar Abbas as a port of commerce. This lent him instant popularity with the traders. British traders in particular appreciated this move.[157] Haji Ahmad used their praises for his self-promotion.

He cited a Mr Mackenzie of the firm of Messrs Gray Paul and Co. at Bushire, who said that on a recent visit to Bandar Abbas and Lingah, he was surprised to find that, as compared to Bushire, the quality of produce shipped by British steamers to and from those ports was high. Mackenzie commented on the 'go ahead' spirit exhibited in Bandar Abbas, which he attributed to the 'friendly feeling' shown by the Governor of that place, Haji Ahmad. He observed that the steamers there obtained higher freights to Bombay than at Bushire, and shippers there preferred sending their goods forward in their steamers to those of the Persian companies. In fact, he was so pleased with the way business was conducted at Bandar Abbas that he said that 'my partner and I will go to reside there for some months, and we make no doubt will work up a better business than we find we can here without encouragement from our own Government'.[158] Indeed, Haji Ahmad was carrying out many reforms to improve the port. He wanted an end to the carrying of merchandise by porters from lighters to the shore and had plans to build a pier at Bandar Abbas.[159]

Later, when the coup at Muscat resulted in the ousting of Sultan Salim and the installation of a non-dynasty member and a collateral of the reigning family, Azan bin Qais, the renewal of the Bandar Abbas lease was annulled. Alongside, Haji Ahmad lost his job as the Vizir of Sultan Salim. This was the time when the niche he had carved at Bandar Abbas as an Arab privateer proved very handy. He was now jobless in Muscat but with a foothold in Bandar Abbas as its revenue contractor and a sterling reputation of being an able administrator and Governor. This was enough for him to renew his efforts with gusto for the independent Governorship of Bandar Abbas.

Haji Ahmad masterfully played his cards, invoking specific strands of his multiple identities and underplaying others as it suited him. He downplayed his rank and status in Oman as well as the allegations that he was a British subject from some Iranians opposed to him. Instead, he forefronted his Persian origin to lay stake to his claim to the Governorship of Bandar Abbas as a Persian subject. And most importantly, he highlighted his wealth by way of promising huge financial investments that he was willing to make in Bandar Abbas in the event of his becoming its Governor.

In 1868, he made a private proposal to the Governor of Fars for the Governorship of Bandar Abbas. He offered to pay 30,000 tomans instead of the earlier 20,000; he was willing to shift his family from Muscat to the port city and govern on his own, not on behalf of Sultan Salim, and that too as a Persian subject. The Persian foreign minister was keen on the proposal as long as he did not claim to be a British subject and invited him to Shiraz to formalize the appointment. By the time Haji Ahmad reached Shiraz, he had already won favour with the minister by paying in instalments the revenues of Bandar Abbas. He had already paid 6000 tomans before reaching Shiraz. He pleaded to the Persians that he had quit the services of the Omani Sultan Salim and would administer Bandar Abbas as a private independent individual and invest in its improvement. The minister wanted him to bring his family to Shiraz so as to reassure himself that he was no longer a British subject but wanted a Persian subjecthood.[160]

Haji Ahmad's growing clout triggered anxiety in both Iranian and British circuits. The Iranian agent in Bombay was wary of Haji Ahmad's claims to improve Bandar Abbas. He wanted the government to ensure the source of his funding for investments in the port city. The agent warned that Haji Ahmad, despite his Persian origin and the invocation of his Persian subject status, was considered a British subject in Bombay and that in the eventuality of his removal or replacement from Bandar Abbas, the British might lay claim to his investments there.[161]

In 1869, in the absence of any other viable alternative for the administration of Bandar Abbas, the Persians granted his wish, and he became the Governor of Bandar Abbas, but as a Persian subject. His seal indicated this very clearly: '*Kadim naliya Ahmad bin Mahomad Ali Nazim Moham Benadur*'. This shot him into the limelight as the chief mediator and broker between Muscat and Persia. He promised to keep Lt Col Pelly, the British Resident in the Persian Gulf, in the loop. But more importantly, he enhanced his power brokering between Muscat and Persia.

While he worked for Persia, it was widely believed that he remained in touch with his former Omani master Sayyid Salim. He used his stature in Bandar Abbas to enable Salim to quietly retain his influence in the port and the country adjacent to it keeping up his old relations and ties with the ousted Sultan.[162] At the same time, it was with his political acumen that he maintained good relations with Persia as well. He clearly was so invested in his new role as the independent Arab Governor of Bandar Abbas that he moved with ease across the diplomatic networks of Persia, following all proper protocol to get his jobs done. He was reported to be collecting presents to take with him to Shiraz for his meeting with the Governor of that province.[163] His ease of handling the Persians as an independent careerist frightened the British, as they feared becoming irrelevant in the politics of the imperial assemblage. A shocked Pelly repeatedly urged him not to commit himself to any arrangement in Bandar Abbas without the consent of the British Indian government. But Haji Ahmad was unconcerned and happy in his new role.[164]

He had nothing to fear, as his administrative and diplomatic acumen had won him friends across the Persian and British commercial community, who applauded his efforts to make business dealings easy at Bandar Abbas. His old British trader friends Mr Mackenzie and others from Messrs Gray Paul and Company were delighted that he was made the independent Governor of the port. They hoped that he would become the permanent administrator of

Bandar Abbas affairs, as his 'arrangements contrasted so favourably with those of the Persian authorities'. They proposed to establish a house and open a separate trade at Bandar Abbas, should Haji Ahmad be there.[165]

The ease with which he could flit through the assemblage invoking multiple identities for private gains was best illustrated when the Persian minister wanted an assurance that he would not claim to be a British subject at any stage. And the minister had every reason to seek this assurance because even as he made an independent career for himself as a Persian subject in Bandar Abbas, he never failed to invoke his earlier stint there as the Arab Governor of the port and also his rank as the Vizir of the Sultanate of Oman.

Neither did he forget to showcase himself as the protector of British commercial interests when it suited him. He always cited Mr Mackenzie of the firm of Messrs Gray Paul and Co. at Bushire, who appreciated the vibrancy in Bandar Abbas and attributed it to the 'friendly feeling shown to us by the Governor of that place [Haji Ahmad]'. Haji Ahmad reminded the British that Mr Mackenzie had observed that the shippers in Bandar Abbas 'prefer sending their goods forward in our steamers to those of the Persian Companies'. In fact, he was so pleased with the way business was conducted at Bandar Abbas that he said that 'my partner and I will go to reside there for some months, and we make no doubt will work up a better business than we find we can here without encouragement from our own Government'.[166] They proposed to establish a house and open a separate trade at Bandar Abbas should Haji Ahmad remain there.[167]

Haji Ahmad continued to brave competitors for his job in Bandar Abbas. Most of them came from his Muscat circle. His old Muscat rival and contender for the spoils of Bandar Abbas, Shaykh Sayyid, who, as we saw in Chapter 3, he had managed to dislodge from the Governorship, continued to try his luck. In 1869, he arrived in Bandar Abbas while Haji Ahmad was away collecting revenues in Minab and claimed to be the new Governor appointed by Muscat. Their respective followers clashed in Bandar Abbas, resulting in rioting in which Haji Ahmad fled in a British ship and his family also had to flee the port city. Later, however, with local support, he was able to recapture Bandar Abbas.[168]

But life remained tense for Haji Ahmad at Bandar Abbas. The inhabitants of Bandar Abbas complained about his oppression to the Shiraz agent. There were also allegations of a deficit of 20,000 tomans in revenue and financial irregularities. He was consequently summoned to Shiraz.[169] In 1871, only three years into his Governorship, his enemies got the better of him. He was dismissed and imprisoned for embezzlement of 30,000 tomans. He remained under guard while his houses and other property were slowly sold.[170]

In 1871, Ahmad Shah Khan Minabi, whose family had been the *kalantar* (mayor) of Minab since time immemorial, succeeded Haji Ahmad. He generally stayed put in his home town of Minab and was known to be aloof. The merchants always complained that they had to arm themselves for protection against the Turkish-speaking tribe of the Baharlurs and other plunderers, as Ahmad Shah was never there for Bandar Abbas.[171] And, thus, it was no surprise that, after his release from prison in 1874, Haji Ahmad pursued his case to be reinstated. Ahmad Shah contested this, and Haji Ahmad did not make much progress. Complaints against Ahmad Shah kept mounting until he died in 1876. Haji Nasir ul mulk remained the Governor of Bandar Abbas until 1881.[172]

But even though without an official position, Haji Ahmad continued to play an important role in Bandar Abbas because of the political and economic capital he had amassed and the wide network of contacts he maintained. Later in the century, Sultan Sayyid Turki made all effort to dislodge Haji Ahmad and regain for Oman the control of Bandar Abbas. But the defence of Haji Ahmad by Persia showed how well he had used the assemblage by invoking his multiple identities to slip in and out of its interstices.

Haji Ahmad's career weathered storms that rocked the imperial assemblage as successive Omani Sultans continued to reassert their control as contractors of Bandar Abbas.[173] This meant the end of formal Omani interest in Bandar Abbas and the end of an era. But clearly, the Arab influence via private interests such as Haji

Ahmad was there to stay. They had a life that outlived the political vicissitudes of the Persian Gulf.

In popular perception, Haji Ahmad was very much the Arab of Persian origin who had grown in stature serving the Sultans of Oman. He was called 'a suitor of a thousand grooms'. The Europeans loved him, as he was known to be liberal and fond of intoxicants and drinking.[174] And not surprisingly, he was accused of governing Bandar Abbas in an Arab fashion: his door at the *firangis* (foreigners) quarters was open to all kinds of people, from workers to merchants, at all times of the day until the evening prayers although, unlike the Arabs, he was more inclined to preach Shi 'ism, which became popular in the port more than ever before. And with him the Arab tag continued also because the slugfest with Oman over the port city revenues never ever came to an end.

Sayyid Turki bin Saʻīd, Sultan of Oman (r. 1871–88), photographed
in Bombay, c. 1866

5

Sultan Barghash:
The Imperial Bridgehead

The Argument

Turki's rule in Muscat overlapped with that of his brother Sayyid Barghash at Zanzibar. Barghash, who was Turki's contemporary, ruled from 1871 to 1889. Like Turki, he too used the tribal bricolage to become the Sultan of Zanzibar. But he was not as successful. Indeed, his unsuccessful political bid for power in Zanzibar led to his deportation, under duress, first to Muscat and then even farther from Zanzibar politics to Bombay.

However, both the failed political bid and the resultant coerced mobility that followed became critical to his later successful installation as the political sovereign of Zanzibar. During his exile in Muscat and Bombay, he was exposed to a wider and more eclectic imperial world that he tapped into to materialize his political ambition. It made him aware of the political dividends of mobility in a world that was seeing the emergence of the nation states. These posed new challenges for survival and the need to refurbish the Sultanate in new ways.

Mobility became the key to his fashioning of the monarchy as a modern political form. He derived his sovereignty by bringing together imperialism, slavery and reformist Islam, all of which he

could access with his exceptional mobility across the British and
the Ottoman imperial cities. From these far-off lands, he brought
back home ideas of urban planning, architecture, coal mining, sugar
processing, educational pedagogy and printing technology.

Most importantly, he was inspired by the British and European
models of monarchy, which were structured around the person
of the ruler as a mother or father figure. He connected equally
well with the imperial networks, using to his advantage the new
technologies of the mail service, the telegraph and the steamship
that came to his door with the slave-hungry Europeans crowding
his island. He squeezed himself into the imperial club by being an
important participant in the discussions on slavery, the steamship
and the telegraph.

He took part in these trans-imperial conversations selectively,
drawing from them to strengthen his political sovereignty and
project his Sultanate as the 'Royal Nation'. This was in sync
with many other monarchs like him, who lived in the age of the
burgeoning nation states and projected themselves both as the
father or mother figures as well as enterprising economic visionaries
who pushed their political imaginaries and were very visible on the
international forums.[1]

In 1890, when Zanzibar became a British protectorate a year
after his death, it was evident that, as part of his vision for commercial
expansion, he had integrated Zanzibar's consumer market to the
Bombay export trade. And yet, Barghash's 'modern' monarchy,
with its overt 'cosmopolitan' stance, was distinct in retaining the Al
Busaidi household and reformist Islam as its guiding core.

Profile: Sayyid Barghash (1837–88)

Sayyid Barghash was born to an Abyssinian mother. He divorced his
wife and had a daughter by a Georgian concubine. He suffered from
the elephantiasis ailment and had gone through surgical operations
to no avail. Like a typical Sultan, he had his favourite courtiers. One
of them particularly close to him was a man called Shaykh Ḥamūd al
Farabi, who was a scholar of the Ibāḍī sect. He became Barghash's

spiritual guide, and it was as his disciple and as the advocate of the *mutawwiʿīn* or reformists of the Ibāḍī sect that he contested for the throne with his brother Majid.

He became the Sultan only after the death of Majid. He performed haj in 1873 and visited Mecca. On his return from Mecca, his ties with Shaykh Ḥamūd strengthened and he began to act as his director in his daily prayers.[2] Given his proximity to the Ibāḍī scholars, it was widely expected that he would act as a zealous religious reformer of ultra Ibāḍī views, that he would ban tobacco, among other such measures. But this did not happen. Indeed, for some time, he even showed laxity in his own religious observance. Barghash remained entangled both in domestic tribal politics as well as in imperial power games. Both these entanglements induced his physical mobility across the Indian Ocean world. It enabled him to survive projecting himself as the modern monarch in the age of the burgeoning nation states.

I

Barghash and the Failed 'Heuric' Moment: Tribes, Revolt and Deportation

Barghash's heart was set on Zanzibar quite early in his life. At the young age of nineteen years, he accompanied his father Sayyid Saʿīd on sail from Muscat to Zanzibar to quell the Barwania rebellion. He was on board the ship when his father suddenly died before they reached Zanzibar. On his death, Barghash immediately laid his eyes on the ruler ship of Zanzibar, as he felt that his brother and in-charge of the island, Sayyid Majid, was epileptic and incapable of keeping peace and order intact.

However, Barghash underestimated Majid's clout in the imperial assemblage as well as his military strength. He surrounded Majid's palace, but his bid was unsuccessful because of the Baluchi garrison, which overpowered him. The British supported Majid and stifled any political aspirations that the Barwania tribe nurtured following Barghash's failed bid to power.[3]

Rigby, the British Consul at Zanzibar, was hostile to Barghash. He viewed him as the 'morose' and 'discontented man' who was not only against his brother, Majid, and never attended his durbar, but also 'inimical to Europeans'. According to him, Majid was often 'low spirited' and frequently expressed the greatest anxiety for the arrival of the British Consul because of the 'intrigues of his brother'. Rigby was of the view that, although Barghash had little support in Zanzibar, he had a faction in Muscat. Their aim was to 'dispossess his brother Sayyid Majid with the aid of the Suri Arabs who visit this place in considerable numbers during the North West monsoon'.[4]

However, Barghash was unrelenting. He moved beyond merely forging tribal alliances. Instead, he waited for the right moment to enter the imperial assemblage and make his political bid by using its networks. His moment arrived in 1857, when the British, writhing in shock with the Indian revolt against their rule, turned their attention away from Zanzibar. There was no British Consul either in Muscat or Zanzibar as a result of the 1857 revolt, which had everyone concentrating on India. Additionally, the news of 1857 had conveyed the impression in the Omani territories that the British rule was folding up in India. This gave political aspirants such as Barghash free play. He was emboldened to prepare for a takeover of Zanzibar after ousting his brother Majid.[5]

Majid had plans to make his brother quit the island. But courtly intrigues ensured that his Vizir Suleiman bin Summund leaked the plan of his ouster. Barghash was forcefully set on sail to Muscat. At the time of his departure, Majid gave him 10,000 rials; he received from the Vizir another 2200 plus 1500 rials that were due to him as per his father's wishes. The Vizir rounded the aggregate to 14,000 rials and handed it to him. Out of this amount, Barghash paid the 7000 rials he owed to Ladda, the Indian trader-banker in Zanzibar, and was left with 7000 rials for his own expenses. He boarded the vessel of Ahmad bin Mubarak, native of Ra's al-Ḥadd, and kept the money there.[6] The Vizir reported that Rigby was so keen on his deportation that he would ask Majid about it on a daily basis.

But Barghash had his own plans. He was in no hurry to leave. He went into the garden which has the house/fort of his deceased brother Wahid and used the money he had received to garner the support of the Al Harth tribals. He then marched towards Majid's house, and an encounter took place between him and his brother's forces. The Al Harth tribe withstood only for half an hour and dispersed. The garden of the house where Barghash was holed up was plundered by Majid's men. The revolt was finally suppressed, with Majid granting them their lives. Brigadier Coghlan, the Political Resident at Aden, prepared a report on the revolt.[7] Both he and Lt Col Rigby felt that the Al Harth were up in arms to reassert their control over Zanzibar and oust the entire family of the late Sayyid Saʻīd. They were merely using the sibling wars for their ends.[8]

But neither of the British officers doubted Barghash's own political ambitions, even if they agreed that he was used as an instrument by the Al Harth. And they were not wrong. In 1859, Barghash made yet another bid to assassinate Majid, firing at his ship from his house on the seafront of Zanzibar town. This too was foiled, and he was kept under house arrest with a British ship, guns pointed at his house, always in attendance. A huge cache of arms and ammunitions was found in his house. In October 1859, he was arrested by Lt Col Rigby while trying to escape. He was asked to leave Zanzibar for Muscat and eventually deported to Bombay.[9]

But he did not leave without resistance. He tapped into the imperial rivalries to garner support. He very much wished to be guided by Britain's arch-rival, the French Consul, in his political plans. In a letter to the Consul, he said that he would foil all efforts of his brothers to hand Zanzibar to the British and French. In an emotional letter, he said, 'if we sell it, we shall do so only at the cost of our blood, and of war to the death'. But he promptly cosied up to the Consul, assuring him that he should not worry, as his investments in the plantations would remain safe.[10]

Whenever the imperial networks became hostile to him, he exploited the sibling rivalry between his Muscat-based brother, Thuwayni, and Majid. He wrote to Thuwayni of the pressure that Majid exerted on him to leave for Oman. He argued that

Col Rigby too was siding with Majid to have him ejected. He alleged that a ship anchored in front of his house and armed retainers of Majid attacked him. His efforts to garner support in Muscat worked. He was granted a one-month 'grace' period to pack and leave Zanzibar even though he had asked for two. In this period, he chartered a bugla, intending to ship the necessary articles for the sea voyage.

Clearly, this was all fraudulent. He was not leaving the island. Shortly, he moved from Zanzibar to a *shamba* (garden/grove/ plantation) outside the city. On hearing this, Majid's troops as well as those of the British surrounded him. They fired at him and burnt the doors of his dwelling. They inflicted injury on him. But once they withdrew, he returned to Zanzibar. Two days later, the combined troops of Majid and the British returned to the shamba and blew it up with gunpowder. Lt Col Rigby met him with parties from the same steam frigate once it was ascertained that he had gone back to Zanzibar town. Barghash alleged that he (Rigby) directed his doors and windows to be broken often with gunfire. They destroyed a good portion of his house.

The elders of the city rallied to intervene and asked him to meet his brother Majid. He met him in the presence of Lt Col Rigby, where he was angrily told to quit Zanzibar within three days. He was asked to give a document written in his own hand, pledging he would never return to Zanzibar. Barghash informed Thuwayni that he wrote this under duress and left for Muscat.[11]

The Barghash revolt was successfully crushed with the help of Rigby and a compliant Majid. The Arab tribes would not fight the British, and their revolt fizzled out once Majid obtained three British war vessels in his defence. In 1859, Rigby informed Thuwayni that Barghash had agreed in the presence of several other British officers and him to leave for Muscat to reside with him. He assured Thuwayni that he swore on the Koran and 'pledged himself solemnly' to repair for Muscat to reside with him, and to never return to Zanzibar. Rigby urged Thuwayni to treat him with respect and assign him a fixed sum of money for his expenses for this first year.[12]

In Muscat, Barghash located himself at the interstices of the local and the imperial networks. He remained in regular touch with Thuwayni and moved freely in Muscat. He even visited the Persian port of Bandar Abbas, on lease to Oman, to meet him soon after his arrival at Muscat.[13] While he built his relations with Thuwayni and grounded himself in Muscat, he also kept in touch with his following in Zanzibar. Thuwayni too owned properties on the island, and a lot of Barghash's followers lived in them. At the time of his departure, his followers and attendants, who were all huddled at Zakhl in the gardens owned by Thuwayni, alleged that they and their property were targeted, and they escaped with 'nothing but our lives'. Only the Koober garden remained in their possession, and all other houses on gardens owned by Thuwayni were razed to the ground: houses at Khuzra and Kamjemina. They wanted Thuwayni to send them baskets and jars with provisions as they were left with nothing.[14]

In 1860, Barghash was sent to Bombay from Muscat as per the agreement of his exit from Zanzibar. The British hoped that the Bombay exile would keep him far removed from Omani politics. But Bombay too was very much integral to the imperial assemblage that framed the lives of Omani princes. Barghash was quick to exploit its dynamics to his best advantage. He continued to live in close contact with the Bombay government. Indeed, he became very Westernized in British company, and his links with his erstwhile Arab tribal chiefs and supporters became fragile. Yet, in Zanzibar in the close circuits of Majid, he was always viewed as a political threat along with his erstwhile rebel allies, the Al Harth chiefs, who were in prison.

Before leaving Zanzibar, Barghash signed a formal engagement swearing on the Koran that he would never return to Zanzibar without Majid's permission. However, he did write to Majid in 1860, asking his permission to return to Zanzibar. Brigadier Coghlan hoped that he would be allowed as he posed no danger: the Al Harth leaders were in prison, and Barghash had conducted himself well in both Muscat and Bombay. Once back, he could be placed under the surveillance of the resident British Consul.[15] Significantly, the return of Barghash to Zanzibar was part of the details of the Canning Award (1861) or partition of the Omani Empire into Muscat and Zanzibar. Clearly, the British wanted to make the very Westernized Barghash their more direct entry point into the island.

Majid resented his return, even if his close alliance with the British made it impossible for him to resist this beyond a point. He complained to the British that about eighty of Barghash's retainers fired at him when his ship, the *Shah Alam*, was preparing to land on nearing the shoreline at the house of Barghash, as was the custom. The three French vessels of war docked at the shore intervened and asked the French Consul to bring about a reconciliation between the warring factions. Majid was reluctant but ultimately agreed to be at the interview. But the reconciliation became void when the British ship *Clive* arrived, and Majid agreed to only British mediation.[16]

A nervous Majid, wary of Barghash's return, repeatedly sought assurances from the British of his good conduct. He clarified that 'he will treat him as a brother and that if he lives here in a peaceable manner he will not be interfered with in any way'.[17] However, he was anxious about his return. He handled the unrelenting British pressure on Barghash's return by conspiring to poison the chief of the Al Harth tribe, a supporter of Barghash, whose release he had earlier agreed to. In the words of Pelly, Political Resident at the Persian Gulf, 'he [Majid] now had the dilemma of return of 2 principal leaders who a short time back had endangered his throne and person'.[18] He feared the Al Harth chief, who still retained power and wealth in the island, and Barghash, the political challenger who was returning after gaining experience in India. The Al Harth chief was separated from his fellow prisoners on the false hope of his release. He was made to sign papers to hand over his money and property to Sultan Majid, and the next morning he was found dead. Majid was convinced this was the only way out as, 'One traitor might be managed—the presence of both could be prelude for expulsion of government itself.'[19] The chiefs of the Al Harth were imprisoned in Zanzibar.

II

Barghash, the 'Modern' Sultan

The Limits to Authority

Majid's deft handling of the Al Harth support base of Barghash ensured that the latter became the Sultan of Zanzibar only in 1870, after his death. In the absence of primogeniture in Omani society, he was chosen to be the Sultan by a small coterie of loyalists from his friend and family circuit. He was called the 'Sultan' by his people but never 'Imam'. Most Arabs called him 'Sayed Barghash', and strangers and outsiders called him Sultan. His authority was absolute on the island, even if he was uneasy in dealing with the Arab families and their dependants. And also, in exercising his control over the trading population, who were under the protection of foreign consulates. He seemed more the Sultan of the coast, as his authority extended little beyond his fortified posts and customs houses.

In the beginning of his reign, Barghash came under the influence of a reformist party of Ibāḍī 'Ulamā called mutawwi'īn. They had a huge influence on his personal and political life. They had very conservative views and forced him to ban tobacco and the Friday prayers led by the Sunnis. By 1873, he had freed himself considerably from their clutches but still his prejudicial attitude towards non-Ibāḍīs remained. He established a printing press that disseminated Ibāḍī views on the island. This was largely done to counter the growth of Sunni beliefs among his Omani subjects.[20]

However, the more serious political challenge to his rule came from outside Zanzibar. The families of Swahili chiefs, though much degenerated, were still numerous and entrenched in society. They posed a threat to Barghash, as his father had allowed them to continue with their land grants and rituals of sovereignty.[21] Indeed, Sayyid Saʿīd had nurtured the wealthier and more influential of them and had purchased their surrender by the promise of pensions and the continuance of certain forms of their sovereignty.

Not surprisingly, the local tribal chiefs reared their head with the change of guard on the island and appeared to be commanding more authority locally than the Sultan. At Kilwa and Kavinja, the Swahili chiefs were very powerful and beyond the reach of Barghash. They levied their dues by a singular process, and the Sultan could not do anything. Caravans of Arabs and Indian subjects coming from the interior were not meddled with beyond the levy of a sort of extra land customs duty.[22]

South of Kilwa, people were much more scared of the tribal petty chiefs than of the Sultan. In these areas, Barghash appeared to have little influence over people in control of land, and he intervened only when they began to fortify it.[23] The writ of the Swahili chiefs, who Sayyid Sa'īd had pensioned on condition of maintaining certain forms of their sovereignty, still prevailed. And very much like in his father's time, the chiefs continued to levy a kind of land customs or transit duty on all caravans from the interior. On rare occasions they paid when the Sultan stopped them forcefully and compelled them to accept a commutation paid through the Customs House, which levied an extra duty on that account. But this was rare and not often a success.

For instance, the Sultan could never enforce the surrender of the chiefs at Kilwa. And they continued to levy transit dues in the area. Every slave caravan was stopped and asked to choose a Swahili patron, and only then could it proceed. The patron's writ prevailed in all slave transactions while the caravan remained in Kilwa. The Sultan was ineffective in putting an end to this practice.

In Mombasa, Barghash was even less successful in superseding the authority of the old ruling family. At Lindy, another significant place on the slave route, the authority of his Arab Governor was of little avail for the protection of life or property beyond the walls of his fort. In one instance, the Banias packed off to exit the city as the chief of the M'gao tribe went on a rampage there and the Governor remained helpless, even though he hired a reinforcement of Arabs from Zanzibar.[24] Similarly, along the Portuguese frontier, towards the mouth of Rovuma and Cape Delgado, the country was in the hands of independent chiefs.

The Sultan's authority in all matters concerning land was even more slippery. He was precluded from his commercial treaties with foreign powers from imposing any tax on land or its produce. He offered a formal grant to anyone on the island and mainland who wanted to expand the cultivation. Arab officials interfered if anyone wanted to settle near his post, especially if he attempted to build. But by and large, the local landed elite asserted in different ways their right over the land. Thus, the Arab 'settlers' needed permission from the local tribal chiefs who generally granted it if they (the settlers) were of friendly disposition.

Local people also dragged in the Europeans to underline their right to landownership. They claimed some annual acknowledgement of their rights from Europeans. At Bagamoyo, the local chiefs always claimed from the French Mission a dollar for a large plantation. But if a chief lived a distance of six or seven days in the interior, hardly ever a claim was made on his behalf. The Universities Mission reported that their small settlement in the Shamballa territory was owned by the interior chief of Fuga. He readily gave the missionaries as much land as they asked for on the sole condition that they would build no fort or stockade where his authority may be defied.[25] In Mombasa, the chief would not even accept a small sum as newcomers' right to settle, as he said, 'we asked you to come here because you are our friend'. They asked them to take land but not meddle with the fields.

Significantly, Barghash too was circumscribed by local authority circuits. The local Swahili chiefs did not grant him the right to impose a tax on land. His assertion of authority was further impeded because unigeniture rather than primogeniture was the established practice followed in determining succession in the Al Busaidi royal family. This made succession open-ended and competitive, with the ruler chosen by the people from within the royal family for his many acts and virtues. This, in the context of the island, meant that a small oligarchy of foreigners (Arabs) looked at the personal qualities of the competitor, his actions and many virtues and formally chose him as the successor. This political practice made Barghash the 'modern monarch' who was viewed as the elected representative of the people. This was used by local chiefs to their advantage, as they ensured he act in consultation with them. This practice of electing the monarch emboldened the locals. It made them feel that they had as much right on the land as him, as he was their Sultan and had been chosen by them and was neither the divine head—Imam—or even Sultan in his own right by direct succession, as was the case in societies with primogeniture.

Barghash's authority was therefore always contested both locally and within the family. This meant that Barghash's sovereignty was not recognized only because it was passed on legitimately from his father. He had earned it in an open-ended competition within the Al Busaidi family and was seen as the representative of the local society. It followed that there was no dynastic obligation to continue with past practices once succession was decided. Thus, if Barghash unhesitatingly repudiated a state obligation incurred by his predecessor for public purposes, as was his proposal to wipe out the debt notoriously due to the customs farmer Jairam Sewji, or when he denied payment of the Muscat subsidy, then it amounted to no faithlessness. Clearly this was in contravention to the Western understanding of political inheritance and the obligations that went with it.[26]

Majid also had to face opposition each time he attempted a land tax, and he eventually gave up. With no right on land, he had limited powers of feudal chiefs, in particular that of being a military chief. He had power only over his ships and the soldiers near his posts.[27] Further, his power was curtailed because it had to be exercised in conformity with the wishes of the trading community, who offered the chief source of revenue to him and were mainly foreigners.

Barghash, later in his reign, set up courts to deal with land disputes, in which he found his hold very slippery. But the locals, so confident over their rights over land, rarely approached these courts. Most of the petitioners who came to his court were British Indian subjects, whose relationship with land was definitely far more tenuous than that of the locals. In 1874, one Saleh bin Sa'īdina, a British subject formerly residing in Zanzibar, complained to the Bombay government about the resumption of certain lands and ferry rights by the Sultan that had been granted to him by Sayyid

Majid. The Sultan wanted written documents of the case from the Consulate, since it happened so long ago. The Consul could not find these, and the case was thus dropped. The Political Agent was of the view that the petitioner should have brought the case back to the Consular court if he was aggrieved instead of raking it up now. In another instance, a complaint against Hamid bin Muhammad bin Abdul Kadir, Barghash said the case was transferred from the Consular court to his court by Dr Kirk. The memorialist did not appear despite repeated warnings, and thus a judgment was given against him by default.[28]

British Indian Subjects and the Sharpening of Political Sovereignty

As part of his vision for commercial expansion, Barghash encouraged ties with Bombay. In the late 1870s, he introduced a line of six steamers to run between Bombay, Zanzibar and Madagascar. He bought these from German and Scottish manufacturers and offered cargo at low rates. Prestholdt has shown how this move integrated Bombay's export economy to the East African consumer market. American cotton (merekani) began to be replaced by Bombay's unbleached merekani lookalike.[29] The economic integration with Bombay offered political dividends as well. The British Indian merchants who kept the wheels of this Bombay-centric commerce going became useful agents through which he could assert his political sovereignty.

Barghash got the opportunity to underline his sovereign status via resolving the disputes brought to his court by the British Indian merchants who lived on the island. In fact, his active involvement in their issues gave him the opportunity to showcase his authority to the tribal chiefs of the interior who, as we saw above, always posed a political challenge. Indeed, he continuously received petitions from local Swahilis of the harassment they experienced at the hands of the 'Hindis and Bania' merchants at Mombasa and other places in his dominions. Some of these locals, such as one Mzee Mwinjw Headj and another Wazee, petitioned that they were $2000 in debt. They

incurred this as they had bad luck, bad bargains or were deceived by
the chiefs of the Wakamba tribe, who took cloth and beads from
them and refused to pay. They complained that the Banias asked
the Wālī to send soldiers to look for them, and if they could not pay,
they were put in prison. They wanted the Sultan to intervene, as
both they as well as the Wakamba were his subjects.[30] Barghash did
intervene and deftly handled their issues, pleasing both the British
as well as showcasing himself as the sovereign in the tribal interiors.

He was also happy to cooperate with British efforts to help
their subjects in his territory. In 1888, some British Indian subjects
were rendered destitute by the bombardment of Minengain by
Portuguese forces. They were offered help by the British agent
and Consul General at Zanzibar. The 'Indian born' tag that was
used to determine their nationality and subsequent rehabilitation
was controversial.[31] Nonetheless, they were provided a subsistence
allowance ranging from Rs 14 to Rs 30—Rs 0.5 per diem for adults
and Rs 0.25 per diem for children—by his consul's agent during the
quarter ending 30 June 1887.[32] Barghash lent his full cooperation.

In 1890, when Zanzibar became a Protectorate of the British
government, the complaints of British Indian subjects increased.
From the island of Lamu as well, there were complaints against
Haridas Runchordas, the Sultan's Customs House master, who
was accused by several Khojas, Banias and Bohra merchants of
maltreatment. He was allegedly using his official position to further
his trade interests. The Indian merchants alleged that he too was a
trader like themselves who imported goods from India and bought
produce locally. But he used the Customs House to store his goods
instead of his own storage depot.

As a result, when their goods reached the Customs House
for duty, they were kept outside in the open. They frequently got
destroyed and spoilt by the rain and thieves as a result. But the
merchants were more concerned about the fact that when their
goods reached the Customs House for duty, they were asked who
the supplier was. Once the name was disclosed, Haridas offered a
higher rate to him and got the goods for himself. He even placed
his own value on the goods that arrived from Bombay or any other

port and valued them at different rates. Thus, our own man having ten bags of rice would be charged duty on Rs 100, the estimated value; others would be charged duty on Rs 150 for the same quantity and description of rice. They complained that duty in kind that was acceptable in the past was no longer agreed upon. And they were asked to pay in cash.[33]

The successor of Barghash, Khalifah bin Sa'īd, intervened. He wrote to the Wālī of Lamu, asking him to return the duty on ivory that he erroneously charged one of the British subjects, who had already paid the duty on the consignment at Mambru.[34] Indeed, on 1 January 1891, when the Imperial British East African Company took over the administration of Lamu, Manda and Patta as per the protectorate agreement, the British Consular Agency at Lamu was abolished. All its documents, stamps and articles were archived along with complaints from Indians addressed to it.[35]

So great was the issue of Indian insolvency that, in 1890, the Consular Judge of Zanzibar suggested that the Consulate Agent should satisfy himself and sell any assets, excepting of course bedding, tools and cooking pots. He was asked to exhibit a notice in the Customs House for fourteen days, call a meeting of creditors and hear any charges of fraud against the insolvent divide among the creditors.[36]

III

The Making of the 'Modern Monarchy' in the Age of the Nation States

Barghash was an extremely well-read Sultan, with a wide vision of the world. His library was extensive, with books from Egypt and Britain in Arabic and English. He read and appreciated British news as well as the news from the Egyptian newspapers the *Al-Rayb*, the *Al-Jawā'ib* and the *Al Nalaqa*.[37] He used the temporal moment of the late nineteenth century that was defined by the proliferation of nation states to fashion a new monarchy that would survive in this milieu. This monarchy was a new political form, as it had the family and religion at its core and a very emphatic outward gaze that entangled him in global conversations on the telegraph, the steamship and slavery.

Barghash placed himself at the centre of this monarchy. He projected himself both as a father figure as well as a 'modern' Sultan who travelled the Ottoman and European cities, met dignitaries and shared forums with the imperial powers. His interventions at the Royal Geographical Society meeting at London, the discussions on slavery, the deliberations on the laying of the telegraph line, the steamship, coal depots and other such pressing global issues showcased him as the 'modern' and 'cosmopolitan' monarch at ease with his Western contemporaries.

Barghash created this new modern monarchy by bringing together the household, slavery, reformist Islam and imperial networks to carve out his sovereign status. This particular conjunctional moment was possible because he was located at the centre of the slave trade, and the European powers made a beeline to his island to dip into its profits. This offered him the perfect opportunity to tap into their networks and make himself globally visible in their company as he articulated the local meaning and relevance of slavery. Indeed, this push into the imperial world, making its issues locally legible and yet remaining firmly heeled in reformist Islam and the household, made his monarchy look very new as he refurbished it to survive in the age of fast-growing nation states.

Randall Pouwels calls the making of this new 'modern monarchy' a kind of cosmopolitanism that inaugurated a 'new secularism and bureaucratic centralization' on the island.[38] This was an administration that linked Zanzibar to the world outside not only in the realm of economy but also in social and ideological aspects. He argues that Zanzibar moved beyond the Muscati political and economic order that Sayyid Sa'īd had introduced and moved to a new 'internationalism'.[39] Jeremy Prestholdt views the making of this cosmopolitanism in the island's 'domesticating' of Western material goods.[40]

However, Barghash's careering reveals the complex making of a 'modern monarchy' that was cosmopolitan in a very specific Zanzibarian way. It reached out to the Western material culture and became entangled with imperial concerns without severing ties with the local referents of religion and the family. Indeed, it remained rooted in the royal household and entangled in Ibāḍī Islam, both of which constituted its core. Barghash, secure in this core, pushed his political frontiers into the wider imperial world by involving himself in its pressing concerns.

The Monarchy and Its Private Core: The Household and the Arab Elite

Observers noted that Barghash was more interested in consolidating the gains of his father and governing rather than concentrating on war and expansion. They reported that he, unlike his father and his coterie who were known as 'men of war from their youth' and did trade only in times of peace, focused on commerce and revenues all year round. He and his men lived a relatively stable life of indolence in the shambas, leaned on Indian traders for money for their plantations and relied on slave labour. Most had houses in Zanzibar but seldom went there unless summoned by the Sultan.[41]

Barghash, his family and their Arab associates constituted the inner core of politics that shaped the Sultanate in no small measure. The monarchy was 'old' in style in that it continued with the Al Busaidi tradition of blurring the private and public spheres in governance. Barghash projected himself as the pivot of his administration. He held a daily durbar and remained accessible to all people. The post of minister was held by another family associate, Nasir bin Sayyid.

Indeed, the household and the extended family controlled the strings of politics. Barghash gave Arabs closely connected to his royal family important positions. The Wālī or Governor of Zanzibar town was an intelligent Arab gentleman, the son of Sayyid Saʿīd's staunch follower. He was assisted by a Jemadar—a Baluchi—also the son of a trusted follower of Saʿīd. A lot of Baluchis with long associations with his family remained integral to his administration. He continued his family tradition of maintaining Arab and Baluch mercenaries on whom his father and brother depended. He added to them a body of about 120 Persians, all artillery men. These constituted his bodyguard.[42]

Indeed, the hold of the Arab elite who were connected in a range of ways to the household was so strong that they constituted a social clique of their own. They lived in their own exclusive quarters away from the local Swahilis. The Arab–Swahili divide was very prominent, with the town divided into two portions occupied by the Arab families and their dependants and the Indian merchants who monopolized the trade respectively. His very limited influence over the Swahili population was evident in the Arab Governor's leanings on the Swahili chiefs for governance. The chiefs catered to all the complaints and disputes of the population.

In some areas, such as Lamu, the divide was even more striking, with the Arab Governor entertaining all affairs of Arabs and foreigners; the local population went for redress to the Swahili chieftains.[43] In Mombasa, his effort to supersede the authority of local chiefs was even less successful. And this was even after Sayyid Sa'īd, with the help of arms from Bombay, had managed to break the stronghold of some Swahili chiefs and tribal patriarchs and deported the troublemakers to Muscat and Bandar Abbas. Farther north, where the Gallas and Somali tribes came down to the coast, his authority was even less recognized beyond the Arab garrison. The tribes seemed willing to befriend the British, having heard of them at Aden. In the towns of Brava, Merka and Magadoxa, Bush Somalis, an internal police force of elders, monitored the place.[44]

The Monarchy and Its Outward Gaze

And yet, the influential role of the household notwithstanding, the monarchy was new in many ways. This was best reflected in Barghash's aspiration to be included as an important member of the imperially crowded world powers. This desire was understandable, given the fact that Zanzibar was the centre of the lucrative slave trade that brought the world to his doorstep. He did not have to strive much to create a niche for himself in the imperial club. In fact, he became the centre of this world as the influential merchant prince who consolidated power largely through negotiating the profits of maritime commerce with the Europeans who thronged his waters. And this international milieu offered him and his people huge opportunities to mingle with the sea captains, European Consuls and Indian, American and European traders who were present at all times on the island. Barghash himself was keenly invested in this diverse ethnic milieu, from which he learnt about pressing global concerns and often plugged into these issues for his self-interest. He was very interested in world affairs, interacted with foreign visitors and, as we saw above, maintained a vast collection of books and newspapers.[45] With an eye to greater connectivity with the world, he showed interest in engaging with the telegraph line that the British were laying across the Western Indian Ocean.

The Telegraph Line

In 1879, Barghash availed of the British India Steamship Navigation Company that started a monthly mail service between Aden and Zanzibar. This was preceded with his keen cooperation in the laying of the telegraph line on the island. In 1877, Mr Pender, the chairman of the Eastern Telegraph Company, offered to lay out a submarine line of cable at Zanzibar by which it was proposed to unite Aden with the South African colonies and Mauritius at an annual payment of 5000 tomans. Barghash expressed his keenness to link Zanzibar to the world outside via the telegraph. He greatly valued this mode of communication.

The route the company wanted to take for the telegraph line was one that linked Aden via Zanzibar to the island of Johanna; from there, branch lines could take it to South Africa and Mauritius. Barghash was hugely attracted to the idea and was willing to cooperate, as it was the best way to connect the local with global affairs and politics. His only reluctance to the acceptance was financial hardship. He declined the offer only on account of his financial condition post the devastating hurricane at Zanzibar.

But he was lucky. By the end of the nineteenth century, Zanzibar had become so central to the imperial world that John

Kirk felt that even if the Sultan was unable to pay the 5000-toman subsidy, the line should pass via Zanzibar instead of the island of Johanna. He argued that this was because Zanzibar was 'the center of a large and daily increasing trade with America, Europe and the East, the headquarter of the British naval squadron in East Africa and the residence of four foreign representatives and many large merchants'. In contrast, Johanna was a small island incapable of any political or commercial importance; it was located close to the French possessions. He was convinced that Barghash, seeing the importance of this means of communication, would like to be placed in direct telegraphic communication with other countries; he would be 'willing to do all he can in order to secure the accomplishment of such a work'.[46]

Private Partnerships with British Firms

Barghash's most lucrative outreach was to British private firms, whom he encouraged to invest in agriculture and use slave labour, which was officially banned. His private estates earned him an income of $25,000 per annum. And he had also started investing in sugar plantations.[47] But the tie-ups with the British firms were more lucrative. He welcomed private British capital being sunk into Zanzibar and entered into partnerships with the firms. In fact, his perfect relationship with the mercantile and banking houses of Britain was reflected when A.A. Buchanan, a partner in the banking house of Messrs I.A. Forbes & Company of London, commented on how the financial bonhomie between Zanzibar, Ireland and the United Kingdom, which received a fillip with the arrival of the steam communications, had 'developed into a recognized feature in the civilized world'.[48]

Significantly, such tie-ups with private firms were useful for building his case for a more formal footing and position in the world crowded by imperial powers. In 1879, Buchanan regretted that, despite this friendly bond, Barghash was not represented either by a diplomatic or Consular Agent in Britain. This was a great lacuna, as his and his subjects' interests remained without the 'consular or diplomatic protection which are so justly deemed the highest privileges of persons visiting a foreign country for commercial or other objects'.

Indeed, Buchanan offered his own services to Barghash for the said appointment. He argued that he had a high social position in Britain and good personal and family ties with the Foreign Office and, therefore, he would be best suited to maintain the political dignity of Barghash. Additionally, he said the status of his firm, Forbes & Co. of London, with operations in Bombay, would 'secure to His Highness' subjects that personal consideration and local attention so desirable where important commercial interests are at stake'.[49]

Buchanan exhorted Barghash to press for a Consular presence in Britain, as the island with its dependencies 'is now regarded in the eyes of the Western nations as the mistress of civilization in Eastern Africa, a certain and no far distant rival to Bombay'. He insisted that the imperial ruler of such a prosperous island 'will no longer forgo those foreign representative dignities which are shared impartially by both Eastern and Western nations'.[50]

Exceptional Mobility: London, Paris, Aden and Cairo

Barghash may not have had Consular presence in Britain and Europe, but he himself travelled widely: London, Birmingham, Windsor in Britain and Paris and Italy in Europe. He was equally invested in the social and intellectual milieu of Aden and the Ottoman Arab cities that he visited: Ismailia, Alexandria and Cairo in Egypt and the Islamic heartland of Mecca. That he was no ordinary visitor, rather someone much sought after, being the Sultan of the lucrative slave island of Zanzibar, was evident when he visited London in 1875 accompanied by British Political Agent John Kirk. This was a trip in connection with the discussion and possible ratification of the slave treaty. Barghash got the global visibility he needed for refurbishing himself as the 'modern' monarch.

The visibility on the wider canvas began soon after he departed for London. After a ceremonial send-off from Zanzibar that included the foreign Consuls and of course John Kirk, who was his travel companion, he was given a twenty-one-gun salute on his halt at Aden. Here, too, the British and German Consuls, along with the elites of the city and trading community, came to meet him.[51] It was not insignificant that, after his stay and royal reception at Aden, he proceeded on his onward journey in a British ship with a Zanzibar flag. After crossing the Suez Canal, he was received royally by the British Consul at Cairo. Both at Aden as well as at Cairo, he had an opportunity to explore the city. He saw the steam engine trains for the first time at Cairo and was impressed by the waterworks of the city; he was much enamoured by the traffic arrangements for ships at the Suez Canal, and the Egyptian city of Ismailia on the western bank of the Suez impressed him. At Port Sayyid, he met many Egyptian dignitaries before he set sail for London.

In London, he was warmly welcomed by the royalty and went sightseeing, where he was impressed by the city's buildings, the gentlemanly conduct of its people and the zoo.[52] But the highlight of his visit was meeting Queen Victoria at her Windsor Palace, and the Duke of Cambridge at the banquets hosted by them in his honour. This, in itself, was a momentous event that brought him wide publicity in the British press and consequent global attention. He travelled to Windsor from London by train and got a royal reception at the railway station by the elites of the town. At Windsor, Queen Victoria's army gave him a full military ceremonial welcome.[53] Several foreign and British dignitaries, including the Japanese Consul, were present to meet him. Barghash was particularly impressed by the hospitality and magnanimity of the Queen, who sat next to him at the banquet and welcomed him personally.

He was inspired by the British model of monarchy. He noted that the technologically advanced and culturally suave British monarchy saw the Queen as the 'mother figure'. Barghash was inspired by this model of monarchy, where Victoria, truly the empress of the world, was loved by her subjects as their mother and not as a lord alone. He noted that she too saw her subjects as sons and not as her slaves.[54] He remarked that he learnt a lot about British political culture from this visit and he was inspired to emulate it back home in Zanzibar.[55]

Barghash was invited as the honoured guest to a meeting of the Royal Geographical Society as well. He attended the meeting along with his friend Rigby, the British Consul at Zanzibar. This forum too exposed him to a wide range of global leaders. He sat on the dais with Henry Lawrence, the Director of the society, and a range of international Consuls, including those from Marrakesh and Japan. He was in the global spotlight as he pledged, as a member of this society, to facilitate travel to Africa and help Europeans explore the geography of the continent. He was applauded for this offer and his support was much appreciated. Slogans of 'long live Zanzibar' were raised and, so was the Zanzibar–Britain friendship lauded.

More importantly, Barghash intervened in the deliberations via his interpreter on emotive issues such as the ivory and slave trade. He made it clear that he always encouraged British traders and supported Britain's political drives, such as the anti-slave trade campaign. He said that he had curtailed slave traffic on his island even before the British drive on abolition began. He wanted the society to praise and thank him for this effort. The society noted that indeed his presence at their meeting had increased the esteem of the society.

On the issue of the delegates raising ethical questions on the extraction of ivory from elephant tusks after killing the animal, Barghash was not at all defensive.[56] Instead, he showed a keen interest in learning from the member who had raised the issue, if any new scientific technique existed that could save the life of the elephant and yet get the bones extracted. He extended an invite to the delegate to Zanzibar for training his people in any such non-invasive extraction technique. He said, 'I invite the delegate to come and teach us how to get the tusk out without killing the animal.'[57] He impressed the society's president when he backhandedly questioned the real intentions of elephant lovers. He argued that if 'someone objects that it's better that elephant [s] be alive than trade in tusks and bones then we will say that if you were really forbidden from killing elephants then by now the ivory market would have collapsed'.[58]

He said that 'if people had the technique of extracting the bones of elephants without killing them then elephants could have been used for transport [instead of] cars'. He said it's difficult to extract bones from the elephants and yet keep them alive.[59]

Rigby supported Barghash in his many interventions at the meeting. In fact, he projected Barghash as a 'pan Africanist', arguing that, because of the Sultan, 'Zanzibar contributed hugely to the success of Africa'. In particular, he pointed to the success of the ivory, sugar and clove production and trade, as well as the urban infrastructure of roads and waterways that Barghash had introduced on the island. Rigby went a step further and hailed Barghash as a world leader. He said the Sultan 'for the welfare of the world left no stone unturned'.

Barghash behaved as the perfect world leader, sensitive to the cultural nuances of the British society he was addressing. He asked his interpreter to thank the society for the honour they had heaped on him. When the interpreter asked if he should start his note of thanks while addressing the women first or the men, he replied, 'Are we in West or East?' On being told that they were in the West, he retorted, 'So follow the culture of the West.' The interpreter proceeded to address the women.

His status as a world leader visiting Britain was reflected when he received the 'Freedom of the City' award at the Guildhall. He attended a state banquet at Mansion House. He attended a garden party at the house of the British interlocutor and former Governor of Bombay, Sir Henry Bartle Frere. And when he left London by train to the city of Birmingham, not surprisingly, he got a royal welcome.

At Birmingham, he was most impressed by the factory for making gold- and silver-plated utensils and ornaments. He showed a keen interest in the production technique and was particularly interested in the electrical gold- and silver-plating machines and technique, as a similar machine existed in Zanzibar as well. As a memento, the government of Birmingham gifted him some coins that he got gold-plated himself by inserting them in the machine. The use of electric power to melt iron was another item that interested him hugely in the city. Visibly impressed by the factories and electric power generation at Birmingham, he said the city should be called, 'Bi'r al-Manham', meaning the centre of Britain's wealth. He entered his generous comments and signature in Arabic in the visitors' register in the city.[60] He was equally excited on seeing coal mining in Britain and told the British that his island too had coal mines, and if they were mined with proper expertise that the British could lend to him, he would benefit from them.[61]

Most significant were the conversations he had with a group of Canterbury padres who visited him while he was in Britain. He shared with them his views on slavery. He had pledged to ban slave trade in his meetings with the Queen and also at the Royal Geographical Society. Conversing with the padres with the help of translators, he once again reiterated his resolve to stop the trade and pledged himself to slave freedom. However, he did not fail to remind them that their rulers had made themselves economically prosperous by depriving slaves of their rights and had conquered cities and ports benefiting from their labour and profits.[62] He was visibly pleased by their praise of Zanzibar and their offer to help him spread a more 'cultured' way of life on the island. He welcomed their efforts to reform society with their etiquette and conduct.

Barghash returned to Zanzibar via Paris and Marseilles after four weeks of sightseeing and entertainment.[63] In Paris too he was royally welcomed and was taken on sightseeing trips, where he was particularly impressed by the zoo.[64]

His next stop was the city of Alexandria in Egypt, from where he took the train to Cairo and then a boat ride on the river Nile to see the sights of the city. While in Cairo, he visited the zoo, the pyramids, the workshop for embalming dead bodies—mummies—and the graveyards with exceptional burial rituals that intrigued him. The visit to the arms factory and its workshop and the printing press left an indelible impression on his mind. He was equally impressed by the city's beautiful parks named after the Ottoman rebel governor who became the Pasha Muhammad Ali. He showed special interest in the books and curriculum of the city library and a tibbi (medical) madrasa that he visited. The chemistry and anatomical charts at the madrasa held his attention. He interacted with the students of a girls-only madrasa where Turkish, French and British alongside music was taught.[65] He also visited the Al Azhar madrasa and mosque, the palace of Muhammad Ali and the grave of Imam Shai'fi. From Cairo, he went to the city of Ismailia on the western bank of the Suez Canal, where he inspected with interest the military practices: *teer andazi* (swordsmanship), display of arms and drills. He met the Khedive and other dignitaries at the city meetings.

Barghash left for Aden after a five-day stint in Egypt. As expected, he was royally received at the port by British Consuls and dignitaries. After a few days' stopover at Aden, where he was busy meeting various sections of British society and local merchant elites, he left for Zanzibar. On reaching home, there was much joy and celebration that he had made it back home safely.

IV

The Making of the Modern Monarchy: Drawing from Multiple Contexts

London and Cairo

Barghash drew upon these multiple contexts and created a niche for himself in the global world even as he remained locally well entrenched. He brought home many influences from his travels abroad. Electric power, coal mining techniques, sugar-processing machines and the gold and silver-plating factories that he had visited in Britain left an indelible impression on his mind. From Egypt, he carried home the impressions he gathered of the efficient water techniques such as the wells and canals, the steam trains and the madrasas, libraries, printing machines and curriculum. Kirk reported that he was laying new roads and had lighted the main stretch and was constructing lighthouses.[66]

Later in 1881, Barghash employed a British geologist, I. Thompson, to tour 60 miles south of Ngomano and the Rovuma river to investigate the availability of coal. He found the coal bituminous and of very poor quality.[67] Clearly, this investment in coal hinted at the significance of the mineral in determining the prosperity of any monarchy that he had learnt from his trip to British coal mines. It revealed the foothold he aspired for in the newly arrived steamship industry. The same year, Barghash's son died, but his development agenda continued unabated. Steamships docked at Aden for refuelling. Barghash explored coal depots in Zanzibar with an eye to divert the ships to the island and corner the refuelling profits.[68]

Barghash was equally impressed by the shipping technology and ship designs of Britain and ordered his yachts to meet those standards even if, once assembled, he did not seem too impressed. He ordered steamships from Scotland and Germany. But a case in point was the HMS *Glasgow* of the Royal Navy, which impressed Barghash hugely when it visited Zanzibar in 1873. This ship became the model for his royal yacht, the HHS *Glasgow* (His Highness Ship). Barghash consulted with Sir William Mackinnon, the founder of the British India Steam Navigation Company. Mackinnon recommended the firm of William Denny and Brothers as the best shipbuilders for this project. Barghash invested heavily in the yacht, which cost him £32,735. It was constructed in Portsmouth, Britain, with state-of-the-art technology. It had an iron frame covered with teak planks and a keel made from rock elm. It had three masts and a steam propulsion system with a lifting propeller.

The yacht landed in Zanzibar in 1878 commanded by Captain Hand of the Royal Navy. It was noteworthy also for its many luxury features: two state rooms, a dining salon, a bathroom and a water closet for the Sultan's use. It was also fitted with seven rifled muzzles loading nine-pounder cannons and a mini barrelled Gatlin gun that was a gift from Queen Victoria. And yet, Barghash seemed unimpressed. He hardly ever used it and it remained docked in Zanzibar for most of its life.

His private steamships, the royal yachts, were very often assembled locally and sent for repairs to the port towns of Bombay, Muscat or Bandar Abbas. They moved around this littoral often as gift items to cement sibling bonds and strengthen the household, and as transport ships carrying Muslims who wished to make their

pilgrimage to Mecca. In all these ways, the steamship—that emblem
of Western modernity—was harnessed to project Barghash as a
'modern' Sultan, whose 'modernity' was exceptional as it was rooted
in the household and the mentorship of Muslims even as it remained
inextricably linked to the world of the imperial powers. The *Dar el-
Salam* yacht reflected this trend beautifully.

In 1878, Barghash presented Turki with a small steam yacht
called the *Dar el-Salam*, as Turki was unable to procure one in
Muscat at a reasonable price. The one available and to his liking and
requirements cost Rs 16,000. Not only was it expensive, but it was
also old and in need of repair. In contrast, the *Dar el-Salam*, which
sailed in from Zanzibar, was about 70 tons and 60 horsepower
and in very good condition.[69] The steam yacht became a symbol
of friendship between Turki and Barghash. It tied Muscat and
Zanzibar in friendly relations. And Lt Col Miles, the British agent
at Muscat, who supplied coal for it from the government depot with
due permission from the Government of India, reflected best the
British role and interest in keeping this bonhomie alive.[70]

Indeed, the British took due interest in the maintenance of
the *Dar el-Salam*, shipping it to Bombay for repairs when it needed
a new boiler. Miles was sympathetic to Turki's request that, since
he could not bear the high cost of replacing the boiler, it be met
by admitting his yacht in the government docks in Bombay and the
alterations carried out at the expense of the British government.
He recommended to the Bombay government that as the *Dar el-
Salam* was small and an addition to the Sultan's 'means of providing
for the security of Muscat and being always at hand would be
available for communication in the event of attacks, wrecks or other
emergencies . . . it would be politic to accede to His Highness'
solicitation'.[71] The Government of India granted permission for its
repair free of cost.[72]

More subtle was the impact of the British model of monarchy
that he imbibed from his visit to Windsor to meet Queen Victoria.
Like the matriarch Queen Victoria, he too became the patriarch,
a father figure around which he centralized his bureaucracy. The
appointment of Lt Lloyd Mathews to reorganize his army was one

of the important takeaways. Kirk was pleased that Barghash gave the duty to Mathews to drill and discipline the recruits. He was a well-regarded naval officer on Her Majesty's ship *London*, and he knew Swahili and got along well with the locals on the East Coast even though he handled slavers strictly. He deputed his commanding officer Captain Sulivan on the job and drilled about 400 men, who showed marked military 'evolution'. Kirk also wanted him to be employed temporarily to tackle the slavers.[73] The reforms in the military were also inspired by his extensive survey and inspection of Egyptian regiments at Ismailia.

Barghash enjoyed the trust of those who were in his pay and those who advised him. His personal character was robust and, with the help of his coterie of advisers, he wielded more authority than Majid. Not surprisingly, he was an enigma to the British as he straddled across the imperial cities, rooted still in the old world of the religious and his family. They viewed him as having a 'good sense' and, for an Arab, a man who is, 'frank and good humored, somewhat brusque and even rude in manner at times and very obstinate, personally inclined to bigotry in religious matters'.[74] Yet, he was perceived as being very just in the dispensation of justice.

Bombay: The Inspiration for Urban Planning

Bombay remained a key inspiration for Barghash as far as his lateral straddling in the ocean was concerned. As an exile in the city, he interacted with eminent Parsi intellectuals such as the scholar and reformer Kharshedji Rustomji Cama. He was inspired by the Parsi attention to detail and their English language skills. He arranged for specialists from the community to move to Zanzibar when he became Sultan.[75]

During his exile to the city, he had seen the opulent wealth of Indian palaces. He tried to emulate these in Zanzibar. He built many palaces, including Chukwani, to the south of Zanzibar town, Maruhubi Palace for his harem to the north of Zanzibar and the iconic *Bayt al Ajaib*—the House of Wonders, named so because of its electric fittings—in the centre of Zanzibar town. Drawing from the

Public Works Departments functioning in Bombay, he introduced the first clean water system to replace rain and well water in the island. He laid out aqueducts and conduits that brought pure water from a spring at Bububu, 6 km from Zanzibar, into town. The town also got its first ice-making factory and electric street lighting.[76] It is not insignificant that one of his Superintendents of health was a Parsi immigrant from Bombay called Sohrabji M. Darukhanawala. Barghash's personal physician was also a Parsi doctor from Bombay called Pestonji B. Nariman. And the Parsi engineer in his Bombay–Zanzibar streamer service, Bomanji M. Darukhanawala, was installed as the island's minister of Public Works.[77]

The Monarchy's Religious Core: Barghash, the Muslim Cosmopolitan?

The 'modern monarchy' that Barghash fashioned, straddling the household and the imperial issues, was very cosmopolitan, and yet, in a very particularistic way, never severing its ties from religion. Indeed, Barghash used the imperial networks that shaped his monarchy to nurture its specific religious core. This was most evident in his exceptional mobility across empires, which was enabled by his imperial connections. He used his contacts and clout in imperial circles to travel, as we saw above, extensively to Ottoman and British cities. He connected with the intellectual hubs in Ottoman Cairo and Mecca and learnt about modernizing religious reforms from these visits.[78]

The visits to Bombay and Cairo introduced him to the printing machine, which he brought back with him to Zanzibar. And while he derived from multiple contexts and lent to the island a truly cosmopolitan hue, he never severed his links with the religious core. Indeed, the printing press, the symbol of his material borrowing from the imperial world, was used to disseminate his religious ideas.

Jeremy Prestholdt views Barghash as epitomizing the culmination of Zanzibar's cosmopolitan culture, which was based on the global experiences of its people, both elite and ordinary, collected via incessant travel, trade and information flows. At the bottom of this cosmopolitanism lay a consumerism that 'domesticated' imported material objects and ideas and used them as tools to fashion a new self-identity.[79] McDow also labels him the 'modernizing Sultan'.[80] He is of the view that Barghash's long stints in exile in cosmopolitan Bombay impacted him and he imbibed lessons of modernization from there. He also highlights the transmission of the printing presses from this British Indian city to Zanzibar.

Both McDow and Prestholdt view Barghash as being heavily influenced by British material and cultural styles due to his exile to Bombay early in his career and his subsequent visits and interactions with British India. His architectural hallmark—the Bayt al Ajaib—reflected British Indian influences, as did his hectic infrastructure projects such as roads and the telegraph and railway line.[81] And yet, as Prestholdt shows, these 'modernities' represented in material objects, languages or ideas were not simply 'derived'. Rather they were inflected with local symbolism and meaning. His Arab subjects, both those who travelled and those who did not, appropriated the global influences and tempered them to local use without being enamoured with them or being simplistically emulative.

But is modernity and cosmopolitanism necessarily Western-derived even if locally inflected? Is there something distinctly non-Western about Zanzibarian cosmopolitanism? Barghash presided over a cosmopolitan Zanzibar that welcomed people and 'domesticated' material objects from around the world; but at its core it retained the local old-world charm as represented in the printing and dissemination of reformist Ibāḍī literature, legal texts and Shai'fi'i literature. Paradoxically, the imperial assemblage and its concomitant 'modernity' that framed the Sultan offered exposure to ideas and technology and travel opportunities that further reinforced his Ibāḍī religious core. This religious core was ironically dependent on the imperial networks of print, steamship and telegraph and was integral to Barghash's cosmopolitanism.

The British portrayal of Barghash as a 'bigot' in a culturally diverse Zanzibar smacked of a particular understanding of cosmopolitan sensibility that was necessarily Western-derived and viewed as hollowed of any form of religion. Annie Bang's work shows the 'fanaticism' attributed to Barghash was reflective of a British mindset that was suspect of everything to do with Islam. Instead, she views Barghash as overseeing the Ibāḍī renaissance that took place in Zanzibar, not more widely in Oman, with his thoughtful interest and investments. Barghash spearheaded a religious reformism that was integral to the Zanzibari cosmopolitanism and not outside it.

This was represented foremost in his travels to Mecca, Cairo, Syria and Palestine by way of providing for his Ibāḍī subjects both the facilities of easy pilgrimage and travel and putting together printed legal and religious texts for their guidance. His travel companion Sayyid Ḥamūd established a *rabat* in Mecca for fellow Ibāḍīs and a madrasa in the town of Bububu just outside Zanzibar. Barghash himself imported both printing presses and printers from Bombay, Syria and Cairo and launched a programme for printing Ibāḍī legal texts written in North Africa and printed in Oman. He undertook the printing of the ninety-volume project *Kitab Qamus al Sharia*, on Ibāḍī theology and law by the Omani scholar Jumayyil b. Khamis b. Lafi al Sa'di. The first volume was published from the Sultanic Press in 1880. In total, seventeen volumes saw the light of day after his demise.[82] Barghash, like his predecessors, Majid and Sa'īd, was always keen on being perceived as the deliverer of justice. He delivered verdicts himself and spent two hours on legal matters every day.[83]

This was a cosmopolitanism that was new in terms of integrating Western materiality and consumerism. But it was also old in adhering to its religious core and its local linguistic and cultural expressions. Thus, not surprisingly, many of the Arab subjects in cosmopolitan Zanzibar were settled in their cultural groove with hardly any first-hand knowledge about Europe. Their impressions were derived only from what they heard from sailors and Europeans they saw around them. Frere, the British missionary and interlocutor in Zanzibar, observed that those who had been to India as exiles and political prisoners a few years after the mutiny of 1857 came back with an idea of the power of Britain, but clearly no love or admiration for it.[84] They certainly did not wish to imitate the British. They had no permanent preference for the French either and use their flag and favours when it suits them. He noted that none of Barghash's courtiers or family knew any European language or had any acquaintance with the Arabic manuals of European history and science, which had been published lately in Egypt and Syria.

His brother and predecessor, Majid, had a few Arab ship captains who spoke a little English. One of them helped Barghash translate the substance of some Indian newspapers for the Sultan's information. The most intelligent and best informed of the Sultan's immediate Arab connections was the son of a French Creole. His owed his knowledge of European affairs and mechanical arts to his mother. But he was a vehement Anglophobe and a very 'bigoted Muhammadan'. Frere felt that the French flag was often used by locals for slave trade. He concluded that by and large the Sultan was a 'bigoted Muhammadan' even if he was inclined towards the British.[85]

Indeed, what was viewed by Frere as Zanzibar's 'bigotry' was the particular form of Muslim cosmopolitan core that Barghash had painstakingly nurtured. Barghash's cosmopolitanism meant that, in his personal life, the Ibāḍī influence stuck to him. His spiritual guide was a man called Shaykh Ḥamūd al Farabi. It was as his disciple and advocate of the mutawwi'īn. or reformists of the Hadiyah sect (of which Ḥamūd was the chief teacher) that Barghash proposed to contest the throne with his brother Majid soon after the latter's succession. And once he succeeded his brother, he gave every indication of being a religious reformer of ultra-conservative views. But he soon gave up this religious agenda and remained 'liberal' in disposition. He performed haj and, after his return from Mecca, he appeared to be once more under the influence of Ḥamūd, who acted as his director in his daily prayers.[86]

He saw the influx into Zanzibar of many religious scholars of the Shafi'i sect from Arabia. He also visited the graves of many Shafi'i saints on his visit to Cairo.[87] Many of these belonged to the Hadhramaut Alawiya Sufi order. They built on earlier networks laid out in the time of his father Sayyid Saʿīd, who too was welcoming of scholars from the Hadhramaut such as Muhyi al Din al Qahtani, who arrived in the 1830s and rose to become the Qadi; he built several

madrasas and the main mosque at Malindi.[88] But he did not encourage
Omani Ibāḍī ʿUlamā converting to the Shafiʿi sect and putting down
roots in Zanzibar. He imprisoned Ali b. Abd Allah al-Mazrui for
such a conversion and deported to Oman another such convert, Ali
b. Khamis al-Barwani.[89] As he increasingly institutionalized the Ibāḍī
faith and brought it under state control, he became even less tolerant
of Shafiʿi Alawi scholars such as Ibn-i-Sumayat. Their rituals, saint
and grave worship and discipleship definitely pushed them beyond the
state control, and their presence became intolerable for Barghash.[90]

   It was this religious world that was anathema to the British. They
viewed him as a bigot connected to the fanatical party in Muscat. And
in Zanzibar, he was bound to the Mutawaa party that consisted of
some six or seven leading individuals whose leaders had an agenda—
the downfall of everything European and the establishment of
Muhammedanism on the Abu Dhabi footing. This sect was based
on the strict interpretation of the Koran. The six leading Mutawaas
determined every branch of administration. They were convinced
that he introduced many changes in the judicial department as per
their advice; wherever there was any departure from the Abu Dhabi
interpretation of law, it was annulled.[91]

Cosmopolitanism's Economic Underpinning: The Indian Merchant Capital

The specific Muslim cosmopolitanism nurtured by Barghash for
his new style monarchy was difficult for the British to dismiss, as it
was heavily financed by British Indian subjects. This put the British
in a curious bind. Large Arab estates were generally mortgaged to
Indian capitalists. Some of them were so deeply entangled as to
belong to the Indian mortgagee.[92] According to Frere, all banking
and mercantile business passed through Indian hands along the
coastline. And there was no guarantee that the loans they advanced
didn't go for purchase and traffic of slaves as well. Indeed, among
the buyers were Arabs in Unyanembe.[93]

   The almost total monopoly of the East African trade in the hands
of Indian merchants was not new. They showed Vasco da Gama the

way to India and assisted the Portuguese as well.[94] They not only drove the strings of commerce in the trade with France, Germany and the Americas but contributed equally to the foreign trade of the Arabian coast: from Aden round to the Euphrates. They were active at every port, but especially at the smaller ports of smaller tribes in the Persian Gulf.

Frere was clear that Africans, Arabs and Europeans all used Indian merchant bankers as agents to manage their buying and selling. Without the intervention of an Indian either as capitalist or petty trader, very little business was done. At Zanzibar, he argued, they had the command of the customs houses along nearly 1000 miles of coast. They generously invested in the country. They kept their records in Gujarati and monopolized the coast from Socotra to the Cape Colony.[95]

Indian traders were not just financing the slave trade but were equally implicated in the island's more wide-ranging foreign trade. The foreign trade of Zanzibar, as distinct from the British, was carried on by two German, one French and three American houses. The German houses were the two Hamburg houses of O'Swald & Co. and Hansing & Co. Most of the imports included cotton goods, glassware and beads, arms and ammunitions, hardware, iron, sundry small ware and sundry merchandise. The American houses were represented by Messrs John Bertram & Co., Messrs Arnold Hines & Co. and Mr John Ropes. American gold was imported to Zanzibar by steamers. The French trade was in the hands of the Marseilles firm of Roux de Fraissinet & Co.[96]

The Banias made this trade possible. They collected from the native traders all the country produce for export and prepared it by packing and sorting it for sale to the European merchants or direct export to India and other foreign parts. Likewise, they were the immediate customers of the European and American importers of foreign produce or manufactures. They purchased the goods wholesale and repacked them for the local markets. They were the main intermediaries in the trade between Europe or Asia and East Africa. They knew the local customs and languages and thus formed the ideal link between Africa and foreigners.

Frere elaborated on the details of the transactions of a single Indian house obtained from a judicial court. The books showed a capital of about 4,54,000 lakhs (L) invested in loans and mortgages in East Africa. Of this, about 60,000L had been advanced in various ways to the Sultan and his family, a rather large sum to Arabs in the interior of Africa and a somewhat smaller amount to Arabs in Zanzibar and on the coast. But the total of advances and loans to Arabs and natives of Zanzibar, all slave owners, and most of them slave dealers was less than 2,00,000 L. This sum was lent and advanced in various ways by loans, advances and mortgages on every kind of property, real and personal, and on various kinds of security by advances of goods for trade, etc. Loans and advances to Europeans and Americans were set down at about 1,40,000 L and those to Indians in Africa at about 1,00,000 L. These were African assets and did not include stock in trade or the capital of the Indian corresponding firms, composed of members of the same family, and doing a very large business with Africa at Mandavi and Bombay. The capital employed in African trade and banking by this one family can be reckoned in millions sterling.[97]

Moreover, slaves were a major source of customs at the Customs House, which was managed by Indians and their associate firms, thereby implicating the Indians directly in the traffic. The Bania influence also existed along the shores of Africa, Arabia, the Persian Gulf and Baluchistan, extending to the western frontier of India. The Banias had not assimilated their methods of commerce to that of the British. They carried on with their proceedings independently, and Europeans knew very little of their affairs.

Frere revealed that a large number of the Banias were by birth subjects of the Rao of Kutch and linked to Kutchi trading families. Few of them were permanent residents and the rest generally the agents or branch managers of mercantile houses whose headquarters were established in India. Many were British subjects or invariably under some sort of British Consular protection. Formerly, they got a passport that certified them as British subjects in Africa. Even though they got this sparingly now, they were always offered protection and help at any British Consulate in Africa. And they were such a close community that invariably some kin or other was a British subject, via whom they always had access to Consular protection. For instance, the agents of the Bombay-based Bania firm Lodha Damji in Zanzibar would not hesitate to approach the consulates if they ran into any trouble. They generally went to Africa as young men and, if married, rarely took their families along. Significantly, the capital for their trade came from India, where their big firms were located. They had to submit their accounts periodically at the Indian headquarters.

V

Slavery and the Creation of the 'Modern Monarchy'

Barghash's interventions in the imperial discussions on slavery, held in Zanzibar and London, played a critical role in the making of his modern monarchy. His defence of slavery, both in the Zanzibar and London conversations, with Frere and the dignitaries at the Royal Geographic Society and other British cities respectively, won him favour with the Arab and British private firms and entrepreneurs and got him instant international visibility. This spotlight on him in the international forums made him project himself as the embodiment of the island's ethos—the quasi 'national monarch' who was its most articulate spokesperson.

Zanzibar's economy was traditionally heavily dependent on the profits of slave trade. Barghash ruled in the period when the treaty for a complete ban on slavery was signed (1873). The treaty monitored carefully the seaborne traffic of slaves and had an adverse bearing on his economy. It proved particularly annoying, as its timing coincided with the devastating hurricane that ruined his clove plantations, causing even more heartburn. This made Barghash bargain hard with the British for the continued use of slave labour to revive his devastated plantations.

Randall Pouwels argues that Barghash resisted the slave ban treaty not so much because of concerns of a fall in his profits, but more because of the reaction of the Arabs and the British subjects that were involved in the trade. He 'pleaded' to Frere, who was negotiating terms of the treaty with him, that the Queen should order him to sign a treaty that would take away all culpability of the action from his shoulders.[98] But a close reading of the negotiations reveal that Barghash was achieving much more than mere protection from local backlash.

Indeed, he was defining his sovereign status on the island. He was more openly against the British restrictions as a competitor for trade profits. He saw the treaty as aimed not to ban slave trade but divert its profits exclusively to the British. Unlike his brother Majid, he did not play any deft diplomacy. Instead, he openly protested against the interventions of the British Navy in his waters in search of slaves; he opposed the new slave treaty and thwarted the British agent. And in an act of insolence, he began to address the British agent Churchill without his title.[99] He was clear that he recognized all treaties with them that were signed by his father, but he wanted to know more details of those signed by Majid.[100] This was particularly true of the slave trade-related negotiations and documentation.

Using the Zanzibar-centric imperial rivalries, politics and financial investments to his advantage, he defended the involvement of his subjects in the slave trade, saying he had no power over them as they had taken the protection of the French.[101] Churchill was incensed at this attitude and reminded Barghash that the treaty had clauses that would 'affect none but those engaged in the slave trade carried on between this coast and the coast of Arabia' and that he and his predecessors had pledged to oppose that trade.[102] He urged him to sign and support the anti-slave treaty.

Barghash was defiant. In 1872, when Sir Bartle Frere went on a mission to Zanzibar to urge him to sign the treaty for the suppression of the slave trade, he found him 'insolent and unyielding'. His bravado derived from the sound economic foundation he had built for himself based on profits of slave trade but also from other favourable commercial treaties he had signed with the British and the Europeans that entangled him in financial networks and were mutually beneficial to both parties.

For instance, his customs house levied duties at the reduced rate of 5 per cent on the copal and ivory trade from the interiors for British traders.[103] At the same time, he benefited from the investments of British Indian subjects, the Banias, in the slave and clove economies of the island. Indeed, as we saw above, the capital of the British Indian trading community was hugely invested in Zanzibar. It oiled and financed not just slave traffic and labour but cultivation and agricultural production of sugar cane and cloves on the shambas and building activities in the coastal areas and the towns. Given these entanglements, Barghash felt emboldened to flex his muscles on slave trade.

He justified slavery by highlighting the very specific political economy of the island that made European-style capitalist infrastructure and the prohibition of slave labour on plantations unfeasible. Underlining the specificity of the island's slave-dependent political economy and culture and sharply contrasting it with slavery in Europe, he projected himself as a 'national monarch' capable of articulating an alternate view on slavery and giving this pressing global issue the requisite local legibility.

This stand made him ground himself in Zanzibar society and offset the opposition he experienced from local Swahili tribal chiefs who posed a challenge to him. It won him credibility in the local community, and he consolidated his hold on Arab slavers and plantation owners who supported him in this move. It also made him an attractive figure for private British firms and capitalists who wanted to sink their capital in the plantations and use its slave labour. The huge investments that the Banias had made in slave trade ensured that he won their support as well.

Diplomacy in the Build-up to the Treaty

Barghash played his diplomacy deftly on the issue of the slave ban treaty. In the process, he won the confidence of John Kirk the acting Secretary to the Government of Bombay and later the Political Agent at the Persian Gulf. This proved useful in his bargaining powers and led to his visit to London accompanied by Kirk to argue his case and get involved in the global conversations on the issue.

In fact, during the build-up to the treaty he gave the impression that he was fully with the British in curtailing slave traffic. Kirk reported that 'nothing is done by him without informing me, or asking my advice, and justice is obtained for all British claims with a rapidity and in a way unknown in the latter days of Sayyid Majid'.[104] He added that the most notable feature was the reduction in corruption and bribery among the Qazis and that the Sultan attended to all complaints forwarded from the Consulate and was convinced that he could not apply the strict Mohammedan law to the Christian subjects.

In fact, Kirk's encouraging appreciation drew from his observation that the Sultan had taken good measures even on the issue of curtailing purchase of slaves by the Arabs. He refused all gratuities to the Arabs of Soor and Muscat, among whom formerly $40,000 and $50,000 were often squandered. The Customs Master indicated that, since his accession to the throne, his expenses had been kept within the income. This was no small feat, considering all the building works and the repair of ships and a new contingent of Persian artillery that he had been maintaining.

Kirk had his misgivings on other issues, such as Barghash not clearing the claims of people of the coast and towns. But he concluded that there was no doubt that he had 'become respectful where before he was insolent, and has set aside in a great measure his *mutawwi'in* advisers on whom at first he relied, and whom he made his tools'.[105] And yet Kirk, wary of the diplomatic manoeuvrings, warned that this sudden change of attitude indicated that he was a 'man devoid of principal or honor' and that he be watched and not trusted entirely even on the question of the suppression of slave trade. This sentiment prevailed when he landed with Barghash in London to ratify the treaty.

Barghash and the Defence of the Slave Trade

Kirk was not entirely wrong. Barghash's defence of the slave trade by pointing to its distinctness and difference from slavery prevalent in the Atlantic and Europe became his style of navigating the old-style Sultanate and his new predicaments in the age of the nation states. As he made his presence felt in the imperial club, he refurbished his monarchy as a new form of political practice that balanced the specifics of Zanzibar with the global concerns on slavery.

A nasty hurricane devastated Zanzibar in 1873 and brought its economy to its knees. Its timing could not have been worse, as this was also the time when Sir Henry Bartle Frere, the former Governor of Bombay, missionary and the main British interlocutor, was negotiating the anti-slave trade treaty with Barghash.

Frere had come well prepared. He had obtained the support of the Rao of Kutch, whose subjects, the Banias, were heavily invested in the slave trade. He hoped that the weaning away of the Banias from the trade would significantly dent the traffic and weaken Barghash. In 1872, a year before the treaty was signed, he arrived in Zanzibar to meet Barghash along with Qazi Shahabuddin—the Indian Muslim prime minister of the Rao of Kutch who had also served the British. They persuaded him to sign the anti-slave treaty. The presence of the Qazi was meant to influence the Banias, many of whom were the Rao's subjects, and in turn have the Sultan yield to his request.[106] The philanthropic and benevolent aspect of the Frere Mission had the approval of the Rao of Kutch. The Qazi was asked to popularize the proclamation of the Rao in Zanzibar and prosecute Kutch Banias who carried on slave traffic.

Barghash was unrelenting. He defended slave trade as integral to his political economy, having been pushed to the wall with the devastating economic fallout of the hurricane and the simultaneous pressure to ban slave trade. His conversations with Frere reflected his political acumen and hard bargaining despite the inequities of power between them. He underlined what slavery meant to him. The slave, he argued, was the bedrock of the island's economy. He was willing to maintain his friendship with the British only if this local meaning of slavery was factored into British policy. He held his ground even as he continued to reach out to their reference of authority for future political gains. As he said, 'Do what you like we will never give up your friendship. We could submit to be cut in bits by degrees for your sake; but you come by the right of the stronger to cut off at once the life and head of the weaker.'[107]

He wanted the British to first control the trade that was in the hands of the northern Arabs and exempt him temporarily because of the hurricane damages. Given the devastation caused by the hurricane, he wondered why, as in the case of the Portuguese, he was not being given an extension to implement the treaty.[108] His forceful defence of his demands reflected his confidence as the Sultan who was calling the shots from a position of strength that his island location lent him. The tone of the conversation revealed that the abolition talk was in practice about competitive politics on the control of trade rather than its ban. On being warned of the forceful implementation by the British and the damage it would do to his legitimate commerce, he replied that his island was anyway in economic crisis and argued that 'in your success lies my ruin. A spear is held at each of my eyes, with which shall I chose to be pierced? Either way it is fatal to me'.

In 1875, Barghash accompanied John Kirk to London at the time of the ratification of the treaty. The significance of the visit was noticeable in that he was no ordinary visitor. As we saw above, he attended many parties hosted for him by the Queen herself and other dignitaries, including Lady Frere, wife of Sir Henry Bartle Frere, who was the chief interlocutor on the slavery discussion with him.

Barghash used this conversation with the British to lend his support to the curtailment of slave trade, but not without defending slavery while keeping his social constituency in mind. He wanted to know from the Consul Rev. G. Badger, who presented the draft of the treaty, what compensation the Arabs would receive for the losses they would suffer with the stoppage of this trade.[109] He bargained hard on the financial implications of the ban even if he was told that only after he signed the treaty could these matters be attended to in a friendly manner.

Barghash used the knowledge he had gained from his international contacts to warn Frere about the violent repercussions of the slave ban. He had been briefed about the civil war in America by Captain Wilson of the United States corvette *Yantie* in an official letter. He was told that this war had arisen out of the slavery question.[110] He used the familiar motif of the American civil war to warn Frere of similar violent repercussions by the Arabs and local chiefs if slavery was banned. Indeed, he warned Frere of an insurrection like the one that had 'happened to the Americans'.

In his articulation of the local meaning of slavery, Barghash put forward a sophisticated argument that laid out the legal and historical contours of his distinct political culture. He contrasted the specifics of Zanzibar's slavery to that familiar to people in Europe. He underlined its distinctness in the social dependence and integration of slaves in society and in his being the familial father figure to all his people, including slaves.[111] This uniqueness made him justify slave labour as non-exploitative.

Justifying slave labour as integral to his political economy, he argued that this was essential to economic life, as no individual on his island was wealthy enough to set up sugar presses and pay wages for labour. Making a case for the uniqueness and exceptional character of Zanzibar, he underlined the non-oppressive and non-exploitative nature of his state, where 'all are protected from seizure and slavery'. He contrasted this to slavery and slaves outside Zanzibar, arguing that the seizures and dark side of slavery was applicable only to those who were in slavery in their own country and had been brought to Zanzibar as slaves.

Barghash made a case for the use of slaves in the agricultural sector by invoking both history as well as the law of his land. He argued that indigenous capital and local investors in agriculture were absent in Zanzibar. The economy was dependent on Indian merchants and private British capital, and this made slave labour justifiable. It also made it necessary for him to attract British capitalists and firms like that of Captain Fraser, who could invest in agriculture. Fraser, he pointed out, had set up a sugar press, extracted oil and manufactured soap, paying the labourers money—wages. He argued that if he attempted this, he would go bankrupt. He warned that he was opposed to the treaty because the withdrawal of slave labour, which was so integral to his political economy, would trigger an insurrection in the ranks of agriculturists whose lands would perish if slaves were withdrawn. If their slaves escaped, it would be difficult to get them back from the mainland owing to the danger of seizure on the sea.

Barghash further pointed out that any treaty with such far-reaching consequences needed to be temporally contingent. In this particular case, the timing of the treaty could not have been worse. The island was hit by a hurricane, and the ruined clove plantations required a renewal. He pointed out that they would yield no profit for a long time until the trees were fully grown. And in this background, the slave ban treaty was a double whammy, as hardly any sum was paid into the Zanzibar treasury derived from the export of slaves.[112] Frere refuted all these explanations, pointing out that his customs had increased from the slave traffic that was routed via his island. He said that were he to sign the treaty, all the fears of insurrection and ruin that he pointed out would be adequately taken care of.[113]

Barghash's Bargaining Counter for Slavery: British Indian Subjects in Slave Trade

Frere was convinced that Barghash's spirited and clever defence of slavery derived from his economic strength on the island. His financial aplomb was largely due to the investments of Indian merchants and bankers, the Banias. His confidence in fighting for his right to continue working with slaves was strengthened as the Banias were legal British Indian subjects. Their involvement itself exposed the hypocrisy of the ban and earned Barghash that extra confidence to put up his defence.

By the time of Barghash, the Indian Bania houses owned most of the capital employed in the date, pearl and grain export trade as well as in the cloth, metal, sugar, indigo and slave import trade. They were the bankers and moneylenders of the petty chiefs, pearl fishers and date growers. Frere was of the view that their capital was so influential that a strike or ganging up of the Banias of his chief town could influence the most independent Arab chief and the most fanatical of his followers.[114]

Frere noted that the most striking part of their modus operandi was their indirect involvement in the slave trade. If an Arab, Portuguese or anyone on the African coast wished to get a commercial or elephant hunting expedition into the interior and had no capital of his own, he took an advance from the Bania. He got this advance in cloth, beads, copper and brass wire. He could also avail muskets and ammunition. No questions were asked as to whether the muskets were for self-defence or elephant hunting. The repayment was to be made in ivory, slaves or other African produce that was brought from a great distance in the interior. The arms and ammunition obtained from the Banias were often loaned to the slave hunters to get slaves from the interior. Indeed, there was no doubt that 'little if any capital is employed in the slave trade which does not pass through the hands of the Banias', many of whom were legal British subjects.[115] The community was further indirectly involved in slave trade by farming the Sultan's customs, of which a large portion was derived from duty on slaves.

Frere revealed the inside working of the Bania financial networks in supporting the slave trade. He detailed the working of a respectable Bania house of A.B. in Zanzibar. This was a branch of the well-known house of the same name in Bombay, which had agencies in Surat and Karachi (British ports), and at Bahrain and Bushire (Arab, Turkish and Persian ports). All the members of the house were British-born subjects whose capital account was balanced at Bombay. They fitted out the caravan of C.D., a respectable Arab merchant of Muscat, ostensibly to buy ivory in the interior. The beads, arms and ammunition were brought from a Zanzibar branch of a great Hamburg house, the cloth and wire from British and American houses. All were to share in the return of ivory and other goods. For two years, the exploits of C.D. in purchasing ivory and fomenting wars and slave hunts in the interior were the general theme of Zanzibar tales. C.D. finally appeared at Zanzibar with large quantities of ivory and other goods brought down by slaves, who were sold on the mainland—some to go to Zanzibar and some to Arabia. After the transactions, C.D. settled accounts with the Banias and his British, American and German connections. He probably prepared for a fresh expedition while the proceeds and profits of his adventures went to Bombay, London, Hamburg and New York and were there accounted for.

Frere was convinced that this case made it clear that the capital employed in the expedition had 'its home primarily under the shelter of the British government in British India'. And the commercial enterprise that brought the goods in the traffic to Zanzibar was directed by Englishmen, Germans and Americans. He showed that the complicity of the British Indian Bania, the slave hunter and dealer was so intact that efforts to suppress slavery were invariably opposed widely in the region. Frere was of the view that the only viable option was to get the Indian government and Her Majesty's government together to exert pressure on the Sultans of Muscat and Zanzibar and get them on board in this anti-slave drive. The issue of subsidy could be raised with the British pitching in to help Zanzibar as bait to get its support in this drive.[116]

Further, the Banias were also largely invested in clove and sugar plantations in Zanzibar, which also worked on slave labour. Therefore, it was no surprise that they were not interested in the suppression of the slave trade. The northern Arab boats were involved in the export of slaves from the east coast. A large amount of capital was used to equip these boats, all of which came from the Indian Bania houses in Arab and Persian ports. Their involvement in the slave trade was much more direct than that of the Banias living in Zanzibar. Frere recommended that the Indian capital clearly had to be redirected or snuffed out in order to control Barghash.

Working Around the 1873 Slave Ban Treaty

The treaty was passed despite Barghash's reservations. It was a watershed, as it did reduce the traffic between the mainland and the islands of Zanzibar and Pemba. The re-export of slaves from Kilwa and Pemba by sea to Eastern Arabia was curtailed. The local trade stagnated, at least temporarily. The estimated number of slaves imported declined from 13,480 in 1874 to 2100 in 1882. However, this decline of slave demand by Arab landholders at Pemba was also due to the great depreciation of the clove market and the Sultan's rigid exactions of the clove tax. Demand for slaves existed in Zanzibar on the clove plantations that were not subject to the same taxation as those in Pemba.[117]

Barghash worked around the treaty to maximize profits even while claiming to abide by its terms. He handled the issue with the utmost diplomacy and caution. The administrative report of Zanzibar for 1873–74 noted that his support for the treaty was phenomenal. Indeed, in 1875, he signed a supplementary treaty giving fuller effect to the treaty of 1873; the following year he issued a proclamation prohibiting the land traffic in slaves and the setting out of slave caravans. He also cooperated with the British by seizing dhows and slave cargoes and by awarding punishment to those implicated. Data also showed that he suffered revenue losses as a consequence of abiding by its terms. By 1877, his list of captures (slaves) was 453 against the 294 of the British.[118]

In 1877, he was particularly praised for arresting, in an open durbar, the Governor of Kilwa, Sayyid bin Abdullah, and putting him in irons on proof being shown that he was actively engaged in slave trading operations. Abdullah was released after an imprisonment of two and a half months because he was suffering from dysentery. Barghash also seized, at Windi, a large body of slave dealers with slaves who were driving north.[119] In fact, he even overlooked the trespassing of British ships bringing gunpowder to maintain vigil against slave traffic. Gunpowder on the British ship *Africa* entered the Zanzibar harbour in wilful violation of port rules. The master of the ship was fined $100, and Barghash refused to accept this amount that was credited to the Agency Treasury Account.[120]

However, Barghash maintained his fine balance of continuing with slave labour in his territory and turning a blind eye to the traffic while at the same time extending support to the British efforts to stop the export trade. His signals to the British were carefully calculated and aimed to ensure his profits of the slave trade. In 1877, he gave land to the missionary societies that were setting up missions for freed slaves in Mombasa and other places on the east coast. Bishop Steere was one such missionary, very active in Zanzibar, who took the slaves back to their home countries after rescuing them from their Arab owners.[121] British officers in Mombasa, such as Commander Russell, often made applications for financial allowances for the maintenance of these freed slaves at the missions.[122] There were reports also of Barghash's officers assisting British naval officers in the rescue of slaves freshly landed on the island of Pemba and lodged in specified houses.[123]

And yet, the British felt that he was doing all this to attract their favourable notice and not because of any 'honest resolve' to do away with the slave trade. Indeed, Lt Col Miles, Consul General at Zanzibar, felt that the real nature of the Sultan's policy was in short exhibited to them in the entire 'absence of any preventive service on the one hand and on the other in his position as one of the most extensive and unsparing employers of the slave labour in his dominion'. He said Barghash 'never employed his small steamers or coast guards for his ports to stop dealers'[124] and that the slave dealers knew that, as long as they could elude the vigilance of the blockade and succeed in landing their ventures, they had every hope of being left to dispose of them unmolested. But Barghash cooperated with the British in stopping the sea traffic of slaves and arrested the imported cargos of slaves and their dealers.

Barghash's diplomatic handling of the treaty provisions guaranteed slave labour in his territory. But the treaty did create a slump in the revenue he collected from the seaborne export trade.[125] Most of his revenue was derived from the customs duties, which were farmed by the Bombay firm of Jairam Sewji. The sum annually paid by this house was $3,00,000. But the total purchase money amounted to $5,40,000. The balance $2,40,000 was deployed in paying off the large debt owed by the ruler of Zanzibar to the customs farmer.

And yet, despite these losses, the British were of the view that it was profits of slave trade and continued supply of slave labour that constituted the base of Barghash's authority. Lt Col Miles, the Consul General at Zanzibar, was of the view that he was the largest landowner and the wealthiest man in his dominion. This was largely because of the large revenue he derived from his estates and the Customs House, and that this consolidation of revenue was largely because of the treaty of 1873, by which he raised himself to an independent position. His authority over people was supreme, and that was the reason he had the 'power and the ability to carry out unopposed any measures of repression or inspection he chooses'.[126] Miles concluded that there was no public voice to oppose him and he was strong enough to 'stand-alone'. He was naturally of an 'aggressive and arbitrary disposition' and had made his will the 'only law of the land'. Miles felt that Barghash had the power to end slave traffic completely if he wanted but lacked the earnest desire to do so as he depended on its profits.

Land Route for Slave Trade Survives the 1873 Treaty

Of course, the treaty only intensified the interest of Barghash in the overland traffic of slaves to avoid British surveillance. A substantial number of slaves arrived under his watch for transaction by the overland route. From 1873 to 1874, the arrivals via this route were as follows: Pangani, 32,000; Pemba, 15,000; Gasi, 16,000; Mombasa and the surrounding district, 13,000; Takaungu, 12,500; Malindi, 6500; Ozy River, 4000. The number of slaves bought locally were as follows: Pemba, 15,000; Tanga District, 1000; Mombasa, 500; Mombash District, 500; Takaungu and district, 5000; Malindi, 1000; Lamo and Kipini District, 1200; Bajunia country, 1000; Banadir and Somali country, unknown.[127]

The land route by which these slaves arrived was always active. Frederic Holmwood, Assistant Political Agent, Zanzibar, alerted the government to the existence of a flourishing traffic on the land route even as the sea route was seeing a drop in transactions. This route moved from Gasi to the Bajunia country. Slave overseers, including both the Arabs and the Swahilis, used the following route: starting from Totana above the northern mouth of the Ozy river, they passed through a marshy country to Kimbu, about eight hours from Lamu. They then came to Makuhe via Kinumbi. This place was on the opposite side of Lamu town, and here the best domestic slaves were bought up by the townspeople. The next station was

Malimaudi. The last station was Jaguani, opposite Paza. Beyond this point, the trade was entirely in the hands of the Somalis.

Very powerful slave dealers, both Swahili and Arab, operated on this land route with the full cooperation of Barghash. For instance, one Mirambo in Unyanembe organized caravans of slaves on this land route. Barghash, to please the British, often sent soldiers to deal with them. But this was for effect as, on the ground, he turned a blind eye to this trade. The Arabs looked for his support in tying up with Mirambo and the Unyanembe, as his political sovereignty extended to this tribal area as well. He clearly obliged. Caravans of Mirambo passed by his Fort Boma and through his country into Karagwe without the slightest molestation or any taxes demanded.

Mirambo also tried to lure the Sultan by sending him a gift of ivory. But Barghash would not allow any such friendly gestures in public. And yet he gave Mirambo free licence to carry on his slave business. The Sultan's encouragement resulted in Mirambo's flourishing business. His caravan often had as many as 1500 raw slaves collected from the interior principally from the Manyema country.[128] He was not the only one. In 1875, an Arab of Nejd was reported to have escorted a large gang of slaves from Kilwa by land to Pangani, from where they were shipped to Pemba and sold. The purchase money was made payable in Zanzibar by draft on an Indian. John Kirk stopped the payment pending on the draft and warned the Indian to desist from indulging in transactions involving the price of slaves.[129]

Barghash's reign saw a spike in the caravan route of the slave trade. But it also triggered competition for the profits of the trade between him and the local Arab Governors, and the Swahili as well as the Arab chiefs. In 1874, Barghash dismissed the Governor of Pemba, Ḥamūd bin Muhammad, who was notorious as a supporter and abettor of the slave trade. This step was taken at the request of the inhabitants of Pemba, who could no longer endure the tyrannical proceedings of the previous Governor.[130]

Barghash remained in continuous confrontation with inland landed chiefs, who tried to draw slave profits to themselves. They continued to levy transit dues on the trade. For instance, in Kilwa,

every 'Negro caravan' was stopped by them and asked to choose a
Swahili patron, and only then could it proceed. The patron's writ
prevailed in all 'Negro transactions' while the caravan remained in
Kilwa. The Sultan was ineffective in putting an end to this practice.
In Mombasa, he was even less successful in superseding the authority
of the old ruling family. Again, at Lindy, the authority of his Arab
Governor was of little avail for the protection of life or property
beyond the walls of his fort. The Banias packed off to leave as the
chief of the M'gao tribe went on a rampage there, and the Governor
remained helpless even though he hired a reinforcement of Arabs
from Zanzibar.[131] Similarly, along the Portuguese frontier, towards
the mouth of Rovuma and Cape Delgado, the country was in the
hands of independent chiefs. The Sultan's authority extended little
beyond his fortified posts and customs houses.[132]

Barghash countered the competition from the inland chiefs by
backing the Arab slavers of Zanzibar to garner the profits of the trade.
Barghash gave all indicators that he wanted to act independently of
the British on the question of slave trade. He made it clear that he
was keener to make friends with the wealthy Arabs of Zanzibar,
who had a vested interest in the maintenance of the slave trade. He
used them as emissaries to influence the wealthy Arab Omanis and
convey to them his intention to continue with the trade for their
benefit. He wanted them to know that he was a supporter of their
slaving intercourse with the East African coast. But at the same time,
he wanted to keep the slavers in his control.

And of course, the British, as the other key contender in the race
for slave profits, never stopped thinking of ways to curb Barghash
and increase their control. According to Holmwood, the land route
was flourishing because it had many advantages, both for the dealer
and buyer. They avoided the expenses of procuring vessels and the
risks of capture at sea. He was of the view that, as compared to the
sea route, this overland trade was relatively cheaper to extinguish.

Holmwood suggested two methods. First, to imitate on land
the repressive measures which had successfully stamped out the sea
traffic on the west coast and between the ports in the dominions of
the Sultan of Zanzibar and Arabia. Since the route and trade between

Kilwa and Pangani was an organized trade, with regularly established resting places, night stations and ferries with fixed charges; in the south, Somali country behind Lamu en route to the port of Banadiris was relatively less organized trade. The establishment of a British settlement at the Banadiris port would be of great advantage. And if a commodious harbour was selected, it might become the much-required naval station for these seas.

The permission of Barghash was required to use it as a temporary base to carry on simple operations. An expedition consisting of a hundred men from Her Majesty's ships, with fifty native carriers and ten baggage animals, would suffice. At least two of those in charge of this force should be Swahili speakers. If selected at once and ordered to repair to Zanzibar, any officers having a slight knowledge of the language might accomplish it. An order in Swahili and Arabic was to be circulated, securing pardon and protection to all persons connected with the caravans, who would peacefully surrender with their slaves or proceed to the nearest large coast town without settling, ill-treating or neglecting those in their charge.

The force was said to camp within convenient distance of the watering place on the point of the land route chosen, and an artesian well was constructed. This camp was meant to be well protected. It was believed that a short occupation of such a post would cause all slave caravans to stop short, and well-organized patrols would readily prevent their turning the position. The caravans would now be thrown back upon the larger coast towns for subsistence, and two host crews commanded by an experienced officer dispatched to each place, if supported by the authority of the Sultan, take charge of the whole. It was thought necessary to have one or more posts on the land route for some time. This would bring pressure on the distant tribes, from whence the great majority of raw slaves were derived. But the great majority of the Arabs would accept service in posts and be useful in this project. The only hitch was that, south of Zanzibar, the Mozambique ports were under Portuguese occupation. It was feared that these efforts may divert traffic there rather than stamp it out altogether.

However, Holmwood argued that the desultory inland traffic of slaves could only be stopped by the opening up of the continent and setting up of strong governments. Another method would be by counteracting the present custom of slave holding by substituting free labour of immigrants from India or China. British Indian subjects who owned land would no doubt welcome this move.[133]

Barghash and the Mixed Impact of the Slave Ban Treaty: The Case of Pemba

An 1875 report on slave owners in Pemba revealed that, despite the treaty, both slave ownership and dealership were rampant. Both the Indians and the Arabs were actively involved in the traffic. Indian Banias and Bohra and Khoja merchants from India owned shambas of cloves and slaves to work on them. For instance, the shamba of Ibrahim Bohra had forty slaves, and two shambas owned by his wife had another forty slaves. Fifteen slaves worked on the two shambas of one Ghulam Hussain Bohra, and sixty on the shamba of Abdullah Khoja, and another six on the second shamba owned by him. Qāsim bin Abdullah Hindī had sixty slaves working in four of his shambas. There were other Banias and natives of Hindustan, such as Easa Bohra, who had 100 slaves and no shambas.

Indians worked in tandem with the Arab slavers, who maintained the flow of slaves from the mainland to Pemba. They used dhows to cart them. This was their permanent vocation. It involved women as well, who used their dhows to cart slaves on a regular basis. A woman who lived in the Wesha port area was 'in the habit of carrying slaves from mainland to Pemba in her dhow'. The nākhodā and the crew were all her slaves.[134] Similarly, Khulfan bin Rāshid Muskasrī of Kolkotomi was similarly active on this route.

Significantly, the Arabs surpassed the Indians in owning slaves. A total of 18,057 slaves were held by Arabs in the shambas. Half the shambas in Pemba were owned by the Arabs, and only about a hundred small shambas were owned by natives.[135] Most slaves worked on clove plantations, which earned the owners well. The price of cloves in 1875 was $4.5 without duty. The owners mortgaged the crops to Indians and Banias in order to pay for the slaves, which they had bought for labour. The prices of shambas was very high and calculated by the number of trees bearing or near bearing. And the price was from $10–15 a tree. By 1875, prices had become so high that shambas that were worth $300 or $1000 three years ago were selling at $25,000.[136]

At the same time, Barghash was playing his cards well and seemingly cooperating with the British administration in curbing corrupt practices related to slaves. In 1881, Barghash, who was said to be in good favour with the British, was asked to cooperate in the case of a corrupt Governor of Pemba, who despite his stern orders, was allowing the traffic of slaves from the island. Barghash agreed to allow the British agent Mr Mathews to proceed to Pemba and take independent action against the slave dealers. Indeed, Barghash asked him to act as 'a Zanzibar officer and Chief of His Highness' police and regular forces'.[137] The mission was successful, and the cooperation of Barghash so appreciated that John Kirk called him a 'most popular Prince; since his accession justice has been fairly administered, which was not the case at any former time'.

However, his tightrope walking had its limits. A decade later, the impact of the slave ban treaty began to be evident in Pemba. The statistics revealed that despite the efforts of Barghash to cushion the ban impact, the treaty restrictions proved ruinous to his Pemba plantations. In 1884, Kirk reported that the island of Pemba 'is an example of enormous waste through death and flight that goes on in a slave plantation'. He pointed out that there were no slaves there for eighteen months. The 'island was deserted . . . jungle where land was once tilled'.[138] Kirk appreciated that Barghash had organized a police force for order in town and remitted tribute collected from people. He also carried out at his own expense many public works and did much for the good of his people, such as 'lighting the principal streets of the town, bringing in a pure supply of water which is distributed freely, and using his own steamers in importing grain thus frustrating combinations of Indian speculators and reducing the price of food on which the bulk of the population depended'. But he warned that his interference in the slave traffic would endanger his position were it not that 'he is known to be supported by us and acting at our instance in what he does'.[139]

And yet reports of 'fugitive slaves' arriving in Pemba in canoes and accosted by Her Majesty's ship *London* kept trickling in.[140] Many of these were taken under the protection of the British, and the Sultan was informed that no application would be entertained for their restitution.

The crippling effect on slave trade and the move against use of slave labour was predictably resented by the Arab landowners of Barghash. Slave trade had supplied them labour for their plantations. But the scarcity of money and the increased vigilance of the Sultan's officers made the slave supply a trickle. Landowners went through a period of great difficulty and incurred huge debts because of a string of measures that put a noose around their necks: they were deprived of their labour supply and thus lost their key means to produce their staple source of wealth—cloves. The market price of cloves fell as Barghash tried to compensate his slave losses by a heavy duty. The landowners had sold the item at high prices in 1875 and 1879 because of the bumper harvest of cloves and the accruing profits. Believing that this would remain the trend, they not only spent their profits recklessly but also borrowed unthinkingly from the Indian moneylenders. But with the treaty regulations restricting profits from slave trade, Barghash increased the duty/tax on cloves from 40 per cent on their value in 1883 to 65 per cent. This was topped by a 5 per cent tax by the Customs House, and the taxes came to almost 75 per cent on their original value. All this came from the growers' pocket.[141] Many Arabs moved from cloves to rice and cut down clove trees. Additionally, the new laws forbade them to sell or mortgage land to foreigners, who were the only people likely to be able to give fair prices for the produce.

If a landowner became insolvent, he was forced to sell in the limited and moneyless market that was available for the Sultan's own subjects at a price generally far below the value. Besides, the ban on transactions with foreigners meant that no local could mortgage or sell land to borrow money as easily as before. Only a few could now borrow money, and that too at a high rate of

interest. Property could be bought only by the rich, as money was
to be brought without security as no mortgages to foreigners were
allowed.[142] The Bania moneylenders were compelled to either
foreclose or to continue the loan on purely personal security.
They raised their interest rates to 15 per cent. The borrowers
fraudulently settled their plantation on a child or their wife and
then allowed whatever remained of their goods to be seized and
sold for the debts. Thus, the measures of the Sultan adversely
impacted their business as well.

The Shift from Slaves to Coolies in the Government Plantations

It was only in 1890, once Zanzibar became a British protectorate
and slavery was formally abolished, that some of these suggestions
could be implemented. Coolie labour from India now became the
substitute for slaves in the Zanzibar government-owned plantations.
In 1897, Mr de Sausmarez, the Assistant Judge in the Consular Court
at Zanzibar, prepared a draft ordinance and a draft of regulations for
regulating the immigration of coolies from India into Zanzibar and
Pemba.[143] This was considered necessary, as the coolies were Indian
subjects/labourers and not under the jurisdiction of the Sultan of
Zanzibar. The ordinance established the contractual relation of
master and servant and narrowed their hiring strictly to British
officers working with the authorization of the Sultan. De Sausmarez
clarified that the ordinance was necessary because of the scheme for
'introducing a limited number of immigrants into Zanzibar to labor
in government plantations'. He felt it necessary to tie the labourers
to the terms of the ordinance as he feared that 'foreigners might
wish to employ Indian immigrants'.[144] He feared that these private
employers of labour may then export them to the German east coast
and elsewhere.

I ndeed, the Government of India agreed to opening immigration
from India to Zanzibar on the condition that 'immigrants will be
in the employ solely at the Zanzibar Government'. But since the
wherewithal for implementation of the Fiji or any similar immigration

ordinance was too complicated and elaborate, and the machinery at the disposal of the Sultan too imperfect, the government wanted to restrict coolies to government employment i.e., at its plantations. It made it a penal offence if any private person employed them.[145] The ordinance gave details of their arrival dates, wages, accommodation, medical facilities and legal redress.[146]

The government was of the view that a year into the opening of immigration into India, the machinery did not exist in Zanzibar for effectively enforcing a labour ordinance against private employers of labour. And, therefore, it insisted that Indian labour be limited and restricted to government plantations and public works alone. It was also wary of the impact the climate of the island would have on Indian labour and wanted to see the immigration as an 'experiment' and confine it within narrow limits. It wanted these provisions factored into the ordinance before it legalized immigration from India to Zanzibar. It was of the view that this limited immigration be tried for two years before legalization. But more importantly, it reiterated that legal sanction would be pending 'until the Governor General in Council was further satisfied that machinery was actually in existence for effectively enforcing the labour ordinance against private employers'.[147]

VI

The Temporal and Spatial Limits of the 'Modern Monarchy'

Barghash and the Loss of Interest in Dar as Salaam

Barghash's cosmopolitan monarchy remained rooted not only in an urban setting but was spatially confined to Zanzibar. It was also temporally framed in the moment of the abolition drive that brought him into sharp focus as he was the Sultan of Zanzibar, the hub of the slave trade. The island remained his stage to showcase his specific modern cosmopolitan monarchy to the detriment of other new cities such as Dar as Salaam. Indeed, Majid's dream city showed

a steady decline in its urban infrastructure and intellectual life as
Barghash remained focused on Zanzibar.

I. Elton, the assistant to the Political Agent, reported that in Dar
as Salaam, Barghash was pronounced as 'the unlucky'.[148] In Majid's
time, caravans headed by flags and men firing guns swaggered
through the streets to receive royal presents. Men from the high
estates of Zanzibar invested their revenues open-handedly in the
new town. But all this ended with Barghash, who was not inclined to
foster any project that he had not initiated. Indeed, he encouraged
the dissenting voices of the Banias and Arab merchants, who were
reluctant to shift base to Dar as Salaam in Majid's reign. The official
neglect and weather slowly destroyed the steps, terraces and wells
that Majid had painstakingly installed in the city.

The devastating hurricane of 1872 made things worse in Dar
as Salaam. It destroyed the fleet inherited from Majid. Barghash's
landed property was also severely damaged. Roads needed to be
renovated.[149] Only two houses were habitable. A low thatched
barn doubled as Customs House in the broad overgrown field
that marked the site allotted by Majid for the erection of a more
permanent structure. Slave caravans passed through Dar as Salaam
in fear of their information reaching Zanzibar. Their number had
increased so much that the akhidah, who normally avoided this topic,
said 'he had never seen anything so shameful it was only killing men
not trading'.[150]

Elton observed that the economic slump and neglect was
reflected in the general decay of houses. The only exception was
one enterprising corner, where a few Indians industriously strove
to revive a failing trade with the interior. House property held no
value. The land around was so deprecated that a plantation of some
extent was shown to him for sale at a price of $40. A plot of land
and a half-finished house in the centre of the town mortgaged about
twenty-seven years ago for $500 would not fetch a reserve of $200
when offered lately at an auction. At the same time, a thatched hut
and 2 acres in a good situation went for $7.[151]

Barghash had very little support of the tribes in and around
Dar as Salaam. A brawl between one of his slaves and the tribes

exposed the animosities. Barghash's support of the slave resulted in the tribes boycotting trade and ending all forms of barter. They completely stopped sending produce from the interior. As a result, many merchants, including Banias and Khojas, shifted out to Magagoni, Tuliani and the neighbouring villages, where a brisk copal trade sprang up to the prejudice of Dar as Salaam.[152] By and large, trade that had shifted to Dar as Salaam moved back to Zanzibar.

But the Sultan did maintain his plantations in and around Dar as Salaam. The soil was alluvial and the plains well wooded, and it was perfect for cultivation. The slaves thrived on the plantation as food was cheap and fish plentifully caught all along the coast and in the river. In the three days they had for themselves, they even collected salt and traded in it.[153] The overland slave caravans moved past Barghash's plantations, skirting close past the town on their coastal journey to reach any island for shipment.[154] The akhidah, Rashkh Allah, an Arab of Shehr who represented the Sultan in the city, was supported by a few Arabs, Baluchis and half-caste mercenaries. A guard was posted at his house, where a substantial number of muskets, matchlocks and old powder horns were stored for the purpose of equipping the 200 slaves who worked on Barghash's extensive plantations. They needed these armaments in the case of disturbances with the neighbouring tribes.

And yet, Dar as Salaam country had admirable facilities for the re-plantation and extension of his clove, sugar, coconut and other gardens that were destroyed in the hurricane. But funds for all this were scarce. Kirk estimated his income as between £60,000 and £70,000. But in the hurricane year, it was much less. He also paid the Muscat subsidy and gave up the £20,000 which he got from the slave trade. But he was heavily in debt and owed Muscat probably £30,000 or £40,000 and to the house of Jairam Sewji £60,000.[155]

And yet, all was not abandoned in Dar as Salaam, even if the focus of the Sultan remained on Zanzibar. Barghash was happy to encourage and support any infrastructural uplift that the British financed. The Mackinnon Road scheme, which was promoted and paid for by W. Mackinnon and Sir Thomas Fowell Buxton to open effective communication for wheeled traffic with Lake Nyasa and connect the coast with the interior, was one such urban project.

The British investment in it checked the hardships of Dar as Salaam and gave it an economic boost. It revived trade by attracting rubber and copal from Zaramo producers. Work on it started in the city with full support of Barghash. He ordered his akhidah to proceed with an armed force and handle the mazungera, a tribal chief who demanded payment to give his permission for the road to pass through his territory. The presence of the disease-producing tsetse fly impeded its progress at a different stretch.[156] Nevertheless, by 1877, it was functional, and about 100 locals used it to bring rice, Indian rubber and copal into Dar as Salaam.

The road was meant to curtail the caravan slave trade as it meandered through the area used by runaway slaves from Kilwa, who marched overland to the ports of Pangani and Tanga, from where they crossed in canoes to Zanzibar and Pemba. John Kirk, the Consul, hoped that Barghash's troops would patrol the road and stop the slave traffic. But this was not to be, as the akhidah did not seem to be interested in this mission and did not cooperate.[157] The Mackinnon Road was abandoned in 1881 after it had reached a length of 81 miles.[158] Dar as Salaam continued to be a spot for the transfer of slaves, even if the numbers remained small unless exceptional circumstances like the 1884 famine saw a spike in the numbers.[159]

The 1882 smallpox outbreak that killed three-quarters of the town's population, coupled with the famine, produced such hardship that slave trade, inter-village kidnapping and pawning of children for food showed an increase.[160] It was not until the German takeover of the town in 1885 that the Arab-handled slave trade was effectively stopped. And yet, despite these hardships, Dar as Salaam grew in its regional economic importance, particularly as an exporter of rice to Zanzibar. Brennan and Andrew demonstrate that by the 1880s, its overall population increased and, after Bagamoyo, it remained the well-established secondary centre.[161]

Credit: Private Collection

Sayyid Barghash, Sultan
of Zanzibar (r. 1871–89).
Photograph by Maull & Co., 1875

Sayyid Barghash, Sultan
of Zanzibar (r. 1871–89),
with his officials in
London. Photograph by
Maull & Co., 1875

Credit: Beinecke Rare Book and Manuscript Library, Yale University

A view of the Zanzibar waterfront showing Sultan Barghash's Bayt al-Ajāʾib
/House of Wonders. Photograph by Coutinho Brothers, c. 1890

Changing the guard at Sultan Barghash's Bayt al-Ajāʾib, c. 1890

Interview between Sir Bartle Frere and Sayyid Barghash, Sultan of Zanzibar, from *Harper's Weekly*, 1873

The Sultan of Zanzibar at Manchester (engraving)

Zanzibar Old Fort, with clove traders in the foreground, c. 1880–90

The waterfront at Dar es Salaam. Photograph for *Zoll &*
Haupt Magazin, 1897

Sorting cloves, Zanzibar, c. 1910

Military parade in front of the Beit al-Hukm
('House of Government'), Zanzibar, c. 1875

'More Slaveries than One', cartoon satirizing relations between Sayyid Barghash, Sultan of Zanzibar, and the British prime minister, Benjamin Disraeli. From *Punch*, 26 June 1875

Acknowledgements

I owe this book to the inspiring scholarship on the Indian Ocean by some of my very dear friends: Enseng Ho, Fahad Bishara, Iza Hussin, Eric Tagliacozzo, Nidhi Mahajan, Sugata Bose, Ayesha Jalal, Sujit Sivasundaram and Sunil Amrith. Their friendship, intellectual camaraderie and companionship triggered my interest in the enchanting world of the Western Indian Ocean. Cynthia Becker, my African art historian-friend, brought back from Zanzibar endless stories of the Omani Sultans on the island. She convinced me that there was a Sultans' tale waiting to be told.

This book is the result of my exciting forays into the waters through the histories of the mobile Sultans of Oman. Their fascinating lives and careers offer fresh insight on the oceanic political culture in the age of Empire.

My intellectual debts and gratitude to Fahad Bishara are huge: his generosity in sending me references, unlocking the many mysteries of the archive, helping with my research trip to Zanzibar and just being there for me at all times in the writing of this book are truly exceptional. I owe special thanks to Eric Tagliacozzo, Upinder Singh and Farhat Hasan for reading parts of the book.

My friend Katherine Prior painstakingly did the picture research alongside offering me her home in London to camp endlessly! My thanks also to Thomas McDow, Steven Fabian and Allen Fromherz, who always replied to my queries with enthusiasm. My students Aakash Awasthi and Pallavi Das helped me think through many of my arguments. Sajjad Rizvi helped in the transliteration.

I owe special thanks to my family members: my cousins Sheeba Zaidi and Sabeena Sagheer who read parts of the book, and my young lawyer niece Ayesha Alavi whose pertinent queries made me reformulate many ideas. And of course my father, Shariq Alavi, continues to be my source of inspiration. His calm and dignified presence in Lucknow, where I wrote this book in the long Covid-19 lockdown years, made its writing ever so special.

Notes

Introduction

1. L. Pelly, Resident Persian Gulf, to Bartle Frere, Bombay, Governor, n.d, Collection 4 of 61/3, L/PS/6/544, British Library [henceforth BL].
2. Karen Stapley, 'Assassination and Intrigue in Muscat 1866–68', Qatar Digital Library, https://www.qdl.qa/en/assassination-and-intrigue-muscat-1866–68 (accessed 9 May 2022); T.F. McDow, *Buying Time: Debt and Mobility in the Western Indian Ocean*, Ohio University Press, Ohio, 2018, pp. 79–80.
3. L. Pelly, Resident Persian Gulf, to Bartle Frere, Bombay Governor, n.d., L/PS/6/544, Collection 4 of 61/3, BL.
4. McDow, *Buying Time*, p. 81.
5. Khalid had backing from his Malabari mother. Hilal was exiled to London.
6. J. Presthold, *Domesticating the World: African Consumers and the Genealogies of Globalization*, University of California Press, Berkeley and Los Angeles, 2008.
7. Lakshmi Subrahmanyam, 'The Ocean and the Historian', *Journal of Indian Ocean World Studies*, Vol. 2, No. 1 (2018), pp. 2–11.
8. Michael Pearson, *The Indian Ocean*, Routledge, New York and London, 2003.
9. Enseng Ho, 'Inter-Asian Concepts for Mobile Societies', *Journal of Asian Studies*, Vol. 76, No. 4 (November 2017), pp. 907–28.

10. Sebastian R. Prange, *Monsoon Islam: Trade and Faith on the Medieval Malabar Coast*, Cambridge University Press, Delhi, 2018.

11. Mahmood Kooria, 'An Abode of Islam under a Hindu King: Circuitous Imagination of Kingdoms among Muslims of 16th Century Malabar', *Journal of Indian Ocean World Studies*, Vol. 1, No. 1 (2017), pp. 90–110.

12. F. Bishara, *A Sea of Debt: Law and Economic Life in the Western Indian Ocean 1780–1950*, Cambridge University Press, Cambridge, 2017.

13. Seema Alavi, 'The Centaur Shipwreck: Law, Politics and Society in the Persian Gulf', *Journal of Colonialism and Colonial History*, Vol. 21, No. 3 (2020); L. Benton, *Law and Colonial Cultures: Legal Regimes in World History, 1400–1900*, Cambridge University Press, Cambridge, 2001; Nurfadzilah Yahaya, *Fluid Jurisdictions: Colonial Law and Arabs in Southeast Asia*, Cornell University Press, Ithaca, 2020.

14. Yahaya, *Fluid Jurisdictions*.

15. See for comparison, Iza Hussin, 'Circulation of Law, Cosmopolitan Elites, Global Repertoires, Local Vernaculars', *Law & History Review*, Vol. 32, No. 4 (2014) pp. 773–95.

16. M. Reda Bhacker, *Trade and Empire in Muscat and Zanzibar*, Routledge Press, London, 2003, pp. 31–38; Presthold, *Domesticating the World*; for piracy, see Patricia Risso, 'Cross Cultural Presence of Piracy', *Journal of World History*, Vol. 12, No. 2 (2001), pp. 293–319; Lakshmi Subramanian, *The Sovereign & the Pirate: Ordering Maritime Subjects in India's Western Littoral*, Oxford University Press, New Delhi, 2016; Sebastian Prange, '"A trade of no dishonor": Piracy, Commerce and Community in the Western Indian Ocean, 12th–16th Centuries', *American Historical Review*, Vol. 116, No. 5 (2011), pp. 1269–93.

17. See John Gordon Lorimer, *Gazetteer of the Persian Gulf*, Bombay, Vol. 1 (1915), p. 656, p. 659.

18. Patricia Risso, 'Cross Cultural Practice of Piracy', pp. 293–319. Her discussions of the British dealing with piracy view Oman as an ally who shared the interest in stability in the Gulf for commercial profits. Its dhows and European-style ships patrolled the Gulf against the Qawasim pirates who came from the pirate coast.

19. McDow, *Buying Time*, 'Introduction', pp. 1–23.

20. Sujit Sivasundaram, *Waves Across the South: A New History of Revolution and Empire*, HarperCollins, London, 2020. I borrow this temporal category of counter-revolutionary imperialism from him.

21. Milinda Banerji, C. Backerra and C. Sarti, eds, *Transnational Histories of the 'Royal Nation'*, Springer, London, 2017, p. 3. In the era of nation states, monarchies transformed into new forms of 'modern national monarchies', or what has been termed as the 'royal nation'.

22. The creation of new modern monarchies that strategized to survive surrounded by nation states was a pattern across the world that included even Queen Victoria, who projected herself as the Queen Mother alongside being Empress. Kipling's stories reveal how the performance aspects of monarchy were becoming fictional and trumped up. See Rudyard Kipling, *The Man Who Would Be King*, 1899, J.J. Little & Co., New York.

23. Ulrike Freitag, *A History of Jeddah: The Gate to Mecca in the Nineteenth and Twentieth Centuries*, Cambridge University Press, Cambridge, 2020.

24. Sivasundaram, *Waves Across the South*. I take the idea of an age of revolution from here and argue for its longer temporality in the ocean. A case for its parallel life.

25. The idea that one speck of sand on the beach can tell the story of the ocean. Total history as a response to the universalizing of Marxist history.

26. Carlo Ginzberg and Lara Putnam spoke about the utility of microhistory for writing big global histories because this experimental discipline relies on the connectedness of individual experience and the collision and conversion of contrasting things. See Carlo Ginzberg, *The Cheese and the Worms: The Cosmos of a Sixteenth-Century Miller*, Johns Hopkins University Press, Baltimore, 1980; Lara Putnam, 'To Study the Fragments/Whole: Microhistory and the Atlantic World', *Journal of Social History*, Vol. 39, No. 3 (Spring 2006), pp. 615–30.

27. Putnam, 'To Study the Fragments/Whole'. As she does for *Atlantic Ocean* studies.

28. Thomas Cohen, 'The Macrohistory of Microhistory', *Journal of Medieval and Early Modern Studies*, Vol. 47, No. 1 (January 2017), pp. 53–73.

29. McDow also alludes to the fact that from 1861, increased imperial hegemony and global economic integration, the bifurcation of the Sultanate into Muscat and Zanzibar challenged older practices of mobility.

30. Tony Ballantyne, *Webs of Empire: Locating New Zealand's Colonial Past*, UBC Press, Vancouver, Toronto, 2014; Jonathan Hyslop, 'Steamship Empire: Asian, African and British Sailors in the Merchant Marine c. 1880–1945', *Journal of Asian and African Studies*, Vol. 44, No. 1 (2009), pp. 44–49. Questioning governmentality and underlining the lateral connections in the Indian Ocean port cities via the career of an Indian seafarer who moved across Calcutta, Cape Town and Colombo.

31. Iza Hussin, 'Introduction, On Translation and Legibility', *in* blog *'Translation and the Afterlives of the Anglophone Theory'*, *Immanent Frame, Secularism, Religion and the Public Sphere*, 15 June 2021. Tif.ssrc.org/2021.32.

32. Borrow the 'forum shopping' concept from Mitra Sharafi. Mitra Sharafi, 'The Marital Patchwork of Colonial South Asia: Forum Shopping from Britain to Baroda', *Law and History Review*, Vol. 28, No. 4 (November 2010), pp. 979–1009.

33. I borrow the term from Fadi A. Bardawil, 'In the Wake of Conscription: Compradors or Bricoleurs?', in blog 'Translation and the Afterlives of the Anglophone Theory', *Immanent Frame, Secularism, Religion and the Public Sphere*, 15 June 2021, Tif.ssrc.org/2021. Also, I use the concept of bricolage from Cemal Kafadar, *Between Two Worlds: The Construction of the Ottoman State*, University of California Press, Berkeley, 1996.

34. See for comparison, Iza Hussin, 'Circulation of Law', pp. 773–95.

35. David Lambert and Alan Lester, eds, *Colonial Lives across the British Empire: Imperial Careering in the Long Nineteenth Century*, Cambridge University Press, Cambridge, 2006.

36. Thongchai Winichakul, *Siam Mapped: A History of the Geo Body of a Nation*, University of Hawaii, Hawaii, 1997.

37. Stefan Tanaka, *Japan's Orient: Rendering Pasts into History*, University of California Press, Berkeley and Los Angeles, 1993.

38. Iza Hussin, 'Introduction'.

39. See M. Reda Bhacker, *Trade and Empire*; A. Sheriff, *Slaves, Spices and Ivory in Zanzibar: Integration of an East African Commercial Empire into*

the World Economy, 1770–1873, Tanzania Publishing House, Dar es Salaam, 1987; Randall L. Pouwels, *Horn and Crescent: Cultural Change and Traditional Islam on the East African Coast, 800-1900*, Cambridge University Press, Cambridge, 1987.

40. Mitra Sharafi, *Law and Identity in Colonial South Asia: Parsi Legal Culture, 1772–1947*, Cambridge University Press, Cambridge, 2014.

41. The port town of Muscat became even more attractive to the imperial powers in this age of increased steamship movement and the telegraph cable that linked Britain to Karachi and Bombay. Muscat opened access to both the Red Sea and the Persian Gulf, enabling steamships to sail freely to Bombay and onwards as far east as China. Zanzibar, too, increased in significance, not only because of the slave trade but also as an important site for the telegraph cable.

42. J.C. Wilkinson, 'The Oman Question: The Background to the Political Geography of South East Arabia', *The Geographical Journal*, Vol. 137, No. 3, (September 1971), p. 71, pp. 361–71. Wilkinson viewed the bond between the Omani interior and the coast contingent on the threat perception to Muscat from the European powers. He viewed its sustainability only in the context of a crisis, when the tribal interior provided the ready supply of men and wherewithal. This link with the interior was severed only in the 1950s, when 'Muscat conquered Oman'. Wilkinson concludes that the longevity of the Imamate owed to the continued relevance of the tribal interiors to the maintenance of the Sultanate. Indeed, the 'iconography of Omani unity was the Ibaāḍī Imamate'.

43. Rudolph Said-Ruete, *Said bin Sultan (1791–1856), Ruler of Oman and Zanzibar. His Place in the History of Arabia and East Africa*, Alexander-Ouseley Limited, London, 1929, p. 146.

44. McDow has shown that the interior and the coastal regions linked like never before when the Sultan shifted to Zanzibar in the 1840s. This encouraged the mobility of people from the interior towns of Nizwa and Al Rustaq to the island. This was especially true in times of drought and famine. McDow, *Buying Time*, p. 31.

45. Hamid ibn Muhammad Ibn Ruzayq d. 1873, *History of Imams and Seyyids of Oman*. G.P. Badger, trans., London, M.DCCC.LXXI., p. 314, p 338, p. 342 and pp. 368–69.

46. The threat perception from the Wahhabis included their encroachments in Muscat (1865) and their demand for a four-

times hike in tribute, their support of the rebel tribals at the old town of Al Rustaq and their capture of the port town of Soor.

47.   Mitra Sharafi, *Law and Identity in Colonial South Asia*. This was very similar to the concept of forum shopping used by Sharafi to describe the Parsi community's effort to push legal jurisdiction to an assemblage of courts they had access to—Persian, British and the local Baroda courts—to get the best lawful deal in marital disputes. Forum shopping reveals the agency, even if momentary and in her case unsuccessfully, that law can impart to subjects to cannibalize available legal networks to their advantage.

48.   Fredrick Cooper, *Plantation Slavery on the East Coast of Africa*, Yale University Press, New Haven, 1977; J. Presthold, *Domesticating the World*, on the hollowness of the abolition narrative.

49.   Banerjee, Backerra and Sarti, eds, *Transnational Histories of the 'Royal Nation'*, p. 3. They carved out new forms of 'modern national monarchies', or what has been termed as the 'royal nation'.

50.   The creation of new modern monarchies that strategized to survive surrounded by nation states was a pattern across the world that included even Queen Victoria, who projected herself as the Queen Mother alongside being Empress. Kipling's stories reveal how the performance aspects of monarchy were getting fictional and trumped up. See Kipling, *The Man Who Would Be King*.

51.   Turki's children married their cousins in Muscat. Of particular significance was the marriage in 1878 in Muscat of Sayyid Turki's daughter to her cousin Hareb, the son of Sayyid Thuwayni.

52.   For the murder of Thuwayni and Salim's expulsion, see McDow, *Buying Time*, pp.79–80.

Chapter 1: Sayyid Saʿīd: The Arab Sultan in the Age of Revolution

1.   Col A. Hamerton, Muscat Agent, to A. Malet, Sec. to Bombay Govt, 24 August 1850, FO 54/14; and also A. Malet, Sec. to Bombay Govt, to H. Elliot, Sec. to Govt of India, 30 November 1850, FO 54/14, National Archives of the United Kingdom, Kew, Richmond (henceforth NA).

2.   Ibn Ruzayq, *History of the Imams and Seyyids of Oman, from A.D. 661–1856*, pp. 189–90.

3. S.B. Miles, 'On the Border of the Great Desert. A Journey in Oman', Part 1, *Geographical Journal*, Vol. 36, No. 2 (1910), p. 175.

4. Ibid., Part 2, p. 411.

5. Ibid., p. 418.

6. Mark Speece, 'Aspects of Economic Dualism in Oman, 1830–1930', *Journal of Middle Eastern Studies*, Vol. 21, No. 4, (November 1989), pp. 495–515, p. 508.

7. Patricia W. Romero, 'Sayyid Said bin Sultan Bu Said and Zanzibar: Women in the Life of this Arab Patriarch', *British Journal of Middle Eastern Studies*, Vol. 39, No. 3 (2012), pp. 373–92, p. 377, p. 378. See also M. Reda Bhacker, 'Family Strife and Foreign Intervention: Causes in the Separation of Zanzibar from Oman: A Reappraisal', *Bulletin of SOAS*, Vol. 54, No. 2 (1991), pp. 269–80, p. 270. His son Khalid was born of a Malabari woman, Khurshid. His son Hilal, with whom he was hostile, had an Assyrian mother in northern Iraq who died at his birth. He had no one in the harem to lobby for him.

8. Vincenzo Maurizi, *History of Seyd Sa'īd, Sultan of Muscat*, Oleander Press, Cambridge, 1984, p. 29.

9. R.F. Burton, *Zanzibar: City, Island and Coast*, Vol. 1, Tinsley Brothers, London, 1872, p. 94.

10. A. Hamerton, Muscat Agent, to A. Malet, Sec. to Bombay Govt, 24 August 1850, FO 54/14; and also A. Malet, Sec. to Bombay Govt, to H. Elliot, Sec. to Govt of India, 30 November 1850, FO 54/14, NA.

11. Nicolini Beatrice, 'Saiyid Bin Sultan Al Bu Saidi of Oman (1791–1856) and His Relationships with Europe', *ARAM*, Vol. 11–12, 1999–2000, pp. 171–80, p. 178.

12. Ibid., p. 179.

13. Shivsundaran, *Waves across the South*, p. 149

14. Ibid.

15. Ibid., p. 154.

16. Maurizi, *History of Seyd Sa'īd*, p. 82, p. 136.

17. Ibid., pp. 141–42.

18. It was these Persian invasions and the constant threat from them and the skirmishes at sea that made the Imam Ahmad bin Said gain acceptance as the Imam. He soon tied up with the Ottomans and allowed the EIC to set up a base at Muscat.

19. Maurizi, *History of Seyd Sa'īd* , p. 35.
20. I borrow the phrase 'legal technologies' from Fahad A. Bishara. He shows that this practice of domesticating the imperial legal repertoire to local use continued until the early twentieth century, when the Muscat dhows used French flags to avoid British surveillance. See Fahad A. Bishara, '"No Country but the Ocean": Reading International Law from the Deck of an Indian Ocean Dhow ca 1900', *Comparative Studies in Society and History*, Vol. 60, No. 2 (2018), pp. 338–66.
21. Beatrice Nicolino, 'The Western Indian Ocean as Cultural Corridor: Makran, Oman and Zanzibar through 19th Century European Accounts and Reports', *Middle East Studies Association Bulletin*, Vol. 37, No. 1, Summer 2003, pp. 20–49, p. 25.
22. Maurizi, *History of Seyd Sa'īd*, pp. 79–80; Ibn Ruzayq, *History of Imams and Seyyids of Oman*, p. 314. Shah sent 3000 cavalries to assist him at Nakhil.
23. Maurizi, *History of Seyd Sa'īd* , pp. 82–83.
24. See Burton, *Zanzibar: City, Island and Coast*, Vol. 1, pp. 292–95.
25. For slave ownership by the Sultan and the Al Busaidis, see Thomas F. McDow, 'Deeds of Freed Slaves: Manumission & Economic and Social Mobility in Pre-Abolition Zanzibar', in Robert Harms, Bernard K. Freamon and David W. Blight, eds., *Indian Ocean Slavery in the Age of Abolition*, Yale University Press, New Haven, 2013, p. 164, p. 173.
26. Said-Ruete, *Said bin Sultan*, p. 74.
27. Pouwels, *Horn and Crescent*, p. 115.
28. Frasila is a unit of weight equal to 35 pounds.
29. Abdul Sheriff, *Slaves, Spices and Ivory in Zanzibar: Integration of an East African Commercial Empire into the World Economy, 1770–1873*, Ohio University Press, Athens, OH, 1987, p. 282.
30. L. No. 26, Hamerton, Consul Zanzibar, to Earl of Aberdeen, 24 July 1849, Col Hamerton's Outward Letters from 31 July 1844 to 10 Nov. 1856, AA1/3, Zanzibar National Archives (henceforth ZNA).
31. A. Hamerton, Consul Zanzibar, to Earl of Aberdeen, 13 April 1844, Col Hamerton's Outward Letters, ZNA.
32. Ibid. Hamerton reported that British subjects encountered serious difficulties in carrying out their operations in Zanzibar firms. There was want of labour, and free people were not available easily.

33. L. No. 9, Col A. Hamerton, Consul Zanzibar, to Earl Aberdeen, 10 March 1846, Col Hamerton's Outward Letters, ZNA.
34. Capt. Cogan to A. Hamerton, Consul Zanzibar, 5 March 1846, Col Hamerton's Outward Letters, ZNA.
35. L. No. 9, Col A. Hamerton, Consul Zanzibar, to Earl Aberdeen, 10 March 1846, Col Hamerton's Outward Letters, ZNA.
36. L. No. 5, A. Hamerton, Consul Zanzibar, to Earl of Aberdeen, 24 March 1845, Col Hamerton's Outward Letters, ZNA.
37. L. No. 3, A. Hamerton, Consul Zanzibar, to Earl Aberdeen, 25 March 1847, Col Hamerton's Outward Letters, ZNA.
38. Matthew S. Hopper, *Slaves of One Master: Globalization and Slavery in Arabia in the Age of Empire*, Yale University Press, New Haven, 2015, pp. 55–56.
39. Biographical sketch of the late Sayyid Saed bin Sultan, Imam of Muscat, by Lt Col S.B. Miles, Administrative Report of the Persian Gulf, Political, Appendix A to Part II, IOR MF 191–92, or IOR V/23/27, No. 128, BL.
40. Bhacker, *Trade and Empire in Muscat and Zanzibar*, pp. 158–59.
41. Sheriff, *Slaves, Spices and Ivory in Zanzibar*, p. 22.
42. Playfair to Committee, 1856, Extracts from State Papers relating to Zanzibar, 1822–67, AA1/78, ZNA.
43. Ibid
44. Said-Ruete, *Said bin Sultan*, p. 75.
45. L. No. 17 of 1860, Brigadier W.M. Coghlan, Incharge Muscat and Zanzibar Commission, to H.L. Anderson, Chief Sec. to Govt of Bombay, 4 December 1860, Report of Commission 1860, Sec. Consultations, 1861, No. 97, PD 33/1861, MSA. Henceforth Coghlan Report, MSA.
46. Said-Ruete, *Said bin Sultan*, p. 76.
47. For details of the date trade to America, see Hopper, *Slaves of One Master*, pp. 51–79.
48. For his dependence of the interior and continued investment in its politics even as he concentrated on the maritime frontier, see Ibn Ruzayq, *History of Imams and Seyyids of Oman*, p. 314, p. 338, p. 342, pp. 368–69. This biography of Sayyid Sa'īd details his politics in the interior for the defence of Bandar Abbas, Muscat and Sohar ports in particular.
49. Said-Ruete, *Said bin Sultan*, p. 75.

50. Pouwels, *Horn and Crescent*, p. 103.

51. Romero, 'Sayyid Said bin Sultan Bu Said and Zanzibar', p. 378.

52. The practice of open-ended succession was not unique to this Indian Ocean rim. It was part of a shared Islamicate political tradition that was common to the early Ottomans and Safavids and continued with the Mughals until the empire's decline in the early eighteenth century. And like in these Islamicate empires, the princely careers were shaped by intense lobbying and factionalism within the household. The household politics often determined their postings and blurred the private and political realms in the Sultanate.

53. Sa'id B. Muhammad Al Hashimy, 'Sayyid Thuwayni's Internal and External Policy: 1856–1866 (Analysis & Evaluation Studies)', *Journal of Documentation and Humanities Research Center* (1989–2004), Issue 14, Qatar University, Qatar, pp. 47–78, p. 52.

54. J.C. Wilkinson, *The Imamate Tradition of Oman*, Cambridge University Press, Cambridge, 1987, p. 51.

55. Maurizi, *History of Syed Sa'īd*, p. 18.

56. Ibid., p. 18, p. 22.

57. Ibid., p. 3.

58. Ibid., p. 6.

59. Major S. Hennell, Resident in Persian Gulf, to A. Malet, Chief Sec. to Govt of Bombay, 2 January 1850, R/15/1/119, Bushire Residency Records, Muscat, No. 2. 1850, BL.

60. Sivasundaram, *Waves Across the South*, p. 133.

61. Ibid., pp. 136–38.

62. Allen James Fromherz, 'The Persian Gulf in the Pre-Protectorate Period 1790–1853', in Mehran Kamrava, ed., *Routledge Handbook of the Persian Gulf Politics*, Routledge, London and New York, 2020, p. 21.

63. Major S. Hennell, Resident in Persian Gulf, to A. Malet, Chief Sec. to Govt of Bombay, 21 May 1850, R/15/1/119, Bushire Residency Records Muscat No.2, 1850, BL.

64. L. No. 223B, Major S. Hennell, Resident in Persian Gulf, to A. Malet, Chief Sec. to Govt of Bombay, 13 June 1850, R/15/1/119, Bushire Residency Records Muscat No.2, 1850, BL.

65. L. No. 184, A. Malet, Chief Sec. to Govt of Bombay to Major S. Hennell, Resident in Persian Gulf, 3 October 1850, R/15/1/119, Bushire Residency Records Muscat No. 2, 1850, BL.

66. L. No. 106. A. Malet to Govt of Bombay, to A. Hamerton, Agent in Muscat, 3 October 1850, R/15/1/119, Bushire Residency Records, Muscat, No. 2, 1850, BL.

67. E.C. Bayley, Under Sec. to Govt of India with Governor General, to H.I. Goldsmid, Sec. to Govt of Bombay, 22 October 1850, R/15/1/119, Bushire Residency Records, Muscat, No.2, 1850, BL.

68. A. Hamerton, Consul Zanzibar, to Sec. to Govt of India, 16 August 1851, FO54/14, NA.

69. A. Hamerton, Consul Zanzibar, to Lt Col Helmeck, 14 August 1851, F/54/14, NA.

70. A. Hamerton to Sec. to Govt of Bombay, 3 February 1851, F/54/14, NA.

71. Pol. Agent and Consul General Zanzibar to C. Aitchinson, Sec. to Govt of India, Zanzibar, 10 December 1873, PD, 1874, Vol. 279, MSA.

72. Matthew S. Hopper has shown the soft attitude of the British themselves in backing the abolition drive with action on the ground. See Hopper, *Slaves of One Master*.

73. Enclosure in Lt Col S. Hennell's letter to A. Malet, Chief Sec. Bombay Govt, 1 August 1850, translated letter from Mullah Hussain, Agent at Sharja, to Lt Col S. Hennell, Resident in Persian Gulf, 25 August or 6 June 1850, R/15/1/123, BL.

74. Bhacker, *Trade and Empire in Muscat and Zanzibar*, p. 62.

75. Moresby Treaty defined jurisdiction for the ban. It did not help stop the trade.

76. For African slaves as labour on Omani date plantations, see Hopper, *Slaves of One Master*.

77. L. No. 296, Lt Col S. Hennell, Resident in Persian Gulf, to A. Malet, Chief Sec. to Govt, Bombay, Bushire, 1 August 1850, R/15/1/123, BL.

78. Enclosure No.1 translated letter from Ahmad bin Mullah Hussain, Agent at Lingah, to Lt Col S. Hennell, Resident in Persian Gulf, 6 June 1850, in letter from Lt Col S. Hennell, Resident in Persian Gulf, to Lt Col Sheil, Envoy Extra-ordinary at the court of Persia, 24 June 1850, R/15/1/123, BL.

79. L. No. 245, Lt Col S. Hennell, Resident in Persian Gulf, to A. Malet, Chief Sec. to Govt, Bombay, 23 June 1850, R/15/1/123, BL.

80. Lt Col S. Hennell, Resident in Persian Gulf, to Lt Col Sheil, Envoy at Persian Court, 10 September 1850, R/15/1/123, BL.

81. Lt Col S. Hennell, Resident in Persian Gulf, to Lt Col Sheil, Envoy at Persian Court, 9 September 1850, R/15/1/123, BL.

82. L No. 353, Lt Col S. Hennell, Resident in Persian Gulf, to Lt Col Sheil, Envoy at Persian Court, 16 September 1850, R/15/1/123, BL.

83. Lt Col S. Hennell, Resident in Persian Gulf, to Lt Col Sheil, Envoy at Persian Court, 10 August 1850, R/15/1/123, BL.

84. Lt Col S. Hennell, Resident in Persian Gulf, to Lt Col Sheil, Envoy at Persian Court, 12 December 1850, R/15/1/123, BL.

85. For details of Mulla Ahmad and his complicity in slave traffic, see F. Jones, Resident Persian Gulf, to H.L. Anderson, Sec. to Govt of Bombay, 9 September 1856, Residency Records, Persian Gulf, Bushire, part 2, R/15/1/157, BL.

86. Translated letter, F. Jones, Resident Persian Gulf, to Mirza Muhammad Khan, Persian Slave Commissioner for suppression of slave trade, 19 August 1856, Residency Records, Persian Gulf, Bushire, part 2, R/15/1/157, BL.

87. Report on the slave trade of the Persian Gulf, H.I. Disbrowe, Asst Resident Persian Gulf, attached to letter from F. Jones, Political Resident Persian Gulf, to H.L. Anderson, Sec. to Govt of Bombay, 15 September 1858, R/15/1/171, BL.

88. Ibid. The Indian Navy was criticized for not being able to send war vessels and aid in the suppression of the Persian Gulf slave traffic.

89. Beatrice Nicolini, 'Sayyid Sa'īd bin Sultan Al Bu Saidi of Oman (1791–1856) and His Relations with Empire', ARAM, Vol. 11–12, 1999–2000, pp. 171–80, p. 179.

90. Lt Col S. Hennell, Resident in Persian Gulf, Bushire, to A. Malet, Chief Sec. to Govt of Bombay, 27 June 1849, R/15/1/117, Part I, BL.

91. Ibid.

92. Translation of Convention concluded between the Amir-i-Nizam and Lt Col Sheil for the detention of the Persian slavers by British cruisers, Political Department 1852/53, Slave Trade, Residency Records, Persian Gulf 1852, Bushire, Part II, R/15/1/130, BL.

93. Extract Para. 5 from a letter from the Honourable Company's agent in the dominions of His Highness the Imam of Muscat, 4 June 1849, R/15/1/123, BL.

94. C. Malet, Chief Sec. Bombay, to Lt Col Sheil, Envoy Extraordinary at Persian court, 31 October 1849, R/15/1/123, BL.

95. L. No. 179, Lt Col Hennell, Resident in Persian Gulf, to H. Malet, Chief Sec. to Govt of Bombay, Bushire, 2 May 1850, R/15/1/123, BL.

96. Biographical sketch of the late Sayyid Sa'īd bin Sultan-Imam of Muscat, by Lt Col S.B. Miles, Administrative Report of the Persian Gulf, Political, Appendix A to Part II, IOR MF 191–92, or IOR V/23/27, No. 128, BL.

97. Precis by Pol. Secretary to Govt of Bombay, 10 March 1866, File no. 136, Foreign Department (FD) Pol. A., May 1866, National Archives of India, Delhi (Henceforth NAI).

98. C.H. Allen Jr, 'The state of Masqat in the Gulf and East Africa 1785–1829', *International Journal of Middle East Studies*, Vol. 14, No. 2 (May 1982), p. 119.

99. Maurizi, *History of Seyd Sa'īd*, p. 35.

100. Kingshuk Chatterji, 'A Tale of Two Ports: Changing Fortunes of Bushehr and Bandar Abbas in Qajar Persia', in K. Hall, R. Mukherjee and S. Ghosh, eds, *Subversive Sovereigns across the Seas: Indian Ocean Ports of Trade from Early Historic Times to Late Colonialism*, The Asiatic Society, Calcutta, 2018, pp. 243–44.

101. Allen, 'The State of Masqat in the Gulf and East Africa', p. 125.

102. Willem Floor, *The Persian Gulf: Bandar Abbas: The Natural Gateway of Southeast Iran*, Mage Publishers, Washington, 2011, p. 1.

103. Ibid., pp. 57–96. Details of lease negotiations.

104. Ibid., pp. 90–91.

105. L. No. 2, Col A. Hamerton, Consul Zanzibar, to Earl of Aberdeen, 24 January 1848, Col Hamerton's Outward Letters 1844–56, AA1/3, ZNA.

106. Emily Ruete, *Memoirs of an Arabian Princess from Zanzibar*, Dover Publications, 2009, p. 58.

107. Col A. Hamerton, Political Agent Zanzibar, to C. Malet, Sec. to Govt of Bombay, 10 May 1848, AA3/8, ZNA.

108. Ibid.

109. Ruete, *Memoirs of an Arabian Princess*, pp. 57–58.

110. Ibid.

111. Ibid., p. 58.

112. Richard Hall, *Empires of the Monsoon: A History of the Indian Ocean and Its Invaders,* HarperCollins, Gurugram, 1996, p. 379. The only stumbling blocks were the large revenues he reaped from the slave trade. His navy was excellent and enabled this trade. And his ships were ordered from the Bombay dockyards.

113. Ibid.

114. L. No. 459 A, Major S. Hennell, Resident in the Persian Gulf, to Lt Col Sheil, British Minister in Persia, 1 November 1847; and A. Malet, Chief Sec. to Govt, to Col A. Hamerton, 6 January 1848, AA12/1A, ZNA. The government wanted Hamerton to report if any such suggestion had been made by the Sultan before it took any review of the situation.

115. L. No. 5, Col A. Hamerton, Consul Zanzibar, to A. Malet, Sec. to Govt of Bombay, 2 April 1847, AA3/8. ZNA.

116. A. Hamerton, Agent in Muscat, to A. Malet, 4 December 1851, Residency Records, Persian Gulf 1852, Bushire, Part II, R/15/1/130, BL.

117. For cases of slave owners that went through his courts and Consular courts right through the reign of Sultan Barghash, see Acting Pol. Agent and Consul General, Zanzibar, to C. Aitchinson, Sec. to the Govt of India, Calcutta, Zanzibar, 10 January 1874, PD, 1874, Vol. 279, MSA.

118. See Seema Alavi, 'The 1852 Centaur Shipwreck'.

119. Translated letter from Haji Yaqub, Agent at Sharjah, to Capt. A.B. Kemball. Resident Persian Gulf, 1 August 1852, Residency Records, Persian Gulf 1852, Bushire, Part II, R/15/1/130, BL.

120. L. No. 27, Major A. Hamerton, Consul at Muscat, to A. Malet, Chief Sec. to Govt of Bombay, 27 August 1852, FD, Pol. 8 October 1852, Files 14–19, NAI.

121. Ibid.

122. Ibid.

123. Ibid.

124. Ibid.

Chapter 2: Sayyid Majid: The Imperious Counter-Revolutionary

1. Frederick Cooper, *From Slaves to Squatters: Plantation Labor and Agriculture in Zanzibar and Coastal Kenya, 1890–1925*, Yale University, New Haven, 1980; Jonathon Glassman, *Feasts and Riots: Revelry, Rebellion, and Popular Consciousness on the Swahili Coast, 1856–1888*, Heinemann, Portsmouth, 1995, pp. 51–52.

2. Coghlan Report, 33/1861.

3. Ruete, *Memoirs of an Arabian Princess*, p. 13.

4. Ibid., p. 23.
5. Ibid., p. 32. At Bet-il Bayt al-Sāḥil, no concubine was allowed to dine with the Sultan, which was a privilege reserved for his wife Azzi and sister only. Among the concubines, too, race and ethnic distinction prevailed. The more fair-skinned Circassians were considered superior and never dined with the dark-skinned Abyssinian concubines.
6. Ibid., p. 44.
7. Burton, *Zanzibar: City, Island and Coast*, Vol. 1, pp. 259–61.
8. Coghlan Report, 33/1861.
9. Minute of Lord Elphinstone, Governor of Bombay, 2 February 1859, Sec. Consult, 21 February 1859, File no. 161, Pol. Dept 1859, Muscat-Zanzibar, Pol, Dept,1859, Vol. 121 Muscat, MSA.
10. Ibid.
11. H.L. Anderson, Sec. to Govt to Brigadier W.H. Coghlan, Pol. Resident Aden, 12 September 1856, Residency Records, Persian Gulf, Bushire, Bk No. 224, Pt 2, FF. 155-297, R/15/1/157, BL. Sharjah and Lingah on the Persian Gulf coast were particularly active in slave traffic.
12. L. No. 43, Capt. C.P. Rigby, British Agent in Zanzibar, to H.L. Anderson, Sec. to Govt of Bombay, Zanzibar, 11 April 1859, File No. 161, PD 1859. Muscat-Zanzibar, PD 1859, Vol. 121, Muscat, MSA.
13. L. No. 39 of 1859, Commodore G. Jenkins, Commissioner Persian Gulf, to Commodore G.G. Wellesley, Commander-in-Chief of Her Majesty's Indian Navy, Muscat, 5 March 1859, File no. 676, Muscat PD 1859, Vol. 120, MSA.
14. Report to Earl of Clarendon, by the Committee on the East African Slave Trade, 24 January 1870, File No. 467, Zanzibar, slave trade, PD 1870, Vol. 3, No. 146, MSA.
15. Commodore L.G. Heath, Indian Navy, to H.A. Churchill, Consul at Zanzibar, 25 August 1868, FD, Pol. A., Nos 114–18, December 1868, MSA.
16. Ibid. Heath, of course, clarified that he did not see any connection between the two issues, which he saw as separate and believed that each should be treated on its own merit.
17. On hollowness of abolition rhetoric, see Cooper, *Slaves to Squatters*, pp. 1–15.

18. Captain H.A. Fraser, 'The East African Slave Trade. Zanzibar and the Slave Trade', in H.A. Fraser, J. Christie and Bishop Tozer, *The East African Slave Trade. And the Measures Proposed for Its Extinction, As Viewed by the Residents of Zanzibar*, Harrison, London, 1871, pp. 9–19, p. 14.

19. C.P. Rigby, Agent Zanzibar, to H.L. Anderson, Sec. to Govt of Bombay, 15 September 1859, R/15/1/171, BL.

20. C.P. Rigby, Agent Zanzibar, to F. Jones, Pol. Resident Persian Gulf, 24 April 1861, R/15/1/171, BL.

21. F. Jones, Resident in Persian Gulf, to H.L. Anderson, Sec. to Govt of Bombay, n.d., R/15/1/168, BL.

22. F. Jones, Acting Resident Persian Gulf, to H.L. Anderson, Sec. to Govt of Bombay, 26 May 1857, Residency Records, Persian Gulf, Bushire, Bk No. 224, Pt 2, FF. 155–297, R/15/1/157, BL.

23. S. Reese, *Imperial Muslims: Islam, Community and Authority in the Indian Ocean 1839–1937*, Edinburgh University Press, Edinburgh 2019, pp. 47–48.

24. H.L. Anderson, Sec. to Govt of Bombay, to F. Jones, Resident in the Persian Gulf, 15 December 1858. See attached extract from Her Majesty's secretary of state for India, 2 December 1858, R/15/1/168, BL. The naval chief agreed to spare vessels for slave trade suppression once his Gulf Squadron was restored to a reasonable strength.

25. L. No. 19, Capt. C.P. Rigby, Agent at Zanzibar, to H.I. Anderson, Sec. to Govt of Bombay, Zanzibar, 24 August 1858, File No. 328, Secret, Muscat, 1858, PD 1858, Vol. 147, MSA.

26. Ibid.

27. Ibid.

28. Souvenir of the International Exhibition of 1862 received by Sultan of Zanzibar, FD, Pol. A. 1865, May, Nos 87–88, NAI.

29. R.L. Playfair, Acting Pol. Agent Zanzibar, to Admiral Sir B. Walker, Commander-in-Chief, Cape Squadron, 20 August 1863, AA3/21, ZNA.

30. Ibid.

31. J. Kirk, Pol. Agent Persian Gulf, to Govt of Bombay, 14 November 1869, File No. 131, Zanzibar, PD 1870, MSA.

32. C.P. Rigby, Consul Zanzibar, to H.L. Anderson, Chief Sec. Bombay, 4 April 1859, File No. 5, FD, Pol. Procds, 17 June 1859, FC 1-11, NAI.

33. 'Slave Dealing and Slave Holdings by Kutchis in Zanzibar', 1870, IOR/L/PS/18/B90, BL.

34. Prestholdt, *Domesticating the World*, pp. 117–46.

35. Bhacker, *Trade and Empire in Muscat and Zanzibar*, pp. 31–38; Frederick Cooper, *Plantation Slavery on the East Coast of Africa*.

36. Report to Earl of Clarendon, by the Committee on the East African Slave Trade, 24 January 1870, File No. 467, Zanzibar, slave trade, PD 1870, Vol. 3, No. 146, MSA.

37. Ibid.

38. H.A. Churchill, Pol. Agent Zanzibar, to Foreign Office, London, 18 August 1870, File No. 467, Zanzibar, slave trade, PD 1870, Vol. 3, No. 146, MSA.

39. Foreign Office, to Pol. Agent Zanzibar, 16 June 1870, File No. 467, Zanzibar, slave trade, PD 1870, Vol. 3, No. 146, MSA.

40. L. No. 19, Capt. Rigby, Agent in Zanzibar, to H.L. Anderson, Sec. to Govt of Bombay, 17 February 1859, Sec. Consultations, File No. 161, PD 1859, Muscat-Zanzibar, PD 1859, Vol. 121, MSA.

41. L. No. 310, F. Jones, Pol. Resident Persian Gulf, to H.L. Anderson, Sec. to Govt of Bombay, 15 September 1858, PD R/15/1/171, BL.

42. L. No. 4 of 1854, Capt. Rigby, Agent in Zanzibar, to H.L. Anderson, Sec. to Govt of Bombay, Zanzibar, 13 April 1854, Sec. Consultations, 1858 PD, File No. 336, Muscat and Zanzibar, PD 1858, Vol. 148, MSA. In 1854, the French dealers would offer the slave broker money to sell the slaves as 'free men' to him. The slaves would then be taken to a judge, or qazi, to get the valid seal of free men and a certificate of the same. This certificate enabled the slaves to be legitimately handed over to the French dealer to be taken away as free labour to Bourbon or any French colony. In the colony, he worked for five years on whatever terms the dealer stipulated. He was paid $2 per month and received rations. After this period, he became a free man. This was a foolproof way to circumvent the British anti-slave export treaties (1822) that prevented the Omani Sultan from exporting slaves from his territories.

43. L. No. 15 of 1858, Capt. C. Rigby, Agent in Zanzibar, to H.S. Anderson, Sec. to Govt of Bombay, 20 August 1858, Sec. Consultations, 1858 PD, File No. 336, Muscat and Zanzibar, PD 1858, Vol. 148, MSA.

44. L. No. not given, Major A. Hamerton, Consul and Agent in the territories of the Imamum of Muscat, to the Earl of Clarendon, Sec. of State for Foreign Affairs, true copy signed by Capt. Rigby, 20 August 1858, Zanzibar, Sec. Consultations, 1858 PD, File No. 336, Muscat and Zanzibar, PD 1858, Vol. 148, MSA.

45. Ibid.

46. Enclosure No. 1, accompanying L. No. 25 of 1858, Translation of French merchant Monsieur Reutone's letter, to Sayyid Majid, Capt. C. Rigby, Company Agent at Zanzibar, Zanzibar, to H.L. Anderson, Sec. to Govt of Bombay, 21 September 1858, Sec. Consultations, 1858 PD, File No. 336, Muscat and Zanzibar, PD 1858, Vol. 148, MSA.

47. Ibid.

48. L. No. 40 of 1858, Capt. C. Rigby, British Agent, Zanzibar, to H.L. Anderson, Sec. to Govt of Bombay, 24 December 1858, File No. 163, 1859, PD, Muscat, Vol. 120, MSA.

49. L. No. 20 of 1859, Capt. C. Rigby, British Consul and Agent at Zanzibar, to H.L. Anderson, Sec. to Govt of Bombay, 16 March 1859, File No. 163, 1859, PD, Muscat, PD 1859, Vol. 120, MSA.

50. Saif bin Ali, Governor of the port of Kilwa, to Sultan Sayyid Majid, Kilwa, 7 March 1859, File No. 163, 1859, PD, Muscat, PD 1859, Vol. 120, MSA.

51. L. No. 21 of 1858, Capt. C. Rigby, Company Agent at Zanzibar, to H.L. Anderson, Sec. to Govt of Bombay, 13 September 1858, Sec. Consultations, 1858 PD, File No. 336, Muscat and Zanzibar, PD 1858, Vol. 148, MSA.

52. L. No. 447 of 1859, Captain C. Rigby, Company Agent at Zanzibar, attached translated letter, Sayyid Thoonee, Ruler of Muscat, to Commodore Jenkins, 4 March 1859, translated on 20 May 1859, Persian Dept, 24 May 1859, File No. 163, 1859, PD, Muscat, Vol. 120, MSA. Sayyid Thuwayni complained to the British Consul that the slave trade was injuring commerce at his ports. For instance, at the Comoro Island, the Arabs who were formally engaged in collecting produce at the numerous ports on the African and Madagascar coasts now found it more profitable to collect slaves from French vessels.

53. Rigby Report, 1860, IOR MF 1/1178, pp. 4–5, BL. In Zanzibar, the Hadramaut Arabs served as porters and labourers and the Omani Suri Arabs were radicalized and out for mischief.

54. Ibid.
55. Ibid.
56. L. No. 20 of 1859, Capt. C. Rigby, British Consul and Agent at Zanzibar, to H.L. Anderson, Sec. to Govt of Bombay, 16 March 1859, File No. 163, 1859, PD, Muscat, PD 1859, Vol. 120, MSA.
57. Lt Col R.L. Playfair to H.L. Anderson, Bombay, 28 November 1864, Procds No. 26, FD Pol. A., February 1865, Nos 25–26, NAI.
58. Lt Col R.L. Playfair, Agent in Zanzibar, to H.L. Anderson, Sec. to Govt of Bombay, 23 May 1863, Consular and Agency Records. Bombay Correspondence, slave trade. Letters Inwards and outwards, AA3/20, ZNA.
59. For the hollowness of the abolition drive, see Prestholdt, *Domesticating the World*; Cooper, *Plantation Slavery on the East Coast of Africa*.
60. Ibid.
61. Lt Col R.L. Playfair, Agent at Zanzibar, to H.L. Anderson, 30 September 1864, Nos 43–106, Procd No. 103, FD Pol. A., Feb. 1865, 100–106, NAI.
62. L. No. 98, Sec. to Govt of Bombay, to Col H.M. Durand, Sec. to Govt of India in FD, Fort William, 28 April 1862, FD Pol. A., May 1862, Nos 88–89, NAI.
63. L. No. 148, L. Pelly to Stewart, 8 March 1862, FD Pol. A., May 1862, Nos 88–89, NAI.
64. H.L. Anderson, Chief Se4c. to Govt of Bombay, to Sec. to Govt of India, FD, with the Gov. Gen., Simla, 13 May 1864, FD Pol. A., May 1864, Nos 173–74, Procds No. 173, NAI. The Inspector General of Ordinance and Magazine at the Presidency said that filed pieces of the pattern mentioned by the Political Agent could not be spared, but that some mountain train guns, obsolete in pattern and in excellent condition and with carriages, could be spared for presentation.
65. Col Durand, Sec. FD, Bombay, to H.L. Anderson, Chief Sec. to Govt of Bombay, 21 May 1864, FD Pol. A., May 1864, Nos 173–74, Procds 174, NAI.
66. Lt Col R.L. Playfair, Consul Zanzibar, to H.L. Anderson, Chief Sec. to Govt of Bombay, 5 October 1863, Enclosure of dispatch to Earl Russell, Principal Sec. of State for Foreign Affairs, 5 October 1863, FD Pol. A., January 1864, Procds 7, Nos 7–8, NAI.

67. Lt Col R.L. Playfair, Agent in Zanzibar, to H.L. Anderson, Sec.
     to Govt of Bombay, 23 May 1863, Consular and Agency Records.
     Bombay Correspondence, slave trade. Letters Inwards and
     outwards, AA3/20, ZNA.
68. Wenlock, C.M. Clarke, W.H. Bliss, J. Grose to Sec. of State for
     India, 13 August 1894, Jud Dept, No.8, File JP1554, IOL.
69. Lt Col R.L. Playfair, Agent in Zanzibar, to H.L. Anderson, Sec.
     to Govt of Bombay, 23 May 1863, Consular and Agency Records.
     Bombay Correspondence, slave trade. Letters Inwards and
     outwards, AA3/20, ZNA.
70. Translated note from Lt Col R.L. Playfair, Agent in
     Zanzibar,14 Sept. 1863, Consular and Agency Records. Bombay
     Correspondence, slave trade. Letters Inwards and outwards,
     AA3/20, ZNA.
71. L. No. 2 E.C. Egerton to H. Merivale. British observers were of
     the view that movement of slaves coastwise from one part of the
     Sultan's dominion to another, and restrictions to limit the number
     of slaves into Zanzibar with a view to stop importation completely
     was a solution to the problem. Papers respecting the slave trade on
     the east coast of Africa and the system pursued for its suppression.
     'Memorandum on Mr Seward's Dispatch of Sept. 9 1866 to the
     Protest of Sultan of Zanzibar against Interference of British Cruisers
     with Slave Vessels in Zanzibar Waters', L/P&S/18/B 87, BL.
72. Seward, Acting Political Agent Zanzibar, to Capt. N.B. Beding,
     Senior Naval Officer, Zanzibar harbour, 13 February 1867, FD,
     Pol., June 1867, Procds File No. 40, NAI.
73. L. No. 447 of 1859, Captain C. Rigby, Company Agent at Zanzibar,
     attached translated letter, Sayyid Thoonee, ruler of Muscat, to
     Commodore Jenkins, 4 March 1859, translated on 20 May 1859,
     Persian Dept, 24 May 1859, File No. 163, 1859, PD, Muscat, Vol.
     120, MSA.
74. Copy of resolution from Europeans and American merchants
     at Zanzibar at a meeting held on 6 March 1865, Consular and
     Agency Records. Bombay Correspondence, Slave Trade: Letters
     inward and outward, 7 June 1862, AA3/20, ZNA.
75. H.A. Churchill, Consul at Zanzibar, to C. Gonne, Sec. of Govt of
     Bombay, 25 January 1869, PD 1869, Zanzibar, Vol. III, No. 155,
     MSA.

76. File No. 977. 'Death of Salim Jebraam, Kawas to Agency at Zanzibar', PD 1868, MSA.

77. F. Jones, Political Resident Persian Gulf, to H.L. Anderson, Sec. to Govt of Bombay, 21 September 1858, Pol. Dept, R/15/1/171, BL.

78. L. No. 10, Lt Col C.P. Rigby, Consul Zanzibar, to H.L. Anderson, Sec. to Govt of Bombay, 11 February 1860, Pol. Dept L/PS/18/ B89. Rigby, incensed with British Indian subjects buying slaves, issued a notice to them, threatening them with dire consequences as per law. The Banias of Kilwa—the chief slave mart—were particularly warned.

79. L. No. 103 of 1874, I. Prideaux, Consul General and Pol. Agent Zanzibar, to Sec. Govt of India, Calcutta, 12 September 1874, PD 1874, Vol. 279, MSA.

80. Notice to all British subjects residing in the Zanzibar Dominions. Lt Col C.P. Rigby, Consul Zanzibar, 15 February 1860, L/PS/18/ B89, BL.

81. L. No. 10, Lt Col C.P. Rigby, Consul Zanzibar, to H.L. Anderson, Sec. to Govt of Bombay, 11 February 1860, Pol. Dept L/PS/18/ B89, BL.

82. L. No. 47, Lt Col C.P. Rigby, Consul Zanzibar, to A.K. Forbes, Acting Sec. to the Govt of Bombay, 12 July 1861, L/PS/18/B89, BL.

83. Extract letter from Lt Col Pelly, Acting Consul and Agent at Zanzibar, 1 February 1862, L/PS/18/B89, BL.

84. L. No. 13, Lt Col C.P. Rigby, Consul Zanzibar, to H.L. Anderson, Sec. to Govt of Bombay, Pol. Dept, 21 March 1860, L/PS/18/ B89, BL.

85. L. Nos 103/488, W.I. Prideaux, Consul General and Pol. Agent Zanzibar, to Sec. Govt of India, Calcutta, 12 September 1874, Outward Letters 1874, Vol. II, AA2/14, ZNA.

86. L. No. 103 of 1874, I. Prideaux, Consul General and Pol. Agent Zanzibar, to Sec. Govt of India, Calcutta, 12 September 1874, PD 1874, Vol. 279, MSA.

87. Ibid.

88. Ibid. Sultan Barghash followed this treaty, with the notable exception of the Kutchis, whose names were entered in the book of 'Sultan's Hindus' as under his protection.

89. L. No. 103 of 1874, I. Prideaux, Consul General and Pol. Agent Zanzibar, to Sec Govt of India, Calcutta, 12 September 1874, PD 1874, Vol. 279, MSA.
90. Ibid.
91. Ibid.
92. Ibid.
93. L. No. 103/488, W.I. Prideaux, Consul General and Pol. Agent Zanzibar, to Sec. Govt of India, Calcutta, 12 September 1874, Outward Letters 1874, Vol. II, AA2/14, ZNA.
94. Ibid.
95. Playfair, to Anderson, 23 May 1863, ZNA.
96. Sheriff, *Slaves, Spices and Ivory in Zanzibar*, p. 279.
97. Jairam Sewji was a canny Indian capitalist who maintained cordial relations with both the Busaidi family and the British. He was based in Zanzibar and often sent gifts to the Bombay Governor to cement his relations. In 1873, he sent an elephant from Zanzibar to Bombay as a gift for the Governor. See Agent to Jairam Sewji, to C. Gonne, Sec. to Govt of Bombay, May 1873, PD 1873, Zanzibar, Vol. II, No. 230, File No. 912, MSA.
98. J. Kirk to W. Wadderburd, Sec. to Govt of Bombay, 18 December 1871, PD 1872, Zanzibar, Vol. I, No. 199, File No. 647, MSA.
99. J. Kirk, Agent and Consul Zanzibar, to Sec. to Govt, 24 March 1871, PD 1872, Vol. II, No. 200, File No. 646, MSA.
100. J. Kirk to W. Wadderburd, Sec. to Govt of Bombay, 18 December 1871, PD 1872, Zanzibar, Vol. I, No. 199, File No. 647, MSA. The Foreign Dept complained about Kirk using his official position to intervene in the dispute between Fraser and Sewji's firm. Leaning in favour of Sewji, he conveyed the impression that contracts, etc. were decided with the influence of British officers in Zanzibar. See From Officiating Registrar Foreign Dept. to the Duke of Argyll, Sec. of State for India, Fort William, 26 April 1872, PD 1872, Vol. II, No. 200, File No. 646, MSA. Kirk denied charges and pleaded that he played the referee.
101. For Majid terminating contract, see L. No. 2352, Chief Sec. to Govt to Consul and Political Agent Zanzibar, 8 August 1864, PD 1864, Vol. 54, MSA.
102. Ibid., p. 282.

103. G.E. Seward, Acting Pol. Agent, Zanzibar, to C. Gonne, Chief Sec. to Govt of Bombay, No. 88–34, 11 July 1866, Procds No. 46, FD, Pol. A., November 1866, NAI.

104. Wenlock, C.M. Clarke, W.H. Bliss, J. Grose to Sec. of State for India, 13 August 1894, Jud. Dept No. 8, File JP 1554, BL.

105. R.L. Playfair, Consul and Political Agent Zanzibar, 'Memorandum on the Trade and Prospects of Zanzibar', 3 October 1864, FD, Pol. A., March 1865, Nos 72–73, NAI.

106. Enclosed the attested contract by Playfair, 25 July 1867, extracts from state papers relating to Zanzibar 1822–67, AA1/78, ZNA.

107. E.C. Egerton, Foreign Office, to Fraser & Co., 19 December 1867, extracts from state papers relating to Zanzibar 1822–1867, AA1/78, ZNA.

108. Ibid.

109. Copy of contract between H.A. Fraser and Company and certain Arab contractors for slave labour, No. 1, date of registration, 10 March 1866, signed by Muhammad bin Abdullah, Abdullah bin Sulmin and Salem Kenery; signed by E. Bishop. Received on account of above contract $1,000. Signed Muhammad bin Abdullah Al Haj, Zanzibar, 7 July 1864, FD, Pol. A., November 1866, NAI.

110. Papers respecting the slave trade on the east coast of Africa and the system pursued for its suppression. 'Memorandum on Mr Seward's Despatch of Sept. 9 1866 to the Protest of Sultan of Zanzibar against Interference of British Cruisers with Slave Vessels in Zanzibar Waters', L/P&S/18/B 87, BL.

111. G.E. Seward, Acting Pol. Agent Zanzibar, to C. Gonne, Bombay, 14 July 1866, FD Pol. A., November 1866, Nos 45–47, NAI.

112. Ibid.

113. Ibid.

114. Ibid.

115. E. Seward, to Lord Stanley, Sec. of State for Zanzibar, London, 6 March 1867, PD 1867, Zanzibar, Vol. 125, File No. 530, MSA.

116. H. Britannia, Consul Zanzibar, to Lord Stanley, Principal Sec. of State for Foreign Affairs, 15 March 1867, PD 1867, Zanzibar, Vol. 125, File No. 530, MSA.

117. H.A. Fraser to E. Seward, Feb. 1867, PD 1867, Zanzibar, Vol. 125, File No. 530, MSA.

118. Ibid; The Bombay govt instituted an inquiry into the alleged use of slave labour by British crew. See Sec. to Govt, to Commissioner of Police, Bombay and Commissioner of Customs, Bombay, 29 May 1867, PD 1867, Zanzibar, Vol. 125, File No. 530, MSA.
119. Opinion of Advocate General, Bombay, No. 89, 12 September 1866, FD Pol. A., November 1866, Nos 45–47, NAI.
120. Resolution, C. Gonne, Sec. to Govt of Bombay, 20 October 1866, FD Pol. A., November 1866, Nos 45–47, NAI.
121. Sec. to Govt of India, FD with Gov General, to the Sec. to Govt, Bombay, No. 1145, Camp Agra, 14 November 1866, Procds No. 47, FD Pol. A., November 1866, Nos 45–47, NAI. For a full discussion on the legality of the firm, see PD 1867, Zanzibar, Vol. 125, File No. 530, MSA.
122. Foreign Office, 6 November 1866, PD 1867, Zanzibar, Vol. 125, File No. 530, MSA.
123. G.E. Seward, Acting Pol. Agent, Zanzibar, to Lord Stanley, Principal Sec. of State for Foreign Affairs, n.d., PD 1867, Zanzibar, Vol. 125, File No. 530, MSA.
124. G.E. Seward, Acting Pol. Agent, Zanzibar, to Lord Stanley, Principal Sec. of State for Foreign Affairs, No. 81–86, FD Pol. A., Procds May 1867, Procds 142, NAI.
125. For currency details, see PD 1868, Zanzibar, Vol. I, File No. 136, MSA.
126. Slave Trade No. 4, Foreign Office, 14 June 1867, translation of Sayyid Majid's letter by Edward Stanley. L/PS/18/B89. For instance, he complied when forced by the Consul to emancipate 711 slaves who were working on contract with the British firm, Fraser & Company.
127. For details of the interception of children slaves at Kutch and Kathiawar en route to Bombay and their rehabilitation by the British authorities, see L. No. 1. Pol Consul, Kathiawar, to Court of Directors for Affairs of the East India Company, London, 1837, Boards Collection 1837–38, File No. 68463, F/4/1699, BL.
128. Petititoner Khakar Damodaran Devji to B.B. Frere, Govt and Supdtt Bombay, 28 January 1863, AA 3/21, ZNA.
129. Ibid.

130. L. No. 399/84, Pol. Dept, H.A. Churchill, Pol. Agent and Consul Zanzibar, to C. Gonne, Sec. to the Govt of Bombay, 22 December 1867, L/PS/18/B89, BL.

131. Translation of a letter of Sayyid Majid, to H.A. Churchill, Pol. Agent and Consul Zanzibar, 21 December 1867, L/PS/18/B89, BL.

132. Ibid.

133. No. 830, Pol. Dept, Bombay Castle, 28 March 1868, L. No. 408/88, C. Gonne, Sec. to Govt, to Political Agent at Zanzibar, 24 December 1867, L/PS/18/B89.

134. L. No. 1298, W.S. Seton-Kabb, Sec. to Govt of India, FD, to C. Gonne, Sec. to Govt of Bombay, 6 November 1868, L/PS/18/B89, BL.

135. L. No. 5/26, H.A. Churchill, Consul at Zanzibar, to C. Gonne, Chief Sec. to Govt of Bombay, 22 January 1869, L/PS/18/B89, BL.

136. L. No. 19/89, H.A. Churchill, Consul at Zanzibar, to C. Gonne, Chief Sec. to Govt of Bombay, 26 February 1869, L/PS/18/B89.

137. Sayyid Majid, to Political Agent and Consul at Zanzibar, 1 February 1869, L/PS/18/B89, BL.

138. L. No. 70, H.A. Churchill, Pol. Agent Zanzibar, to Sultan of Zanzibar, 20 February 1869, L/PS/18/B89, BL.

139. Translated letter, Sayyid Majid to Pol. Agent at Zanzibar, 26 February 1869, L/PS/18/B89.

140. L. No. 960, W.S. Seton-Karr, Sec. to Govt of India, FD, to Sec. to Govt of Bombay, Pol. Dept, 13 July 1869, L/PS/18/B89, BL.

141. J.C. Melvill, Copy of Judicial Letter to the Foreign Office, India Office, 30 July 1869, L/PS/18/B89, BL.

142. L. No. 86/315, J. Kirk, Acting Pol. Agent Zanzibar, to C. Gonne, Sec. to Govt of Bombay, 16 August1869, L/PS/18/B89, BL.

143. L. No. 86/315, J. Kirk, Acting Pol. Agent, Zanzibar, to C. Gonne, Sec. to Govt of Bombay, 16 August 1869, L/PS/18/B89, BL.

144. See for discussion on Consular Jurisdiction in Zanzibar, Hideaki Suzuki, *Slave Trade Profiteers in the Western Indian Ocean: Suppression and Resistance in the 19th Century*, Springer, 2017, pp. 157–58.

145. L. No. 7, J. Kirk to Earl Granville, 8 March 1871, FO 403/717, National Archives (Henceforth NA).

146. Nos 351–63. Extract para 1–3 from a letter from Pol. Resident at
     Aden, 30 May 1867, signed by A. Conner, Asst Sec, Procd No. 55,
     FD Pol. A., July 1867, NAI.
147. L. No. 124–6, G.E. Seward to C. Gonne, 3 September 1866, FD
     Pol. A., October 1866, Nos 169–82, NAI.
148. Ibid. Seward disapproved of the naval officers' conduct.
149. L. No. 273, C. Gonne, to Sec. to Govt. of India, 28 November
     1866, FD, Calcutta, FD Pol. A., January 1867, Procds No. 106,
     NAI.
150. Capt. Pasley, Senior Officer east coast of Africa, to Capt. G.R.
     Goodfellow, Acting Pol. Resident, Aden, 4 October 1866, FD
     Pol. A., January 1867, Procds No. 107, NAI.
151. L. No. 20–127, H.A. Churchill, Consul Zanzibar, to Lord Stanley,
     Sec. of State for Foreign Affairs, 9 July 1868, Procds No. 27, FD
     Pol. A., September 1868, NAI.
152. L. No. 146, A. Mansfield, G.H. Taylor, J. Strachey etc., to Sec. of
     State for India, Simla, 5 September 1868, L/PS/6/565, Collection
     177, BL.
153. Extract para 2 from a letter from the Asst Resident in charge
     of Residency, Aden, 2 October 1866, No. 126–785, FD Pol. A.,
     October 1866, Nos 169–82, NAI; also see 134 A, C. Gonne, Sec.
     to Govt of Bombay, to acting Political Resident, Aden, 13 October
     1866, FD Pol. A., October 1866, Nos 169–82, NAI.
154. L. No. 123, G.E. Seward, Acting Political Resident Zanzibar,
     to Pol. Resident Aden, 3 September 1866, FD Pol. A., October
     1866, Nos 169–82, NAI.
155. L. No. 121–44, L. Seward, Pol. Agent Zanzibar, to C. Gonne, Sec.
     to Govt of Bombay, 31 August 1866, FD Pol. A., October 1866,
     Nos 169–82, NAI.
156. Ibid. See also No. 116, L. Sanders, Acting Pol. Agent, Zanzibar
     and Consul Zanzibar, to Pol. Resident, Aden, 27 August 1866,
     FD Pol. A., October 1866, Nos 169–82, NAI.
157. L. No. 124–26, G.E. Seward to C. Gonne, 3 September 1866, FD
     Pol. A., October 1866, Nos 169–82, NAI.
158. L. No. 988, Officiating Resident, Aden, to Acting Pol. Agent,
     Zanzibar, 29 November 1866, Procds No. 111, FD Pol. A., January
     1867, NAI.
159. Ibid.

160. Ibid.
161. Ruete, *Memoirs of an Arabian Princess from Zanzibar*, p. 91.
162. C.P. Rigby, Consul Zanzibar, to H.L. Anderson, Chief Sec Bombay, 4 April 1859, File No. 5, FD, Pol Procds, 17 June 1859, FC 1-11, NAI.
163. Ibid.
164. L. No. 17 of 1860, Brigadier W.M. Coghlan, In-charge Muscat and Zanzibar Commission, to H.L. Anderson, Chief Secretary to Govt of Bombay, 4 December 1860, Report of Commission 1860, Sec. Consultations, 1861, No. 97. PD 33/1861, MSA.
165. Ibid.
166. C.P. Rigby, Report on the Zanzibar Dominions, 1860, Bombay 1861, Selections from the Records of the Bombay Government, No. LIX. New Series. BL.
167. Ibid.
168. H.A. Churchill, Pol. Agent and Consul, Zanzibar, to C. Gonnes, Sec. to Govt, Bombay, 22 December 1868, PD 1869, Zanzibar, Vol. II, No. 154, MSA.
169. E. Seward, Acting Political Agent Zanzibar, to Capt. N.B. Beding, Senior Naval Officer, Zanzibar harbour, 21 February 1867, No. 48, FD Pol., June 1867, NAI.
170. See Lauren Benton, *Law and Colonial Cultures*, pp. 9–11; Alavi, 'The 1852 Centaur Shipwreck'.
171. E. Seward, Acting Political Agent Zanzibar, to C. Gonne, Sec. to Govt of Bombay, 10 September 1866, Nos 134–49, FD Pol. A., February 1867, NAI.
172. E. Seward, Acting Political Agent Zanzibar, to C. Gonne, n.d., FD Pol. A., February 1867, Procds No. 209, NAI.
173. Ibid.
174. Ibid.
175. Ibid.
176. L. No. 113, L. Pelly, Pol. Resident Persian Gulf, to C. Gonne, 1 December 1866, FD Pol. A., February 1867, Nos 208–10, NAI.
177. Ibid.
178. Enclosure No. 11, The Governor General of India in Council to Sir S. Northcote, 14 May 1868, L/P&S/18/B87, BL.
179. J. Lawrence to Sayyid Majid, 22 May 1867, L/PS/6/560, BL.

180. Enclosure No. 6 in Letter No. 6, L/P&S/18/B87, BL.
181. Enclosure No. 5 in L. No. 6, The Sultan of Zanzibar to the Governor General of India, 11 September 1867, translated, L/P&S/18/B87, BL.
182. Sayyid Majid to the British Consul at Zanzibar, 23 January 1867, L/PS/6/560, BL.
183. B. Frere, 'Dispatches Regarding the Affairs of Muscat and Zanzibar', 15 July 1868, L/PS/6/560, BL.
184. L. No. 29, A.J. Otway to Maj. Gen. Rigby, 16 December 1868, L/P&S/18/B 87, BL.
185. J.W. Kaye, 'Zanzibar, Muscat and Persia', Memorandum by the Political Secretary, 1 July 1868, L/PS/6/560, BL.
186. Burton, *Zanzibar: City, Island & Coast*, Vol. I, p. 195.
187. Bishop W.G. Tozer, 'On the Treatment of Freed Slaves', in Fraser, Christie and Bishop Tozer, *The East African Slave Trade*, p. 29.
188. Ibid., p. 30.
189. Lt Col C.P. Rigby Report, 1860, IOR MF 1/1178, BL.
190. Pol. Agent and Consul General, Zanzibar to C.U. Aitchison, Sec. to Govt of India, FD, 10 December 1873, PD 1874, Vol. 279, MSA.
191. J. Kirk, Pol. Agent Zanzibar, to C.H. Aitchison, Sec. to Govt of India, Calcutta, 1 December 1873, PD 1874, Vol. 279, MSA.
192. Sub-Enclosure No. 1, L. No. 171, Mr B.S. Cave, Marquis of Salisbury, to Foreign Office, Zanzibar, 3 October 1899, IOR/L/PJ/6/525, BL.
193. Ibid. See for a copy of the agreement, Sub Enclosure No. 2. Signed by Khoja representatives, and Aga Khan. Signed also by British Vice Consul Zanzibar, J.H. Sinclair, IOR/L/PJ/6/525. It states: 'The khojas enjoy free right of burial in or upon the said piece of land, and they will hold their usual ceremonies there and on such occasions erect booths temporarily. But not build anything permanent. The Khojas renounce all claim to or right title or interest in the residue of the said land which is outside of and not included in the boundaries of the said piece or parcel of land herein before described. When this said piece of land is full then the government shall at their own expense provide for the Khojas another suitable site for a burial ground within a reasonable distance of the town.'

194. Enclosure I in No. 118, E. Steere, Missionary Bishop, to E. Smith, Acting Consul General, 4 June 1873, L/PS/9/51, BL.

195. H. Waller, *The Last Journal of Dr Livingstone in Central Africa from 1865 to His Death*, Vol. 1, Harper & Brothers, 1874, p. 7.

196. Ibid., pp. 3–8.

197. Burton, *Zanzibar: City, Island & Coast*, Vol.1, pp. 98–99, p. 102.

198. J. Kirk, to Pol. Dept, 24 January 1870, File No. 422, PD, 1870, Vol. III, No. 146, MSA.

199. J. Kirk, Consul Zanzibar and Acting Political Agent, to Acting Sec. to Govt, 20 May 1870, File No. 146, Zanzibar, PD 1870, MSA.

200. James Christie, *Cholera Epidemics in East Africa: An Account of the Several Diffusions of the Disease in that Country from 1821–1872. With an outline of geography, ethnography, ethnology & trade connections of regions through which the epidemic passed*, Macmillan & Co., 1876, p. 119.

201. Christie, *Cholera Epidemics in East Africa*, pp. 101, 117.

202. McDow, *Buying Time*, p. 76.

203. Colin McFarlane, 'Governing the Contaminated City: Infrastructure and Sanitation in Colonial and Post-Colonial Bombay', *International Journal of Urban and Regional Research*, Vol. 32, No. 2 (June 2008), pp. 415–35.

204. No. 2481, Resolution, Bombay Castle, 4 August 1869, signed by C. Gonne, Acting Sec. to Govt, File No. 1052, 'Zanzibar, Cloves & Coconuts. Regarding the tax to carry on Sanitary Improvement at Zanzibar', PD 1869, MSA.

205. J. Kirk, Acting Political Agent and Consul Zanzibar, to C. Gonne, Chief Sec. to Govt, Bombay, 7 January 1869, File No. 1052, 'Zanzibar, Cloves & Coconuts. Regarding the Tax to Carry on Sanitary Improvement at Zanzibar', PD 1869, MSA.

206. No. 2481, Resolution, Bombay Castle.

207. J. Iliffe, *A Modern History of Tanganayika*, Cambridge University Press, 1979, p. 43.

208. G.S. Parker and Freeman Grenville, *East Africa Coast*, Clarendon Press, 1962, p. 234.

209. Chambi Chachage, 'A Capitalizing City: Dar as Salam and the Emergence of an African Entrepreneurial Elite, 1862–2015', unpublished Harvard University PhD, 2018, Chapter 1, pp. 39–86.

210. Glassman, *Feasts and Riots*, p. 57.

211. Letter dated 10 November 1866, reproduced in J.E. Giles Sutton, ed., 'Dar es Salaam: City, Port & Region', *Tanzania Notes & Records,* Vol. 71, 1970, p. 201.
212. Ibid., p. 15.
213. Steven Fabian, 'Curing the Cancer of the Colony: Bagamoyo, Dar as Salam and Socio-economic Struggle in German East Africa', *International Journal of African Historical Studies*, Vol. 40, No. 3 (2007), pp. 441–69, p. 448, p. 459.
214. J.R. Brennan and A. Burton, *'The Emerging Metropolis: A History of Dar es Salam, circa 1862–2000'*, in J.R. Brennan, A. Burton and Y. Lawi, eds, *Dar es Salam: Histories from an Emerging African Metropolis*, Africa Book Collective, 2007.
215. Ibid., p. 16.
216. Memorandum of the Position and Authority of the Sultan of Zanzibar, PD 1875, Vol. 207, MSA.
217. L. Nos 186/67, E. Seward, Agent and Consul Zanzibar, to Chief Secretary to Govt of Bombay, 10 November 1866, AA3/26, ZNA.
218. Memorandum of the Position and Authority of the Sultan of Zanzibar, PD 1875, Vol. 207, MSA.
219. E. Seward, Political Agent Zanzibar to Chief Secretary, Bombay, 10 November 1866, PD 1867, File No. 526, Zanzibar, MSA.
220. J.M. Gray, 'Dar as Salam under the Sultans of Zanzibar', in *Tanganayika Notes & Records*, Vol. 33, 1952, pp. 1–21, p. 9.
221. Ibid., p. 13.
222. Report on Dar as Salam, 9 January 1874, by I. Elton, Asst to Pol. Agent, Zanzibar, PD 1874, Vol. 279, MSA.
223. Political Agent Zanzibar to Chief Secretary, Bombay, 10 November 1866, PD 1867, File No. 526, Zanzibar, MSA.
224. Brennan and Burton, *The Emerging Metropolis*, p. 17; see also Political Agent Zanzibar to Chief Secretary, Bombay, 10 November 1866, PD 1867, File No. 526, Zanzibar, MSA.
225. Political Agent Zanzibar to Chief Secretary, Bombay, 10 November 1866, PD 1867, File No. 526, Zanzibar, MSA.
226. Ibid.
227. Ibid.
228. Report on Dar as Salam, 9 January 1874 by I. Elton, Asst to Pol. Agent, Zanzibar, PD 1874, Vol. 279, MSA.

229. J.M. Gray, 'Dar as Salam under the Sultans of Zanzibar', in *Tanganayika Notes & Records*, Vol. 33, 1952, pp. 1–21, p. 15.
230. L. Nos 186/67, E. Seward, Agent and Consul Zanzibar, to Chief Secretary to Govt of Bombay, 10 November 1866, AA3/26, ZNA.
231. Ibid. Also see Memorandum of the Position and Authority of the Sultan of Zanzibar, PD 1875, Vol. 207, MSA; Political Agent Zanzibar to Chief Secretary, Bombay, 10 November 1866, PD 1867, File No. 526, Zanzibar, MSA.
232. L. Nos 186/67, E. Seward, Agent and Consul Zanzibar, to Chief Secretary to Govt of Bombay, 10 November 1866, AA3/26, ZNA.
233. Brennan and Burton, *The Emerging Metropolis*, p. 17.
234. Gray, 'Dar as Salam under the Sultans of Zanzibar', p. 6.
235. Report on Dar as Salam, 9 January 1874 by I. Elton, Asst to Pol. Agent, Zanzibar, PD 1874, Vol. 279, MSA.
236. Gray, 'Dar as Salam under the Sultans of Zanzibar', p. 7.
237. Brennan and Burton, *The Emerging Metropolis*, p. 21.
238. Brode, Tipu Tib, cited in Gray, 'Dar as Salam under the Sultans of Zanzibar', p. 8.
239. Report on Dar as Salam, 9 January 1874 by I. Elton, Asst to Pol. Agent, Zanzibar, PD 1874, Vol. 279, MSA.

Chapter 3: Sayyid Thuwayni: The Counter-Revolutionary Sultan

1. Mss Eur F. 126/51, BL. This has terms of agreement between Pelly and Thuwayni (1864) for the extension of the telegraph line from Persia to Muscat.
2. Ruete, *Memoirs of an Arabian Princess*, p. 112.
3. S.B. Miles, 'On the Route between Sohar & el Bereymi in Oman with a Note on Zatt or Gipsies in Arabia. 1877', *Journal of Asiatic Society of Bengal*, Vol. XLVI, Part 1, 1877, pp. 41–60, p. 51.
4. No. 89, Abstract of Dispatch to Sec. of State for India, 12 April 1876, FD Pol. A., April 1876, Nos 38–93, NAI. Salim's subsequent attempts to re-enter Muscat failed. He remained a wanderer moving from place to place along the Oman littoral without any party or base for raising one. From 1871, his conflicts focused on Turki when Azan was killed, and the latter became Sultan.
5. L. No. 17 of 1860, Brigadier W.M. Coghlan, in-charge Muscat & Zanzibar Commission, to H.L. Anderson, Chief Secretary to

Govt of Bombay, 4 December 1860, Report of Commission 1860, Sec. Consultations, 1861, No. 97. PD 33/1861, MSA.

6. F. Jones, Pol. Resident, Persian Gulf, Bushire, to Sec. to Govt of Bombay, 21 February 1860, Residency Records, Persian Gulf, Book No. 219, R/15/1/155, BL.

7. Translation of letter from Khojah Haskil, British Agent Muscat, to Capt. F. Jones, Pol. Resident, Persian Gulf, 9 December 1858, Recd. 17 January 1859, translated by I.C. Edwards, Accountant, Residency Persian Gulf, File No. 161, PD 1859, Muscat–Zanzibar, PD 1859, Vol. 121, MSA.

8. L. No. 33 of 1859, H.L. Anderson, Sec. to Govt of Bombay, to Sec. to Govt of India, FD, 28 February 1859, Residency Records, Persian Gulf, Book No. 219, R/15/1/155, BL.

9. Substance of a letter from Sayyid Thuwayni to Lord Elphinstone, Governor of Bombay, 18 February 1859, translated on 24 February 1859, Pol. Dept 1859, Vol. 121, MSA.

10. Ibid.

11. Mitra Sharafi, 'The Marital Patchwork', pp. 979–1009. Very similar to the concept of forum shopping used by Sharafi to describe the Parsi community's effort to push legal jurisdiction to an assemblage of courts to get the best legal deal.

12. L. No. 34, Col C.P. Rigby, Consul Zanzibar, to H.L. Anderson, Sec. to Govt of Bombay, 30 March 1859, PD, 1859, Vol. 121, MSA.

13. L. No. 46 of 1859, Capt. C.P. Rigby, British Consul Zanzibar, to H.L. Anderson, Sec. to Govt of Bombay, 14 April 1859, Sec Dept, PD 1859, Vol. 121, Rigby Report, MSA.

14. Ibid.

15. Ibid.

16. Ibid.

17. Ibid.

18. L. No. 5E of 1859, Capt. Felix Jones, Political Resident, Persian Gulf, to H.L. Anderson, Sec. to Govt of Bombay, Bassedore, 14 May 1859, PD 1859, Vol. 121, MSA.

19. L. No. 114, Lt Col C.P. Rigby, Consul and Resident Zanzibar, to Capt. Felix Jones, Pol. Resident Persian Gulf, Bushire, Residency Records, Persian Gulf, Book No. 219, R/15/1/155, BL. A charge denied by Captain Rigby.

20. L. No. 47 of 1859, Capt. C.P. Rigby, British Consul, Zanzibar, to H.L. Anderson, Sec. to Govt of Bombay, 19 April 1859, PD, 1859, Vol. 121, MSA.

21. Minute of Lord Elphinstone, Governor of Bombay, 2 February 1859, Sec. Consult, 21 February 1859, File No. 161, Pol. Dept 1859, Muscat–Zanzibar, PD 1859, Vol. 121 Muscat, MSA.

22. L. No. 39 of 1859, Commodore G. Jenkins, Commissioner Persian Gulf, to Commodore G.G. Wellesley, Commander in Chief of Her Majesty's Indian Navy, Muscat, 5 March 1859, File No. 676, Muscat Pol Dept, 1859, PD Muscat 1859, Vol. 120, MSA.

23. L. No. 43, Capt. C.P. Rigby, British Agent in Zanzibar, to H.L. Anderson, Sec. to Govt of Bombay, Zanzibar, 11 April 1859, File No. 161, PD 1859. Muscat–Zanzibar, PD 1859, Vol. 121, MSA.

24. L. No. 17 of 1860, Brigadier W.M. Coghlan, in-charge Muscat & Zanzibar Commission, to H.L. Anderson, Chief Secretary to Govt of Bombay, 4 December 1860, Report of Commission 1860, Sec Consultations, 1861, No. 97. PD 33/1861, NAI.

25. L. No. 1070 of 1858, Persian Department, 24 July 1858, Haskil bin Yusuf, Acting Native Agent at Muscat, to H.L. Anderson, Persian Sec. to Govt, 16 June 1858, received to be translated on 20 July 1858, File No. 283, Sec. Muscat, PD, Muscat, Vol. 147, MSA.

26. Muscat PD, Vol. 147, MSA.

27. L. No. 1242 of 1858, Persian Dept, 3 September 1858, Haskil bin Yusuf, Acting Native Agent at Muscat, to H.L. Anderson, Persian Sec. to Govt, 11 July 1858, received and translated on 1 September 1858, File No. 283, Sec. Muscat, PD, Muscat, Vol. 147, MSA.

28. Extract from the Report from Political Resident Persian Gulf while on his tour to Arab ports—May 1858, Enclosure to Secret Despatch No. 184, 6 June 1858, R/15/1/155, BL.

29. Lt W.M. Pengally, Agent Muscat, to Pelly, Sec. to Govt of Bombay, 30 October 1860, R/15/1/155, BL.

30. Khoja Haskīl, British Agent at Muscat, to Capt. Felix Jones, Political Resident, Persian Gulf, Bushire, 9 September 1857, R/15/1/155, BL.

31. L. No. 1391 of 1858, Persian Dept, 18 November 1858, Haskil bin Yusuf, Acting Native Agent at Muscat, to H.L. Anderson,

14 October 1858, translated 26 October 1858, File No. 283, Sec. Muscat, PD, Muscat, Vol. 147, MSA.

32.   Translated Summary of Intelligence, British Agent at Muscat to Capt. Felix Jones, Pol. Resident, Persian Gulf, 4 October 1858, R/15/1/155, BL.

33.   L. No. 15, H. Rafsan, Acting British Agent at Muscat, to A.K. Forbes, Acting Sec. to Govt of Bombay, 29 April 1861, File No. 31, Secret, Muscat, 1861, PD 1861, Vol. 32, MSA.

34   L. No. 25, Lt W.M. Pengally, British Agent at Muscat, to K. Forbes, Sec. to Govt, 11 January 1861, File No. 31, Secret, Muscat, 1861 PD, Vol. 32, MSA.

35.   Lt W.M. Pengally, British Agent at Muscat, to K. Forbes, Sec. to Govt, 21 June 1861, Seeb, near Muscat, File No. 31, Secret, Muscat, PD 1861, Vol. 32, MSA.

36.   L. No. 29, Lt W.M. Pengally, British Agent at Muscat, to K. Forbes, Sec. to Govt, 6 July 1861, File No. 31, Secret, Muscat, PD 1861, Vol. 32, MSA.

37.   L. No. 30, ibid.

38.   L. No. 32, ibid.

39.   L. No. 30, ibid.

40.   L. No. 31, ibid.

41.   Translated Summary of Intelligence, British Agent at Muscat to Capt. Felix Jones, Pol. Resident, Persian Gulf, 4 October 1858, R/15/1/155, BL.

42.   L. No. 1391 of 1858, Persian Dept, 18 November 1858, Haskil bin Yusuf, Acting Native Agent at Muscat, to H.L. Anderson, 14 October 1858, translated 26 October 1858, File No. 283, Sec. Muscat, PD, Muscat, Vol. 147, BL.

43.   L. No. 48, Lt W.M. Pengally, British Agent at Muscat, to K. Forbes, Sec. to Govt, 26 August 1861, File No. 31, Secret, Muscat, 1861, PD PD 1861, Vol. 32, MSA.

44.   Minute by the Hon Governor, 24 September 1861, File No. 31, Secret, Muscat, PD 1861, Vol. 32, MSA.

45.   Resolution by the Honourable Board, 5 December 1861, K. Forbes, Acting Sec. to Govt, R/15/1/155, BL.

46.   Ibid.

47.   Copy of Appendix to Lt Col Pelly's Riyadh Report No. 51, 15 May 1866, Mss Eur F126/60, Pelly Letters, BL.

48. Hopper, *Slaves of One Master*, pp. 61–63. He shows the use of slaves in the date plantations of Al Batinah, a trend that only increased in response to the global demand for dates in the late nineteenth century.

49. L. No. 5, Lt Col A. Hamerton, Consul and Agent at Muscat, to H.L. Anderson, Sec. to Govt, Bombay, 14 March 1857, Pol. Dept, Residency Records, Persian Gulf, Book No. 219, R/15/1/155, BL.

50. Indian Kutchi traders, like Mowji, of the legendary Bhimani firm, and merchants of the Shivji Topan firm were encouraged by successive Sultans of Muscat. Alongside Arab merchants, like Saleh b. Haramil, they were active in the slave and arms trade as well. C. Goswami, *Globalization Before Its Time: The Gujarati Merchants from Kachchh*, Penguin, 2016, pp. 82–84; Sheriff, *Slaves, Spices and Ivory in Zanzibar*, p. 83.

51. Goswami, *Globalization Before Its Time*, p. 102.

52. L. No. 812, R. Spooner, Commissioner of Customs Salt and Opium to L. Anderson, Sec. to Govt of Bombay, Office of Commissioner of Customs Salt & Opium, 1 March 1858; L. No. 1802, B. Crawford, Chief Commissioner of Police, Bombay, to R. Spooner, Commissioner of Customs Salt and Opium, 12 May 1858, File No. 151, Pol. Dept, 1858, Secret, Muscat, PD 147/1858, MSA.

53. Johan Mathew, *Margins of the Market: Trafficking and Capitalism across the Arabian Sea*, University of California Press, 2016, pp. 89–95. The issue of jurisdiction in complaints related to the Kutchis and in petitions they sent in plagued Thuwayni's reign. See Capt. H. Disbrowe, Acting Pol. Agent Muscat, to H.L. Anderson, Chief Sec. to Govt of Bombay, 6 July 1863, PD 1863, File No. 1442, PD 1863, Vol. 38, MSA.

54. F. Jones, Pol. Resident Persian Gulf, to H.M. Chester, British Agent Muscat, 23 March 1860, R/15/1/163, BL.

55. Ibid.

56. L. No. 440 of 1859, Persian Dept, 21 May 1859, copy of letter from Muhammad Jafar Khan, nephew of Aga Khan, to Commodore Jenkins, 4 March 1859, translated 20 May 1859, File No. 676, Muscat, PD 1859, Vol. 120, MSA.

57. Ibid.

58. Ibid.

59. For details, see Muscat Affairs, 13 December 1893–29 December 1894, R/15/1/194, BL.

60. Aga Khan, to Sec. to Govt Pol. Dept, Bombay, May 1869, PD 1869, Vol. III, No. 88, File 799, MSA.

61. L. No. 16, L. Pelly, Pol. Resident in Persian Gulf, to Sec. to Govt of Bombay, 19 October 1872, Mss Eur F 126/39, BL.

62. L. No. 55, British Resident, Bushire, to C. Gonne, Sec. to Govt Pol. Dept, 20 December 1863, Mss Eur F 123/38, BL.

63. Lt Col H. Disbrowe, Pol. Agent Muscat, to C. Gonne, Procds No. 23, FD, December 1865, Nos 22–23, NAI.

64. Government's Observations for Col Pelly's Information, L/PJ/6/219, File No. 155, BL. See also Mss Eur 126/44, Letters of Charles Edwards, Asst Resident Persian Gulf, Folio No. 52, BL.

65. L. No. 55, British Resident, Bushire, to C. Gonne, Sec. to Govt Pol. Dept, 20 December 1863, Mss Eur F 123/38, BL.

66. See correspondence related to the letter of Lt Col L. Pelly, Pol. Resident Persian Gulf, to Sec. to Govt Pol. Dept, Bombay, 21 January 1865, Pol. Consult., 31 March 1865, No. 1650, PD 1865, Vol. 31, MSA.

67. The Bombay government and the Egyptian Pasha had attacked their pirate ports and dented their temporal power in the early nineteenth century. The Imam of Muscat had prevented their expansion into Oman. Comments by B. Frere on the Minute by His Excellency the Governor, 9 October 1865, Mss Eur F126/63, BL.

68. L. No. 196, C. Gonne, Sec. to Govt of Bombay, to Sec. to the Govt of India, Fort William, 19 December 1865, Mss Eur F 123/38, BL.

69. Lt. Col H. Disbrowe, Pol. Agent Muscat, to C. Goume, Sec. to Govt of Bombay, Muscat, 22 August 1865, PD1865, Vol. 31, MSA.

70. L. No. 15, H. Rafsan, Acting British Agent at Muscat, to A.K. Forbes, Acting Sec. to Govt of Bombay, 29 April 1861, File No. 31, Secret, Muscat, 1861, PD 1861, Vol. 32, MSA.

71. L. No. 9A, Capt. F. Jones, Pol. Resident Persian Gulf, to H.L. Anderson, Sec. to Govt of Bombay, 22 May 1860, Residency Records, Persian Gulf, Book No. 219, R/15/1/155, BL.

72. Ibid.

73. Aga Muhammad Bankar Khan, Consul to the Sultan of Muscat, to Sec. to Govt Pol Dept, Bombay, 27 June 1865, FD Pol. A., September 1865, Nos 67/69, NAI.

74. Ibid.

75. Pelly to Bartle Friar, 25 November 1866, Pelly Letters, Mss Eur F 126/43, BL.

76. L. No. 196, C. Gonne, Sec. to Govt of Bombay, to Sec. to the Govt of India, Fort William, 19 December 1865, Mss Eur F 123/38, BL.

77. Lt Col L. Pelly, Pol. Resident Persian Gulf, to Sec. to Govt Pol. Dept, Bombay, 21 January 1865, PD Muscat 1865, Vol. 31, MSA.

78. L. No. 3, Political Resident Muscat to C. Gonne, Sec. to Govt Pol. Dept, Bombay, 16 January 1866, Mss Eur F 123/38, BL.

79. Lt Col L. Pelly, Pol. Resident Persian Gulf, to Sec. to Govt Pol. Dept, Bombay, 21 January 1865, PD Muscat, 1865, Vol. 31, MSA.

80. Ibid.

81. Translated letter of Amir Faisal, Ruler of Nejd, to Asst Resident Persian Gulf, 19 September 1865, L/PS/6/544, Col 61/3, BL.

82. L. No. 66, Sec. Govt of India, FD, to Sec Govt of Bombay, 24 January 1866, L/PS/6/544, Col 61/3, BL.

83. Minute by Governor Elphinstone, concurred in by B.H. Ellis, 9 October 1865, signed H.B.E. Frere, PD 1865, Vol. 31, MSA.

84. L. No. 940, A. Colvin, Under Sec. to Govt of India, to Sec. to the Govt of Bombay, 8 November 1865, Mss Eur F 123/38, BL.

85. L. Pelly, Pol. Resident, Bushire, to Mackmann, 20 April 1866, Mss Eur F 126/43, Pelly Letters, BL.

86. L. Pelly to B. Frere, 2 June 1866, Mss Eur F 126/43, Pelly Letters, BL.

87. L. Pelly, Pol. Resident, Bushire, to Mr Ryan, 2 June 1866, Mss Eur F 126/43, Pelly Letters, BL.

88. L. Pelly to B. Frere, 2 June 1866, Mss Eur F 126/43, Pelly Letters, BL.

89. L. No. 3, Political Resident Muscat to C. Gonne, Sec. to Govt Pol. Dept, Bombay, 16 January 1866, Mss Eur F 123/38, BL.

90. L. No. 361, Sec. to the Govt of India, to the Sec. to the Govt of Bombay, 18 April 1866, Mss Eur F 123/38, BL.

91. P. Ryan, Assistant Sec. to Govt to Nasser bin Ali and Hamid bin Sa'īd Khalifas, undated, Mss Eur F 123/38, BL.

92. Sec. to Govt of India, FD, to Sec. to Govt of Bombay, 14 March 1866, L/PS/6/544, Col. No.2 of 61/3, BL.

93. J. Lawrence and others, Foreign Dept, to Sir C. Wood, Sec. of State, Fort William, 8 February 1866, Wahhabi Report, L/PS/6/544, Collection No.1 of 61/3, BL.

94. L. Pelly, Pol. Resident, Bushire, to Thuwayni, Muscat, 19 January 1868, Mss Eur F 123/38, BL.

95. L. Pelly, Pol. Resident, Persian Gulf, to C. Gonne, Sec. to Govt Pol Dept, Bombay, 4 May 1866, Mss Eur F 123/38, BL.

96. L. Pelly, Pol. Resident, Persian Gulf, to Envoys of the Muscat Government, 18 May 1866, Mss Eur F 123/38, BL.

97. L. Pelly, Pol. Resident, Bushire, to Amir of Nejd, 6 January 1866, Mss Eur F 123/38, BL. See for details of his negotiations with the Wahhabis.

98. L. Pelly, Pol. Resident, Bushire, to C. Gonne, Sec. to Govt of Bombay, 28 April 1866, Mss Eur F 123/38, BL.

99. Extract from letter from Consul General at Baghdad to Ambassador at Constantinople, 1 January 1862, Mss Eur F 123/38, BL.

100. L. No. 7, L. Pelly, Pol. Resident in the Persian Gulf, to C. Gonne, Sec. to Govt, Pol. Dept, Bombay, 12 February 1866, Mss Eur F 123/38, BL.

101. Ibid.

102. L. No. 266, W. Muir, Sec. to the Govt of India, to Sec. to Govt of Bombay, Fort William, 14 March 1866, Mss Eur F 123/38, BL.

103. L. Pelly to Bartle Frere, 22 June 1866, Mss Eur F126/43, BL.

104. A form of currency circulating in the Indian Ocean world.

105. L. No. 73 of 1858, Persian Dept, 3 February 1858, substance of letter from Haskil bin Yusuf, Acting Native Agent at Muscat, to the Persian Secretary to Government, 8 February 1858, translated on 29 January 1858, File No. 283, Sec. Muscat, PD, Muscat, Vol. 147, MSA.

106. Captain H. Disbrowe, Acting Pol. Agent, Muscat, to H. Anderson, Chief Sec. to Govt of Bombay, 10 June 1863, PD 1863, Vol. 38, MSA.

107. Floor, *The Persian Gulf*, pp. 86–87.

108. L. No. 10, G.P. Badger, In-charge of the Muscat–Zanzibar Commission, to A.K. Forbes, Acting Sec. to Govt of Bombay, 5 June 1861, File No. 248, FD Pol. A., January 1864, NAI.

109. Translation of newsletter from Meer Mossun Shah, Makran, 12 February 1857, FD, 27 March 1857 (SC), Nos 98–99, NAI.

110. L. No. 75, Brig. Gen. J. Jacob, Acting Commissioner, Sindh, to Lord Elphinstone, Governor and President in Council, Bombay, 5 March 1857, FD 1857 (SC), 27 March 1857, Nos 98–99, NAI.

111. J. Outram, British Agent of the Queen at Bushire, to Earl of Clarendon, Sec. of State for Foreign Affairs, 2 March 1857, FD, 24 April 1857 (SC) Nos 110–11, NAI.

112. L. No. 125, Govt of India, to Stafford H. Northcote, Sec. of State for India, 1 August 1865, Procds No. 34, FD Pol. A., August 1868, NAI. The overlapping sovereignties at Angaun were part of the Persian treaty and excluded from the Bandar Abbas lease by the Bombay government as they had signed an agreement with it for a telegraph station there.

113. Ibid.

114. George Percy Badger, In-charge Muscat–Zanzibar Commission, to A. Kinloch Forbes, Acting Sec. to Govt of Bombay, Aden, 3 June 1861, FD, Pol. A., July 1863, File No. 123, NAI.

115. H. Disbrowe, Pol. Agent Muscat, to Lt Col Pelly, Pol. Resident, Persian Gulf, 17 November 1864, PD 1865, Muscat, No. 287, MSA.

116. George Percy Badger, In-charge Muscat–Zanzibar Commission, to A. Kinloch Forbes, Acting Sec. to Govt of Bombay, Aden, 3 June 1861, FD, Pol. A., July 1863, File No. 123, NAI.

117. Ibid.

118. Lt Col H. Disbrowe, Pol. Agent, Muscat, to C. Gonne, Sec. to Govt of Bombay, 2 February 1866, File No. 134, FD Pol. A., May 1866, NAI.

119. Floor, *The Persian Gulf*, p. 143.

120. Lt Col L. Pelly, Resident, Persian Gulf, to W.H. Havelock, Officiating Sec. to Govt of Bombay, 16 January 1864, FD, Pol. A., September 1864, Persian Gulf Reports, NAI.

121. Ibid.

122. Ibid.

123. Stephanie Jones, 'British India Steamers and the Trade of the Persian Gulf, 1862-1914', *The Great Circle*, Vol. 7, No. 1 (April 1985), pp. 23–44, p. 33.

124. Ibid., pp. 30–31.

125. Ibid., p. 30.

126. L. No. 296, Lt Col Hennell, Resident in Persian Gulf, to H. Malet, Chief Sec. to Govt of Bombay, Bushire, 1 August 1850, R/15/1/123, BL.

127. Enclosure No. 1, translated letter from Ahmad bin Mullah Hussain, Agent at Lingah, to Lt Col Hennell, Resident in Persian Gulf, 6 June 1850, in letter from Lt Col Hennell, Resident in Persian Gulf, to Lt Col Sheil, Envoy Extraordinary at the court of Persia, 24 June, 1850, R/15/1/123, BL.

128. L. No. 245, Lt Col Hennell, Resident in the Persian Gulf, to H. Malet, Chief Sec. to Govt of Bombay, 23 June 1850, R/15/1/123, BL.

129. Ibid.

130. L. No. 6, Hareb Thuwayni, Qishm, to A.R. Hakim, Asst Surgeon Banidore, 27 Zilhaj 1293 (1877), FD, October 1877, Nos 1–55, NAI.

131. L. No. 415, R.F.Thomson to Earl Granvill, Miscellaneous, Zanzibar Administration, IOR/L/PJ/6/65, File No. 275, BL. As late as 1881, it was decided that any Persian subject who did not notify the fact to the Governor would be punished with six months' imprisonment.

132. Sayyid Thuwayni, Sultan of Muscat, to F. Jones, Pol. Resident, Persian Gulf, 23 October 1860, R/15/1/163, BL.

133. Lt Col Hennel, Resident in Persian Gulf, to Lt Col Sheil, Envoy Extraordinary, at Persian Court, 12 December 1850, R/15/1/123, BL.

134. Precis by Pol Secretary to Govt of Bombay, 10 March 1866, File No. 136, FD, Pol. A., May 1866, NAI.

135. Lt Col L. Pelly, Resident Persian Gulf, to C. Gonne, Sec. to Govt of Bombay, 29 January 1866, File No. 133, FD Pol. A., May 1866, NAI.

136. Ibid.

137. Extract from a letter by Khoja Ibrahim Lalji of Bandar Abbas, to Mr McGill, Agent for British Indian Steam Navigation Company at Muscat, 18–19 January 1866, FD, Pol. A., May 1866, File No. 133, NAI.

138. Extract of letter from Nabandas, Resident of Bandar Abbas, to Mr McGill, Agent for British Indian Steam Navigation Company at Muscat, January 1866, NAI.

139. L. Pelly to Alison, 15 June 1868, Mss Eur F 126/43, Pelly Letters, BL.

140. Lt Col L. Pelly, Resident, Persian Gulf, to C. Gonne, Sec. to Govt of Bombay, 29 January 1866, File No. 133, FD Pol. A., May 1866, NAI.

141. L. Pelly to Ellis, 21 December 1867, Mss Eur F 126/43, Pelly Letters, BL.

142. Lt Col H. Disbrowe, Pol. Agent, Muscat, to H. Anderson, Chief Sec. to Govt of Bombay, 22 June 1864, PD 1864, No. 25, MSA. The government ordered that Haji Ahmad's movement be tracked.

143. Lt Col H. Disbrowe, Pol. Agent Muscat, to Lt Col L. Pelly, Pol. Resident Persian Gulf, 17 November 1864, PD 1865, No. 287, Muscat, MSA.

144. G. Atchinson, Acting Political Agent, Muscat, to Pol. Agent, Persian Gulf, 27 November 1869, PD 1869, Vol. V, No. 90, File No. 96, MSA.

145. G. Atchinson, Acting Political Agent, Muscat, to Pol. Agent, Persian Gulf, 22 November 1868, PD 1869, Vol. V, File No. 96, MSA.

146. G. Atchinson, Acting Political Agent, Muscat, to Pol. Agent, Persian Gulf, 27 November 1869, PD 1869, Vol. V, No. 96, MSA.

147. Extract from the Journal of Shiraz Agent, January 1868, FD Pol. A., June 1868, Procds No. 141, NAI.

148. L. No. 105, Govt of India to Sec of State for India, 22 June 1868, FD Pol. A., June 1868, Procds No. 151, NAI.

149. L. No. 94, Lt Col L. Pelly, Pol. Resident Persian Gulf, to C. Gonne, Sec. to Govt of Bombay, Pol Dept, 26 July 1868, Procds No. 271, FD Pol. A., September 1868, NAI.

150. Lt Col L. Pelly, Pol. Resident Persian Gulf, to Sec. to Govt of Bombay, 25 March 1868, Procds No. 267, FD Pol. A., September 1868, NAI.

151. L. No. 91, Lt Col Pelly, Pol. Resident, Persian Gulf, to C. Gonne, Sec. to Govt of Bombay, Pol Dept, 14 July 1868, Procds No. 269, FD Pol. A., September 1868, NAI.

152. Ibid.

153. L. No. 105, Govt of India to Sec of State for India, 22 June 1868, FD Pol. A., June 1868, Procds No. 151, NAI.

154. Ibid.

155. G.A. Atkinson, Pol. Agent, Muscat, to Pol. Agent Zanzibar, 18 November 1868, PD 1868, Muscat, Vol. I, No. 84, MSA.

156. Memorandum by Captain W.J. Eastwick, 13 July 1868, Zanzibar, Muscat and Persia, L/PS/18/B2/5, BL.

157. Ibid.

158. Sayyid Turki complained to the British that Salim was not entitled to sell Thuwayni's ships, as they were the property of the state, except one of them, which the Sultan owned privately. See Oriental Translation, 1 May 1869, Sayyid Turki to Governor of Bombay, PD 1869, File No. 427, MSA; Sayyid Azan bin Sayyid also wrote to the British demanding the return of the said ship. See Sayyid Azan bin Sayyid to C. Gonne, Sec. to Govt of Bombay, 25 July 1869, PD 1869, File No. 427, MSA.

159. Memorandum by Political Secretary, J.W. Kirk, 14 July 1868, Zanzibar, Muscat and Persia, L/PS/18/B2/5, BL.

160. L. No. 125, Govt of India to Sir S.H. Northcote, Sec. of State for India, 1 August 1865, FD Pol. A., August 1868, File No. 34, NAI.

161. Foreign Sec. Simla to Sec. to Govt of Bombay, 25 June 1868, File No. 188, FD Pol. A., June 1868, NAI.

162. L. No. 125, Govt of India to Sir S.H. Northcote, Sec. of State for India, 1 August 1865, FD Pol. A., August 1868, File No. 34, NAI. This was later denied by Persia, who said that the negotiations were still on for their demand of 30,000 tomans. See Ibid., File No. 36, Telegram, 31 July 1866.

163. See FD Pol. A., July 1868, Files 50–58, NAI.

164. Resident Persian Gulf to Sec. to Govt of Bombay, FD Pol. A., July 1868, File 58, NAI.

165. See for details FD 1879 Pol. A., Procds June 1879, Nos 31–36, NAI.

Chapter 4: Sayyid Turki: The Sultan in the Age of the Nation State

1. L. No. 17 of 1860, Brigadier W.M. Coghlan, In-charge Muscat and Zanzibar Commission, to H.L. Anderson, Chief Sec. to Govt of Bombay, 4 December 1860, Report of Commission 1860, Sec. Consultations, 1861, No. 97, PD 33/186, MSA.

2. Intelligence connected with Imam of Muscat, translated letter, Haji Yaqub, British Agent at Sharjah, to Capt. Felix Jones, Pol. Resident, Persian Gulf, Bushire, 11 November 1857, R/15/1/155, BL.

3. Translated letter, Haji Yaqub, British Agent at Sharjah, to Commander Felix Jones, Pol. Resident, Persian Gulf, 18 November 1857, R/15/1/155, BL.

4. L. No. 415, Captain Felix Jones, Political Resident, Persian Gulf, Bushire, to H.L. Anderson, Sec. to Govt of Bombay, 19 November 1858, R/15/1/155, BL.

5. Ibid.

6. Capt. F. Jones, Pol. Resident Persian Gulf, to H.L. Anderson, Sec. to Govt of Bombay, 5 July 1859, R/15/1/155, BL.

7. Capt. F. Jones, Resident in the Persian Gulf, to Sayyid Thuwayni, 21 July 1859, R/15/1/155, BL.

8. L. No. 17 of 1860, Brigadier W.M. Coghlan, In-charge Muscat and Zanzibar Commission, to H.L. Anderson, Chief Sec. to Govt of Bombay, 4 December 1860, Report of Commission 1860, Sec. Consultations, 1861, No. 97. PD 33/1861, MSA.

9. L. No. 9A, Capt. F. Jones, Pol. Resident Persian Gulf, to H.L. Anderson, Sec. to Govt of Bombay, 22 May 1860, Residency Records, Persian Gulf, Book No. 219, R/15/1/155, BL.

10. L. No. 282, Capt. F. Jones, Pol. Resident in the Persian Gulf, to Sayyid Turki, 22 July 1859, R/15/1/155, BL.

11. Ibid.

12. Sayyid Turki to Capt. Felix Jones, Pol. Resident in the Persian Gulf, 4 June 1859, R/15/1/155, BL.

13. C.P. Rigby, Counsel at Zanzibar, to H.L. Anderson, Sec. to Govt of Bombay, 1 December 1859, Sec Dept, R/15/1/155, BL.

14. Ibid.

15. Translated Summary of Intelligence, British Agent at Muscat to Capt. F. Jones, Pol. Resident in the Persian Gulf, 4 October 1858, R/15/1/155, BL.

16. L. No. 281, Capt. F. Jones, Pol. Resident in the Persian Gulf, to J. Anderson, Sec. to Govt of Bombay, 16 August 1858, R/15/1/155, BL.

17. Comments by B. Frere on the Minute by His Excellency the Governor, 9 October 1865, Mss Eur F 126/63, BL.

18. Ibid. The Bombay government and the Egyptian Pasha had attacked their pirate ports and dented their temporal power in the early nineteenth century. The Imam of Muscat had prevented their expansion into Oman.

19. Haji Yaqub, British Agent at Sharja, to Capt. F. Jones, Pol. Resident, Bushire, 9 August 1858, R/15/1/155, BL.

20. L. No. 17 of 1860, Brigadier W.M. Coghlan, In-charge Muscat and Zanzibar Commission, to H.L. Anderson, Chief Sec. to Govt of Bombay, 4 December 1860, Report of Commission 1860, Sec. Consultations, 1861, No. 97. PD 33/1861, MSA.

21. L. No. 4315, H.L. Anderson, Sec. to Govt of Bombay, to Commander F. Jones, Resident in the Persian Gulf, Bushire, 19 December 1857, R/15/1/155, BL.

22. L. No. 17 of 1860, Brigadier W.M. Coghlan, In-charge Muscat and Zanzibar Commission, to H.L. Anderson, Chief Sec. to Govt of Bombay, 4 December 1860, Report of Commission 1860, Sec. Consultations, 1861, No. 97. PD 33/1861, MSA.

23. L. No. 15, H. Rafsan, Acting British Agent at Muscat, to A.K. Forbes, Acting Sec. to Govt of Bombay, 29 April 1861, File No. 31, Secret, Muscat, 1861, PD 1861, Vol. 32, MSA.

24. L. No. 25, Lt W.M. Pengally, British Agent to Muscat, to K. Forbes, Sec. to Govt, 11 January 1861, File No. 31, Secret, Muscat, 1861 PD, 1861, Vol. 32, MSA.

25. Lt W.M. Pengally, British Agent to Muscat, to K. Forbes, Sec. to Govt, 21 June 1861, Seeb, near Muscat, File No. 31, Secret, Muscat, 1861, PD 1861, Vol. 32, MSA.

26. L. No. 29, Lt W.M. Pengally, British Agent to Muscat, to K. Forbes, Sec. to Govt, 6 July 1861, File No. 31, Secret, Muscat, 1861, PD 1861, Vol. 32, MSA.

27. Substance of a letter from the Bombay government, 21 November 1861, FD Pol. A., December 1861, Nos 20/23, NAI.

28. L. No. 21, H.C. Anderson, Sec. to Govt of Bombay, to Sec. to Govt of India with the Governor General, Secret Department, 1 March 1860, R/15/1/155, BL.

29. L. No. 208, Capt. F. Jones, Pol. Resident in the Persian Gulf, to L. Anderson, Sec. to Govt of Bombay, Pol. Dept, n.d., 1860, R/15/1/155, BL.

30. L. No. 1, Pol. Resident Persian Gulf to C. Gonne, Sec. to Govt, Pol. Dept, Bombay, on board the ship *Bernier* off Sohar, 5 January 1866, Mss Eur F 123/38, BL.

31. Aga Muhammad Bankar Khan, Consul to Sultan of Muscat, to Sec. to Govt, Pol. Dept, Bombay, 27 June 1865, FD Pol. A., September 1865, Nos 67/69, NAI.

32. L. No. 151, Lt Col H. Disbrowe to C. Gonne, Sec. to Govt, Bombay, 4 August 1865, FD Pol. A., September 1865, Nos 67/69, NAI.

33. L. No. 2135, C. Gonne to Pol. Agent, Muscat, 26 August 1865, FD Pol. A., September 1865, Nos 67/69, NAI.

34. Substance of a letter from Turki to the Governor, 15 September 1868, Procds No. 313, FD October 1868, Pol. A., File Nos 307–15, NAI.

35. His Majesty's Viceroy to Bombay Government, 12 February 1869, Procds Nos 239–41, FD Pol. A., February 1869, NAI.

36. Governor of Bombay to Viceroy, 10 February 1869, Procds No. 238, FD Pol. A., February 1869, NAI.

37. W.S. Seton-Karr, Sec. to Govt of India, FD, to C. Gonne, Sec. to Govt of Bombay, 17 February 1869, Procds No. 241, FD Pol. A., February 1869, NAI.

38. L. No. 96, L. Pelly to C. Gonne, 3 October 1866, Procds No. 90, FD, Pol. A., November 1866, Nos 89–95, NAI.

39. L. No. 83, Lt Col Pelly to C. Gonne, Sec. to Govt Pol Dept, Bombay, 21 September 1866, Mss Eur F 123/38, BL.

40. L. Pelly to C. Gonne, Sec. to Govt of India, 29 October 1866, Mss Eur F 123/38, BL.

41. L. No. 93, L. Pelly to C. Gonne, 13 August 1867, Procds No. 153, FD Pol. A., September 1867, NAI.

42. Acting Pol. Agent, Muscat, to Pol. Resident Persian Gulf, 26 August. 1867, Procds No. 149-A, FD Pol. A., September 1867, NAI.

43. L. Pelly to Sec. to Govt of Bombay, 17 February 1867, Pol. Dept No. 35, FD Pol. A., March 1867, Ref. No. 109–110, NAI.

44. L. No. 131, L. Pelly to C. Gonne, Sec. to Govt Pol. Dept, Bombay, Bushire, 18 December 1866, Mss Eur F 123/38, BL.

45. L. No. 305, Bombay Government to L. Pelly, Resident in the Persian Gulf, 26 December 1866, Foreign Pol. A., January 1867, File No. 119/123, NAI.

46. L. No. 117, L. Pelly to C. Gonne, 1 December 1866, Procds No. 120, Foreign Pol. A., January 1867, File Nos 119/123, NAI.

47. L. Pelly to C. Gonne, n.d., Procds No. 93, FD Pol. A., November 1866, Nos 89–95, NAI.

48. Translation of report from Acting Native Agent at Muscat to Pol. Resident in the Persian Gulf, 23 September 1866, FD Pol. A., November 1866, Nos 89–95, NAI.

49. Translation of letter by Sayyid Salim to L. Pelly, 26 November 1866, Foreign Pol. A., January 1867, File Nos 119/123, NAI.

50. Translation of a letter from Sultan Sayyid Salim to L. Pelly, 22 September 1866, FD Pol. A., November 1866, Nos 89–95, NAI.

51. Translation report from Acting Native Agent at Muscat to Pol. Resident in the Persian Gulf, 17 September 1866; and another between them of 20 September 1866, FD Pol. A., November 1866, Nos 89–95, NAI.

52. L. No. 88, L. Pelly to C. Gonne, 23 September 1866, Procds No. 54, FD Pol. A., November 1866, Nos 52/55, NAI.

53. L. No. 1156, Sec. to Govt of India, FD, to Sec. to Govt of Bombay, 16 November 1866, Procds No. 91, FD Pol. A., November 1866, Nos 89–95, NAI.

54. Sec. to Govt of Bombay, Poona, to Foreign Secretary, Simla, 1 November 1868, Telegram, Procds No. 91, FD Pol. A., December 1868, Nos 88–91, NAI.

55. L. No. 2689P, Sec. to Govt of India, FD, to Commissioner Sindh, 5 November 1873, Procds 52, FD Pol. A., December 1873, Nos 44–65, NAI.

56. L. No. 539, A Cotton Way, Pol. Agent and Consul at Muscat, to Lt Col L. Pelly, 7 November 1870, Procds No. 305, FD Pol. A., January 1871, Nos 304–18, NAI.

57. Floor, *The Persian Gulf*, pp. 98–99.

58. Lt Col Miles, Pol. Agent at Persian Gulf and Consul at Muscat, to Lt Col E.C. Ross, Pol. Resident in the Persian Gulf, Muscat, 21 March 1878, IOR: R/15/6/10, BL.

59. L. No. 344, Lt Col Miles, Pol. Agent at Persian Gulf and Consul at Muscat, to Lt Col E.C. Ross, Pol. Resident in the Persian Gulf, Muscat, 23 September 1878, R/15/6/10, BL.

60. L. Nos 432–170, Pol. Agent and Consul Muscat to Pol. Resident in Persian Gulf, 19 September 1873, Procds No. 19, FD Pol. A., November 1873, Nos 16–20, NAI.

61. L. Nos 432–170, Pol. Agent and Consul Muscat, to Pol. Resident in Persian Gulf, 19 September 1873, FD, Pol. A., November 1873, Nos 16–20, Procd No. 9, NAI.

62. L. Nos 346–126, Lt Col S.B. Miles, Pol. Agent and Consul Muscat to Lt Col E.C. Ross, Political Resident, Persian Gulf, 19 August 1875, Procds No. 71, FD Pol. A., November 1875, Procds Nos 61–87, NAI.

63. L. No. 956, Commissioner Sindh to Sec. to Govt of India, 29 September 1873, Procds No. 47, FD Pol. A., December 1873, Nos 44–65, NAI.

64. L. No. 2689P, Sec. to Govt of India, FD, to Commissioner Sindh, 5 November 1873, Procds No. 52, FD Pol. A., December 1873, Nos 44–65, NAI.

65. L. Nos 455–181, Pol. Agent and Consul Muscat, to Acting Political Agent Persian Gulf, 3 October 1873, Procds No. 65, FD Pol. A., December 1873, Nos 44–65, NAI.

66. L. Nos 346–126, Lt Col S.B. Miles, Pol. Agent and Consul Muscat to Lt Col E.C. Ross, Pol. Resident in the Persian Gulf, 19 August 1875, Procds No. 71, FD Pol. A., November 1875, Procds 61–87, NAI.

67. Translated letter, Sayyid Abdul Aziz, to Lt Col Miles, Pol. Agent at Muscat, 9 July 1878, IOR: R/15/6/10, BL.

68. Ibid.

69. Ibid.

70. Lt Col Miles, Pol. Agent at Persian Gulf and Consul at Muscat, to Lt Col E.C. Ross, Pol. Resident in the Persian Gulf, 2 February 1878, IOR: R/15/6/10, BL.

71. L. Nos 346–126, Lt Col S.B. Miles, Pol. Agent and Consul Muscat to Lt Col E.C. Ross, Pol. Resident in the Persian Gulf, 19 August 1875, Procds No. 71, FD Pol. A., November 1875, Procds 61–87, NAI.

72. Lt Col Miles, Pol. Agent at Persian Gulf and Consul at Muscat, to Lt Col E.C. Ross, Pol. Resident in the Persian Gulf, 2 February 1878, IOR: R/15/6/10, BL.

73. Ibid.

74. Lt Col Miles, Pol. Agent at Persian Gulf and Consul at Muscat, to Lt Col E.C. Ross, Pol. Resident in the Persian Gulf, Muscat, 10 July 1878, IOR: R/15/6/10, BL.

75. Translation of a letter from Governor of Sumail to Sayyid Turki, 16 July 1878, IOR: R/15/6/10, BL.

76. Lt Col Miles, Pol. Agent at Persian Gulf and Consul at Muscat, to Lt Col E.C. Ross, Pol. Resident in the Persian Gulf, Muscat, 18 July 1878, IOR: R/15/6/10, BL.

77. Translated letter, Sayyid Faisal bin Turki to Sayyid Turki, 2 July 1878, IOR: R/15/6/10, BL.

78. Translated letter, Sayyid Faisal bin Turki to Sayyid Turki, 6 February 1878, IOR: R/15/6/10, BL.

79. Translated letter, Sayyid Faisal bin Turki to Sayyid Turki, 2 August 1878, IOR: R/15/6/10, BL.

80. Translated letter, Sayyid Faisal bin Turki to Sayyid Turki, 28 July 1878, IOR: R/15/6/10, BL.

81. Translated letter, Sayyid Faisal bin Turki to Sayyid Turki, 4 August 1878, IOR: R/15/6/10, BL.

82. Lt Col Miles, Agent Muscat, to Lt Col E.C. Ross, Pol. Resident in the Persian Gulf, Bushire, 15 August 1878, IOR: R/15/6/10, BL.

83. L. No. 287, Lt Col Miles, Agent at Muscat, to Lt Col E.C. Ross, Political Resident in the Persian Gulf, 7 August 1878, IOR: R/15/6/10, BL.

84. Lt Col Miles, Agent at Muscat, to Lt Col E.C. Ross, Pol. Resident in the Persian Gulf, Bushire, 15 August 1878, IOR: R/15/6/10, BL.

85. Ibid.

86. Lt Col Miles, Agent at Muscat, to Lt Col E.C. Ross, Pol. Resident in the Persian Gulf, Bushire, 31 August 1878, IOR: R/15/6/10, BL.

87. Lt Col Miles, Agent at Muscat, to Lt Col E.C. Ross, Pol. Resident in the Persian Gulf, Bushire, 3 September 1878, IOR: R/15/6/10, BL; see Hopper, *Slaves of One Master*, for significance of export trade in dates from the region.

88. Administrative Report of the Political Agency, Muscat, 1877–78, R/15/6/10, BL.

89. Ibid.

90. Ibid.; See also Administrative report of the Political Agency, Muscat, 1875–76, Part IV, V/23/27, No. 128. Micro Fisch 191–

92. In 1876, wheat imports from Persia increased, as did rice from Calcutta.

91. Administrative Report of the Political Agency, Muscat, 1877–78, R/15/6/10, BL.

92. Ibid.

93. L. No. 367, enclosure to Sayyid Turki's letter to Col L. Pelly, 8 October 1871, Procds No. 346, FD Pol. A., January 1872, Procds Nos 345–49, NAI.

94. Substance of a letter from Sayyid Abdul Aziz bin Saʻīd bin Sultan to Governor of Bombay, 6 June 1872, Procds No. 293, FD Pol. A., July 1872, NAI.

95. L. No. 367–87, Substance of a letter from the Bombay government to FD, 6 September 1873, Procds Nos 367–87, FD Pol. A., September 1873, NAI.

96. L. No. 875, Commissioner of Sindh to Asst Pol. Agent Makran Coast, Karachi, 1 September 1873, Procds No. 375, FD Pol. A., September 1873, NAI.

97. Telegram, Commissioner Karachi to Foreign Sec., Simla, 22 September 1873, Procds No. 382, FD Pol. A., September 1873, NAI.

98. Telegram No. 2267P, 24 September 1873, Foreign Sec, Simla, to Commissioner Karachi, Procds No. 383, FD Pol. A., September 1873, NAI.

99. L. No. 956, Commissioner Sindh to Sec. to Govt of India, 29 September 1873, Procds No. 47, FD Pol. A., December 1873, Nos 44–65, NAI.

100. L. No. 2689P, Sec. to Govt of India, FD, to Commissioner Sindh, 5 November 1873, Procds No. 52, FD Pol. A., December 1873, Nos 44–65, NAI.

101. L. Nos 455–181, Pol. Agent and Consul Muscat, to Acting Pol. Agent in the Persian Gulf, 3 October 1873, Procds No. 65, FD Pol. A., December 1873, Nos 44–65, NAI.

102. No. 89, Abstract of Despatch to Sec. of State for India, 12 April 1876, NAI.

103. Ibid.

104. Sayyid Salim, ex-Sultan of Muscat, to Sec. to Govt of India, FD, 1 May 1873, Procds No. 478, Pol. A., FD, June 1873, Procds Nos 476–89, NAI.

105. L. No. 62. Translated letter from Sayyid Turki to Col Ross, Gwadar, 21 October 1875, FD Pol. A., April 1876, Nos 38–93, NAI.

106. No. 89, Abstract of Despatch to Sec. of State for India, 12 April 1876, NAI.

107. Ibid.

108. L. No. 897, W.L. Merewether, Commissioner Sindh, to C.U. Aitchison, Sec. to Govt of India, FD, 17 November 1875, FD Pol. A., April 1876, Nos 38–93, NAI.

109. L. No. 577P, F. Henney, Under Sec. to Govt of India, FD, to Col W.L. Merewether, Commissioner Sindh, 1 March 1876, FD Pol. A., April 1876, Nos 38–93, NAI.

110. L. No. 2372, R. Wallace, Magistrate of Dist of Hyderabad, to Col Sir W.L. Merewether, Commissioner Sindh, November 1875, FD Pol. A., April 1876, Nos 38–93, NAI.

111. L. No. 996, Col W.L. Merewether, Commissioner Sindh, to C.U. Aitchison, Sec. to Govt of India, FD, 21 December 1875, FD Pol. A., April 1876, Nos 38–93, NAI.

112. Administrative Report of the Political Agency, Muscat, 1877–78, R/15/6/10, BL.

113. Ibid.

114. L. No. 529P, T.H. Thornton, Officiating Sec. to Govt of India, FD, to W.F. Prideaux, Pol. Resident in the Persian Gulf, 9 March 1877, Procds No. 31, FD Pol. A., March 1877, Nos 28–31, NAI.

115. Ibid.

116. L. No. 113, W.F. Prideaux, Political Resident in Persian Gulf, to T.H. Thornton, Officiating Sec. to Govt of India, 4 May 1877, Procds No. 143, FD Pol. A., July 1877, Nos 143–45, NAI.

117. L. No. 172, S.B. Miles, Pol. Agent and Consul Muscat, to W.F. Prideaux, Pol. Resident in the Persian Gulf, 16 April 1877, Procds No. 144, FD Pol. A., July 1877, Nos 143–45, NAI.

118. L. No. 218–92, Pol. Agent and Consul at Muscat to Pol. Resident in the Persian Gulf, 14 May 1874, Procds No. 2, FD Pol. A., July 1874, Nos 1–3, NAI.

119. L. Nos 346/117, Lt Col S.B. Miles, Pol. Agent and Consul Muscat, to Capt. W. Prideaux, Pol. Resident in the Persian Gulf, 17 August 1876, FD Pol. A., 1876, Procds 1876 Nos 34/35, NAI. Prideaux was not keen on the proposal, as he was doubtful if the

Government of India had the authority to detain a vessel that had not transgressed the laws of India.

120. L. Nos 346/117, Lt Col S.B. Miles, Pol. Agent and Consul Muscat, to Capt. W. Prideaux, Pol. Resident Persian Gulf, 17 August 1876, FD Pol. A. 1876, Procds October 1876, Nos 34/35, NAI.

121. Memorandum on Muscat and Zanzibar Subsidy, 3 May 1873, Procds No. 484, Pol. A., FD, June 1873, Nos 476–89, NAI.

122. Ibid.

123. Telegram No. 1537P, Viceroy, Simla, to Sec. of State, London, 10 July 1873, FD Pol., July 1873, Nos 235/236, Procds No. 236, NAI.

124. L. Nos 1645–453, Pol. Resident in Persian Gulf to Sec. to Govt of Bombay, 19 October 1872, Procds No. 260, FD Pol. A., January 1873, Procds Nos 256–88, NAI.

125. L. No. 52, H.B. Frere, Majesty's Special Envoy to Zanzibar and Muscat, to Sec. of State for Foreign Affairs, London, 16 April 1873, Procds No. 477, Pol. A. FD, June 1873, Nos 476–89, NAI.

126. L. No. 18, S.B. Miles, Acting Agent and Consul Gen. Zanzibar, to Earl Granville, KG, Sec. of State for Foreign Affairs, 1 March 1883, Report on the Slave Trade at Zanzibar and Muscat, Procds No. 211, Procds, April 1883, Nos 210–11, FD, A Pol. E, NAI.

127. There was no doubt in British minds about the payment of Zanzibari subsidy to Muscat irrespective of Salim's usurpation. Coghlan's arrangement rested on this agreement between Muscat and Zanzibar, and any change in that threatened the neat and difficult balance of power in the Gulf.

128. J.W. Kaye, 'Zanzibar, Muscat and Persia, 1868', L/PS/18/B2/1, BL.

129. Ibid.

130. L. No. 125, Govt of India to Sir S.H. Northcote, Sec. of State for India, 1 August 1865, FD Pol. A., August 1868, File No. 34, NAI.

131. Foreign Sec. Simla to Sec. to Govt of Bombay, 25 June 1868, File No. 188, FD Pol. A., June 1868, NAI.

132. L. No. 125, Govt of India to Sir S.H. Northcote, Sec. of State for India, 1 August 1865, FD Pol. A., August 1868, File No. 34, NAI. This was later denied by Persia, who said that the negotiations were still on for their demand of 30,000 tomans. See Ibid, File No. 36, Telegram, 31 July 1866.

133. See FD Pol. A., July 1868, Files No 50–58, NAI.

134. Resident Persian Gulf to Sec. Govt of Bombay, FD Pol. A., July 1868, File No. 58, NAI. Salim said they were part of his hereditary possessions and never part of Persia and thus not in the original lease.

135. See for details FD 1879 Pol. A., Procds, June 1879, Nos 31–36, NAI.

136. Floor, *The Persian Gulf*, pp. 98–99.

137. Ibid., pp 94–95.

138. Translation of letter extract from Shiraz Agent to Her Britannie Majesty's Minister at Tehran, 13 July 1871, FD, Secret, October 1871, Procds No. 357, NAI.

139. L. No. 1967 P, C.U. Aitchison, Sec. to Govt of India, to Her Majesty's Minister in Tehran, Telegram dated 28 July 1871, FD, Secret, October 1871, Procds No. 357, NAI.

140. Translation of letter from Agha Muhammad Ali, Malik al-Tujjar, to Sayyid Turki, Sultan of Muscat, 2 November 1872, Procds No. 27, FD, Secret, February 1873, NAI; L. No. 12A, Acting Pol. Resident in Persian Gulf to Sec. to Govt of Bombay, 16 December 1872, Procds No. 28, FD Secret, February 1873, NAI.

141. C.U. Aitchison, Sec. to Govt of India, to Viceroy, 28 July 1871, Telegram, FD, Secret, October 1871, Procds No. 357, NAI.

142. Lt Col L. Pelly, Pol. Resident in the Persian Gulf, to Foreign Sec, Simla, Political Sec. Bombay and Sir William Merewether, Karachi, 25 June 1870, FD Pol. A., Part A, July 1870, Procds No. 203, Telegram, NAI.

143. Resident in the Persian Gulf Reports, 23 February and 7 March 1897, FD 1879, Pol. A., June 1879, Nos 31–36, NAI.

144. L. No. 32, Lt Col S.B. Miles, Consul Muscat, to Lt Col E.C. Ross, Pol. Resident in Persian Gulf, Muscat, 30 January 1879, Procds No. 32, FD 1879, Pol. A., June 1879, Nos 31–36, NAI.

145. Lt Col E.C. Ross, Pol. Resident in Gulf, to T.H. Thornton, Officiating Sec. to Govt of India, 12 February 1876, FD, Pol. A., March 1876, Procds. No. 225, NAI.

146. L. No. 17, W. Taylor Thomson, Minister at Tehran, to C.E. Ross, enclosure translated letter from Persian Minister for Foreign Affairs to British Minister at Tehran, 29 April 1875, Procds No. 366, FD, Pol. A., August 1875, NAI.

147. L. Nos 281–103, Lt Col S.B. Miles, Pol. Agent at Muscat to Lt Col E.C. Ross, Pol. Resident in the Persian Gulf, 8 July 1875, Procds No. 371, FD Pol. A., August 1875, NAI.

148. L. No. 47–12, Lt Col Miles, Consul Muscat, to Lt Col E.C. Ross, Resident in the Persian Gulf, 4 February 1876, Procds No. 226, FD Pol. A., March 1876, NAI; See also in same proceeding, L. No. 98, Ross to Turki, 12 February 1876.

149. L. No. 1423, C. Lyall, Sec. to Govt of India, FD, to E.C. Ross, Pol. Resident in the Persian Gulf, 19 May 1879, FD 1879, Pol. A., June, No. 36, NAI.

150. L. Nos 143 and 153, E.C. Ross, Pol. Resident in the Persian Gulf, to Foreign Dept, 11 and 20 July 1882, FD Pol. A., August 1882, Nos 191/194, NAI.

151. L. No. 95, E.C. Ross, Pol. Resident in the Persian Gulf, to Consul Gen. at Fars, to C. Grant, Sec. to Govt of India, 10 May 1883, FD, A Pol E., June 1883, Nos 24–26, NAI.

152. L. No. 170, E.C. Ross, Pol. Resident in the Persian Gulf, to Sec. to Govt of India, 30 May 1888, FD July 1888, External A, No. 4, NAI.

153. Translation of Head Munshi's Report, 24 June 1889, FD 1889, External A, August 1889, No. 339, NAI.

154. L. No. 234, Pol. Resident in the Persian Gulf to Minister at Tehran, 20 December 1884, FD 1885, External A, Procds January 1885, Nos 110–18, NAI.

155. Translation of a letter from the Hindu community and the British Indian subjects of Bandar Abbas to the Pol. Resident, Persian Gulf, Bushire, 23 November 1884, NAI.

156. L. No. 14, E.C. Ross, Pol. Resident in the Persian Gulf and Consul Gen. for Fars, to H.M. Durand, Sec. to Govt of India, FD, 1886, External A, Procds April 1886, No. 38, NAI.

157. Enclosure from Govt of Bombay, No. 87, 11 March 1869, in FD Pol. A., May 1869, Nos 210–51, NAI.

158. L. No. 28, Lt Col L. Pelly, Pol. Resident in the Persian Gulf, to C. Gonne, Sec. to Govt of Bombay, 13 February 1869, File No. 212, FD, Pol. A., May 1869, NAI.

159. Floor, *The Persian Gulf,* p. 128.

160. Ibid., pp. 94–96.

161. Ibid.

162. L. No. 120, L. Pelly, Pol. Resident in the Persian Gulf, to C. Gonne, Sec. to Govt of Bombay, 4 December 1869, Procds No. 224, FD Pol. A, February 1869, NAI.

163. L. No. 84, Capt. A. Way, Asst Pol. Resident in the Persian Gulf, to Lt Col L. Pelly, Pol. Resident in the Persian Gulf, 28 January 1869,

Procds No. 256, FD Pol. A., March 1869. On Haji Ahmad being appointed Persian Governor of Bandar Abbas, the Government of India gave up hope on Sayyid Salim's recently granted lease of Bandar Abbas and its dependencies being recognized as valid by the Shah of Iran. See L. No. 101, Govt of India to Duke of Argyll, K.T., Sec. of State for India, 20 March 1869, File No. 257, FD, Pol. A., March 1869, NAI.

164. Enclosure from Govt of Bombay, No. 87, 11 March 1869, in FD Pol. A., May 1869, Nos 210–51, NAI.

165. L. No. 45, Lt Col L. Pelly to C. Gonne, 13 March 1869, File No. 219, FD Pol. A., May 1869, NAI.

166. L. No. 28, Lt Col L. Pelly, Pol. Resident in the Persian Gulf, to C. Gonne, Sec. to Govt of Bombay, 13 February 1869, File No. 212, FD, Pol. A., May 1869, NAI.

167. L. No. 45, Lt Col L. Pelly to C. Gonne, 13 March 1869, File No. 219, FD Pol. A., May 1869, NAI.

168. Ibid. p. 98.

169. Translation of letter extract from Shiraz Agent to Her Majesty's Minister at Tehran, 13 July 1871, FD, Secret, October 1871, Procds. No. 357, NAI.

170. Floor, *The Persian Gulf*, p. 99.

171. Ibid.

172. Ibid., pp. 100–01.

173. L. Nos 47–12, Lt Col Miles, Consul Muscat, to Lt Col E.C. Ross, Resident in the Persian Gulf, 4 February 1876, Procds No. 226, FD Pol. A., March 1876, NAI; See also in same proceeding, L. No. 98, E.C. Ross to Sayyid Turki, 12 February 1876.

174. Floor, *The Persian Gulf*, p. 99.

Chapter 5: Sultan Barghash: The Imperial Bridgehead

1. Banerji, Backerra and Sarti, *Transnational Histories of the 'Royal Nation*, pp. 2–3. Barghash was very much like Queen Victoria herself, who was at once both a queen mother as well as an Empress.

2. Memorandum of the Position and Authority of the Sultan of Zanzibar, PD 1875, Vol. 207, MSA.

3. Bhacker, *Trade and Empire in Muscat and Zanzibar*, p. 213.

4. L. No. 19, Capt. C.P. Rigby, Agent at Zanzibar, to H.I. Anderson, Sec. to Govt of Bombay, Zanzibar, 24 August 1858, File No. 328, Secret, Muscat, 1858, PD 1858, Vol. 147, MSA.
5. Bhacker, *Trade and Empire in Muscat and Zanzibar*, pp. 183–84.
6. Sulaiman Bin Summund, Vizir to Sayyid Majid, to Sayyid Thuwayni, Muscat, 24 October 1859, Residency Records, Persian Gulf, Book No. 219, R/15/1/155, MSA.
7. Resolution of the Honourable Board, 21 May 1860, Residency Records, Persian Gulf, Book No. 219, R/15/1/155, BL.
8. L. No. 17 of 1860, Brigadier W.M. Coghlan, In-charge Muscat and Zanzibar Commission, to H.L. Anderson, Chief Sec. to Govt of Bombay, 4 December 1860, Report of Commission 1860, Sec. Consultations, 1861, No. 97. PD 33/1861, MSA.
9. Ibid. See also Barghash's letter to Lord Elphinstone, 19 November 1859, Residency Records, Persian Gulf, Book No. 219, R/15/1/155, BL. In this letter, written from Muscat, he pleads his case to Elphinstone and seeks his help. He vows for his loyalty to Lt Col Rigby, on whose direction he agreed to come to Muscat.
10. L. No. 17 of 1860, Brigadier W.M. Coghlan, In-charge Muscat and Zanzibar Commission, to H.L. Anderson, Chief Sec. to Govt of Bombay, 4 December 1860, Report of Commission 1860, Sec. Consultations, 1861, No. 97, PD 33/1861, MSA.
11. Translated letter, Sayyid Barghash to Sayyid Thuwayni, n.d., R/15/1/155, MSA.
12. Col C.P. Rigby, Agent at Zanzibar, to Sayyid Thuwayni, Imam of Muscat, 24 November 1859, R/15/1/155, BL.
13. L. No. 515, Capt. F. Jones, Pol. Resident in the Persian Gulf, to H.L. Anderson, Sec. to Govt of Bombay, 27 December 1859, Residency Records, Persian Gulf, Book No. 219, R/15/1/155, BL.
14. Translated letter, Servants of Sayyid Thuwayni, to Sayyid Thuwayni, recd at Bushire, 21 February 1860, Residency Records, Persian Gulf, Book No. 219, R/15/1/155, BL.
15. Ibid.
16. Translated letter, British Agent at Muscat to Pol. Resident in the Persian Gulf, 10 May 1859, R/15/1/155, BL.
17. L. No. 40, Lt Col C.P. Rigby, Majesty's Consul and British Agent at Zanzibar, to Forbes, Acting Sec. to Govt of Bombay, 29 June

1861, Zanzibar, File No. 580, Secret PD 1861, Muscat–Zanzibar, PD 1861, Vol. 32, MSA.

18. L. No. 229, L. Pelly, Pol. Resident in the Persian Gulf, to Govt of India, 1 July 1862, File No. 17, Secret, Zanzibar, PD 1862, Vol. 47, MSA.

19. Ibid.

20. Pouwels, *Horns and Crescent*, p. 118.

21. Acting Pol. Agent Zanzibar, to C.H. Aitchinson, Sec. to Govt of India, Calcutta, 16 January 1874, PD 1874, Vol. 279, MSA.

22. L. No. 229, L. Pelly, Pol. Resident in the Persian Gulf, to Govt of India, 1 July 1862, File No. 17, Secret, Zanzibar, PD 1862, Vol. 47, MSA.

23. Enclosure 1 in No. 113, Memorandum on the Position of the Sultan of Zanzibar, FO 403/718, NA.

24. Memorandum of the Position and Authority of the Sultan of Zanzibar, PD 1875, Vol. 207, MSA.

25. Enclosure 1 in No. 113, Memorandum on the Position of the Sultan of Zanzibar, FO 403/718, NA.

26. Ibid.

27. Ibid.

28. Acting Pol. Agent Zanzibar, to C.H. Aitchison, Sec. to Govt of India, Calcutta, 16 January 1874, PD 1874, Vol. 279, MSA.

29. Presthold, *Domesticating the World*, p. 82.

30. R.C. Kamshard, Missionary, to J. Kirk, 10 June 1880, A2/29, 1880, Zanzibar, East Africa, ZNA.

31. Foreign Office to Under Sec of State, India Office, 15 February 1888, L/PJ/6/219, File No. 155, BL.

32. The list included Indian subjects such as Lala Shawa, Ahmad Jamal, Mohammad Devji, Hansraj Damodar, Gooloo Virji, etc. See List of British Indian Subjects Refugees, enclosed in letter from C. Hertolet, to Trevor, 3 January 1888, L/PJ/6/217, File No. 2212, BL.

33. Wellji Bimji, Suleiman Nuttoo, Ludda Bimji, Mdbhoy Moola Ismailji, Adamji Ismaelji, etc. to British Consular Agency, Lamu, 18 February 1890, AA3/10, ZNA.

34. Sultan to Wālī of Lamu, 21 March 1890, AA3/10, ZNA.

35. L. No. 46, Francis de Wintox, Her Majesty's Agency and Consulate Gen, Zanzibar, to F.I. Jackson, Acting British Consular Agent, 22 December 1890, AA3/10, ZNA.

36.   Memo by the Consular Judge on the subject matter of Mr Simon's dispatch No. 58 of 3 January 1890, AA3/10, ZNA.

37.   Zahid bin Sa'īd, *Tanzih Al-Absar wa Al-Afkar fi Rihlat Sultan Zanjibar* (The Exaltation of Visions and Ideas in the Travels of the Sultan of Zanzibar), Muscat, Oman, Ministry of Heritage and Culture, 2007, p. 213.

38.   Pouwels, *Horn and Crescent*, p. 125.

39.   Ibid.

40.   Prestholdt, *Domesticating the World.*

41.   Memorandum of the Position and Authority of the Sultan of Zanzibar, PD 1875, Vol. 207, MSA.

42.   Ibid.

43.   Ibid.

44.   Ibid.

45.   Sa'īd, *Tanzih Al-Absar wa Al-Afkar fi Rihlat Sultan Zanjibar*, p. 213.

46.   L. No. 570, J. Kirk, to Earl of Derby, Zanzibar, 11 April 1877, correspondence with British representatives and agents abroad and reports from naval officers relating to the slave trade, 1877, AA1/22, ZNA.

47.   Enclosure No. 48, Admin Report of Pol. Agent and Consul General at Zanzibar 1873–74, L/PS/9/51. For a copy of the treaty between Her Majesty and Barghash for the suppression of the slave trade, see L/P&S/18/B87, BL.

48.   Memorial of A.A. Buchanan, a partner in the mercantile and banking house of Messrs I.A. Forbes & Co. of London, to Sayyid Barghash, 1879, Miscellaneous Correspondence 1879, AA2/27, ZNA.

49.   Ibid.

50.   Ibid.

51.   Sa'īd, *Tanzih Al-Absar wa Al-Afkar fi Rihlat Sultan Zanjibar*, p. 13.

52.   Ibid., p. 62, p. 126; for international coverage, see *Punch*, 26 June 1875, cartoon titled, 'More Slaveries than One'.

53.   Sa'īd, *Tanzih Al-Absar wa Al-Afkar fi Rihlat Sultan Zanjibar*, pp. 85–88.

54.   Ibid.

55.   Ibid.

56.   Barghash imposed duties on ivory trade and benefited from them. He was always critical of local chiefs of Kilwa and Nyassa, who often plundered and extorted money from traders carrying ivory for sale to the coast. The elders took away sometimes 70 per cent

of the total value of ivory. He sent them letters in Arabic, warning
them to desist, as this was diverting trade away from Zanzibar to
the foreign markets such as Ibo, Mozambique and Quillimane.
He wanted them to adhere to the duties imposed by him. See L.
No. 679, J. Kirk to the Earl of Derby, recd 11 December 1877,
correspondence with British representatives and agents abroad
and reports from naval officers relating to the slave trade, 1877,
AA1/22, ZNA.

57.   Sa'īd, *Tanzih Al-Absar wa Al-Afkar fi Rihlat Sultan Zanjibar*, pp. 143–49.
58.   Ibid.
59.   Ibid.
60.   Ibid., pp. 161–63.
61.   Ibid., p. 160.
62.   Ibid., p. 79.
63.   Edited section of *Zanzibar Travel Guide* Sixth edition, Chris
      Mcintyrem Brabdt Travek Guides, Zanzibar Travel Guide.com/
      bradt-guide.asp.
64.   Sa'īd, *Tanzih Al-Absar wa Al-Afkar fi Rihlat Sultan Zanjibar*, p. 202.
65.   Ibid., p. 213.
66.   J. Klirk, Consul Zanzibar, to Alfred Lyal, 23 July 1879, Alfred Lyal
      Letters, Mss Eur F 132/38-48, 38, BL.
67.   L. No. 339, Lt Col Miles, Consul Muscat, to Earl Granville, 26
      October 1881, Zanzibar Administration, IOR/L/PJ/6/65, File
      275, BL.
68.   L. No. 340, Lt Col Miles, Consul Muscat, to Earl Granville, 21
      October 1881, Ibid.
69.   Lt Col Miles, Consul Muscat, to Lt Col E.C. Ross, Pol. Resident
      in the Persian Gulf, Bushire, 30 May 1878, IOR: R/15/6/10, BL.
70.   Ibid.; L. No. 1575, Under Sec. Govt of India to Pol. Resident in
      the Persian Gulf, Simla, 2 August 1878, IOR, R/15/6/10, BL.
71.   Lt Col Miles, Pol. Agent in the Persian Gulf and Consul at
      Muscat, to Lt Col E.C. Ross, Pol. Resident in the Persian Gulf,
      Muscat, 17 November 1878, IOR: R/15/6/10, BL.
72.   Ibid
73.   J. Kirk to Earl of Derby, recd 15 December 1877, correspondence
      with British representatives and agents abroad and reports from
      naval officers relating to the slave trade, 1877, AA1/22, ZNA.

74. Enclosure 1 in No. 113, Memorandum on the Position of the Sultan of Zanzibar, FO 403/718, NA.

75. Ajay Kamalakaran, 'A Brief History of How Parsis Flourished in Zanzibar (With a cameo from Freddie Mercury)', Scroll.in, 5 February 2022, https://scroll.in/magazine/1016501/a-brief-history-of-how-parsis-flourished-in-zanzibar-with-a-cameo-from-freddie-mercury. Accessed on 9 October 2022.

76. Enclosure 1 in No. 113, Memorandum on the Position of the Sultan of Zanzibar, FO 403/718, NA.

77. Kamalakaran, 'A Brief History of How Parsis Flourished in Zanzibar'.

78. Pouwels, *Horn and Crescent*, p. 127.

79. Prestholdt, *Domesticating the World*, pp. 88–116.

80. McDow, *Buying Time*, p. 75.

81. Prestholdt, *Domesticating the World*, p. 104.

82. Anne Bang, *Sufis and Scholars of the Sea: Family Networks in East Africa 1860–1925*, Routledge, London and New York, 2003.

83. Ibid., p. 119.

84. Enclosure 1 in No. 113, Memorandum on the Position of the Sultan of Zanzibar, FO 403/718, NA.

85. H.B.E. Frere, Memorandum on the Position and Authority of the Sultan of Zanzibar, PD 1875, MSA.

86. Enclosure 1 in No. 113, Memorandum on the Position of the Sultan of Zanzibar, FO 403/718, NA.

87. Sa'īd, *Tanzīh Al-Absar wa Al-Afkar fī Rihlat Sultan Zanjibar*, p. 213.

88. Bang, *Sufis and Scholars of the Sea*, p. 94.

89. Ibid., p. 96.

90. Ibid., p. 119.

91. L. Nos 88–365, H.A. Churchill, Pol. Agent and Consul at Zanzibar, to Acting Sec. to the Govt of Bombay, 5 December 1870, PD, Procds No. 27, FD Pol. A., November 1871, NAI.

92. Enclosure No. 3, Memorandum of Bartle Frere Regarding Zanzibar, FO403/718, NA.

93. Ibid.

94. No. 2, Memorandum by Sir B. Frere, on Connection of British Subjects with East African Slave Trade, FO 403/717, NA.

95. No. 1, B. Frere to Earl Granville, 27 February 1873, FO 403/717, NA. He was of the view that the Indian traders and offenders were complicit in the slave trade and India, therefore, should share with Britain the responsibility for what they did and the obligation to protect them in their lawful callings.

96. Administration Report of Zanzibar and its Dominions 1873–74, Calcutta, 1875, in *Selections from the Records of the Government of India*, Foreign Department, No. CXXI, PD 1875, Zanzibar, Vol. 1, No. 294, MSA.

97. Enclosure No. 3, Memorandum of Bartle Frere Regarding Zanzibar, FO403/718, NA.

98. Pouwels, *Horn and Crescent*, p. 133. In Lamu and Kilwa, his subjects were up in arms against the treaty, and he needed British protection if the treaty was to be implemented.

99. Memorandum of the Position and Authority of the Sultan of Zanzibar, PD 1875, Vol. 207, MSA.

100. Translated letter from Sayyid Barghash to H.A. Churchill, Pol. Agent and Consul at Zanzibar, 24 October 1870, Procds No. 30, FD Pol. A., November 1871, NAI.

101. Sayyid Barghash to H.A. Churchill, Pol. Agent and Consul at Zanzibar, 6 November 1870, Procds No. 32, FD Pol. A., November 1871, NAI.

102. L. No. 331, H.A. Churchill, Pol. Agent and Consul at Zanzibar, to Sayyid Barghash, 10 November 1870, Procds No. 33, FD Pol. A., November 1871, NAI.

103. P.D. Henderson, Under Sec. to Govt of India, to Pol. Agent at Zanzibar, 17 June 1873, PD 1873, No. 767, Zanzibar, Vol. 1, No. 229, MSA. The file has petitions from Indian merchants on the payment of these duties. Barghash exercised a monopoly duty levied at his Customs House on copal and ivory arriving from places outside the limits assigned by the commercial treaty with the British. And British Indian traders, such as Lalji Tower, whose consignment was detained at the Customs House for non-payment, often petitioned to the Consulate, alleging violation of the Commercial Treaty with the British. Barghash was urged to charge the Indian traders with the reduced rates he charged others.

104. Enclosure in No. 8, J. Kirk, to Acting Sec. to Govt of Bombay, 9 March 1871, FO403/717, NA.

105. Ibid.
106. No. 41, B. Frere to Earl Granville, 10 January 1873, FO403/718, NA.
107. Ibid.
108. No. 86, Barghash to Frere, 7 January 1873, FO403/718, NA.
109. Enclosure 19 in No. 85, Report by G. Badger, 1873, FO 403/718, NA.
110. Enclosure 20 in No. 83, The Sultan of Zanzibar to Sir B. Frere, 31 January 1873, FO403/718, NA.
111. For the uniqueness of slavery as a social dependence rather that mere economic category, see Cooper, *Plantation Slavery on the East Coast of Africa*, pp. 5–7. He underlines the personal and social dependence of the slave to his master's family, community and kinship as the distinctive aspect of East African slavery. The integration of the slave into a familial set-up made him more than just an economic category, as was the case in the Atlantic set-up.
112. Enclosure 20 in No. 83, The Sultan of Zanzibar to Sir B. Frere, 31 January 1873, FO403/718, NA.
113. Enclosure 22 in No. 83, B. Frere to Sultan of Zanzibar, 1 February 1873, FO403/718, NA.
114. No. 2, Memorandum by Sir B. Frere, on Connection of British Subjects with East African slave trade, FO 403/717, NA.
115. Ibid. The Banias of the Persian Gulf ports were equally and directly involved in slave trade.
116. Ibid. For his other administrative reorganization suggestions, see details in the memorandum. See also No. 3, Memorandum by Mr Wylde on Sir Barton Frere's memorandum. He alerts the government of the expenditure involved in his suggestions of exercising force on the Zanzibar Sultan to comply with the slave trade ban and also pitch in to help in his subsidy payment to Muscat. He urges Frere to go on a mission to Zanzibar and work out an anti-slave trade treaty with the Sultan.
117. L. No. 18, Lt Col S.B. Miles, Acting Agent and Consul Gen. Zanzibar, to Earl Granville, K.G., Sec of State for Foreign Affairs, 1 March 1883, Procds No. 211, Report on the Slave Trade at Zanzibar and Muscat, Procds April 1883, Nos 210–11, FD, A Pol E, NAI.
118. Ibid.

119. Enclosure No. 592, J. Kirk to Sultan of Zanzibar, 30 May 1877, No. 592, J. Kirk to Earl of Derby, 31 May 1877, Correspondence with British representatives and agents abroad and reports from naval officers relating to slave trade, 1877, AA1/22, ZNA.

120. No. 1044, Sec. to Govt of Bombay, Castle, to Accountant General Bombay and Acting Pol. Agent Zanzibar, 17 February 1873, PD Vol. 1, No. 229, MSA.

121. L. No. 497, J. Kirk, Agent Zanzibar, to Earl of Derby, 10 January 1877, Correspondence with British representatives and agents abroad and reports from naval officers relating to the slave trade, 1877, AA1/22, ZNA. Missionary societies and missions in Mombasa and the east coast of Africa had a tension-prone relationship with the Consulate when it came to the administration of British subjects, in particular, relating to the sanctioning of their marriages by the mission vs the Consulate. See L. No 593 and enclosure, J. Kirk to Earl of Derby, 1 June 1877, ibid.

122. Enclosure 8 in No. 497, J. Kirk to Commander Russell, 10 January 1877, Correspondence with British representatives and agents abroad and reports from naval officers relating to the slave trade, 1877, AA1/22, ZNA. These applications were sent to the government in London for consideration.

123. Enclosure in No. 502. Sir J. Pauncefote to Sec. to the Admiralty, FO, 9 February 1877, Correspondence with British representatives and agents abroad and reports from naval officers relating to the slave trade, 1877, AA1/22, ZNA.

124. L. No. 18, Lt. Col S.B. Miles, Acting Agent and Consul Gen. Zanzibar, to Earl Granville, K.G., Sec of State for Foreign Affairs, 1 March 1883, Procds No. 211, Report on the Slave Trade at Zanzibar and Muscat, Procds, April 1883, Nos 210–11, FD, A Pol E, NAI.

125. Enclosure No. 48. Admin Report of Political Agent and Consul General at Zanzibar 1873–74, L/PS/9/51, BL.

126. L. No. 18, Lt Col S.B. Miles, Acting Agent and Consul Gen Zanzibar, to Earl Granville, K.G., Sec of State for Foreign Affairs, 1 March 1883, Procds No. 211, Report on the Slave Trade at Zanzibar and Muscat, Procds, April 1883, Nos 210–11, FD, A Pol E, NAI.

127. Enclosure 2 in No. 1, Report by Mr Holmwood, L/PS/9/51, BL.

128. No. 150, C.B. Euan Smith, Acting Consul General Smith to the Earl of Derby, 31 July 1875, L/PS/9/51, BL.
129. L. No. 208, J. Kirk to the Earl of Derby, 12 November 1875, L/PS/9/51, BL.
130. H.I. Prideaux, Pol. Agent and Consul General Zanzibar, to C.U. Aitchison, Sec. to Govt of India, Calcutta, 4 May 1874, Foreign Dept Political, PD 1874, Vol. 279, MSA.
131. Memorandum of the Position and Authority of the Sultan of Zanzibar, PD 1875, Vol. 207, MSA.
132. Ibid. Sultan Sayyid Sa'īd managed to drive away the Portuguese, but the families of Swahili chiefs, though much degenerated, still were numerous and entrenched in society. Some were wealthy and influential, and Sayyid Sa'īd continued with their alliance. He purchased their surrender by the promise of pensions and the continuance of certain forms of sovereignty.
133. Enclosure 2 in No.1, Report by Mr Holmwood, L/PS/9/51, BL.
134. Report on the slave owners in Pemba and Mombasa, prepared by Suleiman Sālih, 1875, Consular Agency Records Misc., AA/12/4, ZNA.
135. Ibid.
136. Ibid.
137. L. No. 257, J. Kirk to Earl Granville, 27 April 1881, Zanzibar Administration, IOR/L/PJ/6/65, File 275, BL.
138. British Consulate, Zanzibar, to J. Kirk, 21 February 1884, 'Pemba Report', General Correspondence, Coast Vice Consul, inward and outward, 1884, AA10/1. ZNA.
139. L. No. 200. J. Kirk, to Earl Granville, 5 May 1881, Zanzibar Administration, IOR/L/PJ/6/65, File 275, ZNA.
140. Recd. from HM Ship *London*, to J. Kirk, 2 January 1880, Zanzibar, A2/29, ZNA.
141. C.S. Smith, Vice Consul, Zanzibar, to J. Kirk, 21 February 1884, 'Pemba Report', General Correspondence, Coast Vice Consul, inward and outward, 1884, AA10/1, ZNA. Smith suggested that, for Pemba only, the Arabs should be allowed to sell or mortgage land to foreigners. Abolition of slavery in Pemba was contrary to the 1839 treaty, as most slaves in Pemba were pre-1873. The first measure would release money, and that could be used to buy slaves.

142. C.S. Smith, Vice Consul, Zanzibar, to J. Kirk, 21 February 1884, 'Pemba Report', General Correspondence, Coast Vice Consul, inward and outward, 1884, AA10/1, ZNA.

143. A.H. Hardinge, Diplomatic Agent and Consul General, Zanzibar, to Sec. to Govt of India, Dept of Rev. and Agriculture, 22 May 1897, L/PJ/6/458, File No. 2019, BL.

144. Memorandum, W.H. de Sausmarez, 19 May 1897, L/PJ/6/458, file 2019, BL.

145. D. Ibbetson, Sec. to Govt of India, to Britannic Majesty's Agent and Consul General, Zanzibar, 14 September 1897, L/PJ/6/458, File No. 2019, BL.

146. See 'Ordinance to Regulate the Immigration of Indian Laborers', pp. 1–24, L/PJ/6/458, File No. 2019, BL.

147. D. Ibbeston, Sec. to Govt of India, to Agent and Consular General, Zanzibar, 14 September 1897, L/PJ/6/458, File No. 2019, BL.

148. Report on Dar as Salaam, 9 January 1874 by I. Elton, Asst to Pol. Agent, Zanzibar, PD 1874, Vol. 279, MSA.

149. Ibid.

150. Ibid.

151. Ibid.

152. Gray, 'Dar as Salam under Sultans of Zanzibar', p. 10.

153. Ibid., p. 13; see also Report on Dar as Salaam, 9 January 1874 by I. Elton, Asst to Pol. Agent, Zanzibar, PD 1874, Vol. 279, MSA.

154. Gray, 'Dar as Salam under Sultans of Zanzibar', p. 12.

155. H.B.E. Frere, Special Envoy to Muscat and Zanzibar, Memorandum on the Position and Authority of the Sultan of Zanzibar, PD 1875, Vol. 207. MSA.

156. Gray, 'Dar as Salam under Sultans of Zanzibar', p. 13.

157. Ibid., p. 16.

158. J.R. Brennan, A. Burton and Y. Lawi (eds.), *The Emerging Metropolis. A History of Dar as Salam, circa 1862-2000*, Africa Book Collective, 2007, p. 18.

159. Gray, 'Dar as Salam under Sultans of Zanzibar', p. 17.

160. Brennan, Burton and Lawi, *The Emerging Metropolis*, p. 18.

161. Ibid., p. 19.

Bibliography

Alavi, Seema. 'The Centaur Shipwreck: Law, Politics and Society in the Persian Gulf'. *Journal of Colonialism and Colonial History*, Vol. 21, No. 3 (2020), doi:10.1353/cch.2020.0034.

Al Hashimy, Sa'id B. Muhammad. 'Sayyid Thuwayni's Internal and External Policy: 1856–1866 (Analysis & Evaluation Studies)'. *Journal of Documentation and Humanities Research Center*, Issue 14, Qatar University, Qatar, (1989–2004): 47–78.

Ballantyne, Tony. *Webs of Empire: Locating New Zealand's Colonial Past*. Vancouver, Toronto: University of British Columbia Press, 2014.

Banerji, Milinda., Charlotte Backerra, and Cathleen Sarti, Edited. *Transnational Histories of the 'Royal Nation'*. London: Springer, 2017.

Bang, Anne. *Sufis and Scholars of the Sea: Family Networks in East Africa 1860–1925*. London and New York: Routledge, 2003.

Bardawil, Fadi A. 'In the Wake of Conscription: Compradors or Bricoleurs?'. In blog 'Translation and the Afterlives of the Anglophone Theory', *Immanent Frame, Secularism, Religion and the Public Sphere* (15 June 2021), Tif.ssrc.org/2021.

Benton, Lauren. *Law and Colonial Cultures: Legal Regimes in World History, 1400–1900*. Cambridge: Cambridge University Press, 2001.

Bhacker, M. Reda. *Trade and Empire in Muscat and Zanzibar*. London: Routledge Press, 2003.

Bhacker, M. Reda. 'Family Strife and Foreign Intervention: Causes in the Separation of Zanzibar from Oman: A Reappraisal'. *Bulletin of SOAS*, Vol. 54, No. 2 (1991): 269–80.

Bishara, Fahad A. *A Sea of Debt: Law and Economic Life in the Western Indian Ocean 1780–1950*. Cambridge: Cambridge University Press, 2017.

Bishara, Fahad A. '"No Country but the Ocean": Reading International Law from the Deck of an Indian Ocean Dhow ca 1900'. *Comparative Studies in Society and History*, Vol. 60, No. 2 (2018): 338–66.

Brennan, James R, and Andrew Burton. 'The Emerging Metropolis: A History of Dar es Salam, circa 1862–2000'. Edited James R. Brennan, Andrew Burton and Yusufu Q. Lawi, *Dar es Salam: Histories from an Emerging African Metropolis*. Dar as Salaam: Africa Book Collective, 2007.

Burton, Richard F. *Zanzibar: City, Island and Coast*. Vol. 1, London: Tinsley Brothers, 1872.

Chambi Chachage, 'A Capitalizing City: Dar as Salam and the Emergence of an African Entrepreneurial Elite, 1862–2015'. PhD diss., Harvard University, 2018.

Chatterji, Kingshuk. 'A Tale of Two Ports: Changing Fortunes of Bushehr and Bandar Abbas in Qajar Persia'. Edited Kenneth Hall, R. Mukherjee and S. Ghosh. *Subversive Sovereigns across the Seas: Indian Ocean Ports of Trade from Early Historic Times to Late Colonialism*. Calcutta: The Asiatic Society, 2018: 243–44.

Christie, James. *Cholera Epidemics in East Africa: An Account of the Several Diffusions of the Disease in that Country from 1821–1872. With an outline of geography, ethnography, ethnology & trade connections of regions through which the epidemic passed*. London: Macmillan & Co., 1876.

Cohen, Thomas. 'The Macrohistory of Microhistory'. *Journal of Medieval and Early Modern Studies*, Vol. 47, No. 1 (January 2017): 53–73.

Cooper, Fredrick. *Plantation Slavery on the East Coast of Africa*. New Haven: Yale University Press, 1977.

Cooper, Frederick. *From Slaves to Squatters: Plantation Labor and Agriculture in Zanzibar and Coastal Kenya, 1890–1925*. New Haven: Yale University Press, 1980.

Fabian, Steven. 'Curing the Cancer of the Colony: Bagamoyo, Dar as Salam and Socio-economic Struggle in German East Africa'. *International Journal of African Historical Studies*, Vol. 40, No. 3 (2007): 441–69.

Floor, Willem. *The Persian Gulf: Bandar Abbas: The Natural Gateway of Southeast Iran*. Washington: Mage Publishers, 2011.

Fraser, Captain H.A. 'The East African Slave Trade. Zanzibar and the Slave Trade'. In *The East African Slave Trade. And the Measures Proposed for Its Extinction, As Viewed by the Residents of Zanzibar*. Edited H.A. Fraser, James Christie and Bishop William G. Tozer, pp. 9-19. London: Harrison, 1871.

Freitag, Ulrike. *A History of Jeddah: The Gate to Mecca in the Nineteenth and Twentieth Centuries*. Cambridge: Cambridge University Press, 2020.

Ginzberg, Carlo. *The Cheese and the Worms: The Cosmos of a Sixteenth-Century Miller*. Baltimore: Johns Hopkins University Press, 1980.

Glassman, Jonathon. *Feasts and Riots: Revelry, Rebellion, and Popular Consciousness on the Swahili Coast, 1856–1888*, Portsmouth: Heinemann, 1995.

Goswami, Chhaya. *Globalization Before Its Time: The Gujarati Merchants from Kachchh*. Delhi: Penguin Random House, 2016.

Hall, Richard. *Empires of the Monsoon: A History of the Indian Ocean and Its Invaders*. Gurugram: HarperCollins, 1996.

Ho, Enseng. 'Inter-Asian Concepts for Mobile Societies'. *Journal of Asian Studies*, Vol. 76, No. 4 (November 2017): 907–28.

Hopper, Matthew, S. *Slaves of One Master: Globalization and Slavery in Arabia in the Age of Empire*. New Haven: Yale University Press, 2015.

Hussin, Iza. 'Introduction, On Translation and Legibility'. In blog 'Translation and the Afterlives of the Anglophone Theory', *Immanent Frame, Secularism, Religion and the Public Sphere* (15 June 2021), Tif.ssrc.org/2021.

Hussin, Iza. 'Circulation of Law, Cosmopolitan Elites, Global Repertoires, Local Vernaculars'. *Law & History Review*, Vol. 32, No. 4 (2014): 773–95.

Hyslop, Jonathan. 'Steamship Empire: Asian, African and British Sailors in the Merchant Marine c. 1880–1945'. *Journal of Asian and African Studies*, Vol. 44, No. 1 (2009): 44–49.

Ibn Ruzayq, Hamid ibn Muhammad. *History of Imams and Seyyids of Oman*. Translated by G.P. Badger. London: Hakluyt Society, M.DCCC. LXXI.

Iliffe, John. *A Modern History of Tanganayika*. Cambridge: Cambridge University Press, 1979.

Kafadar, Cemal. *Between Two Worlds: The Construction of the Ottoman State*. Berkeleyand Los Angeles: University of California Press, 1996.

Kipling, Rudyard. *The Man Who Would Be King*. New York: J.J. Little & Co., 1899.

Kooria, Mahmood. 'An Abode of Islam under a Hindu King: Circuitous Imagination of Kingdoms among Muslims of 16th Century Malabar'. *Journal of Indian Ocean World Studies*, Vol. 1, No.1 (2017): 90–110.

Lambert David and Alan Lester, Edited. *Colonial Lives across the British Empire: Imperial Careering in the Long Nineteenth Century*. Cambridge: Cambridge University Press, 2006.

Lorimer, John Gordon. *Gazetteer of the Persian Gulf, Oman and Central Arabia*. Bombay: Govt Press, Vol. 1, 1915.

Mathew, Johan. *Margins of the Market: Trafficking and Capitalism across the Arabian Sea*. Berkeley & Los Angeles: University of California Press, 2016.

Maurizi, Vincenzo. *History of Seyd Sa'īd, Sultan of Muscat*. Cambridge: Oleander Press, 1984.

McDow, Thomas F. *Buying Time: Debt and Mobility in the Western Indian Ocean*. Ohio: Ohio University Press, 2018.

McDow, Thomas F. 'Deeds of Freed Slaves: Manumission & Economic and Social Mobility in Pre-Abolition Zanzibar'. Edited Robert Harms, Bernard K. Freamon and David W. Blight. *Indian Ocean Slavery in the Age of Abolition*. New Haven: Yale University Press, 2013.

McFarlane, Colin. 'Governing the Contaminated City: Infrastructure and Sanitation in Colonial and Post-Colonial Bombay'. *International Journal of Urban and Regional Research*, Vol. 32, No. 2 (June 2008): 415–35.

Miles, Samuel B. 'On the Border of the Great Desert. A Journey in Oman'. Part 1, *Geographical Journal*, Vol. 36, No. 2 (1910): 159–78.

Nicolini, Beatrice. 'The Western Indian Ocean as Cultural Corridor: Makran, Oman and Zanzibar through 19th Century European Accounts and Reports'. *Middle East Studies Association Bulletin*, Vol. 37, No. 1 (Summer 2003): 20–49.

Parker, Greville, S., and Freeman Grenville. *East Africa Coast*. Clarendon Oxford: Clarendon Press, 1962.

Pearson, Michael. *The Indian Ocean*. New York and London: Routledge, 2003.

Pouwels, Randall L. *Horn and Crescent: Cultural Change and Traditional Islam on the East African Coast, 800–1900*. Cambridge: Cambridge University Press, 1987.

Prange, Sebastian R. *Monsoon Islam: Trade and Faith on the Medieval Malabar Coast*. Delhi: Cambridge University Press, 2018.

Prange, Sebastian. '"A Trade of No Dishonor": Piracy, Commerce and Community in the Western Indian Ocean, 12th–16th Centuries'. *American Historical Review*, Vol. 116, No. 5 (2011): 1269–93.

Presthold, Jeremy. *Domesticating the World: African Consumers and the Genealogies of Globalization*. Berkeley and Los Angeles: University of California Press, 2008.

Putnam, Lara. 'To Study the Fragments/Whole: Microhistory and the Atlantic World'. *Journal of Social History*, Vol. 39, No. 3 (Spring 2006): 615–30.

Reese, Scott. *Imperial Muslims: Islam, Community and Authority in the Indian Ocean 1839–1937*. Edinburgh: Edinburgh University Press, 2019.

Risso, Patricia. 'Cross Cultural Presence of Piracy'. *Journal of World History*, Vol. 12, No. 2 (2001): 293–319.

Romero, Patricia W. 'Sayyid Said bin Sultan Bu Said and Zanzibar: Women in the Life of this Arab Patriarch'. *British Journal of Middle Eastern Studies*, Vol. 39, No. 3 (2012): 373–92.

Ruete, Rudolph Said. *Said bin Sultan (1791–1856), Ruler of Oman and Zanzibar. His Place in the History of Arabia and East Africa*. London: Alexander-Ouseley Limited, 1929.

Ruete, Emily. *Memoirs of an Arabian Princess from Zanzibar*. New York: Dover Publications, 2009.

Sharafi, Mitra. 'The Marital Patchwork of Colonial South Asia: Forum Shopping from Britain to Baroda'. *Law and History Review*, Vol. 28, No. 4 (November 2010): 979–1009.

Sharafi, Mitra. *Law and Identity in Colonial South Asia: Parsi Legal Culture, 1772–1947*. Cambridge: Cambridge University Press, 2014.

Sheriff, Abdul. *Slaves, Spices and Ivory in Zanzibar: Integration of an East African Commercial Empire into the World Economy, 1770–1873*. Dar es Salam: Tanzania Publishing House, 1987.

Sivasundaram, Sujit. *Waves Across the South: A New History of Revolution and Empire*. London: HarperCollins, 2020.

Speece, Mark. 'Aspects of Economic Dualism in Oman, 1830–1930'. *Journal of Middle Eastern Studies*, Vol. 21, No. 4 (November 1989): 495–515.

Stapley, Karen. 'Assassination and Intrigue in Muscat 1866–68'. Qatar Digital Library, https://www.qdl.qa/en/assassination-and-intrigue-muscat-1866–68.

Subrahmanyam, Lakshmi. 'The Ocean and the Historian'. *Journal of Indian Ocean World Studies*, Vol. 2, No. 1 (2018): 2–11.

Subramanian, Lakshmi. *The Sovereign & the Pirate: Ordering Maritime Subjects in India's Western Littoral*. Delhi: Oxford University Press, 2016.

Suzuki, Hideaki. *Slave Trade Profiteers in the Western Indian Ocean: Suppression and Resistance in the 19th Century*. New York: Springer, 2017.

Tanaka, Stefan. *Japan's Orient: Rendering Pasts into History*. Berkeley and Los Angeles: University of California Press, 1993.

Wilkinson, John C. 'The Oman Question: The Background to the Political Geography of South East Arabia'. *The Geographical Journal*, Vol. 137, No. 3 (September 1971): 361–71.

Winichakul, Thongchai. *Siam Mapped: A History of the Geo Body of a Nation*. Hawaii: University of Hawaii, 1997.

Yahaya, Nurfadzilah. *Fluid Jurisdictions: Colonial Law and Arabs in Southeast Asia*. Ithaca: Cornell University Press, 2020.

Zahid bin Sa'īd. *Tanzih Al-Absar wa Al-Afkar fi Rihlat Sultan Zanjibar* (The Exaltation of Visions and Ideas in the Travels of the Sultan of Zanzibar). Muscat: Oman, Ministry of Heritage and Culture, 2007.

Primary Sources
London
British Library
Residency Records, Persian Gulf (R)
Secret Letters and Enclosures from India. Secret and Political (L/PS)
Political and Judicial letters from India (L/PJ)

Microfilms: Rigby Report, 1860, IOR MF 1/1178
European Manuscripts Eur/ F 123/38-43; Eur/ F 126/43, Pelly Letters

National Archive of the United Kingdom, Kew, Richmond
Foreign Office Collections 1850–1890 (FO)

Zanzibar, Tanzania
Consular and Agency Records Foreign Office Correspondence (AA1)
Consular and Agency Records General Correspondence (AA2)
Consular and Agency Records Bombay Correspondence (AA3)

Consular and Agency Records. Government of India Correspondence
   (AA4)
Consular and Agency Records Court Records (AA7)
Consular and Agency Records Registers of Correspondence (AA8)
Consular and Agency Records Coast Vice Consuls (AA10)

New Delhi
National Archive of India
Foreign Department Records, Political, 1856–1876 (FD Pol.)

Bombay
Maharashtra State Archive
Bombay Government, Political Department Files, 1848–1875 (PD)

Index